E. F. CODD

The Relational Model

for Database Management

· *Version 2* ·

ADDISON-WESLEY PUBLISHING COMPANY
Reading, Massachusetts • Menlo Park, California • New York
Don Mills, Ontario • Wokingham, England • Amsterdam
Bonn • Sydney • Singapore • Tokyo • Madrid • San Juan

Library of Congress Cataloging-in-Publication Data

Codd, E. F.
  The relational model for database management : version 2 / E.F. Codd.
    p.   cm.
  Includes index.
  ISBN 0–201–14192–2
  1. Data base management.   2. Relational data bases.   I. Title.
QA76.9.D3C626   1990
005.75′6—dc20   89–6793
                                                                  CIP

Reprinted with corrections July, 1991

3 4 5 6 7 8 9 10 HA 9594939291

To fellow pilots and aircrew
in the Royal Air Force
during World War II

and the dons at Oxford.

These people were the source of my determination to
fight for what I believed was right during the ten or
more years in which government, industry, and
commerce were strongly opposed to the relational
approach to database management.

■ *PREFACE* ■

Today, if you have a well-designed database management system, you have the keys to the kingdom of data processing and decision support. That is why there now exists a prototype machine whose complete design is based on the relational model. Its arithmetic hardware is a quite minor part of the architecture. In fact, the old term "computer system" now seems like a misnomer.

My first paper dealing with the application of relations (in the mathematical sense) to database management was a non-confidential IBM research report made available to the general public that was entitled *Derivability, Redundancy, and Consistency of Relations stored in Large Data Banks* [Codd 1969]. I placed a great deal of emphasis then on the preservation of integrity in a commercial database, and I do so now. In this book, I devote Chapters 13 and 14 exclusively to that subject.

Another concern of mine has been, and continues to be, precision. A database management system (DBMS) is a reasonably complex system, even if unnecessary complexity is completely avoided. The relational model intentionally does not specify how a DBMS should be built, but it does specify what should be built, and for that it provides a precise specification.

An important adjunct to precision is a sound theoretical foundation. The relational model is solidly based on two parts of mathematics: first-order predicate logic and the theory of relations. This book, however, does not dwell on the theoretical foundations, but rather on all the features of the relational model that I now perceive as important for database users, and therefore for DBMS vendors. My perceptions result from 20 years of practical experience in computing and data processing (chiefly, but not exclusively, with large-scale customers of IBM), followed by another 20 years of research.

I believe that this is the first book to deal exclusively with the relational approach. It does, however, include design principles in Chapters 21 and 22. It is also the first book on the relational model by the originator of that model. All the ideas in the relational model described in this book are mine, except in cases where I explicitly credit someone else.

Very little is said in this book about the normalization of relations, the normal forms 1NF, 2NF, 3NF that I invented in 1971, the normal forms 4NF, 5NF due to Ronald Fagin in 1976, and the new conceptual normal forms CNF(p) due to me in 1988. I plan to include discussion of these normal forms in a new book on database design.

In developing the relational model, I have tried to follow Einstein's advice, "Make it as simple as possible, but no simpler." I believe that in the last clause he was discouraging the pursuit of simplicity to the extent of distorting reality. So why does the book contain 30 chapters and two appendixes? To answer this question, it is necessary to look at the history of research and development of the relational model.

From 1968 through 1988, I published more than 30 technical papers on the relational model [Codd 1968–Codd 1988d]. I refer to the total content of the pre-1979 papers as Version 1 of the relational model (RM/V1 for brevity).

Early in 1979, I presented a paper to the Australian Computer Society at Hobart, Tasmania, entitled "Extending the Database Relational Model to Capture More Meaning," naming the extended version RM/T (T for Tasmania). My paper on RM/T later appeared in *ACM Transactions on Database Systems* [Codd 1979]. My aim was for the extensions to be tried out first in the logical design of databases and subsequently to be incorporated in the design of DBMS products, but only if they proved effective in database design.

Progress in this direction has been much slower than I expected. Vendors of DBMS products have in many cases failed to understand the first version RM/V1, let alone RM/T. One of the reasons they offer is that they cannot collect all the technical papers because they are dispersed in so many different journals and other publications.

This book collects in one document much of what has appeared in my technical papers, but with numerous new features, plus more detailed explanation (and some emphasis) on those features of RM/V1 and RM/V2 that capture some aspects of the meaning of the data. This emphasis is intended to counter the numerous allegations that the relational model is devoid of semantics. I also hope that this document will challenge vendors to get the job done.

Figure P.1 is intended to show how features of RM/T are expected to be gradually dropped into the sequence of versions RM/V2, RM/V3, ... The dropping will be gradual to allow DBMS vendors and consumers time to understand them.

RM/V2 consists of 333 features. A few of these features are of a proscriptive nature, which may sound surprising or inappropriate. However,

Figure P.1 **Relationship between the Various Versions of the Relational Model**

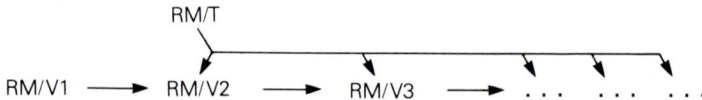

they are intended to improve the understanding of the relational model and help DBMS vendors avoid extensions that at first glance seem quite harmless, but later turn out to block extensions needed to advance the DBMS from a primitive to a basic status. The most famous example of a proscriptive feature in the computing field was Dijkstra's assertion that new programming languages should exclude the GO TO command.

The features of RM/V2 include all of the features of RM/V1, roughly 50 of them. Thus, this book covers both versions of the relational model. However, except for some of the advanced operators in Chapter 5, there is no sharp boundary between RM/V1 and RM/V2. This is partly due to changes in some of the definitions to make them more general—for example, entity integrity and referential integrity. Incidentally, the new definitions [Codd 1988a] were available to DBMS vendors well before their first attempts to implement referential integrity.

Domains, primary keys, and foreign keys are based on the meaning of the data. These features are quite inexpensive to implement properly, do not adversely affect performance, and are extremely important for users. However, most DBMS vendors have failed to support them, and many lecturers and consultants in relational database management have failed to see their importance.

Most of the new ideas in RM/V2 have been published in scattered technical journals during the 1980s. What is different about this version of the relational model? Is all of RM/V1 retained?

Versions 1 and 2 are at the same high level of abstraction, a level that yields several advantages:

- independence of hardware support;
- independence of software support;
- occasionally, vendors can improve their implementations "under the covers" without damaging their customers' investment in application programs, training of programmers, and training of end users.

A strong attempt has been made to incorporate all of RM/V1 into RM/V2, allowing programs developed to run on RM/V1 to continue to operate correctly on RM/V2. The most important additional features in RM/V2 are as follows:

- a new treatment of items of data missing because they represent properties that happen to be inapplicable to certain object instances—for example, the name of the spouse of an employee when that employee happens to be unmarried (Chapters 8 and 9);
- new features supporting all kinds of integrity constraints, especially the user-defined type (Chapter 14);
- a more detailed account of view updatability, which is very important for users but has been sadly neglected by DBMS vendors (Chapter 17);

- some relatively new principles of design applied to DBMS products and relational languages (Chapters 21 and 22);
- a more detailed account of what should be in the catalog (Chapter 15);
- new features pertaining to the management of distributed databases (Chapters 24 and 25);
- some of the fundamental laws on which the relational model is based (Chapter 29).

A few of the ideas in RM/T have been incorporated into RM/V2. Many, however, are being postponed to RM/V3 or later versions, because the industry has not been able to maintain an adequate pace of product development and improvement. Additionally, errors made in the design of DBMS products along the way are also hindering progress—often it is necessary to continue to support those errors in order to protect a customer's heavy investment in application programs.

In this book, I attempt to emphasize the numerous semantic features in the relational model. Many of these features were conceived when the model was first created. The semantic features include the following:

- domains, primary keys, and foreign keys;
- duplicate values are permitted within columns of a relation, *but duplicate rows are prohibited*;
- systematic handling of missing information independent of the type of datum that is missing.

These features and others go far beyond the capabilities of pre-relational DBMS products.

Except in Chapter 30, very little is said about models for database management other than the relational model. The relational model, invented in 1969, was the first model for database management. Since then, it has become popular to talk of many other kinds of data models, including a network data model, a hierarchical data model, a tabular data model, an entity-relationship model, a binary relationship model, and various semantic data models.

Historically, it has often been assumed that the hierarchic and network data models pre-dated not only the relational model, but also the availability of hierarchical and network DBMS products. Actually, judging by what has been published, no such models existed before the relational data model was invented or before non-relational DBMS products became available. With the sole exception of relational systems, database management system products existed before any data model was created for them.

The motivations for Version 2 of the relational model included the following five:

1. all of the motivations for Version 1;
2. the errors in implementing RM/V1, such as the following:
   a. duplicate rows permitted by the language SQL;
   b. primary keys have either been omitted altogether, or they have been made optional on base relations;
   c. major omissions, especially of all features supporting the meaning of the data (including domains);
   d. indexes misused to support semantic aspects;
   e. omission of almost all the features concerned with preserving the integrity of the database.
3. the need to assemble all of the relational model in one document for DBMS vendors, users, and inventors of new data models who seem to be unaware of the scope of the relational model and the scope of database management;
4. the need for extensions to Version 1, such as the new kinds of joins, user-defined integrity, view updatability, and features that support the management of distributed databases;
5. the need for users to realize what they are missing in present relational DBMS products because only partial support of the relational model is built into these products.

In Appendix A, the features index, there is a specialized and comprehensive index to all of the RM/V2 features. This index should facilitate the cross-referencing that occurs in the description of several features. In addition to the exercises at the end of each chapter, simple exercises in predicate logic and the theory of relations appear in Appendix B. The reference section, in addition to full citations to the many papers and books cited in the text, includes a short bibliographical essay.

I have tried to keep the examples small in scale to facilitate understanding. However, small-scale examples often do not show many of the effects of the large scale of databases normally encountered.

Finally, I would like to acknowledge the encouragement and strong support provided by friends and colleagues, especially Sharon Weinberg, to whom I am deeply indebted. I also wish to thank the reviewers of my manuscript for their many helpful comments: Nagraj Alur, Nathan Goodman, Michel Melkanoff, Roberta Rousseau, Sharon Weinberg, and Gabrielle Wiorkowski.

I hope that all readers of this book—whether they are students, vendors, consultants, or users—find something of value herein.

E. F. Codd

Menlo Park, California

■ CONTENTS ■

CHAPTER 3

Domains as Extended Data Types   43

CHAPTER 4

The Basic Operators   61

CHAPTER 5

The Advanced Operators   97

CHAPTER 6

Naming   145

CHAPTER 7

Commands for the DBA   155

CHAPTER 8

Missing Information   169

CHAPTER 9

Response to Technical Criticisms Regarding Missing Information 197

CHAPTER 10

Qualifiers 207

CHAPTER 11

Indicators 221

CHAPTER 16

Views   285

CHAPTER 17

View Updatability   293

CHAPTER 18

Authorization   325

CHAPTER 19

Functions   337

CHAPTER 20

Protection of Investment   345

CHAPTER 21

Principles of DBMS Design   351

CHAPTER 22

Principles of Design for Relational Languages   361

CHAPTER 25

More on Distributed Database Management   417

CHAPTER 26

Advantages of the Relational Approach   431

■ *CHAPTER 1* ■

Introduction to Version 2
of the Relational Model

1.1 ■ What Is a Relation?

The word "relation" is used in English and other natural languages without
concern for precise communication. Even in dictionaries that attempt to be
precise, the definitions are quite loose, uneconomical, and ambiguous. *The
Oxford English Dictionary* devotes a whole page of small print to the word
"relation." A small part of the description is as follows:

> That feature or attribute of things which is involved in considering
> them in comparison or contrast with each other; the particular way
> in which one thing is thought of in connexion with another; any
> connexion, correspondence, or association, which can be conceived
> as naturally existing between things.

On the other hand, mathematicians are concerned with precise communication, a very high level of abstraction, and the economy of effort that
stems from making definitions and theorems as general as possible. A special
concern is that of avoiding the need for special treatment of special cases
except when absolutely necessary. The generally accepted definition of a
relation in mathematics is as follows:

> Given sets S1, S2, . . ., Sn (not necessarily distinct), R is a relation
> on these n sets if it is a set of n-tuples, the first component of which
> is drawn from S1, the second component from S2, and so on.

More concisely, R is a subset of the Cartesian product S1 × S2 × . . . × S*n*. (For more information, see Chapter 4.) Relation R is said to be of *degree n*. Each of the sets S1, S2, . . ., S*n* on which one or more relations are defined is called a *domain*.

It is important to note that a mathematical relation is a set with special properties. First, all of its elements are tuples, all of the same type. Second, it is an unordered set. This is just what is needed for commercial databases, since many of the relations in such databases are each likely to have thousands of tuples, sometimes millions. In several recently developed databases, there are two thousand millions of tuples. In such circumstances, users should not be burdened with either the numbering or the ordering of tuples.

The relational model deals with tuples by their information content, not by means extraneous to the tuples such as tuple numbers, tuple identifiers, or storage addresses. The model also avoids burdening users with having to remember which tuples are next to which, in any sense of "nextness."

As one consequence of adopting relations as the user's perception of the way the data is organized, application programs become independent of any ordering of tuples in storage that might be in effect at some time. This enables the stored ordering of tuples to be changed whenever necessary without adversely affecting the correctness of application programs.

Changes in the stored ordering may have to be made for a variety of reasons. For example, the pattern of traffic on the database may change, and consequently the ordering previously adopted may no longer be the most suitable for obtaining good performance.

A mathematical relation has one property that some people consider counter-intuitive, and that does not appear to be consistent with the definition in *The Oxford English Dictionary*. This property is that a unary relation (degree one) can conform to this definition. Thus, a mathematical relation of degree greater than one does inter-relate two or more objects, while a mathematical relation of degree one does not. In some cases, intuition can be a poor guide. In any event, whether the concept of a unary relation is counter-intuitive or not, mathematicians and computer-oriented people do not like to treat it any differently from relations of higher degree.

In applying computers effectively (whether in science, engineering, education, or commerce) there is, or should be, a similar concern for precise communication, a high level of abstraction, and generality. If one is not careful, however, the degree of generality can sometimes be pursued beyond what is needed in practice, and this can have costly consequences.

A relation R in the relational model is very similar to its counterpart in mathematics. When conceived as a table, R has the following properties:

■ each row represents a tuple of R;

■ the ordering of rows is immaterial;

■ all rows are distinct from one another in content.

From time to time, objects are discussed that violate the last item listed, but that are mistakenly called relations by vendors of database management systems (abbreviated DBMS). In this book, such objects are called *improper relations* or *corrupted relations*. Reasons why improper relations should *not* be supported in any database management system are discussed in Chapter 23.

The fact that relations can be perceived as tables, and that tables are similar to flat files, breeds the false assumption that the freedom of action permitted with tables or flat files must also be permitted when manipulating relations. The manipulation differences are quite strong. For example, rows that entirely duplicate one another are not permitted in relations. The more disciplined approach of the relational model is largely justified because the database is shared by many people; in spite of the heavy traffic, all of the information in that database must be maintained in an accurate state.

The concept of a relation in the relational model is slightly more abstract than its counterpart in mathematics. Not only does the relation have a name, but each column has a distinct name, which often is not the same as the name of the pertinent set (the domain) from which that column draws its values. There are three main reasons for using a distinct column name:

1. such a name is intended to convey to users some aspect of the intended meaning of the column;
2. it enables users to avoid remembering positions of columns, as well as which component of a tuple is next to which in any sense of "nextness;"
3. it provides a simple means of distinguishing each column from its underlying domain. A column is, in fact, a particular use of a domain.

One reason for abandoning positional concepts altogether in the relations of the relational model is that it is not at all unusual to find database relations, each of which has as many as 50, 100, or even 150 columns. Users therefore are given an unnecessary burden if they must remember the ordering of columns and which column is next to which. Users are far more concerned with identifying columns by their names than by their positions, whether the positions be those in storage or those in some declaration. It makes much more sense for a user to request an employee's date of birth by name than by what its position happens to be (for example, column # 37).

One reason for discussing relations in such detail is that there appears to be a serious misunderstanding in the computer field concerning relations. There is a widely held misconception that, for one collection S of data to be related to another collection T, there must exist a pointer or some kind of link from S to T that is exposed to users. A pointer to T, incidentally, has as its value the storage address of some key component of T. A recent article [Sweet 1988] shows that this false notion still exists.

Table 1.1 **Relations in Mathematics Versus Relations in the Relational Model**

Mathematics	Relational Model
Unconstrained values	Atomic values
Columns not named	Each column named
Columns distinguished from each other by position	Columns distinguished from each other and from domains by name
Normally constant	Normally varies with time

For many reasons, pointers are extremely weak in supporting relations. In fact, an individual pointer is capable of supporting no more than a relation of degree 2, and even then supports it in only one direction. Moreover, pointers tend to foster needlessly complex structures that frustrate interaction with the database by casual users, especially if they are not programmers. The slow acceptance of artificial intelligence (AI) programs has been largely due to the use of incredibly complex data structures in that field. This supports the contention that AI researchers write their programs solely for other AI researchers to comprehend.

It is therefore a basic rule in relational databases that there should be no pointers at all in the user's or programmer's perception. For implementation purposes, however, pointers can be used in a relational database management system "under the covers," which may in some cases allow the DBMS vendor to offer improved performance.[1]

The term "relation" in mathematics means a fixed relation or constant, unless it is explicitly stated to be a variable. In the relational model exactly the reverse is true: every relation in the relational model is taken to be a variable unless otherwise stated. Normally it is the extension of relations (i.e., the tuples or rows) that is subject to change. Occasionally, however, new columns may be added and old columns dropped without changing the name of the relation.

The distinctions between the relation of mathematics and that of the relational model are summarized in Table 1.1.

A final note about relations: every tuple or row coupled with the name of the relation represents an assertion. For example, every row in the EMPLOYEE relation is an assertion that a specific person is an employee of the company and has the immediate single-valued properties cited in the row. Every row in the CAN_SUPPLY relation is an assertion that the cited supplier can supply the cited kind of part with the cited speed in the cited minimum package and at the cited cost. It is this general fact that makes relational databases highly compatible with knowledge bases.

---

1. Occasionally it is necessary in this book to discuss some features of database management that are at too low a level of abstraction to be included in the relational model. When this occurs, such features are said to be *under the covers* or *hidden from the user's view*.

In a reasonably complete approach to database management, it is not enough to describe the types of structure applied to data. In the recent past, numerous inventors have stopped at that point, omitting the operators that can be used in query and manipulative activities, data-description techniques, authorization techniques, and prevention of loss of integrity (see [Chen 1976] for an example). All of these capabilities should be designed into the DBMS from the start, not added afterwards. If a similar approach were adopted in medical science, all that would be taught is anatomy. Other important subjects such as physiology, neurology, and cardiology would be omitted. Database management has many facets in addition to the types of structure applied to data. Of key importance is the collection of operators that can be applied to the proposed types of data structure.

The relational model provides numerous operators that convert one or more relations into other relations; these are discussed in Chapters 4 and 5. Very few of these operators were conceived by mathematicians before the relational model was invented. One probable reason for this was the widely held belief that any problem expressed in terms of relations of arbitrary degree can be reduced to an equivalent problem expressed in terms of relations of degree one and two. My work on normalizing relations of assorted degrees shows this belief to be false.

1.2 ■ The Relational Model

A database can be of two major types: production-oriented or exploratory. In commerce, industry, government, or educational institutions, a production-oriented database is intended to convey at all times the state of part or all of the activity in the enterprise.

An exploratory database, on the other hand, is intended to explore possibilities (usually in the future) and to plan possible future activities. Thus, a production-oriented database is intended to reflect reality, while an exploratory database is intended to represent what might be or what might happen. In both cases the accuracy, consistency, and integrity of the data are extremely important.

Database management involves the sharing of large quantities of data by many users—who, for the most part, conceive their actions on the data independently from one another. The opportunities for users to damage data shared in this way are enormous, unless all users, whether knowledgeable about programming or not, abide by a discipline.

The very idea of a discipline, however, is abhorrent to many people, and I understand why. For example, I have encountered those who oppose a special feature of the relational model, namely, the prohibition of duplicate rows within all relations. They declare, "Why shouldn't I have duplicate rows if I want them? I am simply not prepared to give up my freedom in this regard." My response is as follows. If the data were a purely private concern (to just this single user), it would not matter. If, on the other hand, the data is shared or is likely to be shared sometime in the future, then *all of the users of this data* would have to agree on what it means for a row to be duplicated (perhaps many times over). In other words, the sharing of data requires the sharing of its meaning. In turn, the sharing of meaning requires that there exist a single, simple, and explicit description of the meaning of every row in every relation. This is necessary even though one user may attach more importance to some facet of the meaning than some other user does.

Returning to the questionable support of duplicate rows, if the DBMS supports duplicate rows or records, it must be designed to handle these duplicates in a uniform way. Thus, there must be a general consensus among *all of the users of a DBMS product* regarding the meaning of duplicate rows, and this meaning should *not* be context-sensitive (i.e., it should not vary from relation to relation). My observation is that no such consensus exists, and is not likely to exist in the future.

For this reason and others, the discipline needed for the successful sharing of important data should be embodied within the database management system. The relational model can be construed as a highly disciplined approach to database management. Adherence to this discipline by users is enforced by the DBMS provided that this system is based whole-heartedly on the relational model.

As a normal mode of operation, if a user wishes to interpret the data in a database differently from the shared meaning, the DBMS should permit that user to extract a copy of the data from the database for this purpose (provided that the user is suitably authorized), and should disallow re-entry of that data into the database.

The management of shared data presents significantly tougher problems than the management of private data. Also, the role of shared data in efficiently carrying out business and government work is rapidly becoming a central concern. These two facts strongly suggest that no compromises be made on the quality of systems that manage the sharing of data simply to support a small minority of users of private data.

1.2.1 Relation as the Only Compound Data Type

From a database perspective, data can be classified into two types: atomic and compound. Atomic data *cannot* be decomposed into smaller pieces by the DBMS (excluding certain special functions). Compound data, consisting of structured combinations of atomic data, *can* be decomposed by the DBMS.

In the relational model there is only one type of compound data: the relation. The values in the domains on which each relation is defined are required to be atomic with respect to the DBMS. A relational database is a collection of relations of assorted degrees. All of the query and manipulative operators are upon relations, and all of them generate relations as results. Why focus on just one type of compound data? The main reason is that any additional types of compound data add complexity without adding power.

This is particularly true of the query and manipulative language. In such a language it is essential to have at least four commands: **retrieve, insert, update,** and **delete.** If there are N distinct types of compound data, then for these four operations $4N$ commands will be necessary. By choosing a single compound data type that, by itself, is adequate for database management, the smallest value (one) is being selected for N.

In non-relational approaches to database management, there was a growing tendency to expose more and more distinct types of compound data. Consequently, the query and manipulative languages were becoming more and more complicated, and at the same time significantly less comprehensible to users, even those who were knowledgeable about programming.

Relational databases that have many relations, each with few rows (tuples), are often called *rich,* while those that have few relations, each with many rows, are called *large.* Commercial databases tend to be large, but not particularly rich. Knowledge databases tend to be rich, but not particularly large.

About six years after my first two papers on the relational model [Codd 1969 and 1970], Chen [1976] published a technical paper describing the entity-relationship approach to database management. This approach is discussed in more detail in Chapter 30, which deals with proposed alternatives to the relational model. Although some favor the entity-relationship approach, it suffers from three fundamental problems:

1. Only the structural aspects were described; neither the operators upon these structures nor the integrity constraints were discussed. Therefore, it was not a data model.

2. The distinction between entities and relationships was not, and is still not, precisely defined. Consequently, one person's entity is another person's relationship.

3. Even if this distinction had been precisely defined, it would have added complexity without adding power.

Whatever is conceived as entities, and whatever is conceived as relationships, are perceived and operated upon in the relational model in just one common way: as relations. An entity may be regarded as inter-relating an object or identifier of an object with its immediate properties. A relationship may be regarded as a relation between objects together with the immediate properties of that relationship.

1.2.2 Inter-relating the Information Contained in Distinct Relations

Some people who are used to past approaches find it extremely difficult to understand how information in distinct relations can possibly be inter-related by the relational model without the explicit appearance in the user's perception of pointers or links.

The fundamental principle in the relational model is that all inter-relating is achieved by means of comparisons of values, whether these values identify objects in the real world or whether they indicate properties of those objects. A pair of values may be *meaningfully compared,* however, if and only if these values are drawn from a common domain.

Some readers may consider the "common domain" constraint to be an unnecessary restriction. The opportunities for comparing values even with this constraint, however, are vastly superior in numbers and quality over the old approach of requiring pointers, links, or storage contiguity. Regarding the numbers, it should be remembered that not only object-identifiers can be compared with each other, but also simple properties of objects. Regarding the quality, those relational operators that involve the comparing of values require the values that are compared to be drawn from a common domain. In this way, these operators protect users from making very costly kinds of errors.

An example may help. Suppose the database contains serial numbers of suppliers and serial numbers of parts. Then, the immediate properties of a supplier contained in the SUPPLIER relation can be inter-related to the immediate properties of a supplier's capability contained in the CAPABIL-ITIES relation by means of a single relational operator. This operator is the **equi-join,** and its application in this case involves comparing for equality the serial numbers of suppliers in the SUPPLIERS relation with those serial numbers in the CAPABILITIES relation.

Suppose that values for the serial numbers of suppliers and parts happen to have the same basic data type (i.e., character strings of the same length). Naturally, it is not meaningful to compare the supplier serial number in the SUPPLIER relation with the part serial number in the CAPABILITIES relation, even though they happen to have the same basic data type. Thus, the domain concept plays a crucial role in the inter-relating game. In fact, in Chapter 3 I discuss the general problem of determining of a given collection of relations whether they are all inter-relatable; domains are an essential and central concept in that discussion.

1.2.3 Examples of Relations

Two examples of relations in the relational model, described next, are intended to convey the structural uniformity of the approach to representing the information in relational databases for users (including application pro-grammers). The first of these examples is the parts relation P, which iden-tifies and describes each kind of part carried in inventory by a manufacturer.

P#	Part serial number
PNAME	Part name
SIZE	Part size
QP	Quantity of parts

OH__QP   Quantity of parts on hand

OO__QP   Quantity of parts on order

MOH__QP   Minimum quantity of parts to be in inventory

There are only four domains: P#, PNAME, SIZE, and QP.

P	P#	PNAME	SIZE	QP		
				OH__QP	OO__QP	MOH__QP
	p1	nut	10	500	300	400
	p2	nut	20	800	0	300
	p3	bolt	5	400	200	300
	p4	screw	12	1200	0	800
	p5	cam	6	150	150	100
	p6	cog	15	120	200	100
	p7	cog	25	200	50	100

This relation has six columns and therefore is of degree six. All of the rows (seven in this example) constitute the *extension* of the parts relation P. Sometimes the extension of a relation is called its *snapshot*. The remaining descriptive information constitutes the *intension* of the parts relation P.

The second example, the capabilities relation C, is intended to provide information concerning which suppliers can supply which kinds of parts.

In many approaches to database management, such a concept is treated entirely differently from the information concerning parts, differently from both the structural and the manipulative points of view. (Most of these approaches are pre-relational.) Parts are called entities, while each capability is called a relationship between suppliers and parts. The problem is that capabilities have immediate properties just as parts do. Examples of properties that are applicable to capabilities are the speed of delivery of parts ordered, the minimum package size adopted by the supplier as the unit of delivery, and the price of this unit delivered.

This example may help the reader understand why, in the relational model, precisely the same structure is adopted for capabilities as for parts— and, more generally, precisely the same structure is adopted for entities as for relationships between entities.

S#   supplier serial number

P#   part serial number

SPEED   number of business days to deliver

QP   quantity of parts

UNIT__QP   minimum package

MONEY   U.S. currency

PRICE   price in U.S. dollars of minimum package

There are five domains: S#, P#, TIME, QP, and MONEY.

C	S#	P#	SPEED	UNIT_QP	PRICE
	s1	p1	5	100	10
	s1	p2	5	100	20
	s1	p6	12	10	600
	s2	p3	5	50	37
	s2	p4	5	100	15
	s3	p6	5	10	700
	s4	p2	5	100	15
	s4	p5	15	5	300
	s5	p6	10	5	350

This relation has five columns and is therefore of degree five. All of the rows (nine in this example) constitute the *extension* of the capabilities relation C. The remaining descriptive information constitutes the *intension* of relation C.

1.2.4 Omission of Features

When implementing a relational database management system, many questions arise regarding the relational model. Occasionally, support for some basic feature has been omitted due to it being assessed as useless. Unfortunately, the relational model has always had features that are inextricably intertwined. This means that omission of one feature of the model in a DBMS can inhibit implementation of numerous others. For example, omission of support for primary keys and foreign keys (defined in Section 1.8) jeopardizes the implementation of

■ view updatability (see Chapter 17),
■ the principal integrity constraints (see Chapter 13), and
■ logical data independence (see Chapter 20).

1.2.5 The Goals of RM/V2

Version 2 of the relational model (abbreviated RM/V2) now has 333 features, which are even more inextricably intertwined than the approximately 50 features of Version 1 (see Appendix A.4). Most of the original definitions and features of RM/V1 have been preserved unchanged in Version 2. A very few of the original definitions and features have been extended to become broader in scope!

In late 1978 I developed an extended version of the relational model called RM/T [Codd 1979]. A principal aim was to capture more of the meaning of the data. Acceptance of the ideas in this version has been exceptionally slow. Consequently, it seems prudent to develop a sequence of versions V1, V2, V3, . . . that are more gradual in growth. As the development of this sequence proceeds, certain features of RM/T will be selected and incorporated in appropriate versions.

My goals in developing Version 2 of the relational model included all those for the original relational model, RM/V1. Three of the most important of these goals were, and remain,

1. simplifying interaction with the data by users
   a. who have large databases,
   b. who need not be familiar with programming, and
   c. who normally conceive their interactions independently from all other users;
2. substantially increasing the productivity of those users who are professional programmers;
3. supporting a much more powerful tool for the database administrator to use in controlling who has access to what information and for what purpose, as well as in controlling the integrity of the database.

If these goals were attained, and I believe they have been, the market for DBMS products would be expanded enormously. This suggests one more goal, namely, that a very strong emphasis be placed on the preservation by the DBMS of database integrity. Chapters 13 and 14 are devoted to the treatment of integrity by the relational model. The DBMS products available so far have supported very few of the integrity features of the model.

It is the database administrator (abbreviated DBA) who is responsible for imposing controls on the database: controls that are adequate for the DBMS to maintain the database in a state of full integrity, as well as controls that permit access for specified purposes to only those users with authorized access for those purposes. The DBMS, however, must provide the DBA with the tools to carry out his or her job. Pre-relational DBMS products failed to provide adequate tools for this purpose.

Implementation of a high-performance DBMS that supports every feature of RM/V2 is not claimed to be easy. In fact, it is quite a challenging task. There are already clear indications that the DBMS products leading in performance and in fault tolerance will be those based on new hardware and software architectures, both of which exploit the many opportunities for concurrency provided by the relational model.

1.2.6 The Relational Model as an Abstract Machine

The term "abstract" scares many people who work in computing or data processing, even though they deal with abstractions every day. For example, speed and distance are abstractions. An airline reservation is an abstraction. Bits and bytes are abstractions. So are computer commands.

In my book *Cellular Automata* [Codd 1968], I make use of at least four levels of abstraction to explain concisely how a self-reproducing computer that is capable of computing all computable functions might be designed from a large number (in fact, millions) of simple identical cells, each of which interacts with only its immediate neighbors.

It is useful to think of RM/V2 as an abstract machine. Its level of abstraction is sufficiently high that it can be implemented in many distinctly different ways in hardware, in software, or in both. This machine can be advantageously treated by all DBMS vendors, standards committees, and DBMS users as an abstract machine standard.

For example, consider the structural features introduced in Chapter 2. Their level of abstraction is necessary for enabling different types of hardware and software (possibly from different vendors) to communicate with one another about their databases. The abstract machine must be complemented with standards that deal with the following:

- the physical representation of data for inter-computer communication;
- transaction-control signals to facilitate adequate control of each transaction that straddles two or more computer systems (e.g., the signal from one system to the other "Are you ready to commit your data?");
- specific relational languages that have specific syntax.

These topics are discussed in detail in Chapters 24 and 25.

1.2.7 The Structured Query Language (SQL)

Many people may contend that a specific relational language, namely SQL, already exists as a standard. SQL, standing for structured query language, is a data sublanguage invented by a group in IBM Research, Yorktown Heights, N.Y. [IBM 1972].

SQL was invented in late 1972. Although it was claimed that the language was based on several of my early papers on the relational model, it is quite weak in its fidelity to the model. Past and current versions of this relational language are in many ways inconsistent with both of the abstract machines RM/V1 and RM/V2. Numerous features are not supported at all, and others are supported incorrectly. Each of these inconsistencies can be shown to reduce the usefulness and practicality of SQL.

The most noteworthy error in several current implementations is that SQL permits the use and generation of improper or corrupted relations, that is, "relations" that contain duplicate tuples or rows. In Chapter 23 this problem is examined in sufficient detail to demonstrate the seriously adverse consequences of this very simple infidelity to the model. As each feature of RM/V2 is introduced in this book, the attempt is made to comment on SQL's support, non-support, or violation of the feature.

Several relational languages other than SQL have been developed. An example that I consider superior to SQL is Query Language (abbreviated QUEL). This language was invented by Held and Stonebraker at the University of California, Berkeley, and was based on the language ALPHA [Codd 1972]. More attention is devoted to SQL, however, because it has been adopted as an ANSI standard, and is supported in numerous DBMS products.

1.2.8 An Abstract Machine Standard

The computing field clearly needs an abstract machine standard for database management for at least the following reasons:

■ The intrinsic importance of computer-based support for the sharing of business information interactively and by program.

■ The users involved in this sharing normally conceive their modifications of the information independently of one another.

■ Clearly the field of database management is moving toward the management of distributed databases, and at each of the sites involved there may be hardware and software from a variety of vendors. Intercommunication among these systems will be a vital requirement.

■ The boundary between hardware and software is moving out from the von Neumann position. Hardware is taking on more of the tasks previously handled by basic software, and already there are products in which numerous components of operating systems and DBMS are supported by hardware. An abstract machine standard for database management should enable this boundary to move without the necessity of continual reformulation of a new standard.

The relational model deals with database management from an abstract, logical point of view only, never at the detailed level of bits and bytes. Does this make the relational model incomplete? If incomplete in this sense, the model is intended to be this way. It is important to stop short of prescribing how data should be represented and positioned in storage, and also how it should be accessed. This not only makes users and programmers more productive, but also permits both hardware and software vendors to compete in lower-level techniques for obtaining good performance.

This is an area of considerable technical significance in which DBMS vendors can productively compete with one another. In the case of DBMS products that are carefully based on the relational model, such competition need not adversely affect the users' investment in training and application development, precisely because their perception is at a high level of abstraction.

One final reason for a high level of abstraction is that the choice of representation for data in storage and the choice of access methods depend heavily on the nature and volume of the traffic on the database.

Publication of the relational model in the June 1970 issue of *Communications of the Association for Computing Machinery* [Codd 1970] preceded the completion of development of relational DBMS products by at least a decade. The model is more abstract than these systems and has an existence that is completely independent of them.

This is an advantage in many ways. First, it provides a useful goal, target, and tool for the designers and developers of new DBMS products. Second, it provides a special kind of standard against which dissimilar DBMS products can be measured and compared. No DBMS product or data sub-language marketed in the western world today fully supports each and every feature of the relational model, even Version 1 [Codd 1969, 1970, 1971a–d, 1974a]. Third, it provides a foundation upon which theoretical work in database management has been and will continue to be based.

1.3 ■ The Transaction Concept

Brief reference was made to the concept of a transaction in the preceding discussion of the additional kinds of standards that are now needed. In the relational model, this concept has a precise definition.

A *transaction* is a collection of activities involving changes to the database, all of which must be executed successfully if the changes are to be committed to the database, and none of which may be committed if any one or more of the activities fail. Normally, such a collection of activities is represented by a sequence of relational commands. The beginning of the sequence is signaled by a command such as BEGIN or BEGIN TRANSACTION. Its termination is signaled by a command such as END or COMMIT—or, if it is necessary to abort the transaction, ABORT.

A simple example of a transaction is that in which a bank customer requests the bank to transfer $1,000 from his checking account into his savings account. In the bank's computer program the first action is to check that there is at least $1,000 in the customer's checking account. If so, this amount is deducted from the balance in that account. The next action is to credit the customer's savings account with the $1,000.

If the first action were successful and the second action failed (due to hardware malfunction, for example), the customer would lose the $1,000; this would be unacceptable to most customers. Therefore, this is a case in which both actions must succeed or neither must cause any change in the database.

In DBMS products two methods of handling a transaction are as follows:

1. to delay storing in the database any data generated during execution of a transaction until the DBMS encounters a COMMIT or END TRANSACTION command, and then store all of this data;

2. to write details of each change in the recovery log as each change is generated, and immediately record the change in the database. This log

is then used for recovery purposes if an ABORT TRANSACTION command is to be executed.

1.4 ■ Classification of RM/V2 Features

Each feature of the relational model RM/V2 is assigned to one of the 18 classes listed in Table 1.2. The table includes the number of the chapter in which each class of features is described. Each letter identifies the class. Each feature has a unique label. Thus, in the feature RS-9, R stands for relational, S for the structure class, and 9 for the ninth feature in that class. The numbering of features within a class should be interpreted as a distinctive label only, not as an ordering of importance.

There is no claim that the features of RM/V2 are all independent of one another. In fact, as discussed earlier, there are numerous inter-dependencies among the features. A minimal, totally non-redundant set would be more difficult to understand, would probably reduce user productivity significantly, and would probably lead to even more errors by vendors in designing their relational DBMS products. Of course, I am not advocating

Table 1.2 **The 18 Classes of Features and the Pertinent Chapters**

Chapter	Label	Class
2	S	Structural
3	T	Extended data types
4	B	Basic operators
5	Z	Advanced operators
6	N	Naming
7	E	Elementary commands
10	Q	Qualifiers
11	J	Indicators
12	M	Manipulative
13,14	I	Integrity
15	C	Catalog
16,17	V	View
18	A	Authorization
19	F	Scalar and aggregate functions
20	P	Protection of user investment in the DBMS, the database, application programming, and user training
21	D	DBMS design principles
22	L	Language-design principles
24,25	X	Distributed database management

the other extreme, namely complexity, since this runs counter to comprehensibility.

Two very important concepts of relational DBMS products are the *catalog* and *views*. Some think that the basic relational model does not mention the catalog or views, but these concepts were discussed in my early papers on the relational model, although not by these names. I referred to the catalog as the *relational schema* and to views as *derived relations* whose definitions were stored in the schema. In this book I have adopted the System R terms "catalog" and "view" [Chamberlin et al. 1981] because they are concise and very usable, and are now quite widely used. System R was one of three DBMS prototypes developed in distinct divisions of IBM and based on the relational model.

When DBMS products are evaluated today, the evaluation should include fidelity of the product to the relational model, and specifically RM/V2. In part, this is required because almost all vendors claim that their DBMS products are relational. Therefore, one important concern for potential users of these products is that they reap all the benefits of fidelity to the relational model.

As with RM/V1, the features that are included in RM/V2 are intended to be helpful for all users of relational DBMS, both application programmers and end users. Also, as with RM/V1, they are intended to help the designers, implementors, and evaluators of relational DBMS products. RM/V2 features include all the features of RM/V1, together with the following:

■ new features that cover important aspects of relational DBMS not previously included in RM/V1, either because they were overlooked or because I considered them too obvious to mention, until I discovered that many people had not realized their obvious importance;

■ new features that are in line with the original RM/V1, but at a slightly lower level of abstraction.

A DBMS product is *fully relational* in the 1990s if it fully supports each and every one of the features of RM/V2 defined in this book. A DBMS product that is not fully relational can nevertheless qualify to be called *relational* in the early 1990s by fully supporting each one of the roughly 67 features listed in Sections A.4 and A.5 of Appendix A.

Like the basic relational model RM/V1, all the features of RM/V2 are based on the practical requirements of users, database administrators, application programmers, security staff, and their managers. Along with the description of each feature, I attempt to explain the practical reasons for that feature.

The relational model RM/V2 is based on the original model RM/V1 and on a single fundamental rule, which I call Rule Zero:

For any system that is advertised as, or claimed to be, a relational database management system, *that system must be able to manage databases entirely through its relational capabilities,* no matter what additional capabilities the system may support.

This must hold *whether or not* the system supports any non-relational capabilities of managing data. Any DBMS that does *not* satisfy this Rule Zero is *not* a *relational* DBMS.

The danger to buyers and users of a system that is claimed to be a *relational* DBMS and fails on Rule Zero is that these buyers and users will expect all the advantages of a truly relational DBMS, but will fail to receive them.

One consequence of Rule Zero is that any system claimed to be a relational DBMS must support database insert, update, and delete at the *relational* level (multiple-record-at-a-time). (See Feature RM-6 in Chapter 12.) Another consequence is the necessity of supporting the information feature and the guaranteed-access feature. (See Feature RS-1 in Chapter 2 and Features RM-1 and RM-2 in Chapter 12.)

Incidentally, "multiple-record-at-a-time" includes the ability to handle those situations in which zero or one record happens to be retrieved, inserted, updated, or deleted. In other words, a relation (often carelessly called a table) may have either zero tuples (rows) or one tuple (row) and still be a valid relation. Note that although it may be unusual for a relation to have either zero rows or one row, it does not receive special treatment in the relational model, and therefore users do not have to treat such a relation in any special way either.

1.5 ■ Tables versus Relations

Actually, the terms "relation" and "table" are not synonymous. As discussed earlier, the concept of a relation found in mathematics and in the relational model is that of a *special kind of set*. The relations of the relational model, although they may be *conceived* as tables, are then special kinds of tables. In this book they are called *R-tables,* although the term "relation" is still used from time to time to emphasize the underlying concept of mathematical sets, to refer to the model, or to refer to languages developed as part of implementations of the model.

R-tables have no positional concepts. One may shuffle the rows without affecting information content. Thus, there is no "nextness" of rows. Similarly, one may shuffle the columns without affecting information content, providing the column heading is taken with each column. Thus, there is no "nextness" of columns.

Normally, neither of these shuffling activities can be applied with such immunity to arrays. That is why I consider it extremely misleading to use the term "array" to describe the structuring of data in the relational model.

Those relations, or R-tables, that are internally represented by stored data in some implementation-defined way are called the *base relations* or *base R-tables.* All R-tables other than base R-tables are called *derived relations* or, synonymously, *derived R-tables.* An example of a derived relation is a *view.* A view is a virtual R-table defined in terms of other R-tables, and is represented by its defining expression only.

In both RM/V1 and RM/V2, *duplicate rows are not permitted in any relations,* whether base relations, views, or any other type of relations. For details, see Features RS-3 and RI-3 in Chapters 2 and 13, respectively. This rule has been applied in all of my technical papers on the relational model, even the first one [Codd 1969].

In RM/V2, duplicate rows are still excluded from all relations. They are excluded from *base R-tables,* primarily as a step to retain integrity of the database: each row in such a table represents an object whose distinctiveness is lost if duplicate rows are allowed in these R-tables. A very fundamental property of the relational model is that each object about which information is stored in the database must be uniquely and explicitly identified, and thereby distinguished from every other object. As we shall see, the unique identifier is the name of the R-table, together with the primary key value. This fundamental property, an integrity-preservation feature, is not enforced by any other approach to database management.

Duplicate rows are still excluded from all *derived R-tables* for semantic reasons (see Fundamental Law 20 in Chapter 29). They are also excluded because such duplicates severely reduce the interchangeability of sequencing of operators within a relational command or in a sequence of commands. This reduction in interchangeability has two serious consequences (see Chapter 23 for more detail):

1. it reduces the optimizability of relational commands;
2. it imposes severe conceptual problems and severe constraints on users.

Two of the early prototypes of relational DBMS products were developed in the mid-1970s by the System R team at IBM Research in San Jose, Calif. [Chamberlin et al. 1981] and the INGRES team at the University of California Berkeley [Stonebraker 1986]. Curiously, both of these teams made the same two criticisms of the relational model:

1. the expected loss of performance if duplicate rows had to be eliminated in several types of relational operations without the user explicitly requesting that elimination;
2. the alleged impossibility of applying statistical functions correctly to columns that happen to have duplicate values legally.

Based on the first point, I conditionally agreed to the idea that duplicate rows should be permitted in derived R-tables *only,* not in base R-tables. The condition for this concession was that all of the effects upon the relational operators be carefully examined for possibly damaging consequences.

On the second point, I found myself in strong disagreement, because the mistake made in these two prototypes was to apply as a first step the projection operator (see Chapter 4) on the column or columns for which statistics were needed. Instead, I advised the researchers to apply the statistical function first in the context of whatever relation was given, and then apply the projection operator, only if such action were necessary for other reasons.

It now appears that neither project adequately examined the severely damaging effects of duplicate rows (1) on the operators and (2) on common interpretability by users (see Chapter 23).

This latter concern is related to the fact that, when hundreds, possibly thousands, of users share a common database, *it is essential that they also share a common meaning for all of the data therein that they are authorized to access.* There does not exist a precise, accepted, context-independent interpretation of duplicate rows in a relation. These adverse consequences are the reason that I still find that duplicate rows in any relation are unacceptable.

Let us turn our attention to a table that is extracted from a non-relational source for storage in a relational database. If it happens to contain duplicate rows, these duplicate rows can easily be removed by means of a special operator (see Feature RE-17 in Chapter 7). This operator removes all except one occurrence of each row that has multiple occurrences. It leaves the table unchanged if it happens to contain no duplicate rows.

From an evaluation standpoint, the RM/V2 features defined in this book have been created with primary concern for those DBMS products that are designed to support multiple users concurrently accessing shared data and engaged in tasks that can be (and often are) conceived independently of one another. Therefore, some of the features are not applicable to a DBMS intended for very small computer systems, particularly single-user systems such as personal computers.

An example of such a feature is concurrency control. Although locking as a form of concurrency control is mentioned in very few features of RM/V2, it is accompanied by the phrase "or some alternative technique for concurrency control that is at least as powerful as locking (and provably so)." I plan to say more about the subject of locking in a forthcoming book on computer-aided development (CAD) and engineering extensions to the relational model.

The logic that is usually encountered in data processing is propositional logic, often called Boolean logic, which deals with only two truth-values: TRUE and FALSE. In the field of database management, one reason that propositional logic was considered adequate in the past is that, before the relational model, logic was considered relevant to query products only, and such products normally supported the use of logic in the querying of single files only. Two truth values were considered adequate because no attempt was made to handle missing values in a uniform and systematic manner across the entire database.

Mathematical logic plays a central role in the relational model. In RM/V1 the logic is *three-valued,* first-order predicate logic, where the three truth-values are TRUE, FALSE, and MAYBE. This logic is substantially more powerful than propositional logic. The MAYBE truth-value means that the DBMS cannot decide whether a truth-valued expression is TRUE or FALSE due to values missing from the database.

In RM/V2 this logic is extended to *four-valued,* first-order predicate logic, where the four truth-values are TRUE, FALSE, MAYBE BUT APPLICABLE, and MAYBE BUT INAPPLICABLE. This is especially relevant when it becomes necessary to handle information that may contain some database values that are applicable but missing because they have not been entered yet, and some values that are missing because the property in question is inapplicable to the pertinent object (see Chapter 8 on missing information).

1.6 ■ Terminology

In this account of RM/V2, several terms that are now popular in database management are used, instead of the longer established and more carefully defined mathematical terms. Any ambiguity that is perceived in the use of the database-oriented terms can be resolved by referring to Table 1.3.

The degree *n* of a relation is the number of columns, which can be any positive integer, including the special case of a unary relation for which *n* = 1. A relational database is perceived by all users, whether application programmers or end users, as a collection of relations of assorted degrees. Each relation can be thought of as inter-relating the identifying properties of a type of object with the other immediate properties of that type of object. Every value appearing in a relation is treated by the DBMS as atomic, except for certain special functions that are able to decompose certain kinds of values (see Chapter 19).

The phrases "delete duplicates" and "delete redundant duplicates" mean *delete all occurrences except one* of an object (the object is determined by the context in which this phrase is used, and it is usually a complete row of an R-table).

Table 1.3 **Mathematical and Database Terms**

Mathematical Term	Database Term
Relation of degree *n*	R-table with n columns
Attribute	Column of R-table
Domain	Extended data type
Tuple	Row of R-table
Cardinality of relation	Number of rows in R-table

In this book the terms "interrogation," "query," and "retrieval" are used synonymously. Each of these terms denotes a read-only operation. No data modification is involved. Notwithstanding their names, identifying the database languages SQL and QUEL as just query languages is quite incorrect, since both support much more than interrogation.

The terms "modification" and "manipulation" are used whenever data modification is involved, whether it be data entry, deletion, or updating. Except where otherwise indicated, the term "updating" denotes a particular kind of modification, namely, modification applied to values already within the database. Therefore, updating is normally an operation that is distinct from both data entry and deletion.

When applied to any database activity, the term "dynamically" means *without* bringing any database traffic to a halt.

1.7 ■ Role of Language in the Relational Model

Early in the development of the relational model (1969-1972), I invented two languages for dealing with relations: one algebraic in nature, and one based on first-order predicate logic [Codd 1971a]. I then proved that the two languages had equal expressive power [Codd 1971d], but indicated that the logic-based language would be more optimizable (assuming that flow tracing was not attempted) and easier to use as an interface to inferential software on top of the DBMS.

During subsequent development of the relational model, I have avoided the development of a specific language with specific syntax. Instead, it seemed appropriate that my work remain at a very high level of abstraction, leaving it to others to deal with the specific details of usable languages. Thus, the relational model specifies the semantics of these languages, and does not specify the syntax at all.

The abbreviation RL denotes the principal relational language supported by the DBMS—a language intended specifically for database management, and one that is not guaranteed to be usable for the computation of all computable functions. RM/V2 specifies the features that RL should have, and the specification is (as we just saw) semantic, not syntactic. Examples of existing relational languages are SQL and QUEL, although neither of these supports more than half the relational model.

The power of RL includes that of four-valued, first-order predicate logic [Church 1958, Suppes 1967, Stoll 1961, Pospesel 1976]. The complete power of RL should be fully exploitable in at least the following contexts:

■ retrieval (database description, contents, and audit log);

■ view definition;

■ insertion, update, and deletion;

■ handling missing information (independent of data type);

- integrity constraints;
- authorization constraints;
- if the DBMS is claimed to be able to handle distributed data, distributed database management with distribution independence, including automatic decomposition of commands by the DBMS and automatic recomposition of results by the DBMS (see Feature RP-4 in Chapter 20).

One of the main reasons that "object-oriented" DBMS prototypes and products are not going to replace the relational model and associated DBMS products is these systems appear to omit support for predicate logic. It will take brilliant logicians to invent a tool as powerful as predicate logic. Even then, such an invention is not an overnight task—once invented, it might well take more than a decade to become accepted by logicians. Thus, features that capture more of the meaning of the data should be added to the relational model [Codd 1979], instead of being proposed as replacements.

In the development of application programs, a relational language normally needs as a partner a host language such as COBOL, PL/1, FORTRAN, or some more recently developed programming language. Some relational DBMS support several such host languages to be used as partners, although the user is normally required to select just one for developing an application program. In this book I occasionally use the term "HL" (for "host language") to denote such a language.

Languages are being developed that are significantly higher in level than COBOL, PL/1, and FORTRAN; such languages frequently include statements that must be translated into RL. Thus, an important requirement for RL is that it be both convenient and powerful in two roles: as a source language and as a target language.

Sometimes I am asked why I do not extend relational languages to include the features of PROLOG or of someone's favorite "fourth-generation" language. My usual reply is that I do not wish to tie the destiny of the relational model to any tool that has not been overwhelmingly accepted or does not appear to be defined at the same level of abstraction as the relational model. Moreover, I believe that the days of monstrous programming languages are numbered, and that the future lies with specialized sublanguages that can inter-communicate with one another.

1.8 ■ Keys and Referential Integrity

The term "key" has been used in the computing field for a long time, and with a great variety of meanings. In the relational model the term is normally qualified by the adjectives "candidate," "primary," and "foreign," and each of these phrases has a precisely defined meaning.

Each base R-table has exactly one primary key. This key is a combination of columns (possibly just one column) such that

- the value of the primary key in each row of the pertinent R-table identifies that row uniquely (i.e., it distinguishes that row from every other row in that R-table);
- if the primary key is composite and if one of the columns is dropped from the primary key, the first property is no longer guaranteed.

Sometimes these two properties are called the *uniqueness property* and the *minimality property,* respectively. Note, however, that "minimality" in this context does not mean the shortest in terms of bits or bytes or the one having the fewest components.

It is equally valid to interpret the uniqueness property in terms of object identification: the value of the primary key in each row of the pertinent R-table identifies the particular object represented by that row uniquely within the type of objects that are represented by that relation. Everywhere else in the database that there is a need to refer to that particular object, the *same* identifying value drawn from the *same* domain is used. Any column containing those values is called a *foreign key,* and each value in that column is called a *foreign key value.*

Referential integrity is defined as follows:

Let D be a domain from which one or more primary keys draw their values. Let K be a foreign key, which draws its values from domain D. Every unmarked value which occurs in K must also exist in the database as the value of the primary key on domain D of some base relation.

Incidentally, a value in the database is *marked* if and only if it is missing. The subject of missing information is discussed in some detail in Chapters 8 and 9.

The case in which K is a combination of columns, and some (perhaps all) of the component values of a foreign key value are allowed to be marked as missing, needs special attention. *Those components of such a foreign key value that are unmarked should adhere to the referential-integrity constraint.* This detail is not supported in many current DBMS products, even when the vendors claim that their products support referential integrity.

To make use of this definition, it is necessary to understand primary keys (PK) and foreign keys (FK). The example in the following subsection is intended to give the reader some understanding of the semantic nature of these keys.

1.8.1 Semantic Aspects of Primary and Foreign Keys

Notice that referential integrity applies to pairs of keys only, one a primary key PK and the other a foreign key FK. The keys may be simple (single-column) or composite (two or more columns). The DBMS should not require that each and every combination of simple keys within a single relation be treated as a foreign key, even if that combination appears as a composite primary key in the database. This is clearly an issue that is related to the meaning of the data.

Suppose, for example, that a database contains the relations listed in Table 1.4.

Table 1.4 **Example Relations in a Database**

Relation	Meaning	Primary Key
R1	Suppliers	S#
R2	Parts	P#
R3	The *capabilities* of suppliers to supply parts, including price and speed of delivery	(S#,P#)
R4	*Orders* for parts placed with specified suppliers, including date the order was placed	(S#,P#, DATE)

To avoid an extra relation and keep the example simple, assume that every order is a one-line order (that is, only one kind of part appears on any order) and that it is impossible for two orders with the same order date to refer to identical kinds of parts.

Suppose that each of two companies has a database of this kind. In company A, however, the relation R3 is used as advisory information, and there is no requirement that every combination of (S#,P#) that appears in R4 must appear in R3. In company B, on the other hand, R3 is used as controlling information: that is, if an order is placed for part p from supplier s, it is company policy that there must be at least one row in relation R3 stating that p is obtainable from s, and incidentally indicating the price and the speed of delivery. Of course, there may be other rows in R3 stating that p is obtainable from other suppliers. Thus, if referential integrity were applied to the combination (S#,P#) as primary key in R3 and foreign key in R4, it would be correct in company B, but incorrect in company A.

There are two ways in which this example (and similar ones) could be handled:

1. Make the referential integrity constraint applicable to all PK-FK pairs of keys (whether simple or composite) in which one key PK is declared to be primary, and the other key FK is declared to be foreign. In company B, declare the (S#,P#) combination in R4 as a foreign key that has as its target the (S#,P#) primary key of R3. In company A, avoid altogether the declaration that (S#,P#) in R4 is a foreign key.

2. Make the referential integrity constraint applicable to simple PK-FK pairs of keys only, and require the DBA to impose a referential con-

straint on just those compound PK-FK pairs of keys for which the constraint happens to be applicable in his or her company—by specifying a user-defined integrity constraint, expressed in the relational language.

Method 1 is the approach now adopted in the relational model. It makes the foreign-key concept a more semantic feature than does Method 2. After all, the concepts of keys in the relational model were always intended to identify objects in the micro-world that the database is supposed to represent. In other words, keys in the relational model act as surrogates for the objects being modeled. Once again, Method 1 is adopted.

1.8.2 Primary Keys on a Common Domain

Let us consider an example of the fact that primary keys on a given domain can occur in more than one base relation. This is the database in which there are two base R-tables that provide the immediate properties of suppliers: one for the domestic suppliers, one for the foreign suppliers. There would normally be some properties in the foreign suppliers table that do not occur in the domestic suppliers table. Each R-table has as its primary key the supplier serial number. Nevertheless, the database may contain several R-tables that include the supplier serial number as a foreign key without making any distinction regarding the R-tables in which the corresponding primary key value resides. In general, that value may reside as a primary key value in one, two, or even more R-tables.

No assumption is made in either RM/V1 or RM/V2 concerning the adoption of the tighter discipline of the extended relational model RM/T [Codd 1979]. For example, there is no requirement that type hierarchies be incorporated in the database design, wherever they are appropriate. Moreover, there is no requirement that, for each primary key, a unary relation (called the *E-relation* in RM/T) exists to list all of the distinct values in use for that primary key.

A second example in the non-distributed case is that of a base relation R that happens to have many columns, but a large amount of traffic on only 20% of these columns (call this A) and a very modest amount on the remaining 80% (call this B). In such a case the DBA may decide to improve performance by storing the data in the form of two base relations instead of one:

1. a projection of R onto its primary key together with A;
2. a projection of R onto its primary key together with B.

A specific feature of the relational model that requires support in the DBMS for multiple primary keys from a common domain is RS-10, described in the next chapter.

In the case of distributed database management, it is not at all uncommon to have the information distributed in such a way that several relations at several sites all have a primary key based on a common domain. See Section 24.4 for a detailed discussion of the relational approach to distributing data.

1.8.3 Comments on Implementation

Referential integrity is discussed further in Chapter 13. It should be implemented as far as possible as a special case of user-defined integrity (see Chapter 14) because of their similarities. One such common need, for example, is to give the DBA or other authorized user the freedom to specify linguistically how the system is to react to any attempt to violate these integrity constraints, whether the constraints are referential or user-defined.

Further, it should be remembered that referential integrity is a particular application of an *inclusion constraint* (sometimes called an inclusion dependency). Such a constraint requires that the set of distinct values occurring in some specified column, simple or composite, must be a subset of the values occurring in some other specified column (simple or composite, respectively). In the case of referential integrity, the set of distinct simple FK values should be a subset of the set of distinct simple PK values drawn from the same domain.

Inclusion constraints, however, may apply between other pairs of attributes also (e.g., non-keys). When declared and enforced, such additional constraints reflect either business policies or government regulations. One would then like the DBMS to be designed in such a way as to provide reasonably uniform support for referential integrity and these additional (user-defined) inclusion constraints.

1.9 ■ More on Terminology

The following terms are used in connection with relational languages and user-defined functions.

- *retrieval targeting:* specifying the kinds of database values to be extracted from the database, and then possibly specifying transformations to be applied to occurrences of these values;
- *retrieval conditioning:* specifying a logical condition in a retrieval or manipulative statement of a particular relational language for the purpose of conditioning access;
- *PK-targeting:* finding the primary key(s) corresponding to any given foreign key;
- *FK-targeting:* finding the foreign key(s) corresponding to any given primary key;

■ *PK-based projection:* a projection that includes the *primary key* of the operand R-table;

■ *non-PK projection:* a projection that does not include the *primary key* of the operand R-table.

1.10 ■ Points to Remember

Four important points concerning relations follow:

1. every relation is a set;
2. *not* every set is a relation;
3. every relation can be perceived as a table;
4. *not* every table is a correct perception of a relation.

Designers of the relational DBMS products of many vendors appear to be ignorant of these facts or to have ignored them.

Exercises

Note that, for some exercises, additional chapters are identified as sources of more information.

1.1 Identify the 18 classes of features in RM/V2. Supply a brief description of each class.

1.2 When a relation is perceived as a table, what are the special properties of that table? Is the ordering of columns crucial? Is the ordering of rows crucial? Can the table contain duplicate rows?

1.3 The terms "table" and "relation" are not synonymous. Supply a simple example of a table that is neither a relation of the relational model nor a relation of mathematics.

1.4 What is your position on the entity-relationship approach? (See also Chapter 30.) Will it replace the relational model? Give five technical reasons for your answer.

1.5 What is a transaction in the relational model? Describe an application that illustrates that there is a practical need for this concept.

1.6 Are either of the following statements true about the structures of the relational model?

They are merely flat files.
They are merely tables.

In each case, if your answer is no, give an example of a flat file that is not a relation or an example of a table that is not a relation.

1.7 What is your position on the object-oriented approach? (See also Chapter 30.) Will it replace the relational model? Give five reasons for your answer. You may wish to postpone this exercise, as well as Exercise 1.8, until you have absorbed Chapter 28.

1.8 Can any object-oriented concepts be added to the relational model without violating any of the principles on which the model is based? Which concepts? (See also Chapter 30.)

1.9 When designing a database, is it possible to anticipate all of the uses to which the data will be put? Is it possible to anticipate the batch load, on-line teleprocessing load, and interactive query load for the next three, five, or seven years? Conclude from your answer what properties the DBMS should have if it is to protect the user's investment in application programs. (See also Chapter 26.)

1.10 Are duplicate rows needed in a relation? If so, what for? Supply an example. Should duplicate rows be allowed in any relation? State reasons why or why not, whichever is applicable, and supply examples. (See also Chapters 2 and 23.)

1.11 In RM/V2 does the prohibition of duplicate rows within every relation imply that no duplicate values (e.g., currency values) can occur in any column? Explain.

■ *CHAPTER 2* ■

Structure-Oriented and Data-Oriented Features

Chapters 2 through 25 describe and explain the 333 features of RM/V2. In this chapter attention is focused on the way a relational database is structured and how the information in various parts of the database is inter-related. Each feature has a brief title and a unique label of the type R*Y-n*, where *Y* is a character that denotes the pertinent class of features and *n* is the feature number within this class.

Reference is made occasionally to "the 1985 set" [Codd 1985]. This set of 12 rules, a quick means of distinguishing the DBMS products that are relational from those that are not relational, can still be used for coarse distinctions. The features of RM/V2, however, are needed for distinctions of a finer grain.

2.1 ■ Databases and Knowledge Bases

As explained in Chapter 1, both a commercial database in the relational sense and a knowledge base consist largely of assertions. In commercial databases most of the assertions contain no variables. There are few distinct kinds of assertions, and very many assertions of each type (perhaps hundreds of millions). In knowledge bases, on the other hand, most of the assertions contain variables that are bound in the logician's sense. Moreover, there are many distinct kinds of assertions, and very few of each type (often just one).

The relational model is intended to be applied primarily to commercial and industrial databases. Thus, it takes advantage of the large numbers of assertions all of the same type. The predicate in the logician's sense that is common to all the assertions of one type is factored out and becomes the relation name.

There is a component of every relational database, however, that is very similar to a knowledge base, and that is the database description. Further discussion of this subject is postponed until Chapter 15. In any event, due to the focus of the relational model on cleanly expressed assertions unencumbered with irrelevant structural details (for example, the clutter of pointers), this model has an outstandingly clean interface to knowledge bases.

2.2 ■ General Features

RS-1   The Information Feature

See Rule 1 in the 1985 set. The DBMS requires that all database information seen by application programmers (AP) and interactive users at terminals (TU) is cast explicitly in terms of values in relations, and *in no other way* in the *base relations.* Exactly one additional way is permitted in *derived relations,* namely, ordering by values within the relation (sometimes referred to as inessential ordering).

This means, for example, that, in the database, users see no repeating groups, no pointers, no record identifiers (other than the declared primary keys), no essential (i.e., non-redundant) ordering, and no access paths. Obviously this is not a complete list. *Such objects may, however, be supported for performance reasons under the covers* because they are then not visible to users, and hence impose no productivity-reducing burden on them.

2.2.1 Repeating Groups

Many people experienced with pre-relational systems express shock or dismay at the exclusion of repeating groups from the relational model. Repeating groups had their origin in the trailer cards of the punched-card era. Thus, it seems worthwhile to consider an example that illustrates how repeating groups can be avoided.

Suppose that, at database-design time, it is decided that the database is to contain information concerning parts in the inventory and orders placed for more parts to be added to the inventory. An order usually consists of heading information such as the name and address of the supplier with whom the order is to be placed, an appropriate employee in the supplier company, the telephone number of this employee, the date when the supplier promises to ship the parts, the expected cost, and possibly other items of information. The line items then follow, and it is here that some think that a repeating group is needed.

In the relational approach the heading information for all orders is incorporated into a single relation, the *heading relation*. Similarly, the line items for all orders are incorporated into a single relation, the *trailing relation*. Each distinct order in the heading relation includes an order serial number as a unique identifier of the order. This identifier is, of course, the primary key of the heading relation. Every line item in the trailing relation includes the pertinent order serial number as a foreign key. This identifier, together with the line number for the pertinent line item, constitute the primary key of the trailing relation.

It will be seen that in eliminating repeating groups from the database design no information has been lost. Now the question arises, "Why eliminate repeating groups? Surely, they are both natural and harmless!"

In fact, they are not harmless. One of the principal penalties is that each repeating group must be positioned next to its heading information, and all members of a group must be positioned next to each other. The relational model avoids all decisions regarding positioning of information, allowing positioning to be used purely for performance purposes.

A second penalty is that repeating groups represent an additional way of representing information. Hence, one more retrieval command, one more insertion command, one more update command, and one more deletion command are needed in the data-manipulation vocabulary.

A third penalty is that logical database design now involves more decision making without a theoretical foundation upon which to base those decisions. Thus, if repeating groups were adopted, it would be necessary to conceive clear, concise, and rigorously established criteria for the database designers to choose whether or not to exploit repeating groups.

2.2.2 More on the Information Feature

Returning to the information feature RS-1, even R-table names, column names, and domain names are represented as character strings in some R-tables. R-tables containing such names are normally part of the built-in database catalog (see Chapter 15). The catalog is accordingly a relational database itself—one that is dynamic and active and that represents the *meta-data*. Meta-data consists of data that describes all of the data in the database, as well as the contents of the catalog itself.

The information feature is supported for several reasons. First, as explained in Chapter 1, this feature makes a simpler data sublanguage possible, and therefore supports user productivity. Second, it greatly simplifies the interface between the DBMS and software packages "on top of" the DBMS.

Examples of such software packages are application-development aids, expert systems, and dictionaries. These packages must not only interface with relational DBMS but, by definition, must be well integrated with the DBMS. This integration is necessary because these packages retrieve information already existing in the database (including the catalog) and, as needed, put new information in the database (and possibly in the catalog also).

An additional reason is to simplify the database administrator's task of maintaining the database in a state of overall integrity and to make this task more effective. There is nothing more embarrassing to a DBA than being asked whether the database contains certain specific information, and, after a week's examination of the database or of documents that allegedly describe the database, of having to reply that he or she does not know.

RS-2 Freedom from Positional Concepts

The DBMS protects the application programmers and terminal users from having to know any positional concepts in the database.

Examples of positional concepts follow:

- Where is a particular relation stored?
- Which row is next to a given row?
- Which column is next to a given column?

In dealing with databases that contain R-tables with thousands (sometimes millions) of rows, as well as hundreds of columns, it would place a heavy and unnecessary burden on users if the DBMS required them to remember which row or which column is next. User productivity would suffer seriously.

RS-3 Duplicate Rows Prohibited in Every Relation

The DBMS prohibits the occurrence of duplicate rows in any relation (whether base, view, or derived), and in this way protects the user from the subtle complexities and reduced optimizability that stem from permitting duplicate rows.

As mentioned in Chapter 1, for duplicate rows there is no precise, accepted definition that is context-independent. Consequently, there is no common interpretation that all users can share. Many of the present versions of SQL fail to support Feature RS-3. The adverse consequences are discussed in some detail in Chapter 23. Note that Feature RS-3 refers to entire rows being duplicated. It does *not* prohibit the occurrence of duplicate values in any column.

RS-4 Information Portability

If a row of a base R-table is moved in any kind of storage by the DBMS, its information content as perceived by users remains unchanged, and therefore need not be changed. The entire information content of the DBMS as seen by users must not be dependent upon the site or equipment in which any of the data is located.

An example of such a move is the archiving of a portion of an R-table. Another example is the re-distribution to different sites of parts of a distributed database. Thus, any hashing of data done by the system must not be perceptible to users. Similarly, if the primary key value is ever system-generated, that value cannot be a pointer or an address, and cannot be location-dependent in any way.

For the time being, this feature is not intended to include the case of vendor-independent physical representation of data stored in or retrieved from databases, especially on communication lines. This topic should be treated by standards organizations as a matter needing urgent attention. This feature is also not intended to apply to performance-oriented objects such as indexes.

2.2.3 Three-Level Architecture

About 1976 the SPARC committee of the American National Standards Institute (ANSI) announced with great fanfare something called the "three-schema architecture." The definitions of the three levels supplied by the committee in a report were extremely imprecise, and therefore could be interpreted in numerous ways. Upon reflection, however, I believe the idea had been already conceived and published as part of the relational model and as part of the System R architecture [Chamberlin et al. 1981]. Of course, the definitions in the relational model and in System R were much more precise, but the terminology was different.

Base relations are those relations represented directly by stored data (not by formulas or relational commands). *Views* are virtual relations defined in terms of the base relations and possibly other views using the relational operators. It is these definitions (either by formulas or by relational commands) that are stored in the catalog. *Storage representation* is the representation in storage for the information contained in base relations.

With an appropriate interpretation of the ANSI definitions, the correspondence in terms is as follows:

ANSI term	R-term
External schema	Views
Conceptual schema	Base relations
Internal schema	Storage representations

RS-5 Three-Level Architecture

A relational DBMS has a three-level architecture consisting of views, base relations, and storage representations.

This feature is concerned with the structural aspect only. Full support of the three-level architecture includes full support of view-manipulative Features RV-4, RV-5, and RV-6. It also includes a systematic approach to view updatability, which is the subject of Chapter 17.

2.3 ■ Domains, Columns, and Keys

Let us turn our attention to the concepts upon which the relations of the relational model are built.

RS-6 Declaration of Domains as Extended Data Types

Each semantically distinct domain is distinctly named and declared separately from the R-table declarations (since it may be used in several R-tables). Each domain is declared as an extended data type, not as a mere basic data type.

For an explanation of the differences between basic data types and extended data types, see the introductory text in Chapter 3 (preceding Feature RT-1). Feature RC-3 states in detail the kind of domain declaration that should be stored in the catalog.

The concept of a domain is quite fundamental. It is essential in determining whether a given relational database can be split into two or more independent databases without loss of meaningful derivable information—or, to express it another way, without loss of inter-relatedness (see Chapter 3).

Many features of RM/V2, as well as the original RM/V1, depend on the domain concept. Some of the advantages of supporting domains as extended data types are as follows:

- a large component of the description of every column that draws its values from a given domain need be declared only once in the domain declaration (this is called the *factoring advantage*);

- for every operator that involves comparing pairs of database values, the DBMS can ensure that each of the two components are semantically comparable by checking either at the start of the operation or (when possible) at compile time that both columns involved draw their values from a common domain (see Feature RM-14 in Chapter 12);

- integrity checks are facilitated (see Chapters 13 and 14, and Feature RD-7 in Chapter 21).

RS-7 Column Descriptions

For each column of each base R-table, there should be the capability of declaring (1) from which domain that column draws its values (thus identifying the extended data type) and (2) what additional constraints, if any, apply to values in that column.

When the DBMS fully supports the domain concept, it can detect errors resulting from users forgetting which columns have values of a given extended data type. Therefore, users can depend on the system to check whether the values in two given columns are semantically comparable (i.e., of the same extended data type).

RS-8 Primary Key for Each Base R-table

For each and every base R-table, the DBMS must require that one and only one primary key be declared. All of the values in this simple or composite column must be distinct from one another at all times. No value in any component column is allowed to be missing at any time.

Whether the primary key is indexed or not is a purely performance concern, and therefore a decision to be made by some authorized user quite separately (see Feature RD-3 in Chapter 21). The primary key is constrained by the DBMS to contain distinct primary key values in distinct rows, and (because of Feature RI-3 in Chapter 13) is not permitted to have missing values.

The constraints that values must be distinct and that missing values must be excluded may also, at the discretion of the DBA, be enforced on columns other than the primary key. Therefore, the mere existence of these constraints on some column or combination of columns does not identify which column(s) constitute the primary key.

A primary key may consist of a simple column or a combination of columns. When it consists of a combination of columns, the key is said to be *composite*. Each column participating in a composite primary key may be, but need not be, a foreign key.

RS-9 Primary Key for Certain Views

For each view the DBMS must support the declaration of a single *primary key* whenever the DBA observes that the definition of that view permits the existence of such a key, including adherence to the entity-integrity feature (see Feature RI-7 in Chapter 13). Where possible, the DBMS must check that a primary key declaration for a view is consistent with primary key declarations for the base R-tables.

Note that, in some cases, views can have instances of missing information *in every column* (although not all in one row, of course). In these cases, it is impossible to declare a primary key for the view and have it adhere to the entity-integrity feature. A simple example is a view that is a projection of a base R-table that does not include any column of the table from which missing values are prohibited (and thus does not include the primary key of that R-table). In these circumstances and in the view thus defined, use is made of the concept of a *weak identifier*, defined at the end of Section 5.3.

Generally, it is clearer to limit the specification of all kinds of integrity constraints to *base R-tables*. It is helpful to users, however, to have a primary key declared for each view whenever possible, because such a key plays a significant role as a unique identifier of objects during user interaction with a relational database. Further, it is reasonable to expect users to interact with views rather than with base R-tables, because in this way they enjoy more logical data independence. (See Feature RP-2 in Chapter 20.)

RS-10 Foreign Key

The DBMS permits the declaration of any column or combination of columns of a base R-table as a *foreign key* (where this is semantically applicable). Included in this declaration are the target primary keys (usually just one) for this foreign key. However, the DBMS must *not*, through its design, constrain the target to be just one primary key for a given foreign key, even though the most frequently occurring case may be just one.

In supporting more than one primary key as the target for a given foreign key, the DBMS must *not* assume that the corresponding primary key values are partitioned into disjoint sets in distinct R-tables. Moreover, the DBMS must *not* deduce foreign keys and their targets from the declared primary keys and their domains. In the case of composite foreign keys, the DBMS could be in error because of the semantic nature of key targeting (i.e., the association of foreign keys with primary keys). An example of this semantic nature is described in Section 1.8.1.

RS-11 Composite Domains

A user-chosen combination of simple domains can be declared to have a name, providing that name is distinct from that of any other domain (simple or composite). The sequence in which the component domains are cited in this declaration is part of the meaning of the combination.

An example of a composite domain is the combination of two simple domains: the supplier serial number domain and the part serial number domain. Several composite columns in a database may draw their values from this composite domain.

This declaration of combinations of domains enables them to be treated as unit pieces of information without specifying their components (in other words, as if they were simple domains). For example, if an **equi-join** (see Chapter 4) is required that involves comparing one combination of columns with another, and if both combinations happened to be based on the same composite domain, the user would be able to gain confidence more rapidly concerning the correctness of the **join,** and the DBMS would be able to check this correctness more rapidly.

For each composite domain, of course, the sequence in which the domains are specified is a vital part of the definition. For any composite column based on a composite domain, the sequence in which the combination of columns is specified must match the sequence in which the simple domains are specified that participate in the composite domain.

RS-12 Composite Columns

A user-chosen combination of simple columns within a base R-table or view can be declared to have a name, providing that name is distinct from that of any other column (simple or composite) within that R-table, and providing a composite domain has already been declared from which this composite column is to draw its values. The sequence in which the component columns are cited in this declaration is part of the meaning of the combination, and it must be identical to the sequence cited in the declaration of the corresponding composite domain.

An example of a frequently needed composite column is a postal address: the combination of an apartment or suite number in a building, the building number on some street, the street name, the city name within a state or country, and finally the state or country.

Note that, if a composite column is declared to contain every column of some R-table (admittedly a rare event), that combined column is not itself an R-table and should not be treated as if it were. In this case, the name of the R-table and the name of the composite column should be distinct.

The naming and declaration of combinations of columns enables them to be treated as unit pieces of information without specifying their components (in other words, as if they were simple columns). For example, if an **equi-join** (see Chapter 4) is required that involves comparing one combination of columns with another, and if these combinations happened to be declared and each named as such, it would be easier to express the comparison in terms of the combination names. For each composite column, of course, the sequence of simple domains corresponding to the sequence of components in each combination would have to be identical in order for the values to be comparable with one another.

Note that a composite column is restricted to combining simple columns within a single base R-table. This restriction should be interpreted in the sense that at present I am not taking a position either for or against the kind of composite columns that combine columns that may be simple or composite. Such columns are sometimes loosely referred to as "composites of composites." So far, I fail to see the practical need for them.

The name of the composite column can be the same as the name of the composite domain from which the composite column draws its values (barring ambiguity within the pertinent R-table). The name, however, should be distinct from that of any R-table (base or view), and it *must* be distinct from

- any simple column within the pertinent base R-table, and
- any other composite column already declared and still in effect for that R-table, and
- any word assigned special meaning within the relational language (i.e., any keyword of RL).

To explain the meaning of a comparator such as LESS THAN (<) applied to a pair of composite columns, suppose that the composite column C, consisting of C1, then C2, then C3, is to be compared with a composite column D, consisting of D1, then D2, then D3. The condition C < D is equivalent to making a sequence of tests:

C1 < D1, then C2 < D2, then C3 < D3.

The first test that fails causes the whole test to fail for the truth-valued expression C < D and that application of it. If duplicate values occur in some or all of these columns, there is no guarantee that a request for an ordering based on them will deliver exactly the same sequence of tuples in repeated execution of the request. To obtain precise repeatability, requests for ordering should be based on columns, which contain values that are distinct from one another.

The treatment is tantamount to C1 and D1 being treated as high-order, C2 and D2 as middle-order, and C3 and D3 as low-order in the usual arithmetic sense (whether the operands are numeric or character strings). The LESS THAN comparator applied to a pair of character strings makes use of a collating sequence established as a standard for database management and for data processing.

2.4 ■ Miscellaneous Features

RS-13   Missing Information: Representation

Throughout the database, the fact that a database value is missing is represented in a uniform and systematic way, independent of the data type of the missing database value. Marks are used for this purpose. (Note that RS-13 is the structural part of Rule 3 in the 1985 set; see Feature RM-11 in Chapter 12 for the manipulative part.)

The semantics of the fact that a database value is missing are quite different from the semantics of the value that is missing. See Chapters 8 and 9 or [Codd 1986a and 1987c] for more details. Marks were previously called nulls, and occasionally null values—which is even more misleading because it suggests that nulls behave just like other database values. To be independent of data type, they must be distinguishable from all database values of all types. Thus, any value whose bit representation lies within the bit boundaries of a database value is unacceptable in the role of representing the fact that a database value is missing. For example, if the following are stored in the same R-column as the corresponding non-missing database values, they are unacceptable as representations of missing values (whether built-in, default, DBA-declared, or user-declared):

- the empty character string,
- a string of blank characters or any other character string,
- zero or any other number,
- any string of bits.

An example of a conforming representation for missing information is that adopted in IBM's DB2. In this system, any column in which database values are permitted to be missing is assigned an extra byte outside the bit boundaries of the database values. This byte is reserved to indicate to the DBMS whether the corresponding value, which is represented by the bits within the bit boundaries of the database values in this column, is to be taken seriously as an actual value or as a fictitious value left over from some previous use.

To support database integrity, the DBMS should deduce from the primary key declaration that marks are not allowed for that column or combination of columns. It must be possible, however, for the DBA or some other suitably authorized user to specify "marks not allowed" for any other columns for which this happens to be an appropriate integrity constraint. An example would be certain foreign key columns.

Note that the "marks not allowed" declaration is *not* an alternative to an explicit declaration of the primary key. By itself, such a declaration is inadequate to distinguish primary key columns from other columns.

Techniques in database management before the relational approach required users to reserve a special value peculiar to each column or field to represent missing information. This would be most unsystematic in a relational database because users would have to employ different techniques for each column or for each domain. This is a difficult task because of the high level of language in use, and one that would lower the productivity of users significantly.

RS-14 Avoiding the Universal Relation

Neither the collection of all base relations nor the collection of all views should be cast by the DBMS in the form of a single "universal relation" (in the Stanford University sense) [Vardi 1988]. The DBA, however, should have the option of creating such a relation as one of the many views.

Generally, the database should be perceived as a collection of base relations and a collection of virtual relations (views), all of assorted degrees.

If all of the base relations or all of the views are each cast as a single universal relation (in the Stanford University sense), there are at least three adverse consequences:

1. waste of space (disk and memory) due to the large number of values that must be marked "property inapplicable," and waste of channel time for the same reason;

2. loss of adaptability to changes in the kinds of information stored in the database:

   a. more human effort is required when the counterpart of a new base R-table or view is defined,

   b. application programs will be adversely affected because their logic is not immune to the restructuring of the "universal relation," and

   c. more of a reorganizing load at the storage level is likely to be involved;

3. the need for joins on non-key values is not decreased, and their counterpart is more difficult for the user to request, because the key-based **join** built into the "universal relation" must be decomposed before the **join** based on non-keys is constructed.

In the relational model a database is treated as a collection of relations of assorted degrees. The Stanford University research on the universal relation concept was, I believe, motivated by the desire to eliminate the need for joins. In the universal relation approach, however, the combining of several relations (perhaps many) into a single relation is necessarily based on only one method of combination, and the method normally selected is by key-based equi-joins.

One of the great advantages of the relational approach is that it supports joins of all kinds, whether based on keys or not. It is quite likely that a database that adheres to the relational model has more distinct kinds of non-key-based joins than key-based ones. The approach adopted in the relational model is far more flexible and more adaptable to change.

When new kinds of information are introduced into a database, one can merely define new domains, new columns, and new R-tables as necessary. On the other hand, using the Stanford approach, this new information would have to be carefully fitted into the existing universal relation, which is a much more complicated problem. For more detail, see Chapter 30.

Exercises

2.1 Does RM/V2 permit any information to be carried solely in the ordering of rows in base relations? State reasons why or why not, whichever is applicable.

2.2 What is the precise definition of a domain in the relational model? Which of the following statements is always true, which always false, and which can be true in some cases and false in others?
1. A domain determines the type and range of values that may occur in one or more columns.
2. A domain determines the type and range of values that may occur in exactly one column.
3. Exactly one column determines the type and range of values that may occur in a domain.
4. One or more columns determine the type and range of values that may occur in a domain.

2.3 How should domains be supported? What is wrong with storing for each and every domain all of the values that belong to it? (**10, 17**)

2.4 IBM's DB2 supports the language SQL for database interrogation, manipulation, and control. Should the declaration of a primary key for each base relation be optional, as in the SQL of Version 2 of IBM's DB2? Give reasons for your answer.

2.5 Define the candidate-key concept. Define the primary-key concept.

2.6 Why does the primary-key concept preclude there being two or more primary keys in a base table? Explain the problems that result from having two or more primary keys per relation.

2.7 Why is a single primary key mandatory for each base relation? Does this requirement reduce the range of applicability of the relational model?

2.8 Does the fact that a column has been declared to be the primary key of some base relation mean that the column must be indexed? How about the reverse implication?

2.9 Does RM/V2 *require* a relation to be stored as (1) a table, (2) an array, (3) a flat file, or (4) a collection of records connected by pointers? (See also Chapter 20.)

2.10 Does RM/V2 *require* a relation to be stored row by row? Does RM/V2 *require* the components to be ordered within each row in storage in the same sequence as the columns are declared in the catalog? (See also Chapter 20.)

2.11 What does it mean for a value to be atomic with respect to the DBMS? Is not an atomic value always atomic?

2.12 Supply two reasons why the DBA should always control the introduction of new types of values into the database to ensure that these values are atomic in meaning as well as atomic with respect to the DBMS.

▪ *CHAPTER 3* ▪

Domains as Extended
Data Types

3.1 ▪ Basic and Extended Data Types

The concept of domains has played a very important role in the relational model since the model was conceived. It is not overstating the case to say that the domain concept is fundamental. It participates crucially in the definition of numerous features of RM/V1 and RM/V2. *Consequently, many of these features cannot be fully supported by a DBMS unless that DBMS supports domains.* Omission of support for domains is the most serious deficiency in today's relational DBMS products.

In my first two papers on the relational model [Codd 1969 and 1970], domains and columns were inadequately distinguished. In subsequent papers (e.g., Codd 1971a, 1971b, and 1974a), I realized the need to make this distinction, and introduced *domains* as declared data types, and *attributes* (now often called *columns*) as declared specific uses of domains. It has become clear that domains as data types go beyond what is normally understood by data types in today's programming languages. Consequently, as noted in Chapter 2, when domains are viewed as data types, I now refer to them as *extended data types*. With regard to the data types found in programming languages (excluding PASCAL and ADA), I refer to them as *basic data types*.

An extended data type is intended to capture some of the meaning of the data. It is conceptually similar to a basic data type found in many programming languages. If, however, two semantically distinguishable types of real-world objects or properties happen to be represented by values of

43

the same basic data type, the user nevertheless assigns distinct names to these types and *the system keeps track of their type distinction.*

The description of an extended data type includes its basic data type together with information concerning the range of values permitted, and whether the less than comparator (<) is *meaningfully applicable* to its values. The distinction between extended data type and basic data type is *not* that the first is user-defined and the second is built into the system, even though many of the extended data types will, in practice, be user-defined.

Note that, unless it is built into the system, a domain, and hence an extended data type, must be declared as an object itself before any use can be made of it. Whenever an extended data type is built into the system, its name as an object must be available to users.

In contrast, a basic data type is normally a property associated with an object at the time of the declaration of that object. As an aside, given the present state of the data sublanguages SQL and QUEL, a CREATE DOMAIN command must be added to each language. Table 3.1 lists some of the distinctions between basic and extended data types.

By now it should be clear that it is quite incorrect to equate either (1) basic data types with built-in data types, or (2) extended data types with user-defined data types.

The distinction between built-in data types and user-defined data types is a purely temporary consideration based largely on the kind of hardware that is economically available; this boundary moves at least every decade, possibly more frequently. On the other hand, the distinction between basic and extended data types is both non-temporary and conceptual in nature: it is closely related to the question of levels of abstraction.

In apparent opposition to the first row of Table 3.1, it has been contended that both basic data types and extended data types have names. In a sense this is true. The "names" of basic data types, however, can be used only in designating certain properties of data (e.g., in a program). On the other hand, the names of extended data types can be used not only in designating properties of data, but also as objects themselves, when the user

---

Table 3.1 **Basic versus Extended Data Types**

Basic Data Type	Extended Data Type
No object-oriented name	Object-oriented name
A property of an object	An object
Not independently declarable	Independently declarable
Range of values is *not* specifiable	Range of values is specifiable
Applicability of <, > is *not* specifiable	Applicability of <, > is specifiable

Two database values with the same basic data type need not have the same extended data type.

---

wishes to interrogate them or modify them either interactively from a terminal or by using a program. This holds true of extended data types because their names and descriptions are stored as data in the catalog.

3.2 ■ Nine Practical Reasons for Supporting Domains

Full support for many of the features of the relational model depends on full support of the domain concept. Some of the advantages of supporting domains fully follow.

First, full support of the domain concept is the single most important concept in determining whether a given relational database is integrated. Consider the consequences of alleging that a relational database viewed as a collection CD of domains and a collection CR of relations could be split into two databases, without any loss of information or of retrieval capability. How would one check whether this assertion were true?

One way of solving this problem is to look for a subset cd of the domains CD and a subset cr of the relations CR with the following two properties:

1. the relations in cr make use of domains in cd only (no other domains);
2. the relations in (CR - cr) make use of domains in (CD - cd) only (no other domains).

Note that in Property 1 a relation makes use of a domain if at least one of its columns draws its values from that domain. In Property 2, the symbol "-" in (CR - cr) and (CD - cd) denotes set difference.

When both these properties hold, the relational operators will not permit the derivation of any relations that include information from cr as well as information from (CR - cr), whether these two collections are regarded by the DBA or by anyone else as a single database or as two databases. There is a sound reason for this related to (1) value-comparisons that make sense and (2) value-comparisons that do not. (See the third practical reason for supporting domains later in this section.)

This first reason for supporting domains can be concisely stated as follows: *domains are the glue that holds a relational database together.* Notice that I said *domains,* not primary keys and foreign keys. The concept of keys in the relational model provides an important additional and specialized kind of glue.

Second, support of domains is necessary if the factoring advantage is to be realized in declaring the types of data permitted in columns.

A large component of the description of *every column* that is defined on a given domain need be declared only once for that domain. As an example, consider a financial database that has 50 columns containing currency of some type (e.g., all U.S. dollars).

Using pre-relational DBMS, it was usually necessary to store 50 declarations, one for each column; this task was often left to numerous application programmers, who inserted these declarations into their programs. With this approach, the usual result was that no two currency declarations were in precise agreement, placing an immense and unnecessary burden on the DBA and on the community of users.

It was this phenomenon that spurred the development of add-on packages called *dictionaries*. Control over names and declarations, however, should be handled by the DBMS itself, making it much more difficult for any user to circumvent such control.

Using the relational approach, just one declaration of semantic data type for the currency domain will suffice for all 50 currency columns. Then, for any currency column that needs tighter control (an interval of permitted values more narrow than that declared for the domain), an extra range constraint can be declared for that column (type C or column integrity). All domain declarations and all additional constraints applicable to specified columns are stored by the DBA in the catalog, which is where they belong if users are to receive the important benefit of not having to change application programs whenever integrity constraints are changed.

Third, support of domains is necessary if domain integrity is to be supported. Domain integrity consists of those integrity constraints that are shared by all the columns that draw their values from that domain. Three kinds of domain integrity constraints that are frequently encountered are (1) regular data type, (2) ranges of values permitted, and (3) whether or not the ordering comparators greater than (>) and less than (<) are applicable to those values.

Fourth, full support of domains includes domain-constrained operators and domain-constrained features of other kinds to protect users from costly blunders. For every operator that involves comparing pairs of database values, the DBMS ensures that the two components to be compared are semantically comparable. It does this by checking either at the start of the operation or (when possible) at compile time that both columns involved are defined on a common domain. This constraint is supported by a relational DBMS to help protect users from incorrectly formulating commands such as **joins** (for example, a **join** in which quantities of parts are being compared with quantities of people). If a special need arises "to compare apples with oranges," with special authorization—and a DBA would grant such authorization rarely and for only short intervals—a user may employ the DOMAIN CHECK OVERRIDE qualifier in his or her command.

RT-1 Safety Feature when Comparing Database Values

When comparing a database value in one column with a database value in another, the DBMS checks that the two columns draw their values from a common domain, unless the domain check is overridden (see Feature RQ-9 in Chapter 10). When comparing (1) a computed value with a database value or (2) one computed value with another computed value, however, the DBMS checks that the basic data types are the same.

The main reason for checking the weaker basic data types when computed values are involved is that the computing is likely to be expressed in some host-programming language. Most such languages do not yet support the extended data types of the relational model.

The following operators and features of the relational model require implementation of domains to ensure that data is handled properly by the DBMS and by the user:

■ Operators for retrieval and modifying:
  ■ **theta-select** (whenever two components of a tuple are being compared),
  ■ **theta-join,**
  ■ **t-join,**
  ■ **relational division,**
  ■ **relational union, intersection,** and **difference,**
  ■ all of the outer operators (**outer join, outer union, outer intersection, outer difference**),
  ■ **primary key update.**
■ Integrity features:
  ■ referential integrity (type R),
  ■ other inclusion dependencies,
  ■ user-defined integrity constraints (type U) involving any of the operators just listed,
  ■ every integrity constraint involving cascading the action to all equal values in all columns defined on the same domain (e.g., **cascade delete, cascade update, cascade insert**).

Fifth, in the highly dynamic environment supported by a fully relational DBMS, it is necessary to support domains in order to support transactions that single out all occurrences of some value as a value of a specified extended data type. Consider an example: business activity with supplier s3 has been terminated in a completed state (no shipments are still due from this supplier and all bills have been paid). A company executive requests that all rows of a certain kind (wherever they occur in the database) be archived—specifically, all rows of all relations that contain s3 as a supplier serial number.

In executing this action, it is important to avoid archiving rows that happen to contain s3 as something other than a supplier serial number (say, a part serial number), if these rows do not also contain s3 as a supplier serial number. It is inadvisable to expect any application programmer to remember the information as to which columns draw their values from the supplier serial number domain: this information may change even while the programmer is thinking about the transaction because of activities by other users and programmers. A relational DBMS supports a great variety of users engaged concurrently in actions conceived independently of one another. Most of these actions may be simple changes to the data, but some may be changes in the database description. Thus, while the application programmer is thinking about the transaction needed to archive all rows that contain s3 as a supplier serial number, some other user may be introducing a new relation or adding a new column containing supplier serial numbers. That user or another one may then insert s3 in such a column.

Consequently, it is essential that the DBMS retain in an extremely up-to-date state the information as to which columns draw their values from the supplier serial number domain. It is also essential that the relational language contain a command that is capable of referring to all columns currently drawing their values from a specified domain *without the user having to list these columns within the command or elsewhere.* At present, SQL and its dialects lack such a command.

Sixth, support of domains facilitates certain user-defined integrity checks by the DBMS. An example is an inclusion constraint, in which the values appearing in one column C1 (simple or composite) are required to be a subset of the values appearing in another column C2. In this case, the relational model requires that C1 and C2 draw their values from a common domain.

Seventh, the domain concept participates in many definitions in the relational model, including the definitions of primary domain, foreign key, all value-comparing operators (as noted earlier in the third reason), union compatibility, referential integrity, and inclusion constraints.

Eighth, domains can be used by the DBMS to establish the extent of naming correspondence needed from the user when a **union** or similar relational operator is requested. When forming R UNION S in the relational model, it is required not only that the degree of R is equal to the degree of S, but also that there exist at least one mapping (one-to-one) of the columns of R onto the columns of S, such that the two columns of each pair belonging to the mapping have a common domain.

Clearly, if all the domains of columns of R are distinct, then all the domains of S must also be distinct, and the domains can be used by the DBMS to determine the mapping of columns on columns completely. Thus, in this case, the user need not become involved at all in the pair of column names.

If two or more domains of columns of R are identical, however, the same must be true of S, and the user is faced with alternatives. He or she must therefore be involved in column correspondence between R and S to the extent of having to specify a mapping for just those columns of R that share a common domain and just those columns of S that share a common domain. Obviously, determining this correspondence can also affect the naming of columns of the result.

Ninth, and last, it is necessary to support domains in order to support an important performance-oriented tool, namely domain-based indexes. While this tool is not itself part of the relational model, it is important because it can cause certain types of relational DBMS (specifically those that make use of indexes under the covers) to perform competitively with non-relational DBMS.

A domain-based index is a single index on the combination of all the columns that draw their values from the specified domain. Such an index is usually a multi-relation index. However, not every multi-relation index is a domain-based index. It provides immediate direction for the DBMS to find all occurrences of each currently active value from that domain.

Once such an index has been declared by the DBA, the introduction into the database of a new column drawing its values from the pertinent domain causes automatic expansion by the DBMS of the domain-based index. Similarly, whenever the DBA requests the dropping of a column that is referenced by a domain-based index, the DBMS automatically removes references to this column from the pertinent index.

It is worth noting that domain-based indexes can do more than improve the performance of certain kinds of DBMS in the execution of **joins** and other value-comparing operations. Also, when applied to *primary domains* (domains from which primary keys draw their values), they can improve the performance of tests of referential integrity.

One extreme case may be interesting, although I am not advocating it as a preferred approach: the case in which the entire collection of values in the database is stored in domain-based indexes only. Of course, in this case such indexes cannot be dropped without losing information from the database.

3.3 ■ RM/V2 Features in the Extended Data Type Class

3.3.1 General Features

RT-2   Extended Data Types Built into the System

The DBMS supports calendar dates, clock times, and decimal currency as extended data types, including the various kinds of dates and time units in common use, the computation of date intervals and time intervals, and the use of partial as well as full dates (see Features RT-3–RT-9, following). The DBMS must have access to the date of the current day and the time of day at all times.

A justification for this feature is that very few institutions, whether commercial, industrial, or governmental, can manage themselves without these types of data. Incidentally, each built-in extended data type must have a name that is usable in the catalog for appending integrity constraints of type D to the data type.

RT-3 User-defined Extended Data Types

The DBMS permits suitably authorized users to define extended data types other than those for which it provides built-in support in accordance with Feature RT-2. These data types can be used to enrich the retrieval-targeting and retrieval-conditioning capabilities of the principal relational language (e.g., with respect to text manipulation and computer-aided development/computer-assisted manufacturing).

3.3.2 Calendar Dates and Clock Times

As described in Features RT-4–7, the treatment of dates and clock times (separately and in combination) in the relational model is intended to be flexible enough to be suitable for managing databases of any of the following types, among others:

- genealogical types at the headquarters of the Mormon church in Salt Lake City, Utah;
- air-traffic control at major air-traffic-control centers of the Federal Aviation Administration;
- commercial databases used by institutions operating in a variety of different time zones (possibly many time zones).

RT-4 Calendar Dates

From the user's standpoint, dates appear to be treated by the DBMS as if they were atomic values. However, the DBMS supports functions that are capable of treating as separate components the year, month, and day of the month.

The services provided by Feature RT-4 include the 14 that follow:

4.1. Independence of date and time from particular time zones in which users are located, by use of Greenwich dates and Greenwich mean time.

4.2. The function called NOW yields for any site the current date and time that are in effect in the time zone of the site.

4.3. Extraction of any one or any pair of the three components, a form of *truncation*.

4.4. Extraction with *rounding* of either year alone or year followed by month.

4.5. Conversion of the combination year, month, day of the month to the year followed by day of the year, as well as conversion in the opposite direction.

4.6. Computation of the difference between two dates of similar or distinct external types, where each argument is expressed as
   a. years only, or
   b. years and months, or
   c. years, months, and days of the month, or
   d. years, and days of the year.

These four options must be available to users, and *the result must be of the same external type as the argument that is coarser.*

4.7. Conversion of date intervals into years only or months only or days only, using truncation or rounding as specified, if the conversion is from fine units to coarser units.

4.8. Arithmetic on dates, including computation of a date from a given date plus or minus a date interval, without the adoption of dates and date intervals as distinct data types.

4.9. Pairwise comparison of dates, including testing of pairs of dates to see which is the more recent and which is the less recent.

4.10. Finding the most recent date of a collection.

4.11. Finding the least recent date of a collection.

4.12. All varieties of **joins** based on comparing dates.

4.13. The ability to report dates in at least one of the following formats:
   a. European format: D,M,Y;
   b. North American format: M,D,Y;
   c. computer format: Y,M,D;
   d. in the Indian calendar with lunar months.

4.14. Two types of date-conversion functions:
   a. DATE__IN for transforming dates from external representation of dates to the internal representation;

b. DATE—OUT for transforming dates in the reverse direction, with the DBA having the option of putting into effect functions defined and specified by the DBA either for all users of a given DBMS or for specified classes of users (instead of or in addition to those supplied by the DBMS vendor).

This option is needed because users with different responsibilities and those located in different countries (even within a single country) may employ different kinds of dates externally with respect to the DBMS. Table 3.2 shows an example of two distinct types of conversions that may be needed in countries that use the Gregorian calendar.

Of course, the DBMS must know how many days there are in each of the calendar months, and which years are leap years. The DBMS should also have a standard internal representation of dates oriented toward arithmetic on dates. The preferred representation is a date origin established by the DBA (such as the first day of the year 1900), coupled with the number of days following that day. This representation is compatible with the handling of arithmetic operations upon dates (while abiding by all the usual laws of arithmetic) and of comparisons between pairs of dates (such as LESS THAN). Such a standard would ease the problem of communication between heterogeneous DBMS products. Finally, the DBMS must know the date of the current day.

Note that the DBA may impose bounds, both lower and upper, on acceptable values of dates using type D and type C integrity constraints. Dates occur in the numerous examples included in this book. The standard representation adopted is the computer format Y,M,D (year, month, day) cited earlier in the discussion of Feature RT-4.13.

RT-5 Clock Times

From the user's standpoint, clock times appear to be treated by the DBMS as if they were atomic values. The DBMS however, supports

---

Table 3.2 **Examples of Date Conversions**

		Two examples	
	Type of Date	**Any Year**	**Non-Leap Year**
	Internal date	September 31	February 29
DOWN →	Closest earlier date	September 30	February 28
UP →	Closest later date	October 1	March 1

functions that are capable of treating as separate components the hours, minutes of the hour, and seconds of the minute. The services provided include counterparts to the first 12 of the 14 services listed in the discussion of RT-4.

Whenever it is necessary to store fractions of a second (e.g., milliseconds or microseconds) in one or more columns of the database, a user-defined extended data type should be established for each distinct and pertinent unit of time.

RT-6 Coupling of Dates with Times

The DBMS supports a composite data type consisting of the data type DATE coupled with the data type TIME, allowing the functions applicable to dates alone or times alone to be applied to combinations in which DATE plays the role of the high-order part and TIME the low-order part.

RT-7 Time-zone Conversion

The DBMS supports (1) the conversion of every date-time pair from any specified time zone to Greenwich date and Greenwich mean time, and (2) the inverse conversion of Greenwich date-time pairs back into a specified time zone.

3.3.3 Extended Data Types for Currency

RT-8 Non-negative Decimal Currency

The DBMS supports non-negative decimal currency as a built-in extended data type, but does not necessarily support automatic conversion between currencies of different countries. The basic data type is non-negative integers.

This extended data type permits the DBMS to distinguish those non-negative integers representing currency from those that represent anything else (e.g., numbers of people). The basic data type represents the monetary amount expressed in terms of the smallest monetary unit in the currency (cents in U.S. currency, new pence in British sterling).

Monetary amounts can be expressed in larger units in selected columns. For example, there may be a need to express such amounts in units of one thousand dollars or one million dollars. If the DBMS does not support conversion functions to convert a monetary amount expressed in small units into much larger units (including either rounding up or truncation according to the user's request), a user-defined extended data type will be necessary for each column that employs units different from the smallest.

If an attempt is made to introduce a negative number into any column drawing its values from the non-negative currency domain, the DBMS rejects the request with an explanatory error message.

RT-9   Free Decimal Currency

The DBMS supports decimal currency (in which values may be negative, zero, or positive) as an extended data type. The basic data type is integer.

The DBMS does not necessarily support automatic conversion between currencies of different countries. This requires user-defined functions, together with a relation of degree of at least three, containing the current conversion rates.

With some databases, the DBA may choose to use just one of the two built-in extended data types for currency, namely the free version, because of the need to compare currency values involving pairs of currency columns, for which one column is not permitted to have negative values and the other can accept both negative and positive values. If such comparisons are routine, the DBA may with good reason decide that the pairs of columns involved should be declared to have a common domain. Whenever the DBA makes this choice, the prohibition of negative values in certain currency columns be expressed as an extra constraint of type C for those columns only (not for the domain).

Two additional extended data types (Features RF-9 and RF-10) built into the DBMS are described in this chapter and in Chapter 19. These types pertain to the names of functions and the names of arguments of functions. They make the relational model easier to interface with activities that really do not belong in the model. Their definitions are given here for ease of reference, but are expressed differently.

RF-9   Domains and Columns Containing Names of Functions

The DBMS supports names of functions as an extended data type. The DBMS can use any one of these names to (1) retrieve the corresponding code for the function, (2) formulate a call for this function as a character string, and (3) execute the string as an invocation of the function.

Note that, prior to execution, the names of appropriate arguments must be plugged into the character string that represents the invocation.

RF-10 Domains and Columns Containing Names of Arguments

The DBMS supports names of arguments of functions as an extended data type. These arguments can be variables used in a host-language program. The names are character strings that can be incorporated with the name of a function to formulate a call for this function to be applied to the pertinent arguments. The names can also be incorporated in a source program expressed in RL, in the HL, or in both.

3.4 ■ The FIND Commands

In the next two chapters the basic operators and the advanced operators of RM/V2 are described. Each of these operators transforms either one or two relations into a relation. None of them deals with the entire database, which may contain any number of relations.

The FIND commands presented here are different in type, because:

1. each has an operand that consists of all of the columns in the database that draw their values from a specified domain; and

2. although the result is a relation, at least two of the columns are concerned with database descriptive values.

The FIND commands are also intended for the DBA and his or her staff. That is why as features of RM/V2 they are labelled RE-1 and RE-2 (see Chapter 7).

In the relational model what does it mean to find something? Disk addresses and memory addresses are concepts that do not belong to the model. However, each occurrence of every atomic value in a relational database has a uniquely identified "location." The identification of this location is the combination of a relation name, a primary key value, and a column name. The first two of these identify a row uniquely with respect to the entire database, while the third identifies a component of that row. Now it is possible to introduce the FIND commands one by one.

Normally the FIND commands are limited to finding character strings, because finding numeric values or the truth values of logic is not usually an interesting thing to do.

3.4.1 The FAO__AV Command

RE-1 The FAO__AV Command

This command is intended to find all occurrences of all active values drawn from a specified domain. Note that for any domain (with the possible exception of those domains that have very few legal values) it is highly unlikely that all of its values are active (i.e., exist in the database) at any one time.

Suppose the DBA believes that certain city names in the database are incorrectly spelled, and he wants to check all of them either by reading a list of all of them or by means of a spelling checker program along with a dictionary of city names. Then, the following query would be appropriate:

Example: find all occurrences of all city names that exist *anywhere* in the database.

If the domain of city names happens to be called CITY, and if the resulting relation is to be called CITY__DOM, this query could be expressed as: CITY__DOM← FAO__AV domain CITY.

The result is a relation CITY__DOM (RELNAME COLNAME PK VALUE) where the RELNAME and COLNAME columns are always simple columns, (degree one) the VALUE column is either simple or composite depending on the example, and the PK column is usually a composite column of degree n (consisting of n simple columns), where n is adequate to hold values for the primary key of highest degree in the entire database. Note that, whenever the value of a primary key of degree p is inserted in the result and p < n, the excess components in that row (there are n-p of them) are marked as inapplicable (see chapter 8).

To find all these city names the DBMS takes the first step of searching the catalog to find a column in some base relation that draws its values from the domain CITY. Suppose it finds that column C1 of relation R1 is such a column, and that R1 has N1 rows. It then copies the value part of the primary key column of R1 (possibly composite) along with the value part of column C1 into the relation CITY__DOM being developed. To this partial relation it appends a pair of columns containing the name of the relation R1 and the name of the column C1 repeated N1 times. It names these two columns RELNAME AND COLNAME.

The DBMS then takes the second step searching the catalog again and finds another column C2 of a relation R2 that draws its values from the domain CITY. If R1 happens to have two such columns, then R1 and R2 are the same relation. However, the pair R1 and C1 cannot be identical to the pair R2 and C2. It copies the value part of the primary key column of R2 (possibly composite) along with the value part of column C2.

This process continues step by step until the last column in the database based on the CITY domain has been treated. Now a spelling checker program along with a dictionary of city names can be used as a utility to check the spelling of each and every occurrence of the city names as listed in a column of the relation CITY_DOM.

This FIND command (FAO_AV) can be applied not only to a simple domain, but also to a composite domain: for example, the domain CITY-STATE. Then the VALUE column is also composite (in this case, degree 2), since it has to hold pairs of simple values, where each pair consists of a city name together with a state name.

3.4.2 The FAO_LIST Command

RE-2   The FAO_LIST Command

This command is intended to find all occurrences in the database of each of the currently active values in a given list of distinct values, all of which are drawn from one domain, and that domain is specified in the command.

Suppose the DBA wishes to inquire whether any of ten city names occur in the database, and if so where they occur.

Example: find all occurrences in the database of each of the eight city names in a given list L drawn from the domain CITY (where L is a unary relation).

Suppose that the resulting relation is to be called OCC. Then, this command could be expressed as:

OCC ← FAO_LIST L domain CITY.

The result is a relation OCC (RELNAME COLNAME PK VALUE), where PK is usually a composite column consisting of n simple columns and n is adequate for the primary key of highest degree in the entire database. Note that, whenever the value of a primary key of degree p is inserted in the result and p < n, the excess components in that row (there are n-p of them) are marked as inapplicable (see chapter 8).

Incidentally, when the FAO_LIST command is executed, it is possible that the resulting relation OCC is entirely empty. This means that each and every one of the eight city names does not occur at all in the database. Of course, the list L could have contained any strictly positive number of city names.

Just like the FIND command introduced in section 3.4.1, this FIND command (FAO_LIST) can be applied not only to a simple domain, but also to a composite domain: for example, the CITY-STATE domain. Then the VALUE column is also composite (in this case, degree 2), since it has to hold pairs of simple values, where each pair consists of a city name together with a state name.

Another feature of this FIND command is that a qualifier called SUBSTRING may be attached to it, and this indicates that the list of values is actually a list of substrings that the DBMS must search for in all columns of the database that draw their values from the specified domain. Whenever a value is found in such a column that has as a substring one of the strings in the given list, then that value and its location in the database are included as a row in the resulting relation.

In both types of FIND command, if a domain is specified that the DBMS discovers does not exist in the catalog, it turns on the DOMAIN NOT DECLARED indicator (see chapter 11), and the relation that is generated is empty.

Frequently, people get confused about the meaning of the following two questions, although they are quite different. The first question is Q1: "Is v a legitimate value for currency in this database?" The second question is Q2: "Is v in the database at this time as a currency value?"

To check Q1 the user simply examines the declaration pertaining to currency for this database, and of course this declaration is stored in the catalog. Then he or she examines the value v to determine if its data type is within the scope of the currency data type. If and only if it is, v is a legitimate value for currency in the database.

Before checking Q2 let us assume that Q1 has been answered affirmatively. Then one can (1) establish v as a single member of a unary relation L; and (2) issue the request FAO_LIST L CURRENCY. This will find all occurrences of v in the entire database as a value drawn from the currency domain. If the result is an empty relation, the proper conclusion is that v is admissible as a currency value, but v does not occur in this role in this database at this time.

Of course, if Q1 is answered negatively, then the proper answer for Q2 is that v does not occur in the database as a value of currency, but it is also inadmissible in this role.

Exercises

3.1   Give at least eight reasons why domains should be fully supported in a DBMS. List at least 10 features of RM/V2, other than Feature RS-5, that a DBMS will be unable to support if it does not support domains as extended data types.

3.2 Your DBA makes the whole of the catalog available to you for reading. How would you determine where there exist parts of the database that are not inter-relatable?

3.3 A critic has stated that basic data types and extended data types are really built-in and user-defined, respectively. Supply the pertinent definitions and defend whatever position you take on this subject.

3.4 According to Feature RT-1, which extended data types are required to be built into the DBMS?

3.5 List 10 of the 14 requirements for full support of calendar dates.

3.6 Assume that you have currency values expressed as follows:

- in U.S. dollars in column C of R-table S,
- in British sterling in column D of R-table T.

By introducing a currency-conversion relation, develop a method of supporting automatic conversion to pounds sterling whenever a **join** between S and T is executed using columns C and D as comparand columns.

▪ CHAPTER 4 ▪

The Basic Operators

The basic operators are intended to enable any user to retrieve information from all parts of the database in a very flexible and powerful way, but without requiring him or her to be familiar with programming details. First-order predicate logic is a standard against which such power can be measured. (See the listing under "Texts Dealing with Predicate Logic" in the reference section.) It has been proved [Codd 1971d, Klug 1982] that, collectively, these operators have the same expressive power as first-order predicate logic.

This logic is the standard adopted by the relational model. The operators are not intended to be directly incorporated into a relational language. Instead, a language based more directly on first-order predicate logic, such as ALPHA [Codd 1971a], is more capable of supporting better performance, because in use its statements are more likely to be optimizable to a greater degree.

The operators of the relational model transform either a single relation or a pair of relations into a result that is a relation. The operators are designed to be able to express a class of queries that, if expressed in terms of a logic, would require the power of at least four-valued, first-order predicate logic. Such a logic is more powerful than any supported by pre-relational database management systems.

The main reason for insisting on operators that yield relations from relations is that this form of operational closure permits an interrogator to conceive his or her ongoing sequence of queries based on the information gleaned to date. In this "detective" mode, it is essential that any result produced so far in the activities be capable of being used as an operand in

61

later activities. This operational closure is similar to the operational closure in arithmetic: every arithmetic operator acting upon numbers yields numbers (except for the case of dividing by zero). It would be next to impossible to handle accounting were it not for the operational closure in integer arithmetic. In a few decades, I predict, we shall comment similarly on the virtual impossibility of managing databases if the operational closure property in relational DBMS were abandoned.

In this chapter we adopt the algebraic approach to explaining how a relational language works, for two reasons:

1. upon first encounter, that approach appears easier to understand;

2. it is much easier to explain integrity constraints, the authorization mechanism, and the view-updatability algorithms described in Chapter 17 using the relational algebra than in terms of predicate logic.

It should not be assumed, however, that an algebraic approach is to be preferred over a logic-based approach when it comes to designing a relational language, even though both approaches are at the same level of abstraction. Quite the contrary—a logic-based approach encourages users who have complicated queries to express each query in a single command, whereas an algebraic approach seems to encourage users to split their queries into several commands per query. The optimizers of existing relational DBMS products are unable to optimize more than one command at a time. Therefore, they accomplish more if more activity is packed into each single command. The net result is that improved performance can be obtained with a logic-based approach over that achievable with an algebraic approach.

In this connection, it is important to remember that very few optimizers in the compilers for programming languages, and even fewer optimizers in relational DBMS, attempt to optimize across more than a single command. Otherwise, the optimizers would have to engage in flow tracing—a difficult problem at best, and often impossible because the flow may not be traceable at all when it is expressed in certain programming languages.

Some consider it incongruous that the algebra is used as an explicative tool, when logic is preferred as the basis for a relational language. The example at the end of Section 4.2 illustrates the algebraic and logic-based alternatives. It may also show the reader why it is easier to introduce the query and manipulative capabilities step by step using the algebra.

Every relational operator in the relational model is designed to work with operands that are relations free of duplicate rows, and to generate as a result a relation that is also free of duplicate rows.

The feature of permitting duplicate rows in any relation, base or derived, was added to SQL with the idea of making that language more powerful in some sense. In fact, this feature made SQL less powerful, because duplicate rows made use of the language more error-prone and damaged the interchangeability of ordering of the relational operators (see Chapter 23 for more detail). I call this mistaken belief—that one more feature cannot possibly detract from a system's usability and power—the "one-more-feature trap."

Section 4.1 deals with the techniques used in explaining the operators. Section 4.2 describes the *basic operators,* which may help the reader to understand the power of relational languages. Section 4.3 discusses the *manipulative operators* such as **relational assignment, insert, update,** and **delete.** Chapter 5 deals with certain *advanced operators,* including outer equi-joins, outer unions, T-joins, user defined joins, and recursive joins.

The explanation of each operator includes a rough idea of what it does and how it is intended to be used. Also included are a precise definition, a formal algebraic notation, and some practical examples.

The notations used in this chapter are not intended to be taken as a serious proposal for a data sublanguage, but as illustrative and primarily for conceptual purposes. The operators are, however, intended to be interpreted as one definition of the power a relational language should possess. In Chapter 8, the way these operators deal with operands, from which certain kinds of information are missing, is discussed.

4.1 ■ Techniques for Explaining the Operators

Consider a relation S of degree m that has the following attributes:

Attribute A1 drawing its values from domain D1.
Attribute A2 drawing its values from domain D2.

. . .   .

Attribute Am drawing its values from domain Dm.

The relation S is abbreviated

S (A1:D1 A2:D2 . . . Am:Dm),

and often

S (A1 A2 . . . Am)

when the domains are listed separately.

It must be remembered that the ordering

A1, A2, . . . Am

is insignificant in practice even to the user (except in the few cases where the command being explained requires the column ordering to be made explicit). Normally, we shall make use of column ordering for explanatory purposes only, just as is done in mathematics. There is no implication that components of tuples (i.e, rows) must be *stored* in any of the sequences used in explaining how the operators transform the operands into results.

In explaining the basic relational operators, we shall make use of the relation S of degree *m* just cited, and also a relation T of degree *n*, denoted

T (B1:E1 B2:E2 . . . B*n*:E*n*).

We shall consider the example of **Cartesian product** to illustrate the explanatory techniques. Incidentally, the major use of this operator is itself explanatory. Definitions of some of the other operators (such as **relational division**) make conceptual use of it. The designer of a DBMS product is advised to implement **Cartesian product** as a special case of the **theta-join** discussed later because it is rarely needed in practice.

To introduce the relational version of **Cartesian product** gradually, let us consider a simple example first. Suppose that a database contains information about suppliers and shipments received from these suppliers. The supplier relation S contains the serial number S# of all the suppliers in the database, their names SNAME, and other immediate properties (marked ". . ."). The shipment relation SP contains the serial number S# of the supplier making each shipment, the serial number P# of the part shipped, the date SHIP—DATE the shipment was received, and other immediate properties of the shipment (marked ". . .").

To keep the example simple, suppose that relation SP″ is SP restricted to those shipments with SHIP—DATE between 89-01-01 and 89-03-30 inclusive. Relation S has three rows; relation SP″, four rows:

S	(S#	SNAME	. . .)
	s1	Jones	. . .
	s2	Smith	. . .
	s3	Clark	. . .

SP″	(S#	P#	SHIP—DATE	. . .)
	s1	p1	89-03-31	. . .
	s1	p2	89-03-20	. . .
	s2	p7	89-02-19	. . .
	s3	p2	89-01-15	. . .

In the relational model, the **Cartesian product** C of relation S with relation SP″ is as shown in the following 12-row relational table:

C	(. . .	SNAME	S#	S#	P#	SHIP—DATE	. . .)
	. . .	Jones	s1	s1	p1	89-03-31	. . .
	. . .	Jones	s1	s1	p2	89-03-20	. . .
	. . .	Jones	s1	s2	p7	89-02-19	. . .
	. . .	Jones	s1	s3	p2	89-01-15	. . .
	. . .	Smith	s2	s1	p1	89-03-31	. . .
	. . .	Smith	s2	s1	p2	89-03-20	. . .
	. . .	Smith	s2	s2	p7	89-02-19	. . .
	. . .	Smith	s2	s3	p2	89-01-15	. . .
	. . .	Clark	s3	s1	p1	89-03-31	. . .
	. . .	Clark	s3	s1	p2	89-03-20	. . .
	. . .	Clark	s3	s2	p7	89-02-19	. . .
	. . .	Clark	s3	s3	p2	89-01-15	. . .

The ordering of columns shown is there merely because the result must be displayed on paper. This ordering should be ignored. Note how each row of S is combined with each and every row of SP″. The same result is generated if the relational version of the **Cartesian product** of SP″ with S is requested.

Clearly, the **Cartesian product** has two operands, each one a relation. Consider the **Cartesian product** of S and T, denoted S × T. To form the **Cartesian product** U = S × T, concatenate each and every tuple of S with each and every tuple of T. In textbooks on mathematics the usual explanation is that U is the set of all tuples of the form

$$< < a1,a2,. . .,am >,< b1,b2,. . .,bn > >,$$

where $< a1,a2,. . .,am >$ is a tuple of S and $< b1,b2,. . .,bn >$ is a tuple of T. In this case, U would be a binary relation whose pairs have an m-tuple as the first component, and an n-tuple as the second component. For purposes of database management, it is more useful to adopt a slightly different definition, and to say that U is the set of all tuples of the form

$$< a1,a2,. . .,am,b1,b2,. . .,bn >.$$

In this case, U is a relation of degree $m + n$. Actually, because positional concepts are de-emphasized in the relational model, it is preferable to define U as a relation of degree $m + n$ that has the form

$$U (A1:D1 \ A2:D2 \ . \ . \ . \ Am:Dm \ B1:E1 \ B2:E2 \ . \ . \ . \ Bn:En),$$

where column names and domain names are used rather than the positioning of typical elements of these columns in tuples. Note that, with this de-emphasis on positioning concepts, a surprising consequence is that

$$S × T = T × S,$$

which holds true for all relations S and T.

It is necessary, however, to face up to the problem that, for some i and some j, it may happen that the pair of names in the expression Ai:Di may be the same as the pair of names in the expression Bj:Ej—the A and D names come from S, whereas the B and E names come from T. According to Feature RN-3 of the relational model (see Chapter 6), it is required that, given any relation, every one of its columns must have a distinct name.

Assume that S and T do not refer to one and the same relation. Then, all we need do to make sure the columns of the result are distinctly named is to attach the prefix S to Ai (where S is the name of the relation from which Ai came), and attach the prefix T to Bj (where T is the name of the relation from which Bj came). Prefixing in these cases means adopting a syntax such as S.Ai and T.Bj.

This technique will not work if S = T. In this case, if m is the degree of S, there will be m pairs of columns having the property that each member of the pair has the same name, as well as precisely the same database values. To make the column names distinct for each of the members of these pairs of columns, each column name is qualified by the name of the source relation (namely S in each case), followed by a punctuation mark (such as a period), followed by a citation number, followed by a second punctuation mark (this can be a period also). The citation number is either 1 or 2, depending on whether the first-cited or the second-cited occurrence of relation S is the source of the pertinent column in the result. In Chapter 6 we discuss column naming and column ordering in more detail.

RB-1   De-emphasis of Cartesian Product as an Operator

A relational DBMS must not support **Cartesian product** as an explicitly separate operator. A relational command, however, may have an extreme case that is interpreted by the DBMS as a request for a **Cartesian product.**

Note that the **Cartesian product** U contains no more information than its components S and T contain together. However, U consumes much more memory or disk space and channel time than the two relations S and T consume together. These are two good reasons why, in any implementation of the relational model, **Cartesian product** should be de-emphasized, and used primarily as a tool for explanatory or conceptual purposes. The main purpose in discussing this operator in some detail at this point is to show how the relational operators will normally be treated.

One may ask, "Why is it necessary to discuss column naming and column ordering at all?" The simple answer is that every result of executing a relational operation can be either an intermediate or a final result of a relational command. In either case, a subsequent relational operation may employ this result as an operand, and, as we shall see, the specification of some kinds of relational operation involves employing the names of columns of one or other of the operands and sometimes the ordering of these columns also.

Of course, we are not referring to "stored ordering" when we speak of column ordering. We are referring either to the *citation ordering* (the ordering in which columns are cited in some relational command) or to an ordering derived from such citation.

4.2 ■ The Basic Operators

The basic operators of RM/V2 include **projection, theta-selection, theta-join, natural join, relational division, relational union, relational difference,** and

relational intersection. Projection and **theta-selection** act upon one operand only, while each of the remaining operators acts upon two operands. In every case, operands and results are true relations with no duplicate rows.

Figure 4.1 is a simple guide to the Basic operators of the relational model. All of the operators except **Cartesian product** are intended to be implemented in a relational DBMS. **Cartesian product,** although a good conceptual tool, wastes storage space and channel time if implemented in the DBMS and used by application programmers or invoked interactively from terminals.

RB-2   The Project Operator

The **project** operator employs a single R-table as its operand. The operator generates an intermediate result in which the columns listed by name in the command are saved, and the columns omitted from the command are ignored. From this R-table it then generates the final result by removing all occurrences except one of each row that occurs more than once.

Suppose that the **project** operator is applied to the following R-table EMP of degree five. Suppose that the columns are named as follows:

EMP# (primary key), ENAME, BIRTH__DATE, SALARY, and H__CITY.

EMP	(EMP#	ENAME	BIRTH__DATE	SALARY	H__CITY	)
	E107	Rook	23-08-19	10,000	Wimborne	
	E912	Knight	38-11-05	12,000	Poole	
	E239	Knight	38-11-05	12,000	Poole	
	E575	Pawn	31-04-22	11,000	Poole	

Note that there are two employees named "Knight," and that these two Knights have the same birthdate, earn the same salary, and live in the same city. The only piece of information that tells us that these are distinct employees is the primary key EMP# (E912 for one person, E239 for the other). If the primary-key values were not in the database, there would be clear ambiguity in the data: specifically, do the two rows represent two distinct persons, or are the duplicate rows there by accident? This is one of the many reasons why the primary-key concept should be explicitly supported in every relational database management system.

The intermediate result that is generated when applying **project** onto ENAME, BIRTH__DATE, SALARY, and H-CITY is a table (but not an R-table) obtained by selecting only those columns cited in the **project** command:

X	(ENAME	BIRTH_DATE	SALARY	H_CITY)
	Rook	23-08-19	10,000	Wimborne
	Knight	38-11-05	12,000	Poole
	Knight	38-11-05	12,000	Poole
	Pawn	31-04-22	11,000	Poole

The final result, in which duplicate rows are removed, is the following R-table:

Y	(ENAME	BIRTH_DATE	SALARY	H_CITY)
	Rook	23-08-19	10,000	Wimborne
	Knight	38-11-05	12,000	Poole
	Pawn	31-04-22	11,000	Poole

Notice how, in generating the R-table Y from the table X, the duplicate row for "Knight" was removed. It has been asserted that duplicate rows should not be removed, and in fact the language SQL fails to remove duplicate rows unless the user adds to the command the qualifier DISTINCT. When the user fails to add this SQL qualifier, the result is then no longer a true relation in the mathematical sense. If such tables are permitted, the consequences are devastating. The power of any relational language is severely reduced because of the reduced interchangeability in the ordering of relational operators (see Chapter 23). The form of projection in which duplicate rows are not removed from the result is called a corrupted version of the **project** operator.

If the user must retain the two occurrences of rows containing the name "Knight," he or she should retain the primary key EMP# as well by projecting onto EMP#, ENAME, together with zero or more of the remaining columns of EMP. In Chapter 17 on view updatability, much emphasis is placed on retaining the primary key in defining a virtual relation (usually called a view). When this is done, the user normally gains the advantage of being able to perform **inserts, updates,** and **deletes** on this view.

A second example shows that removing duplicates can be precisely what the user needs. Suppose we wish to find the cities in which the employees live. By taking the projection of EMP onto H_CITY, we obtain

Z	(H_CITY)
	Wimborne
	Poole

which is exactly what was requested. If 100 employees happen to live in Poole, why obtain 100 copies of the name Poole? If the number living in each city is needed, the DBMS should be capable of counting these numbers (as is RM/V2) and capable of providing the information as output in the form of a second column (this one computed).

Using the notation I introduced in early papers on the relational model

[Codd 1970, 1971a–d], the three applications of the **project** operator just introduced are represented as follows:

Example 1:   Z ← EMP [ENAME, BIRTH__DATE, SALARY, H__CITY]

Example 2:   Z ← EMP [EMP#, SALARY, H__CITY]

Example 3:   Z ← EMP [H__CITY]

The naming and virtual ordering of columns pertinent to the result of a **project** operation are discussed in Chapter 6.

The version of the **project** operator just described is useful whenever few columns are to be *saved* (and possibly many dropped). A second version is useful whenever few columns are to be *dropped* (and possibly many saved). In this version the columns to be dropped are listed, instead of the columns to be saved. However, this version is less adaptable to changes in the source relation. For example, if a new column is added to the source relation, its name may have to be added to the list of columns to be dropped in the projection.

RB-3–RB-12   The Theta-Select Operator

The **theta-select** operator, originally called **theta-restrict,** employs a single R-table as its operand. In normal use the term **theta-select** is abbreviated to **select,** and this means that the equality comparator '=' should be assumed unless there is an explicit alternative comparator specified. It generates as a result an R-table that contains some of the same complete rows that the operand contains—those rows, in fact, that satisfy the condition expressed in the command. To distinguish **theta-select** from the **select** command of SQL, we shall sometimes refer explicitly to **theta-select** as the algebraic **select,** and refer explicitly to SQL's **select** as the **select** of SQL. It is important to remember that the operand contains no duplicate rows, and that therefore neither does the result.

The complete class of **select** operators is called **theta-select,** where **theta** stands for any of the 10 comparators listed on page 70. Features RB-3–RB-12 are the 10 types of **theta-select** operators corresponding respectively to the 10 comparators. An extension of the **select** operator (Feature RB-13) and an extension of the **join** operator (Feature RB-25) are also discussed. These extensions permit Boolean combinations of comparisons.

Suppose that the **select** operator is applied to the same R-table as used in the explanation of **project,** and that the rows specified to be saved are those for which the SALARY has a specified value. In the three examples of this kind of query cited next, I again use the notation introduced in my early papers on the relational model [Codd 1970, 1971a–d]. The result for each query is listed immediately after the query.

Example 4: Z ← EMP [SALARY = 12,000]

Z	(EMP#	NAME	BIRTH_DATE	SALARY	H_CITY	)
	E912	Knight	38-11-05	12,000	Poole	
	E239	Knight	38-11-05	12,000	Poole	

Example 5: Z ← EMP [SALARY = 11,000]

Z	(EMP#	NAME	BIRTH_DATE	SALARY	H_CITY	)
	E575	Pawn	31-04-22	11,000	Poole	

Example 6: Z ← EMP [SALARY = 20,000]

Z	(EMP#	NAME	BIRTH_DATE	SALARY	H_CITY	)

Example 6 yields an R-table that happens to have no rows at all (since no employee earns this amount); the five columns have the same headings as the R-table EMP. An R-table of this kind is perfectly legitimate. It represents an empty relation of degree five with the same column headings as EMP. In each of the three examples (4, 5, and 6), the result is union-compatible with EMP (see RB-26 for an explanation of union-compatibility).

All of the **select** operators discussed so far involve the comparison of database values, on the one hand, with a constant, on the other hand; the comparator in each case has been equality. The **theta-select** operator can be used to compare a database value within a row of an R-table with another database value within the same row, and to execute this comparison for all rows of that R-table (see Example 8).

Further, any of the following 10 comparators may be used:

1. EQUALITY
2. INEQUALITY
3. LESS THAN
4. LESS THAN OR EQUAL TO
5. GREATER THAN
6. GREATER THAN OR EQUAL TO
7. GREATEST LESS THAN
8. GREATEST LESS THAN OR EQUAL TO
9. LEAST GREATER THAN
10. LEAST GREATER THAN OR EQUAL TO

In the following example of **theta-select, theta** is taken to be the LESS

THAN comparator ($<$):

Example 7:   Z ← EMP [SALARY $<$ 12,000].

Z	(EMP#	ENAME	BIRTH_DATE	SALARY	H_CITY	)
	E912	Rook	23-08-19	10,000	Wimborne	
	E575	Pawn	31-04-22	11,000	Poole	

The relational model provides a very important safety feature, introduced at the beginning of Chapter 3 and repeated here for convenience:

RT-1   Safety Feature when Comparing Database Values

When comparing a database value in one column with a database value in another, the DBMS checks that the two columns draw their values from a common domain, unless the domain check is overridden (see Feature RQ-9 in Chapter 10). When comparing (1) a computed value with a database value or (2) one computed value with another computed value, however, the DBMS merely checks that the basic data types are the same.

Table 4.1 shows the columns of EMP and the domains from which the columns draw their values. Note that no two columns of EMP draw their values from a common domain. Therefore, let us expand the EMP relation by appending another column with the heading BONUS, and assume certain values for the bonus component. All of the BONUS values are drawn from the currency domain. The modified version of EMP follows:

EMP″	(EMP#	ENAME	BIRTH_DATE	SALARY	H_CITY	BONUS)
	E107	Rook	23-08-19	10,000	Wimborne	15,800
	E912	Knight	38-11-05	12,000	Poole	6,700
	E239	Knight	38-11-05	12,000	Poole	13,000
	E575	Pawn	31-04-22	11,000	Poole	3,100

Table 4.1   Columns of EMP and Domains from which Values are Drawn

Column	Domain
EMP#	Employee serial numbers
ENAME	Employee names
BIRTH_DATE	Dates
SALARY	Currency
H_CITY	City names

Now consider Example 8:

Z ← EMP″ [BONUS > SALARY].

This command yields the following R-table:

Z	(EMP#	ENAME	BIRTH_DATE	SALARY	H_CITY	BONUS)
	E107	Rook	23-08-19	10,000	Wimborne	15,800
	E239	Knight	38-11-05	12,000	Poole	13,000

The naming and virtual ordering of the columns in the result of a **select** operator are discussed in Chapter 6.

RB-13 The Boolean Extension of Theta-Select

Let R denote any relation whose simple or composite columns include A and B. Let @ denote one of the 10 comparators used in **theta-select,** and let x denote a host-language variable or constant. Suppose that R [A @ x] and R [A @ B] denote **theta-select** operations. Then A @ x and A @ B are called *comparing terms,* and each comparing term is truth-valued.

The usual comparing terms in all 10 types of **theta-select** can be used in any Boolean combination within a single operator. Such an operator is called **extended theta-select.** A Boolean combination of the comparing terms, each of which is truth-valued, is any combination of these terms using the elementary logical connectives NOT, OR, AND, and IMPLIES.

Clearly, this operator is redundant from the user's viewpoint in the sense that a query involving **extended theta-select** can be re-expressed in terms of simple **theta-selects,** together with some combination of relational unions, differences, and intersections. However, it permits such queries to be expressed more clearly and concisely.

Consider a simple example of the practical use of this extended **join.** Suppose that a database includes a relation E describing employees, and that two of the immediate properties recorded are the gender (male M or female F) and present salary. The Boolean extension of **theta-select** can be used to place a request for the names of the employees who are female and earn more than $20,000:

E [(GENDER = F) ∧ (SALARY > 20,000)].

One DBMS product on the market in the mid-1980s supported this single feature of the relational model and no others. The vendor falsely advertised that the product was a relational DBMS.

RB-14–RB-23 The Theta-Join Operator

The **theta-join** operator employs two R-tables as its operands. It generates as a result an R-table that contains rows of one operand (say S) concatenated with rows of the second operand (say T), but only where the specified condition is found to hold true. For brevity, this operator is often referred to as **join.**

The condition expressed in the **join** operator involves comparing each value from a column of S with each value from a column of T. The columns to be compared are indicated explicitly in the **join** command; these columns are called the *comparand columns.* This condition can involve any of the 10 comparators cited in the list presented on page 74 (after a description of the operator applied with equality as the comparator).

Suppose that the **join** operator is applied to the following two relational tables:

S (EMP#	ENAME	H_CITY)
E107	Rook	Wimborne
E912	Knight	Poole
E239	Pawn	Poole

T (WHSE#	W_CITY)
W17	Wareham
W34	Poole
W92	Poole

For this example, we shall assume that the only pair of columns having a common domain are S.H_CITY and T.W_CITY; each of these two columns draws its values from the CITY domain. Therefore, in this example, these are the only two columns that can be used as comparand columns in a **join** of these two relations. Normally, there are several pairs of potential comparand columns, not just one pair.

The **join** operator based on equality that is now being discussed is called **equi-join.** An **equi-join** of S on H_CITY with T on W_CITY finds all of the employees and warehouses that are located in the same city. The formula for this **join** is

$$U = S [H\_CITY = W\_CITY] T.$$

The result obtained assuming the values cited earlier is as follows:

U	(EMP#	NAME	H_CITY	WHSE#	W_CITY)
	E912	Knight	Poole	W34	Poole
	E912	Knight	Poole	W92	Poole
	E239	Pawn	Poole	W34	Poole
	E239	Pawn	Poole	W92	Poole

Some people find it easier to think of the **equi-join** of S on H_CITY with T on W_CITY as the **Cartesian product** of S with T, followed by the selection of just those rows for which

H_CITY = W_CITY.

Naturally, if the goal is good performance, the designer of a DBMS should not implement **equi-join** in this way.

Any of the following 10 comparators may be used in a **join:**

1. EQUALITY
2. INEQUALITY
3. LESS THAN
4. LESS THAN OR EQUAL TO
5. GREATER THAN
6. GREATER THAN OR EQUAL TO
7. GREATEST LESS THAN
8. GREATEST LESS THAN OR EQUAL TO
9. LEAST GREATER THAN
10. LEAST GREATER THAN OR EQUAL TO

The complete class of **joins** is called **theta-join,** where **theta** stands for any of the 10 comparators just listed. As an example, consider

U = PART [OH_Q < SHIP_Q] SHIP.

The result U is generated from the following operands:

PART	(P#	PNAME	OH_Q)		SHIP	(WHSE#	SHIP_Q)
	N12	nut	1000			W34	1200
	B39	bolt	1500			W92	2000

U	(P#	PNAME	OH_Q	WHS#	SHIP_Q)
	N12	nut	1000	W34	1200
	N12	nut	1000	W92	2000
	B39	bolt	1500	W92	2000

Just as mentioned in the discussion of the **select** operator, when comparing a database value in one column with a database value in another, the DBMS checks that the two columns draw their values from a common domain, unless the domain check is overridden (see Feature RQ-9 in Chapter 10 and Feature RJ-6 in Chapter 11). The practical reasons for this check and its override were discussed in Chapter 3 (see the fourth reason to support domains in a DBMS together with Feature RT-1).

It is possible to conceive of each of the 10 **theta-joins** of S with T as a subset of the **Cartesian product** of S with T. However, as stated for **equi-**

join, Cartesian product should not be used in the implementation of any one of the 10. The result of each of the 10 **theta-joins** has a degree equal to the sum of the degrees of the operands.

The result of a **join** based on Comparators 3, 4, 5, or 6 in the preceding list is often quite large in terms of the number of rows. Not surprisingly, this number is often nearly as large as the number of rows in the **Cartesian product.** If, on the other hand, any one of Comparators 7, 8, 9, or 10 in the list is selected, the resulting relation is quite modest in size. That is one of the more important reasons why a user may choose one of these comparators instead of Comparators 3, 4, 5, or 6.

It is certainly possible to join a relation with itself, provided that it has two or more columns on a common domain. Let us modify the relation EMP by adding a column that identifies the immediate manager for each and every employee.

EMP	(EMP#	ENAME	BIRTH__DATE	SALARY	CITY	MGR#)
	E107	Rook	23-08-19	10,000	Poole	E321
	E912	Knight	38-11-05	12,000	Wareham	E321
	E239	Knight	38-11-05	12,000	Wareham	E107
	E575	Pawn	31-04-22	11,000	Poole	E239
	E321	Queen	27-02-28	20,000	Wimborne	—

In this table, MGR# is the employee serial number of the immediate manager of the person designated by the left-most component (EMP#). The employee designated E321 appears to be "top dog," since the serial number of his or her immediate manager is unknown.

Because the columns EMP# and MGR# both draw their values from the common domain of employee serial numbers, it is clear that we may join EMP with itself, using the EMP# and MGR# columns as comparands. The assignment could be

Z ← EMP [EMP# = MGR#] EMP,

but fewer columns are needed in the final result. Suppose that projection is applied to the result from the **join,**

Z ← (EMP [EMP# = MGR#] EMP)[EMP#, ENAME, CITY, MGR#, MGR__NAME],

where MGR__NAME denotes the employee name ENAME of the manager. The result of this evaluation is as follows:

Z	(EMP#	NAME	CITY	MGR#	MGR__NAME)
	E107	Rook	Poole	E321	Queen
	E912	Knight	Wareham	E321	Queen
	E239	Knight	Wareham	E107	Rook
	E575	Pawn	Poole	E239	Knight

The tuple < E321, Queen, Wimborne, —, — > is omitted because it does not satisfy the equality condition. The query "Who earns a higher salary than his immediate manager?" can be answered by a **join** of EMP with itself, once again using EMP# and MGR# as comparand columns.

Under certain quite broad conditions, the **project, select,** and **join** operators can be executed in any sequence and yield a result that is independent of the sequence chosen. This fact is important when the DBMS is attempting to generate the most efficient target code from a relational language acting as source code. This process is called *optimization;* the DBMS component involved is called the *optimizer. This inter-changeability of ordering of the operators is damaged when duplicate rows are allowed.* More is said about this point in Chapter 23.

The following observations are intended to complete the discussion of **theta-joins.** Users who are wedded to the approaches of the past often think that the only kind of **join** in the relational model is either the **equi-join** or the **natural join** (discussed later in this section), and that the only comparand columns allowed are primary keys or foreign keys. In other words, these users see **joins** as key-based **equi-joins** only. This tunnel vision may be due to the fact that DBMS products of the pre-relational variety tended to support pointers or links only where the relational model supports primary and foreign keys.

Theta-joins are the algebraic counterparts of queries that use the existential quantifier of predicate logic. A brief explanation of these quantifiers appears later in the explanation of **relational division** (Feature RB-29). Incidentally, the result of an **equi-join** can be empty, even if neither of its operands is empty.

Note the following identities:

$$R [A = B] S = S [B = A] R$$
$$R [A < B] S = S [B > A] R.$$

Equi-join is commutative, whereas **join** on LESS THAN (<) is related simply to **join** on GREATER THAN (>), and is not commutative.

RB-24 The Boolean Extension of Theta-Join

Let R, S denote any relations whose simple or composite columns include R.B and S.C. Suppose that R.B and S.C draw their values from a common domain. Let @ denote one of the 10 comparators used in **theta-join.** Suppose that R [B @ C] S denotes a **theta-join** operation. Then B @ C is called a *comparing term,* and each comparing term is truth-valued.

The usual comparing terms in all 10 types of **theta-join** can be used in any Boolean combination within a single operator of the extended type. It is important to remember that each pair of comparand columns cited in the comparing terms must draw their values from a domain common to the pair. Such an operator is called **extended theta-join.** A Boolean combination of the comparing terms, each of which is truth-valued, is any combination of these terms using the elementary logical connectives NOT, OR, AND, and IMPLIES.

Consider a simple example of the practical use of this **extended join.** Suppose that a database includes two relations T1 and T2, respectively describing the members of two teams of employees (each team is assigned to a different project). Suppose that the need arises to pair off individual members of Team 1 with individual members of Team 2 based on both of the following:

- equality in jobcode (abbreviated J1, J2);
- birthdate B1 of the Team 1 member being earlier than the birthdate B2 of the Team 2 member.

The Boolean extension of **theta-join** can be used to place a request for all the eligible pairs of team members who satisfy both of these conditions:

$$T1 \ [(J1 = J2) \wedge (B1 < B2)] \ T2.$$

Note that, if jobcode happened to have the same column name in T1 as in T2, the name would have to be prefixed by the pertinent relation name (e.g., T1.J). The same applies to the birthdate columns.

RB-25 The Natural Join Operator

As described in the last section, an **equi-join** generates a result in which two of the columns are identical in values, although different in column names. These two columns are derived from the comparand columns of the operands; of course, the columns may be either simple or composite. Of the 10 types of **theta-join, equi-join** is the only one that yields a result in which the comparand columns are completely redundant, one with the other. The **natural join** behaves just like the **equi-join** except that one of the redundant columns, simple or composite, is omitted from the result. To make the column naming clear and avoid impairing the commutativity, the retained comparand column is assigned whichever of the two comparand-column names occurs first alphabetically.

The degree of the result generated by **natural join** is less than that generated by **equi-join** on the same operands. The degree of the former result is the sum of the degrees of the operands reduced by the number of simple columns in the comparand column of either operand.

Natural join is probably most useful in the theory of database design, especially in normalizing a collection of relations. It is included here primarily for that reason.

As an aid to understanding the following three operators—**relational union, relational intersection,** and **relational difference**—the reader may wish to refer to Figure 4.1.

RB-26   The Union Operator

The **relational union** operator is intentionally not as general as the union operator in mathematics. The latter permits formation of the union of a set of buildings with a set of parts and also with a set of employees. On the other hand, **relational union** permits, for example, (1) a set of buildings to be united with another set of buildings, (2) a set of employees to be united with another set of employees, or (3) a set of parts to be united with another set of parts.

Figure 4.1   **The Basic Operators of the Relational Model**

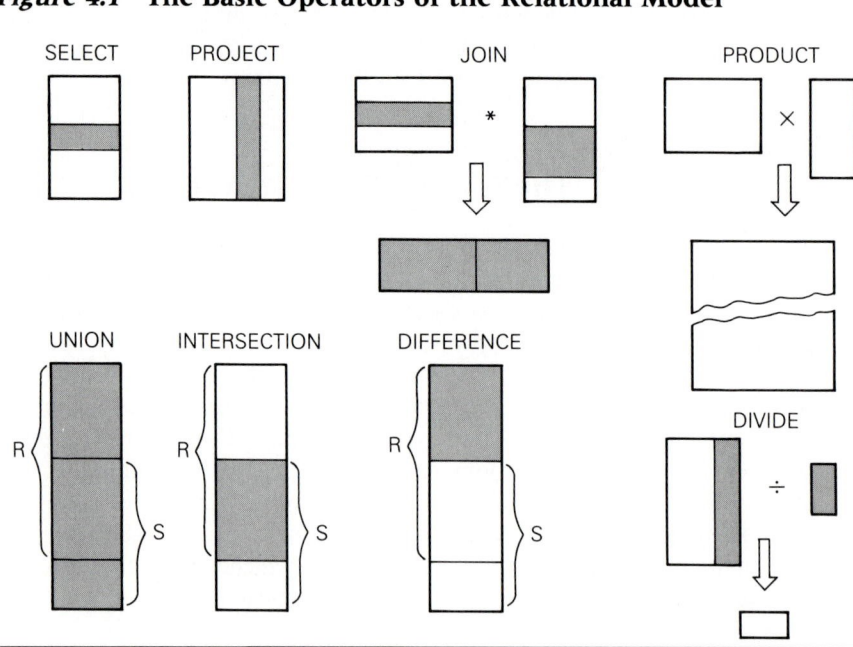

Relational union is intended to bring together in one relation all of the facts that happen to exist in whatever two relations are chosen to be its operands, provided these two relations contain the same kind of facts. It does this by copying rows from both of its operands into the result, but *without generating duplicate rows in the result.* The relations that are combined by the **relational union** operator must be compatible with one another in having rows of similar type, thus ensuring that the result is a relation. It must be remembered that all relations are sets, but that not all sets are relations. Thus, **relational union** is intentionally *not* as general as set union. Union compatibility is now discussed in more detail.

Suppose that S and T are two relations. Then, S and T are *union-compatible* if they are of the same degree and it is possible to establish at least one mapping between the columns of S and those of T that is one-to-one, and with the property that, for every column A of S and every column B of T, if column A is mapped onto column B, then A and B draw their values from a common domain. Of course, the number of such mappings between S and T may be zero, one, two, or more. If it happens that no such mapping exists, then S and T are not union-compatible, and any request from the user to form S **union** T causes an error code to be returned.

The **union** operator requires that its two operands (which are relations, of course) be union-compatible. In practice, it is rare that two base relations are union-compatible, but not at all rare that two derived relations are. The **union** operator also requires that the column alignment for its two operands, whether explicit or implied, be in conformity with one of the mappings that guarantees union compatibility (this is discussed further later in this section).

The result of applying **union** to relations S and T is a relation containing all of the rows of S together with all of the rows of T, but with duplicate rows removed. The removal of duplicate rows becomes necessary when it happens that relation S has some rows in common with relation T. Those DBMS implementations that either require or permit the retention of duplicate rows in the final result of a **union** will give rise to the same severe problems cited earlier in the description of the **project** operator.

The principal reason why **relational union, intersection,** and **difference** are not as general as their mathematical counterparts is that, in a relational system, it must be easy to find any desired information in the result. Hence, the result is required to be a relation. The result of these operators is also constrained to be a relation because this is necessary for operational closure (see Feature RM-5 in Chapter 12).

Consider an example involving domestic suppliers S and overseas suppliers T. These relations are likely to be separated from one another because certain properties are applicable to one but not the other. For the example, suppose that we take the projection S″ of S and the projection T″ of T on certain columns common to both S and T, namely, supplier serial number and supplier name.

Suppose that the corresponding snapshots are as follows:

S" (S#	NAME)
S11	Peter
S12	Smith
S17	Clark
S23	Rock
S25	Roth

T" (S#	NAME)
S2	Jones
S17	Clark
S3	Blake
S7	Tack

Applying the operator **union,** we obtain the following:

Z (S#	NAME)
S11	Peter
S12	Smith
S17	Clark
S23	Rock
S25	Roth
S2	Jones
S3	Blake
S7	Tack

Z ← S" union T"

We observe that Clark, with the serial number S17, is both a domestic and an overseas supplier. Note that the row < S17, Clark > is not repeated in the result.

The designer of a relational language must face the difficulty that, when applying the **union** operator in some circumstances, the user must specify in some detail which columns of one relation are to be aligned with which columns of the second relation. This alignment is particularly relevant when two or more columns of one operand have the same domain. When this is true of one operand, it must be true of the other, if they are to satisfy the requirement of union compatibility.

The simplest approach appears to be as follows:

■ if all the domains of one relation are distinct, then the DBMS aligns the columns by ensuring that aligned pairs have the same domain;

■ if not all the domains of one relation are distinct, then

1. for those columns of one operand that have distinct domains within that operand, the DBMS aligns them with the columns of the other operand by ensuring that aligned pairs have the same domain; and

2. it aligns the remaining columns by accepting the pairing of these columns as specified by the user in his or her request or, if no such pairing is specified, it pairs columns by name alphabetically (lowest alphabetically from one operand with lowest alphabetically from the other, and so on).

The relational model requires this approach to be adopted within the DBMS for the operators **relational union, intersection,** and **difference.**

In countries that do not use the Roman alphabet, it may be necessary to replace the alphabetic default by some other kind of default.

The DBMS sends an error message if either the implicit alphabetic ordering or the explicit alignment declared by the user fails to satisfy the constraint that pairs of columns that are aligned for the **union** operator must draw their values from a common domain. This approach to column alignment is required by the relational model until such time as a simpler technique is devised to deal with this column-alignment problem.

The following special case is noteworthy. Whenever the two operands of a **union** have primary keys PK1 and PK2, which draw their values from a common domain, and whenever PK1 and PK2 happen to be aligned for a requested **union,** then the DBMS deduces that the primary key of the result is a column PK that is formed by uniting PK1 with PK2. One consequence of this is that the DBMS rejects duplicate values in column PK of the result.

RB-27   The Intersection Operator

Suppose that S and T are two relations that are union-compatible. Then, they are sufficiently compatible with one another for the **intersection** operator to be applicable. Columns have to be aligned in the same way as for the **union** operator. The result of applying **intersection** to relations S and T is a relation containing only those rows of S that also appear as rows of T. Of course, the resulting relation contains no duplicate rows, since neither of the operands contain any.

Consider the same example as before involving domestic suppliers S and overseas suppliers T. Assume that the same projections as before have been made to generate relations S″ and T″.

S″ (S#	NAME)
S11	Peter
S12	Smith
S17	Clark
S23	Rock
S25	Roth

T″ (S#	NAME)
S2	Jones
S17	Clark
S3	Blake
S7	Tack

Applying the operator **intersection,** we obtain the following R-table:

Z (S#	NAME)
S17	Clark

Z ← S″ intersection T″

The supplier Clark with the serial number S17 is both a domestic and an overseas supplier. Note also how the row < S17, Clark > was not repeated in the result.

The approach to column alignment is the same as with **union:**

- if all the domains of one relation are distinct, then the DBMS aligns the columns by ensuring that aligned pairs have the same domain;
- if not all the domains of one relation are distinct, then
  1. for those columns of one operand that have distinct domains within that operand, the DBMS aligns them with the columns of the other operand by ensuring that aligned pairs have the same domain; and
  2. it aligns the remaining columns by accepting the pairing of these columns as specified by the user in his or her request or, if no such pairing is specified, it pairs columns by name alphabetically (lowest alphabetically from one operand with lowest alphabetically from the other, and so on).

In countries that do not use the Roman alphabet, it may be necessary to replace the alphabetic default by some other kind of default.

The DBMS sends an error message if either the implicit alphabetic ordering or the explicit alignment declared by the user fails to satisfy the constraint that pairs of columns that are aligned for the **intersection** operator must draw their values from a common domain.

RB-28 The Difference Operator

Suppose that S and T are two relations that are union-compatible. Then, they are sufficiently compatible with one another for the **relational difference** operator to be applicable. Columns must be aligned in the same way as for the **union** operator. The result of applying **relational difference** to relations S and T is a relation containing only those rows of S that do not appear as rows of T. Of course, the resulting relation contains no duplicate rows.

Consider the same example involving domestic suppliers S and overseas suppliers T. Assume that the same projections as before have been made to generate relations S″ and T″:

S″ (S#	NAME)
S11	Peter
S12	Smith
S17	Clark
S23	Rock
S25	Roth

T″ (S#	NAME)
S2	Jones
S17	Clark
S3	Blake
S7	Tack

Applying the operator **relational difference,** we obtain the following:

$$Z \; (\; S\# \quad NAME \;) \qquad\qquad Z \leftarrow S'' - T''$$

Z (S#	NAME)
S11	Peter
S12	Smith
S23	Rock
S25	Roth

The supplier Clark with the serial number S17 is both a domestic and an overseas supplier, which explains why the row < S17, Clark > does not appear at all in the result.

The approach to column alignment is the same as with **union:**

- if all the domains of one relation are distinct, then the DBMS aligns the columns by ensuring that aligned pairs have the same domain;
- if not all the domains of one relation are distinct, then
  1. for those columns of one operand that have distinct domains within that operand, the DBMS aligns them with the columns of the other operand by ensuring that aligned pairs have the same domain; and
  2. it aligns the remaining columns by accepting the pairing of these columns as specified by the user in his or her request or, if no such pairing is specified, it pairs columns by name alphabetically (lowest alphabetically from one operand with lowest alphabetically from the other, and so on).

In countries that do not use the Roman alphabet, it may be necessary to replace the alphabetic default by some other kind of default.

The DBMS sends an error message if either the implicit alphabetic ordering or the explicit alignment declared by the user fails to satisfy the constraint that pairs of columns that are aligned for the **relational difference** operator must draw their values from a common domain.

RB-29 The Relational Division Operator

Relational division is similar in some respects to division in integer arithmetic. In **relational division,** just as in integer arithmetic division, there is a dividend, a divisor, the quotient, and even a remainder. Thus, relational division has similarly named operands and results. Instead of being integers, however, these operands and results are all relations. None of them need contain any numeric information at all, and even if the operands do contain such information, it need not be the numeric components that play a crucial role in relational division.

Consider an example of division in integer arithmetic. Suppose that we are dividing 29 by 7. One must find the largest multiplier for 7 that yields a product that is equal to or less than 29. That multiplier is 4, since $4 \times 7 = 28$, and 28 is less than 29; while $5 \times 7 = 35$, and 35 is greater than 29.

In **relational division** the relational operator corresponding to multiplication is **Cartesian product**. The relational comparator corresponding to LESS THAN OR EQUAL TO ($\leq$) is SET INCLUSION.

When dividing one relation by another, at least one pair of columns (one column of the pair from the dividend, the other column from the divisor) must draw their values from the same domain. Such a pair of columns can be used as comparand columns (just as if we were attempting an **equi-join**).

Suppose that (1) relation S is the dividend, (2) relation T is the divisor, (3) the comparand columns are B from S and C from T, and (4) the column A from S is to be the source of values for the quotient. Then suppose that Q is the quotient obtained by dividing S on B by T on C. The assignment to Q is represented by

$$Q \leftarrow S\,[\,A,\,B\,/\,C\,]\,T,$$

and we obtain the largest relation Q, such that $Q[A] \times T[C]$ is contained in $S[A,B]$. The term "largest relation" in this context means the relation that has the most tuples (rows), while still satisfying the specified condition.

As an example, suppose that we have a list of parts required for a certain job, and that the list is presented as a unary relation named LIST containing part serial numbers. LIST is an R-table with one column named P#. Suppose also that CAP has the same meaning as the CAPABILITY relation used in Section 1.2.3. Suppose that CAP and LIST have the following extensions:

CAP	(S#	P#	SPEED	UNIT_Q	PRICE)
	S1	P1	5	100	10
	S1	P2	5	100	20
	S1	P6	12	10	600
	S2	P3	5	50	15
	S2	P4	5	100	15
	S3	P6	5	10	700
	S4	P2	5	100	15
	S4	P3	5	50	17
	S4	P5	15	5	300
	S4	P6	10	5	350

LIST	(P#)
	P2
	P5
	P6

Note that SPEED denotes speed of delivery in number of working days.

Consider the query "Find the suppliers each of whom can supply every one of the parts listed in the given R-table LIST." This query is equivalent to

QUOT ← CAP [S#, P# / P#] LIST.

This query calls for CAP on S#, P# to be divided by LIST on P#. The result obtained is as follows:

QUOT	(S#	SPEED	UNIT_Q	PRICE)
	S4	5	100	15
	S4	15	5	300
	S4	10	5	350

Note that the relation QUOT [S#] contains only one row, and this row contains only one component S4. Thus, the **Cartesian product**

CP ← QUOT [S#] × LIST [P#] is as follows:

CP	(S#	P#)
	S4	P2
	S4	P5
	S4	P6

This is contained in CAP [S#, P#]. The quotient is accordingly the relation QUOT of degree four just shown. The remainder is simply the dividend with some of its rows removed—namely, those appearing in the quotient QUOT with the P# column removed:

RMDR	(S#	P#	SPEED	UNIT_Q	PRICE)
	S1	P1	5	100	10
	S1	P2	5	100	20
	S1	P6	12	10	600
	S2	P3	5	50	15
	S2	P4	5	100	15
	S3	P6	5	10	700
	S4	P3	5	50	17

Note the degrees of the relations:

Dividend CAP	Degree 5
Divisor LIST	Degree 1
Quotient QUOT	Degree 4
Remainder RMDR	Degree 5

More generally, the degree of the quotient is equal to the degree of the dividend minus the degree of the divisor. The degree of the remainder is equal to the degree of the dividend.

Relational division is the principal algebraic counterpart of queries that involve the universal quantifier of predicate logic. Now follows the promised and brief explanation of the quantifiers of predicate logic. The example just used to explain **relational division** is now used with more concise notation to explain the two quantifiers: the *existential* and the *universal*.

Suppose that the relations in a database include S, P, and C, where S describes suppliers, P describes parts, and C describes capabilities of suppliers in supplying parts. Let the primary key of suppliers be supplier serial numbers S#; for parts, the primary key is part serial numbers P#; for capabilities, the primary key is the combination of S# and P#. Let the description of suppliers include for each supplier its name; the corresponding column is called SNAME. Suppose also that a list of parts needed for some project is given as a unary relation L whose only column P# draws its values from the part serial number domain P#.

Two quite different kinds of queries are now discussed from the standpoint of a relational language ALPHA [Codd 1971a], which is based on predicate logic, rather than algebra, and uses tuple variables, rather than domain variables. Q1 requires the existential quantifier, and Q2 requires the universal quantifier.

> Q1: Retrieve the names of all suppliers, each of whom can supply at least one of the parts listed in L.

```
range of s is S
range of p is L
range of c is C
s, p, and c are tuple variables.
get s.SNAME where
EXISTS p EXISTS c (c.s# = s.s# AND c.p# = p.p#).
```

The term "EXISTS" denotes the existential quantifier of predicate logic. It corresponds to the **theta-join** operators. It does *not* denote the same use of the term "EXISTS" as in the language SQL.

> Q2: Retrieve the names of all suppliers, each of whom can supply all of the parts listed in L.

Assuming the same three range statements as listed under Q1,

```
get s.SNAME where
FOR ALL p EXISTS c (c.s# = s.s# AND c.p# =p.p#)
```

The phrase "FOR ALL," which denotes the universal quantifier of predicate logic, corresponds to **relational division.** Present versions of the language SQL cannot express **relational division** in any direct manner. Consequently, SQL users must translate Q2 into the following:

Q2″:   Retrieve the name of every supplier, for whom it is not true that there exists a part in the list L that it cannot supply.

This kind of translation represents a significant burden on users that is completely unnecessary. (Refer back to Figure 4.1 on page 78 for a summation of all the basic operators.)

4.3 ■ The Manipulative Operators

The manipulative operators are those concerned with making changes to the contents of the database. Eight such operators are described:

RB-30   **Relational assignment**

RB-31   **Insert**

RB-32   **Update**

RB-33   **Primary key update with cascaded update**

RB-34   **Primary key update with cascaded marking**

RB-35   **Delete**

RB-36   **Delete with cascaded deletion**

RB-37   **Delete with cascaded marking.**

In contrast to pre-relational DBMS, each one of these operators is capable of handling multiple-records-at-a-time, where "multiple records" means zero, one, two, or more rows of a relation. No special treatment is given to any data on account of the number of records.

RB-30 Relational Assignment

When querying a database, the user may wish to have the result of the query (a relation, of course) retained in memory under a name of his or her choosing. The user may also wish to be able to require this retained relation to participate in some later relational query or manipulative activity. Both of these desires are satisfied to a certain extent by **relational assignment**. This operator is denoted by ← in the expression T ← rve, where (1) rve denotes a *relation-valued expression* (an expression whose evaluation yields a relation), and (2) T denotes a user-selected name for the relation that is specified by rve and that is to be retained in memory.

Note that the relation obtained by executing rve may, as usual, contain zero, one, two, or more rows.

Since a relation may consist of a very large number of rows, and since each row is likely to consist of a combination of character strings, numbers, and logical truth-values, a **relational assignment** is beyond the capability of most programming languages. However, a fully relational language must be able to express **relational assignment,** while a fully relational DBMS must be able to execute such an assignment.

If the qualifier SAVE is attached to the command, the DBMS establishes the data description of T in the catalog, unless an appropriate description of T is already there. The domain of any column of T in which the values are derived by means of a function is identified as *function-derived,* because the DBMS usually cannot be more specific than that.

When the qualifier SAVE is attached, the user should be required to declare which simple column or combination of simple columns constitutes the primary key.

If the user needs this relation only temporarily (within a particular interactive session or within a single execution of an application program), the qualifier SAVE may be omitted. Then,

1. the DBMS does not record the description of T in the catalog;
2. if T still exists, T is dropped by the DBMS at the end of the interactive session or at the end of execution of the program.

RB-31 The Insert Operator

The **insert** operator permits a collection of one or more rows to be inserted into a relation. The user has no control, however, over where these rows go. They may even be appended by the DBMS "at one end or the other" of the target relation. I place this phrase in quotation marks because there is no concept of the end of a relation in the relational model. It is the responsibility of the DBMS alone to determine exactly where the rows should be stored, although this positioning may be affected by the access paths already declared by the DBA for that relation. It is assumed that, for insertion of new rows into a relation T, the catalog already contains a detailed description of T.

If the collection of rows to be inserted includes two or more rows that are duplicates of one another, only one of these rows is inserted. If the collection of rows to be inserted includes a row that duplicates any one of the rows in the receiving relation, that row will not be inserted. Thus, at the end of the insertion the resulting relation contains no duplicate rows; to achieve this, several rows in the collection to be inserted may have been withheld. Whenever rows are withheld by the DBMS from insertion (to avoid duplicate rows in the result), the *duplicate row indicator* is turned on (see Feature RJ-8 in Chapter 11, "Indicators").

One or more rows in the collection to be inserted may be withheld by the DBMS for another reason: the resulting relation is not allowed to have duplicate values in its primary key. In the event that such a withholding occurs for this reason, the *duplicate primary-key indicator* is turned on (see Feature RJ-9 in Chapter 11). This constraint is more restrictive than the no-duplicate-row constraint, since it is entirely possible that the non-primary-key components may be different from one another, even though the primary-key values are identical.

If one or more indexes exist for the target relation, the DBMS will automatically update these indexes to support the inserted rows.

If the new rows for relation T are derived from one or more other relations in the same relational database in accordance with a relation-valued expression rve, then an alternative way of obtaining the result of inserting these rows into T is by using the **union** operator and **relational assignment:**

$T \leftarrow T$ UNION rve.

However, to be able to use this method, T must be either a base relation or a special kind of view—the kind that the DBMS at view-definition time has determined can accept insertions. It is worth noting that not all views can accept insertions, a point discussed in detail in Chapter 17, "View Updatability." It is worth noting that the **insert** operator eliminates duplicate rows and duplicate primary-key values just as the **union** operator does.

RB-32 The Update Operator

In managing a database, it may be necessary occasionally to change the values of one or more components of one or more rows that already exist within a relation. This is usually distinguished from inserting entirely new rows because the components to be changed in value may represent a very small percentage of the number of components in each row.

This observation is the justification for the **update** operator. The information that must be supplied with this operator consists of the name of the relation to be updated, the specification of the rows in that relation to be updated, and the column names that identify the row components of these rows to be identified, and the new values for these components. The DBMS should provide two options for identifying the rows to be updated; the user should supply either a list of primary key values or an expression that (1) is a valid condition for a **select** operation and that (2) involves the DBMS in conducting a search for those rows that satisfy this condition.

Existing indexes for the target relation are automatically updated by the DBMS to reflect the requested update activity.

Referential integrity may be damaged if the column to which the update is applied happens to be the primary key of the pertinent relation or a foreign key. Normally, Feature RB-33 should be used to update a primary-key value. When updating a foreign-key value only, the user should make sure that the new value for this key exists as the value of a primary key defined on the same domain. Otherwise, the DBMS will reject the update.

RB-33 Primary-Key Update with Cascaded Update of Foreign Keys and Optional Update of Sibling Primary Keys

It is seldom necessary to update the value of a primary key, but, when this is necessary, it is very important that it be done correctly. Otherwise, integrity in the database will be lost, and it will be quite difficult to recover from the damage.

An important check made by the DBMS is that each allegedly new value for a primary key is not only of the data type specified for that key, but is also new with respect to that simple or composite column: that is, at this time the new value does not occur elsewhere in that primary-key column.

When a primary-key value is changed, it is usually necessary to make the same change in value of all of the matching foreign-key values drawn from the same domain. Why cannot this be programmed as a transaction that includes an **update** command for the row that contains the primary key value followed by an **update** command for each of the rows in the database that contain that same value as a foreign key whose domain is the same as that of the primary key? To prepare such a transaction correctly, the user must have extremely recent knowledge of which columns in the entire database draw their values from the domain D of the given primary key; "recent" means down to the millisecond level or some shorter time interval.

It is important to remember that the relational approach is highly dynamic, and that users who are appropriately authorized can at any time request new columns be added to one or more relations. Thus, it would be very risky to assume that any user (even the DBA) knows at any time precisely which columns draw their values from any given domain. It is precisely for this reason that

- the kind of transaction cited in the preceding paragraph is unacceptable;
- the relational model includes the *cascading option* in some of its manipulative operators and in the reaction of the DBMS to attempted violation of certain integrity constraints.

If a DBMS is fully relational, it maintains in the catalog the knowledge concerning which columns draw their values from any given domain in a state that is consistent with the most recently executed relational command.

This means that the DBMS is in a better position than any user to handle correctly the updating of *all* the matching foreign-key values drawn from the pertinent primary domain.

The **primary-key update** command not only updates a primary-key value, but also updates in precisely the same way all of the matching foreign-key values drawn from the same domain as the primary-key value. For the DBMS to support this command, it is essential that the DBMS support domains.

This command is not included in the present version of the language SQL. In fact, it is impossible to express a precisely equivalent action in SQL. Moreover, it is extremely cumbersome to express any action in SQL that is even superficially similar, but is based on the false assumption that some user knows precisely which columns draw their values from a given domain. Such an expression takes about three pages of commands, some expressed in SQL and some in a host language. This is just one of the severe penalties stemming from the failure of SQL to support domains as extended data types (see Chapters 3 and 23).

A more detailed account follows. The **primary-key update** operator is intended to simplify the updating of primary-key values. The DBMS finds from the catalog which domain (say D) is the domain of the specified primary key. It then finds all of the columns in the entire database that draw their values from domain D. From this set of columns, it selects two subsets:

S1:D   Those columns that are primary-key columns for other relations, but defined on D

S2:D   Those columns that are declared to be foreign-key columns with respect to the given primary key

The set S1:D is called the set of *sibling primary keys*. The set S2:D is called the set of *dependent foreign keys,* where "dependent" refers to the fact that foreign-key values are existence-dependent on their primary key counterparts.

Unless the qualifier EXCLUDE SIBLINGS is attached to the command, the DBMS takes primary-key action as follows. It hunts in each column cited in S1:D for the value of the given primary key. It then updates this value in precisely the same way as the original primary key was updated. Unconditionally, the DBMS takes foreign-key action as follows. It hunts in each column cited in S2:D for the value of the given primary key, now occurring in a foreign-key role. Whenever such a value is found, it is updated in precisely the same way as the primary key was updated. In this way, referential integrity is maintained.

Thus, the DBMS executes all of these primary- and foreign-key updates in addition to the update of the specified primary-key value, except that the action on other primary keys is omitted if the qualifier EXCLUDE SIB-LINGS is attached to the pertinent command. Whenever an index involves any of the keys (primary or foreign) being updated, that index is also automatically updated by the DBMS to reflect the updating of the actual key.

The entire sequence of activities is treated as if it had been requested as a transaction. Thus, either the whole series of updates is successful, or none of it is successful. This is what one should expect in any case, since only a single relational command is involved.

Existing indexes for all of the columns of all of the relations involved are automatically updated by the DBMS to reflect the requested update activity. These changes are committed to the database if and only if the aforementioned changes are committed.

RB-34   Primary-key Update with Cascaded Marking of Foreign Keys

This operator behaves in the same way as that of Feature RB-33, except in regard to all of the foreign keys based on the same domain as the primary key. Instead of updating the matching foreign-key values, the DBMS marks each foreign-key value as missing-but-applicable. Of course, if one or more of these foreign keys happens to have a DBA-declared constraint that there be no missing values, then the whole command is rejected by the DBMS.

RB-35   The Delete Operator

The **delete** operator permits a user to delete multiple rows from a relation: "multiple" includes the special cases of zero and one, and these cases do not receive special treatment. Why include zero as a possibility? One reason is that a condition that the user has incorporated in the **delete** command might not be satisfied by any row. Of course, it is necessary for the user to specify the pertinent relation and identify the rows to be deleted in either of the two ways permitted by the simple **update** operator.

Existing indexes for the target relation are automatically updated by the DBMS to reflect the requested deletion activity.

Users of the **delete** command are advised to be very cautious, since every row of a base relation that is deleted results in the deletion of some primary-key value. Then, if in the database there happen to be matching values of foreign keys, referential integrity can be damaged: hence, the next two commands.

RB-36 The Delete Operator with Cascaded Deletion

This **delete** operator is similar to that of Feature RB-35, except that it takes into account the fact that a simple or composite component of each of the rows being deleted happens to be the value of the primary key of a base relation. This is true even if the deletion is executed through a view (a virtual relation). Thus, execution of RB-35 will often violate referential integrity. Since usually referential integrity is not fully checked until the end of a transaction, this violation may be just a transient state that is permitted to exist within the pertinent transaction only. (See Chapter 13 for more details.)

When a primary-key value of a base relation participates in a deletion, referential integrity is normally violated if any foreign keys exist elsewhere in the database, in that relation or in others, that are drawn from the same domain as that primary key and are equal in value to it. There is no violation if the primary-key value still exists as a *sibling primary-key value.* This is the primary key of some other relation, provided that key draws its values from the same domain. Use of the **delete with cascaded deletion** operator causes the DBMS to propagate deletions to those rows in the database that happen to contain dependent foreign-key values as components.

If the qualifier EXCLUDE SIBLINGS is attached to the command, no action is taken with respect to the other occurrences of this value as a sibling primary key from this domain. If this qualifier is not attached, the rows that contain the same value in the role of a sibling primary key are deleted also.

Existing indexes for all of the relations involved are automatically updated by the DBMS to reflect the requested deletion activity.

This operator should be used with great care. In fact, few people in any installation should be authorized to use it; they should probably be on the staff of the DBA. The reason is simple. The deletions can occur in wave after wave, all automatically. (See Chapter 18, "Authorization," for more details.)

The deletion of each row that contains a pertinent foreign-key value must also result in the deletion of a value of some primary key; this primary key will often be different from the primary key that initiated the cascading action. Quite often, the initial deletion of one row results in the deletion of many other rows elsewhere in the database. Then, each of these deletions results in the deletion of many other rows in the database, and so it proceeds.

RB-37 The Delete Operator with Cascaded A-marking and Optional Sibling Deletion

This operator is similar to that of Feature RB-36, but is far less dangerous, because the initial cycle of cascading does not trigger any subsequent cycles of deletion. This reduced danger is a strong reason why foreign keys should be allowed to have missing values, unless the DBA has an overriding reason why not.

The DBMS finds all of the columns that draw their values from the domain of the primary key involved: primary domain D. From these columns it selects the two subsets S1:D (the sibling columns) and S2:D (the dependent foreign-key columns) as defined earlier. The DBMS then examines the catalog to see whether any column cited in S2:D has the declaration that missing values are prohibited.

Suppose that one or more of the columns cited in S2:D is of the missing-values-prohibited type. If the value v (say) found in the primary key of the row or rows to be deleted does not occur at all in any of the missing-values-prohibited columns, then execution of the command may proceed. If, however, there is at least one occurrence of the value v in these missing-values-prohibited columns, then the DBMS aborts the deletion and marking altogether. It also turns on an indicator asserting that the deletion has been aborted. If the command participates in a transaction, then the transaction is aborted also.

Assume that the tests just described are satisfactorily passed, and that no abortion occurs. Then, the DBMS searches all of the foreign-key columns cited in S2:D to find all occurrences of the pertinent value and marks each one as missing-but-applicable.

If the qualifier EXCLUDE SIBLINGS is attached to the pertinent command, no action is taken on the columns cited in S1:D. If this qualifier is not attached, however, all of the rows containing the pertinent primary key value in each of the columns cited in S1:D are deleted. Then, regardless of any attached qualifier, all of the columns cited in S2:D that permit missing values are searched for the value v, and each such value is A-marked.

Existing indexes for each of the relations involved are automatically updated by the DBMS to reflect the requested deletion activity. Of course, these changes are committed if and only if the aforementioned changes are committed.

In subsequent chapters frequent use is made of the basic operators described in this chapter. A good understanding of these operators is essential to any real understanding of the relational model.

Exercises

4.1 The connectives LESS THAN, EQUAL TO, GREATER THAN participate in almost every programming language. *In that context* they are often called the relational operators. Are the relational operators of the relational model simply these connectives revisited? If not, explain.

4.2 In the relational model why is row selection called **select,** while column selection is called **project?** Hint: do not confuse the **select** of the relational model with the **select** of SQL.

4.3 Execution of a **join** usually involves comparing values drawn from pairs of columns (each simple or composite) in the database. These are called the comparand columns for this operator.
- What is wrong with requiring for every **join** that the comparand columns in a **join** be identically named?
- What constraints, if any, are placed by the relational model on pairs of comparand columns? Why?

4.4 Is it adequate for the DBMS to check that the comparand columns involved in **joins** contain values of the same basic data type? State reasons for your answer.

4.5 Consider the following query: find the suppliers, each of whom can supply every part in some given list of parts. What relational operator provides the most direct support for this query? Is this a brand-new operator? What is the shortest SQL representation of this request?

4.6 In what sense are the **union, intersection,** and **difference** operators of the relational model different from their counterparts in set theory?

4.7 What is union compatibility? To which of the operators does the relational model apply this as a constraint? Why does the model make union compatibility a requirement in these cases? Can this constraint be overridden?

4.8 In what sense are the operators of the relational model closed? Does this mean that no new operators may be invented? How is this closure useful in the real world?

4.9 What are the sibling primary keys of a given primary key? Does every primary key have a sibling primary key?

4.10 Is updating a primary key any more complicated than updating any other piece of data? If so, state why, and then describe how RM/V2 handles the problem.

4.11 Do present versions of the SQL language handle the problem stated in Exercise 4.10 correctly without requiring the assistance of the host language? Do present versions of SQL handle this problem correctly with assistance from the HL? Explain.

▪ *CHAPTER 5* ▪

The Advanced Operators

The operators discussed in this chapter are intended to meet some practical needs and, in so doing, increase the flexibility and power of the relational model without introducing programming concepts. Any reader who finds this chapter difficult to understand can, and should, skip it on first reading; most of the following chapters are simpler.

The advanced operators include **framing a relation,** the **extend** operator, **semi-join, outer join, outer union, outer difference, outer intersection,** the **T-joins, user-defined selects, user-defined joins,** and **recursive join.** The set of advanced operators is intentionally open-ended. When conceiving extensions, however, it is very important to adhere to the operational closure of all relational operators. See Feature RM-5 in Chapter 12, as well as Chapter 28.

In this chapter, unlike its predecessors, the sample relations that explain each operator involve the use of abstract symbols to denote values. For each column, however, the values must be assumed to be all of one declared data type. For example, all the values may be character strings, integers, floating-point numbers, or the truth-values of some logic. On the other hand, the collection of columns belonging to a relation can have any mixture of these data types. A reader who is unfamiliar with the use of symbols to denote values of these types may wish to take the time to substitute actual values of his or her choosing in place of the symbols, taking care to abide by any domain constraints explicitly mentioned.

Thus, in the example in Section 5.1.2—namely R1 (K A C D E)—K is intended to be the primary key, so all of its values must be distinct from one another, and C is specified as a numeric column, so all of its values must be numeric. Thus, a specific case of the relation R1 would be the PARTS relation with K as the part serial number (character-and-digit strings of length 8); A as the part name (strings of characters only, of fixed length 12); C as the quantity-on-hand (modest-sized non-negative integers); D as the quantity-on-order (of the same extended data type as quantity-on-hand); and E as the minimum quantity that should be maintained in inventory (of the same extended data type as quantity-on-hand).

5.1 ■ Framing a Relation

5.1.1 Introduction to Framing

Occasionally users must partition relations into a collection of subrelations, whose comprehensive union restores the original relation. Each of the subrelations is a member of the partition. A well-known property of a partition is that every pair of these subrelations has an empty intersection.

Consider a relation that contains information about employees in a company. Suppose that it includes a column containing the employee's present annual salary, and another column indicating the department to which that employee is assigned. With this database, consider a request that involves a partition: find the total salaries earned in each department along with the department identification. A user may wish to find for each department the sum of all the present salaries earned by employees in that department, and may want the corresponding totals to appear in one of the columns of the result, along with other columns such as the department number.

Many subrelations may be involved in partitioning a given relation. The approach described next avoids generating these subrelations as a collection of separate relations, for two reasons:

1. each of the subrelations would have to be assigned a distinct name;

2. a new type of operand and result would have to be introduced—namely, a collection of relations. This type appears in RM/T, an earlier extended version of the relational model [Codd 1979], but for other reasons.

Instead of the approach just described, a *frame* is placed on the relation to be partitioned.

RZ-1 Framing a Relation

A frame separates the set of rows in any one member of the partition from the set of rows in any other member. This separation is achieved by appending a new column to the relation and, within this column, assigning a distinct value for each distinct member of the partition. The standard name for this column is FID, or *frame identifier.*

In the relational model, in line with the emphasis on basing all operators on explicit values in the database, the act of partitioning is always based on values. In generating partitions, RM/V2 offers the options of using the individual values that occur in a column, simple or composite, or else specified ranges of values that occur therein. Since individual values are simpler to understand, let us consider them first.

5.1.2 Partitioning a Relation by Individual Values

The following steps are taken to generate a simple partition of a relation R by changes in values within a simple or composite column C:

1. The DBMS reorders the rows of relation R into ascending order by the values encountered in column C, whether these values are numeric, alphabetic, alphanumeric, or even the truth-values of some logic. (In the last case, the ascending sequence is FALSE, TRUE, MAYBE-AND-APPLICABLE, and MAYBE-BUT-INAPPLICABLE pending the establishment of a standard.);

2. The DBMS appends the new frame-identifier column FID to R. The initial value in the frame identification column (FID) is 1; this value is increased by one each time that a distinct value in C is encountered in the ascending order cited in Step 1.

In the case of alphabetic and alphanumeric columns, the DBMS uses some standard collating sequence for ordering purposes.

The result is a single relation with a frame that represents partitioning of R according to the distinct values in C. The frame is identified by the integers in column FID. Let R /// C denote relation R framed according to column C.

For example, relation R2 is R1 framed according to column C in the simple sense just described. The dotted lines portray the frame. In this example the pivotal column C happens to contain numeric values. Those readers who like "real" examples can assume the following denotations:

R1   PARTS relation

K   Part serial number

A   Part name

C   Quantity on hand

D   Quantity on order

E   Quantity for triggering reorder

R2 = R1 /// C

R1 (K	A	C	D	E	)
k1	a1	13	d1	e3	
k2	a1	9	d2	e7	
k3	a2	37	d1	e2	
k4	a3	24	d2	e6	
k5	a3	13	d3	e1	

R2 (K	A	C	D	E	FID)
k2	a1	9	d2	e7	1
----	----	----	----	----	----
k5	a3	13	d3	e1	2
k1	a1	13	d1	e3	2
----	----	----	----	----	----
k4	a3	24	d2	e6	3
----	----	----	----	----	----
k3	a2	37	d1	e2	4

Column FID identifies the interval and makes it unnecessary for the DBMS to keep the row ordering illustrated. Note that relation R1 has five tuples, but that column C has just four distinct values. Consequently, R1 framed according to C by individual values has precisely four members. Of course, each of these four members is a subrelation, which is a set. Three of the members of the partition are sets consisting of just one tuple, while the fourth member is a set containing two tuples.

5.1.3 Partitioning a Relation by Ranges of Values

A more complicated partitioning involves a sequence of ranges of values in the pivotal column C. Suppose the desired ranges for this new partitioning are as follows:

1–10, 11–20, 21–30, 31–40, and so on.

This sequence could be expressed more concisely as follows:

Begin at 1; the range interval is 10.

When the range interval is not constant, a ternary relation may be used as a listing of all the range intervals. For example,

RANGE	(FROM	TO	FID)
	1	11	1
	12	25	2
	26	32	3
	33	48	4

Note that in such a table it is required that the intervals do not overlap one another.

Thus, a user may wish to request the DBMS to use the RANGE relation (any name that satisfies the naming features will do) for determining the starting value and intervals. Now, a different result R3 is generated. Once again, the dotted lines portray the frame.

R3 = R /// C per RANGE

R3	(K	A	C	D	E	FID)
	k2	a1	9	c2	87	1
	---	---	---	---	---	---
	k5	a3	13	c3	81	2
	k1	a1	13	c1	93	2
	k4	a3	24	c2	76	2
	---	---	---	---	---	---
	k3	a2	37	c1	52	4

Column FID identifies the interval and makes it unnecessary for the DBMS to keep the row ordering illustrated. Note that the values in FID determine membership in various elements of the partition. Thus, there is no need for the DBMS to preserve the ascending ordering based on column FID as illustrated in the preceding table.

5.1.4 Applying Aggregate Functions to a Framed Relation

Assume that the relation R1 discussed in Section 5.1.2 is framed on column C according to the ternary relation RANGE discussed in Section 5.1.3. Let the result be R3. Normally, applying the function SUM to column E in any of the relations R1, R2, R3 (whether framed or not) yields the sum of all the values in column E. If, however, a relational command requests that the function SUM be applied to column E of either relation R2 or R3 *according to the frame implied by column FID,* then SUM is applied to each member of the partition; that can yield as many resulting values as there are distinct values in column FID.

SUM	R1.E		SUM-per-FID	R2.E		SUM-per-FID	R3.E
	389			87			87
				174			250
				76			52
				52			

Of course, it is quite likely that in the third case the user would like to have the pertinent range from the RANGE relation with each of the three totals. This can easily be accomplished by requesting column R3.FID along with the SUM according to FID(R3.E), and then requesting either the **natural join** or the **equi-join** of this relation, with the RANGE relation, using the pair of FID columns (one from each of the operand relations) as the comparand columns.

The result is relation R4:

R4	(FROM	TO	FID	SF(R3.E))
	1	11	1	87
	12	25	2	250
	33	48	4	52

SF denotes the function SUM-per-FID.

The following example illustrates partitioning and applying an aggregate function to the members of the partition. Assume that the following base relation provides the identification EMP# and immediate properties of employees:

EMP1	(EMP#	ENAME	DEPT#	SALARY	H_CITY)
	E107	Rook	D12	10,000	Wimborne
	E912	Knight	D10	12,000	Poole
	E239	Knight	D07	12,000	Poole
	E575	Pawn	D12	11,000	Poole
	E123	King	D01	15,000	Portland
	E224	Bishop	D07	11,000	Weymouth

Consider the following two steps:

1. Partition the relation EMP1 according to the DEPT# column:

EMP2 ← EMP1 /// DEPT#

EMP2	(EMP#	ENAME	DEPT#	SALARY	H_CITY	FID)
	E123	King	D01	15,000	Portland	1
	E224	Bishop	D07	11,000	Weymouth	2
	E239	Knight	D07	12,000	Poole	2
	E912	Knight	D10	12,000	Poole	3
	E107	Rook	D12	10,000	Wimborne	4
	E575	Pawn	D12	11,000	Poole	4

2. Find for each department the department serial number and the total salary earned by all employees assigned to that department:

DSAL(DEPT#, TOTSAL) ← EMP2(DEPT#, SUM-per-FID(SALARY))

DSAL	(DEPT#	TOTSAL)
	D01	15,000
	D07	23,000
	D10	12,000
	D12	21,000

Although the GROUP BY feature of SQL is quite concisely expressed, it is neither as powerful nor as flexible as the framing feature of RM/V2.

5.2 ■ Auxiliary Operators

One reason to introduce the auxiliary operators here is to keep the definition of the three outer set operators in the next section reasonably concise. Another reason is that these operators can be useful in other contexts.

Common to all three outer set operators—**outer union, outer difference, and outer intersection**—is an initial step that makes the two operands union-compatible. This step is explained by introducing the operator discussed in Section 5.2.1. (see [GOOD]).

5.2.1 Extending a Relation

RZ-2   Extend the Description of one Relation to Include all the Columns of Another Relation

The relation cited first in the command is the one whose description is altered to include all the columns of the second-cited relation that are not in the first. The columns thus introduced into the first relation are filled with A-marked values, unless the VALUE qualifier RQ-13 (see Chapter 10) is applied to specify a particular value.

Considerable care must be taken in using the **extend** operator. A column of one of the operands may have the same name and certain other properties (such as the domain) as a column of the second operand, but the two columns may have different meanings. Such columns are called *homographs* of one another.

The **extend** operator may not be able to distinguish between the different meanings, and may incorrectly assume that they are identical. The only known solution to this problem is for the DBA to be continually concerned about the possibility of homographs and try to avoid them altogether. Homographs can be deadly in other contexts also.

It is possible, although unlikely, for the DBMS to discover that no new columns need be added to the first-cited relation. To make a pair of relations (say S and T) mutually union-compatible, it is normally necessary to extend the columns of both relations by requesting

St ← S **per** T and Ts ← T **per** S,

where "**per**" denotes the **extend** operator. Note that, in general, union compatibility is attained only after two applications of the **extend** operator.

Two applications of this kind constitute the first step in each of the outer set operators.

This **extend** operator is used in defining the **outer joins** and the **outer set** operators. Of course, it may be used independently of these operators.

It is quite common for some banks to record accounts in more than one way. For example, the following two types might have been established (they are simpified for exposition):

			%	$
ACCOUNT	(ACCOUNT#	NAME	INTEREST_RATE	BALANCE)

				$
ACCT	(ACCOUNT#	NAME	MATURITY_DATE	BALANCE)

The first type is unique in having INTEREST_RATE as a column, while the second is unique in having MATURITY_DATE as a column. Thus, these two relations are *not* union-compatible. They can be converted into a pair of relations that are union-compatible by applying the **extend** operator to each one.

A1 ← ACCOUNT EXTEND **per** ACCT

A2 ← ACCT EXTEND **per** ACCOUNT

Both A1 and A2 have as their columns ACCOUNT#, NAME, MATURITY_DATE, INTEREST_RATE, and BALANCE. The relation A1 UNION A2 may be exactly what the headquarters planning staff needs for analysis and planning purposes.

An unlikely special case, which is not given special treatment, does not permit the operands (relations S and T) to have any domains in common. Hence, there are no comparable columns at all.

5.2.2 The Semi-theta-join Operator

The idea for the **semi-join** operator has been circulating for many years; it is not clear who originated the concept. One discussion is found in a paper by Bernstein and Chiu [1981]. In this section, a slight generalization of the **semi-join** operator is discussed: the EQUALITY comparator that is normally assumed is replaced by **theta,** where "theta" can be any one of the 10 comparators:

1. EQUALITY
2. INEQUALITY
3. LESS THAN
4. LESS THAN OR EQUAL TO
5. GREATER THAN

6. GREATER THAN OR EQUAL TO
7. GREATEST LESS THAN
8. GREATEST LESS THAN OR EQUAL TO
9. LEAST GREATER THAN
10. LEAST GREATER THAN OR EQUAL TO

Once again, it is important to recall that the relational model provides a very important safety feature, first cited in Chapter 3:

RT-1 Safety Feature when Comparing Database Values

When comparing a database value in one column with a database value in another, the DBMS merely checks that the two columns draw their values from a common domain, unless the domain check is overridden (see Feature RQ-9 in Chapter 10). When comparing (1) a computed value with a database value or (2) one computed value with another computed value, however, the DBMS checks that the basic data types (not the extended data types) are the same.

Several of the advanced operators involve comparing of database values. The following operators are examples of this.

Let n = 3,4, . . . ,12. Then the RZ feature with n as its number is a semi-theta-join that makes use of the comparator numbered n-2 in the list of comparators cited at the beginning of this section.

RZ-3 through RZ-12 Semi-Theta-Join

Suppose that the operands of a **theta-join** are S and T, where **theta** is any one of the 10 comparators listed earlier, and the columns to be compared are simple or composite column A of S with simple or composite column B of T. Suppose that relation T is projected onto column B. The result of this projection contains only those values from B that are distinct from one another. The **semi-join** of S on A with T on B yields that subrelation of S whose values in column A are restricted to just those that qualify in accordance with the comparator **theta** with respect to the projection of T onto B.

Suppose that, when **theta** happens to be EQUALITY, the operator **semi-theta-join** is denoted by **sem=**. Then, S **sem=** T is that subrelation of S containing all of the rows of S that match rows of T with respect to the comparand columns. The remaining rows of S are those that fail to match any row of T in accordance with the comparand columns. When the comparand columns are not explicitly specified (as in the preceding case), the DBMS assumes that the set of these columns is maximal with respect to the given operands, disregarding keyhood. (Incidentally, I use the term "match" only when values are being compared for equality.)

The **semi-join** can be useful when relations S and T happen to be located at different sites as part of a distributed database. Suppose that relation T has many more rows than relation S. Then, the load on the communication lines between the site containing S and the site containing T can often be reduced by (1) transmitting the projection of S onto A to the site containing T, (2) executing the semi-join of T with S [A] at this site, yielding a subset of relation T, and then (3) transmitting this subset of relation T back to the site containing S for the full **join** to be completed there.

It is the responsibility of the optimizer in the DBMS to select this method of handling a **join,** whenever it happens to be the most efficient. Such a selection certainly should not be a burden on end users or on application programmers.

The following example shows the **semi-join** operator in action. The operands are as follows:

S (EMP#	ENAME	H_CITY)
E107	Rook	Wimborne
E912	Knight	Poole
E239	Pawn	Poole

T (WHSE#	W_CITY)
W17	Wareham
W34	Poole
W92	Poole

Consider this query: find the employee information and the warehouse information for every case in which an employee's residence is in the same city as a company warehouse. The formula for the **join** is

$$U \leftarrow S [H\_CITY = W\_CITY] T,$$

and the result obtained assuming the values just cited is as follows:

U	(EMP#	NAME	H_CITY	WHSE#	W_CITY)
	E912	Knight	Poole	W34	Poole
	E912	Knight	Poole	W92	Poole
	E239	Pawn	Poole	W34	Poole
	E239	Pawn	Poole	W92	Poole

5.3 ■ The Outer Equi-join Operators

Several operators referred to as the **outer join** are supported in the relational model. The **join** operators introduced in Chapter 4 are henceforth called **inner joins,** when a need arises to refer to them as a collection.

The **outer joins** are based on a proposal made in 1971 by Ian Heath, then of the IBM Hursley Laboratory in England [Heath 1971]. In this section and Section 5.4, examples of the **inner** and **outer equi-join** with and without the MAYBE qualifier are described, and the close relationship of the **inner** and **outer joins** is explained. The MAYBE qualifier pertains to the four-valued logic supported by a relational DBMS, assuming its fidelity to the model with respect to the treatment of missing information. This qualifier is discussed in detail in Chapters 8, 9, and 10.

The following two simple relations are used as sample operands in explaining the **outer join** operators. Notice that values in column B of relation S are to be compared with values in column C of relation T. More concisely, S.B and T.C are the comparand columns. Further, b1 occurs in S.B but not in T.C, while b4 occurs in T.C but not in S.B.

S (A	B)		T (C	D)
a1	b1		b2	d1
a2	b2		b2	d2
a3	b3		b3	d3
			b4	d4

Columns S.B and T.C draw their values from the same domain. Thus, it is meaningful to compare values from S.B with those from T.C.

There are three kinds of **outer joins: left outer equi-join** (Feature RZ-13), **right outer equi-join** (Feature RZ-14), and **symmetric outer equi-join** (Feature RZ-15).

RZ-13 Left Outer Equi-join

The **left outer join** of S on B with T on C, denoted U = S [B /= C] T, is defined in terms of the inner **equi-join** (IEJ) and the left outer increment (LOI). LOI is defined as follows: pick out those tuples from S whose comparand values in the comparand column S.B do not participate in the **inner join,** and append to each such tuple a tuple of nothing but missing values and of size compatible with T.

In more formal terms,

LOI = (S − IEJ [A, B]) **per** IEJ.

Then, U is defined by

U = IEJ ∪ LOI.

Its extension is as follows:

U	(A	B	C	D)	
	a1	b1	—	—	} left outer increment
	a2	b2	b2	d1	
	a2	b2	b2	d2	} inner equi-join
	a3	b3	b3	d3	

RZ-14 Right Outer Equi-join

The **right outer join** of S on B with T on C, denoted V = S [B = \ C] T, is defined in terms of the **inner equi-join** (IEJ) and the right outer increment (ROI). ROI is defined as follows: pick out those tuples from T whose comparand values in the comparand column T.Y do not participate in the inner join, and append to each such tuple a tuple of nothing but missing values and of size compatible with S.

In more formal terms,

ROI = (T − IEJ [B, C]) **per** IEJ.

V is then defined by

V = IEJ ∪ ROI.

Its extension is as follows:

V	(A	B	C	D)	
	a2	b2	b2	d1	
	a2	b2	b2	d2	} inner equi-join
	a3	b3	b3	d3	
	—	—	b4	d4	} right outer increment

RZ-15 Symmetric Outer Equi-join

The **symmetric outer equi-join** of S on B with T on C, denoted W = S [B / =\ C] T, is defined by W = LOI **union** IEJ **union** ROI. This implies that W = U **union** V.

Its extension is as follows:

```
             W   (A    B    C    D  )
                  a1   b1   —    —
                  a2   b2   b2   d1
left outer join   a2   b2   b2   d2   right outer join
                  a3   b3   b3   d3
                  —    —    b4   d4
```

Note that this particular result contains an A-marked value in every column, which is not necessarily true of other examples of **symmetric outer join.** Also note that the following identity holds for **outer join** results:

outer join = **left outer join** ∪ **right outer join.**

It is important to observe that the result of a **symmetric outer join** is likely to contain one or more missing values in each and every column, although no single row contains a missing value in every column. This is why such a result cannot have a primary key that satisfies the entity-integrity rule—namely, that a primary key must have no missing values (see Chapter 13).

Because duplicate rows are prohibited in every relation of the relational model, however, it is still true that every row is distinct from every other row in the result of a **symmetric outer join.** Thus, for every relation R of this type, an identifier is defined that consists of every column of R; this is called the *weak identifier* of R.

Even though **outer joins** are not well supported in many of today's DBMS products, they are frequently needed and heavily used. Consider the following example.

A database contains information about suppliers and shipments received from these suppliers. The supplier relation S contains the serial number S# of all of the suppliers in the database, their names SNAME, and other immediate properties. The shipment relation SP contains the serial number S# of the supplier making each shipment, the serial number P# of the part shipped, the date SHIP_DATE the shipment was received, and other immediate properties of the shipment, such as the quantity received SHIP_Q.

A company executive requests a report listing all the shipments received in the first six months of 1989. The report must include, for each shipment, the supplier's serial number and name, together with the serial number of the part, the quantity shipped, and the date received. The executive also requests that the report include those suppliers on record in the database from which the company received no shipments at all, accompanied by an indication that each one shipped nothing at all during the specified period. Such a request can be expressed in terms of a **left outer join.**

Suppose that the supplier relation S is as shown below, and relation SP″ is derived from the shipment relation SP by row selection, retaining exclusively those rows that pertain to shipments with SHIP__DATE between the dates 89-01-01 and 89-06-30 inclusive.

S	(S#	SNAME	. . .)		SP″	(S#	P#	SHIP__DATE	SHIP__Q)
	s1	Jones	. . .			s1	p1	89-05-31	1000
	s2	Smith	. . .			s1	p2	89-03-20	575
	s3	Clark	. . .			s2	p7	89-02-19	150
	s4	Rock	. . .			s4	p2	89-06-15	900
	s5	Roth	. . .			s4	p4	89-04-07	250
						s4	p8	89-02-28	650

The **left outer join** of S on S# with SP on S# is denoted,

$$\text{SSP} \leftarrow \text{S} \ [\text{S\#} \ / = \ \text{S\#}] \ \text{SP},$$

in which the relation S is the left operand. Alternatively, the operands may be switched and the **right outer join** may be used,

$$\text{SSP} \leftarrow \text{SP} \ [\text{S\#} \ = \backslash \ \text{S\#}] \ \text{S},$$

in which the relation S is the right operand.

In either case the extension of SSP is as follows:

SSP	(. . .	SNAME	S#		S#	P#	SHIP__DATE	SHIP__Q)
	. . .	Jones	s1		s1	p1	89-05-31	1000
	. . .	Jones	s1		s1	p2	89-03-20	575
	. . .	Smith	s2		s2	p7	89-02-19	150
	. . .	Clark	s3		—	—	—	—
	. . .	Rock	s4		s4	p2	89-06-15	900
	. . .	Rock	s4		s4	p4	89-04-17	250
	. . .	Rock	s4		s4	p8	89-02-28	650
	. . .	Roth	s5		—	—	—	—

Note that, to conform with the request, the suppliers Clark and Roth in this report have designations of missing items in the shipments-half of their rows—no shipment was received from either of these suppliers in the first six months of 1989.

In Section 17.5.4, it is argued that, in certain circumstances, the **outer equi-join** operator is clearly superior as a view to its inner counterpart. I am confident that this use of the **outer equi-join** was not conceived when the operator was invented.

5.4 ■ Outer Equi-joins with the MAYBE Qualifier

A common characteristic of real databases is that values are missing in various rows and columns for a variety of reasons. As a result, a DBMS that has only two truth values (TRUE and FALSE) designed into it may be unable to determine in a non-guessing mode the truth value of a truth-valued expression in the condition part of a relational request. A relational DBMS that supports all of the features of RM/V2 has four truth values designed into it:

TRUE (t), FALSE (f), MAYBE-APPLICABLE (*a*),

and

MAYBE-INAPPLICABLE (*i*)

Both of the latter two truth values reflect the fact that missing data can make it impossible for the DBMS to determine whether the truth value is TRUE or FALSE. These truth values are distinguished by whether a value is missing but applicable (simply unknown at this time) or missing and inapplicable (e.g., the sales commission earned by an employee who is not a salesman).

While describing the **outer equi-joins,** it is worthwhile to consider the effect of the MAYBE qualifier on the operator. The MAYBE qualifier should be distinguished from the MAYBE truth values. For data to be retrieved, it is normally required that the specified condition evaluate to TRUE. The MAYBE qualifier alters the truth value that is required for data to be retrieved. The alteration is from the truth value TRUE to one of the MAYBE truth values (see Chapters 8 and 10 for more details). In other words, the data retrieved is that for which the condition is evaluated to be neither TRUE nor FALSE.

Let a1 and b3 in S be missing but applicable (A-marked). Let d1 and the second occurrence of b2 in T be missing but applicable (A-marked). Thus, the new operands are as follows:

S″	(A	B)		T″	(C	D)
	—	b1			b2	—
	a2	b2			—	d2
	a3	—			b3	d3
					b4	d4

The 12 possible comparisons between the values from S″.B and the values from T″.C have the following truth-values:

S″.B	b2	b1	b2	—	—	—	—	b1	b1	b1	b2	b2
T″.C	b2	—	—	—	b2	b3	b4	b2	b3	b4	b3	b4
truth	t	m	m	m	m	m	m	f	f	f	f	f

where t, f, m respectively denote the truth values TRUE, FALSE, and MAYBE.

The **symmetric outer equi-join** of S on B with T on C accompanied by the MAYBE qualifier is denoted

$$U'' = S'' [B╱=\backslash C] T'' \text{ MAYBE}.$$

Its extension is as follows:

U″	(A	B	C	D)
	—	b1	—	d2
	a2	b2	—	d2
	a3	—	b2	—
	a3	—	—	d2
	a3	—	b3	d3
	a3	—	b4	d4

Note that < a2 b2 b2 — > is the only tuple that belongs to the **inner equi-join** with no MAYBE qualifier. It does *not* belong to either the **inner** or **outer equi-join** with the MAYBE qualifier.

In this example, the **outer join** with MAYBE happens to be equal to the **inner join** with MAYBE. In other words, the left outer increment and the right outer increment happen to be empty in the MAYBE case. In the next example, all four of the following results are distinct:

inner equi-join TRUE,   **inner equi-join** MAYBE,

outer equi-join TRUE,   **outer equi-join** MAYBE.

To provide some additional explanation of these operators, consider the **outer equi-join** of S on X with T on Y, where the comparand columns are S.X and T.Y.

The increment over the **inner equi-join** contributed by the *left outer increment* (LOI) is defined as follows:

LOI with or without the MAYBE qualifier: pick out those tuples from S whose comparand values in the comparand column S.X do not participate in the **inner join,** and append to each such tuple a tuple of nothing but missing values and of size compatible with T.

Non-participation of a comparand value in the MAYBE case means that no comparison involving that value yields the truth-value m. Non-participation in the true case (reflected by the absence of the MAYBE qualifier) means that no comparison involving that value yields the truth value t.

The increment over the **inner equi-join** contributed by the **right outer increment** (ROI) is defined as follows:

ROI with or without the MAYBE qualifier: pick out those tuples from T whose comparand values in the comparand column T.Y do not participate in the **inner join,** and append to each such tuple a tuple of nothing but missing values and of size compatible with S.

Now for the promised example. Assume the operands are as follows:

S2 (A	B)		T2 (C	D)
a1	—		b2	d1
a2	b2		b2	d2
a3	b3		b3	d3
			b4	d4

The 12 possible comparisons between the occurrences of values in S2.B and T2.C have the following truth-values:

S2.B	b2	b2	b3	—	—	—	—	b2	b2	b3	b3	b3
T2.C	b2	b2	b3	b2	b2	b3	b4	b3	b4	b2	b2	b4
truth	t	t	t	m	m	m	m	f	f	f	f	f

The results obtained by applying the four operators are as follows:

Inner equi-join TRUE

a2	b2	b2	d1
a2	b2	b2	d2
a3	b3	b3	d3

Inner equi-join MAYBE

a1	—	b2	d1
a1	—	b2	d2
a1	—	b3	d3
a1	—	b4	d4

Outer equi-join TRUE

a1	—	—	—	} LOI
a2	b2	b2	d1	
a2	b2	b2	d2	} inner
a3	b3	b3	d3	
—	—	b4	d4	} ROI

Outer equi-join MAYBE

a2	b2	—	—	} LOI
a3	b3	—	—	
a1	—	b2	d1	
a1	—	b2	d2	
a1	—	b3	d3	} inner
a1	—	b4	d4	

Note that ROI is empty in the **outer equi-join** with MAYBE. All four of these relations are distinct.

5.5 ■ The Outer Natural Joins

Consider two relations S and T that happen to have extensions as follows:

S (P	A)		T (Q	B)
k1	a1		m1	a2
k2	a2		m2	a2
k3	a2		m3	a4
k4	a3			

Suppose that columns S.A and T.B draw their values from a common domain, and it is therefore meaningful to compare values from one column with values from the other. Consider two kinds of joins: the **symmetric outer natural join** of S on A with T on B, and the **symmetric outer equi-join** of S on A with T on B.

$$U = S [A / *\backslash B] T$$
$$V = S [A / =\backslash B] T$$

	Symmetric outer natural join				Symmetric outer equi-join			
	U (P	AB	Q)		V (P	A	B	Q)
left outer join	k1	a1	—		k1	a1	—	—
	k4	a3	—		k4	a3	—	—
	k2	a2	m1	right outer join	k2	a2	a2	m1
	k3	a2	m1		k3	a2	a2	m1
	k2	a2	m2		k2	a2	a2	m2
	k3	a2	m2		k3	a2	a2	m2
	—	a4	m3		—	—	a4	m3

In table U, the **left outer** and **right outer natural joins** are shown as subrelations of the **symmetric outer natural join.** The three **outer natural joins** are defined constructively (Features RZ-16–RZ-18)—that is, in terms of an algorithm that will generate the appropriate result. An implementation can make use of this algorithm, but is not required to do so. It is only necessary that the implementation generate the same result as the defining algorithm.

RZ-16 Left Outer Natural Join

First, form the **inner natural equi-join** W of S on A with T on B. Then, form the **relational difference** W1 = S − W [P, A]. Then, **extend** W1 **per** S to yield W2. Finally, form the **left outer natural join** LONJ = W **union** W2.

RZ-17 Right Outer Natural Join

First, form the **inner natural equi-join** W of S on A with T on B. Then, form the **relational difference** W3 = T − W [A, Q]. Then, **extend** W3 **per** S to yield W4. Finally, form the **right outer natural join** RONJ = W **union** W4.

RZ-18 Symmetric Outer Natural Join

First, form W and W2 as in the first three steps of Feature RZ-16. Then, form W4 as in the first three steps of Feature RZ-17. Finally, form the **symmetric outer natural join** by taking the **union:** SONJ = W2 **union** W **union** W4. Alternatively, **symmetric outer join** = LONJ **union** RONJ. Note that **union** in the relational model always includes removal of duplicate rows from the result.

It may be recalled that the **inner natural join** is a simple projection of the **inner equi-join,** in which one of two mutually redundant comparand columns is removed. The **outer joins,** however, are not related to one another so simply.

The columns in the **outer equi-join** that stem from the comparand columns in the operands are not necessarily mutually redundant columns. In fact, in this example columns A and B are clearly *not* mutually redundant. Thus, the **outer natural join** is not necessarily a projection of the **outer equi-join**—a fact that may decrease the usefulness of the **outer natural join.**

5.6 ■ The Outer Set Operators

In this section I define the three outer set operators in the relational model—**union, set difference,** and **set intersection**—and compare them with their inner counterparts. A close correspondence is shown to exist between an identity that pertains to the inner operators and one that pertains to the outer operators.[1]

5.6.1 The Inner Operators Revisited

In the relational model, each of the inner set operators—**union, set difference,** and **set intersection**—is applied exclusively to a pair of relations of precisely the same type. In other words, between the two operands (relations S and T, say) there must exist a one-to-one correspondence between the columns of S and the columns of T, such that each of the pair of columns in this correspondence draws its values from a common domain. Any pair of relations that are of precisely the same type are said to be *union-compatible.* When restricted in this way, these operators are called **relational union, relational difference,** and **relational intersection,** respectively.

This correspondence must be specified in the expression that invokes the pertinent relational operator. The reason is as follows. The domains from which the columns of S and T draw their values are, in general, inadequate to establish such a correspondence, because two or more of the columns of either S or T may draw their values from the same domain.

---

1. I am grateful to Nathan Goodman [1988], who contributed to the definitions in their final form.

An important relationship called the *inner identity* holds between these three inner relational operators:

$$(S \cup T) = (S - T) \cup (S \cap T) \cup (T - S)$$

for any relations S and T that are union-compatible, where the minus sign denotes relational difference.

5.6.2 The Outer Set Operators

With the inner set operators, the operands S and T are required to be union-compatible, that is, of exactly the same type. One important reason for the outer set operators is to allow the operands S and T to differ somewhat in type, and even in degree. Thus, S may include columns not found in T, and T may include columns not found in S.

In the context of the inner set operators, two rows (one from S, the other from T) are duplicates of one another if there is pairwise equality between corresponding components. In the context of the outer set operators, however, equality between a row in S and a row in T is seldom encountered, because S and T are not required to be union-compatible. Therefore, it is necessary to include the following concept, which is more general than row equality.

A row from relation S is a *close counterpart* of a row from relation T if all the following conditions hold:

■ the operands S and T have primary keys defined on the same domain;
■ the two rows (one from S, one from T) have equal primary-key values;
■ pairwise equality in non-missing values holds for those properties of S that correspond to properties of T.

This concept is heavily used in the outer set operators: **union, difference, and intersection.**

The outer set operators are potentially important in distributed database management. For example, consider a bank that stores customer accounts in a distributed database. Suppose that customer accounts are represented using logical relations of different types in different cities or in different states. The differences may be slight, or may be quite significant. An extreme case, not likely to be found in banks, and not part of this example, is that S and T have no domains at all in common. In the discussion following Feature RZ-19, the bank example is pursued in more detail with explicit data.

For each of the three outer set operators, a precise definition is presented followed by an example and some informal discussion. The definitions of the outer operators are crafted so that the identity cited for the three inner operators applies also to the outer operators.

The following sample relations are used as operands to illustrate the outer set operations:

S	(A	B	)
	a1	b1	
	a1	b2	
	a2	b3	

T	(E	C	)
	a2	c3	
	a3	c4	

T″	(E	C	)
	a1	c1	
	a1	c2	
	a2	c3	
	a3	c4	

For generality, columns A, B, C, and E may be either simple or composite. B is assumed to consist of all—and nothing but—the simple columns whose domains do not occur in T. C is similarly assumed to consist of all—and nothing but—the columns whose domains do not occur in S. Thus, A consists of all—and nothing but—the simple columns whose domains occur in both S and T. A similar remark applies to column E.

In the examples, either the pair S and T or the pair S and T″ is used as the two operands. All of the columns S.A, T.E, T″.E draw their values from a common domain, whether simple or composite. Columns B and C draw their values from domains that are different from one another and from the domain of A.

RZ-19   Outer Union

Suppose the operands of **outer union** are S and T. As the first step, apply the **extend** operator to both S and T: **extend S per** T and call it St; **extend T per** S and call it Ts. Now, St and Ts are of the same degree, and each contains columns based on all the domains in S and all the domains in T. In fact, St and Ts are completely union-compatible. As the second and final step, form St **union** Ts, which yields the **outer union** $S \backslash \cup / T$.

The **outer union** $S \backslash \cup / T$ of relation S with relation T is generated by means of the following three steps:

1. form St = S **per** T;
2. form Ts = T **per** S;
3. form $S \backslash \cup / T$ = St $\cup$ Ts.

The close-counterpart concept (see p. 116 for its definition) is used instead of row equality to remove duplicate rows.

By definition,

$$S \backslash \cup / T = (S \textbf{ per } T) \cup (T \textbf{ per } S).$$

And clearly,

$$S \backslash \cup / T = T \backslash \cup / S.$$

Take the sample relations as operands, and apply the **outer union.** The results are as follows:

S \U/ T (A	B	C)
a1	b1	—
a1	b2	—
a2	b3	—
a2	—	c3
a3	—	c4

S \U/ T″ (A	B	C)
a1	b1	—(1)
a1	b2	—
a2	b3	—
a1	—	c1(2)
a1	—	c2
a2	—	c3
a3	—	c4

Note that rows of $S\backslash U/T''$ marked (1) and (2) in the preceding R-table are not coalesced into < a1, b1, c1 >, primarily because the operands S and T″ do not have primary keys with a common domain. Judging from their present extensions, S and T″ merely have weak identifiers. Lacking a common primary key means that a typical row of S and a typical row of T″ represent quite different types of objects in the micro-world. Under these circumstances, it would be very risky to assume that the missing B-component of row < a1, —, c1 > of operand T″ is equal to b1, and that the missing C-component of row < a1, b1, — > of operand S is equal to c1.

In the following example, the coalescing of rows is acceptable. In this example, a bank has accounts of two different types. Suppose that one type is recorded in relation ACCOUNT; the other, in relation ACCT. The primary key of each relation is ACCOUNT#. No claim is made, of course, that the few columns in each relation are adequate for any bank. The small number was selected to keep the example simple.

ACCOUNT	(ACCOUNT#	NAME	(ANNUAL) INTEREST_RATE	($) BALANCE)
	121-537	Brown	7.5	10,765
	129-972	Baker	8.0	25,000
	126-343	Smith	7.5	15,000
	302-888	Jones	8.0	18,000

ACCT	(ACCOUNT#	NAME	MATURITY_DATE	BALANCE)
	645-802	Green	95-12-31	35,680
	645-195	Hawk	94-09-30	50,000
	640-466	Shaw	96-03-31	22,500
	642-733	Piper	97-10-30	30,900
	302-888	Jones	96-07-31	18,000

Note that the first table is unique in having INTEREST_RATE as a column, while the second table is unique in having MATURITY_DATE as a column. Thus, these two relations are not union-compatible. Part of the **outer union** operation is to convert them into a pair of relations that are union-compatible by applying the **extend** operator to each one.

For purposes of exposition, not implementation, the **outer union** A of these two relations is developed in two stages. First is the generation of a temporary result A':

A' (ACCOUNT#	NAME	MATURITY_DATE	(ANNUAL) INTEREST_RATE	($) BALANCE)
121-537	Brown	—	7.5	10,765
129-972	Baker	—	8.0	25,000
126-343	Smith	—	7.5	15,000
645-802	Green	95-12-31	—	35,680
645-195	Hawk	94-09-30	—	50,000
640-466	Shaw	96-03-31	—	22,500
642-733	Piper	97-10-30	—	30,900
302-888	Jones	—	8.0	18,000
302-888	Jones	96-07-31	—	18,000

The final result A differs from A' in only one respect: the DBMS attempts to coalesce the two rows describing accounts held by Jones, because the two operands have a primary key in common, and these rows have a common primary-key value. The attempt succeeds because each of the corresponding non-missing properties in the two rows has pairwise equal values. Thus, the two Jones rows in A' are close counterparts. The end result A contains the row < 302-888, Jones, 96-07-31, 8.0, 18,000 > instead of the two Jones rows in A'.

RZ-20   Outer Set Difference

The **outer set difference** S \ − / T between relations S and T, with S as the information source and T as the reducing relation, is generated by means of the following steps:

1. form St = S **per** T;
2. form Ts = T **per** S;
3. form the **semi-equi-join** U = St[**sem** =]Ts;
4. form S \ − / T = St − U.

The close-counterpart concept (p. 116) is used instead of row equality.

By definition,

S \ − / T = St − (St **sem** = Ts).

And clearly,

$$S \setminus - / T \neq T \setminus - / S.$$

Take the sample relations as operands, and apply the **outer set difference:**

S \ -/ T (A	B	C)
a1	b1	—
a1	b2	—

S \ -/ T" (A	B	C)
	empty	

T \ -/ S (A	B	C)
a3	—	c4

T" \ -/ S (A	B	C)
a3	—	c4

Once again, consider the operands ACCOUNT and ACCT in the bank example. Suppose that a user requests all of the accounts information from the ACCOUNT relation, but excluding those rows that have close counterparts in the ACCT relation. The DBMS responds by extending each operand in accordance with the other, and then removing those rows in the extended ACCOUNT relation that have close counterparts in the extended ACCT relation. The result is defined by

DIFF ← ACCOUNT \ – / ACCT.

Its extension is as follows:

DIFF (ACCOUNT#	NAME	MATURITY_DATE	(ANNUAL) INTEREST_RATE	($) BALANCE)
121-537	Brown	—	7.5	10,765
129-972	Baker	—	8.0	25,000
126-343	Smith	—	7.5	15,000

RZ-21 Outer Set Intersection

The **outer set intersection** S \∩/ T of relations S and T is generated by means of the following steps:

1. form St ← S **per** T;
2. form Ts ← T **per** S;
3. form U ← St **sem** = Ts;
4. form V ← Ts **sem** = St;
5. form S \∩/ T ← U ∩ V.

The close-counterpart concept (p. 116) is used instead of row equality.

By definition,

$$S \setminus \cap / T = ((S \text{ per } T) \text{ sem} = (T \text{ per } S)) \cup ((T \text{ per } S) \text{ sem} = (S \text{ per } T))$$

and clearly,

$$S \setminus \cap / T = T \setminus \cap / S.$$

Take the sample relations as operands, and apply the **outer set intersection:**

S \∩/ T	(A	B	C)
	a2	b3	—
	a2	—	c3

S \∩/ T″	(A	B	C)
	a1	b1	—
	a1	b2	—
	a2	b3	—
	a1	—	c1
	a1	—	c2
	a2	—	c3

T \∩/ S	(A	B	C)
	a2	b3	—
	a2	—	c3

T″ \∩/ S	(A	B	C)
	a1	b1	—
	a1	b2	—
	a2	b3	—
	a1	—	c1
	a1	—	c2
	a2	—	c3

The sample operands S and T, displayed at the beginning of this section, will now be used again to show that the **symmetric outer join** yields a quite different result from that generated by the **outer union, difference,** and **intersection** operators. The composite columns labeled A and E are used as comparands:

$$U = S [A \setminus = / E] T.$$

U	(A	B	E	C)
	a1	b1	—	—
	a1	b2	—	—
	a2	b3	a2	c3
	—	—	a3	c4

Once again consider the operands ACCOUNT and ACCT in the bank example. Suppose that a user requests all the accounts information that is common to the ACCOUNT relation and the ACCT relation. The DBMS responds by extending each operand per the other, and then preserving those rows in the extended ACCOUNT relation that have close counterparts in the extended ACCT relation.

The result is defined by

INT ← ACCOUNT \∩/ ACCT.

Its extension is as follows:

INT (ACCOUNT#	NAME	MATURITY_DATE	ANNUAL INTEREST_RATE	$ BALANCE)
302-888	Jones	96-07-31	8.0	18,000

5.6.3 The Relationship between the Outer Set Operators

It should now be clear that, for any pair of relations S and T, the following identity holds:

$$S \setminus \cup / T = (S \setminus - / T) \cup (S \setminus \cap / T) \cup (T \setminus - / S).$$

This outer identity is very similar to the relationship between the inner set operators; the latter identity was defined at the end of Section 5.6.1.

This outer identity can be seen in action by applying it to the two cases of **outer union.** The first case makes use of the sample relations S and T.

```
S \∪/ T      (A      B      C )

             a1      b1      —   ⎫
             a1      b2      —   ⎬  S \ - / T
            ----------------------
             a2      b3      —   ⎫
             a2      —      c3   ⎬  S \∩/ T = T \∩/ S
            ----------------------
             a3      —      c4   } T \ - / S
```

The second case makes use of the relations S and T":

```
S \∪/ T"     (A      B      C )

                                  }  S \ - / T" empty
            ----------------------
             a1      b1      —   ⎫
             a1      b2      —   ⎪
             a2      b3      —   ⎪
             a1      —      c1   ⎬  S \∩/ T" = T" \∩/ S
             a1      —      c2   ⎪
             a2      —      c3   ⎭
            ----------------------
             a3      —      c4   } T" \ - / S
            ----------------------
```

5.7 ■ The Inner and Outer T-join

The well-known **inner joins** are based on the 10 comparators:

1. EQUALITY
2. INEQUALITY
3. LESS THAN
4. LESS THAN OR EQUAL TO
5. GREATER THAN
6. GREATER THAN OR EQUAL TO
7. GREATEST LESS THAN
8. GREATEST LESS THAN OR EQUAL TO
9. LEAST GREATER THAN
10. LEAST GREATER THAN OR EQUAL TO

These **inner joins,** together with the corresponding **outer joins,** are readily accepted today. The **T-join** operators about to be described are new kinds of joins, principally based on the four ordering comparators (numbered 3–6 in the preceding list). The **inner T-join** produces a subset of that produced by the corresponding **inner join;** the **outer T-join** produces a subset of that generated by the corresponding **outer join.** The **T-joins** should be regarded as a proposed enrichment of the relational model, not a replacement for any of the original **inner joins** or **outer joins.**

The topic of **T-joins** is a complicated one. The reader may wish to skip to Section 5.8, which is much simpler.

5.7.1 Introduction to the T-join Operators

The four ordering comparators are as follows:

Strict:	LESS THAN	GREATER THAN
Non-strict:	LESS THAN OR EQUAL TO	GREATER THAN OR EQUAL TO

Full joins based on these comparators frequently yield a result that is not very informative because it includes too many concatenations of the tuples of the operands. For example, consider the following relations S and T:

S (P	A)		T (Q	B)
k1	4		m1	3
k2	6		m2	5
k3	12		m3	9
k4	18		m4	11
k5	20		m5	13
			m6	15

Suppose that A and B draw their values from the same domain, and that the comparator LESS THAN ($<$) is applicable on this domain. One of the full **joins** is

$$U = S [A < B] T.$$

Its extension is as follows:

U	(P	A	B	Q)
	k1	4	5	m2
	k1	4	9	m3
	k1	4	11	m4
	k1	4	13	m5
	k1	4	15	m6
	k2	6	9	m3
	k2	6	11	m4
	k2	6	13	m5
	k2	6	15	m6
	k3	12	13	m5
	k3	12	15	m6

Of the items being compared (A and B), if both are calendar dates, times of day, or combinations of dates and times, a **join** is often needed that is "leaner" than this full **join** ("leaner" in the sense that it has fewer rows or tuples). **T-joins** are intended to fill this role.

Each of the new **joins** is defined constructively—that is, in terms of an algorithm that will generate the appropriate result. An implementation can make use of this algorithm, but is not required to do so. All that is necessary is that the implementation generate the same result as the defining algorithm.

An important first step in the defining algorithm is to order the rows in each operand on the basis of the values in the comparand column of that operand. If the comparand column in each of the operands is guaranteed by a declaration in the catalog to contain no duplicate values, then precisely the same ordering will be generated again if the command is re-executed later, provided the data in the operand relations has not changed. If, however, duplicate values are permitted in one or both of these columns, the DBMS must be able to make use of values in other columns to resolve ties in the comparand columns.

These other columns are called *tie-breaking columns.* The need for resolving these ties stems from the need to make the operation precisely repeatable, if it should be re-executed later with the operands in exactly the same state at the relational level, but not necessarily in the same state at the storage level. Precise re-executability of relational commands is required by Fundamental Law 15 (see Chapter 29).

To be a good tie-breaker, a tie-breaking column should be of a *highly discriminating character:* that is, the number of distinct values in such a column divided by the number of rows in the operand must be as close as possible to one. Clearly, the best tie-breaking columns are the primary-key column (or for certain kinds of views, the weak identifier) and any other column for which there is a declaration in the catalog that each of its values must be unique within that column.

Every datum in a computer-supported database is represented by a bit string of some length. Now, every bit string of length L bits (say) can be interpreted as a binary integer, whether that bit string represents a number, a string of logical truth-values, or a string of characters. This integer can therefore be arithmetically compared with every other bit string of length L if this latter string is also interpreted as a binary integer.

Thus, it might be proposed that, whenever a tie is encountered in which two equal values from the comparand columns are competing to qualify as representatives of two candidate rows of one of the operands, the tie can be broken by (1) descending to the bit level in other items of data and (2) comparing the corresponding binary integers arithmetically. To achieve precise repeatability of the operation, however, this approach assumes too much—namely, that the representation of data by the DBMS in storage remains constant. This approach departs from the principle that all actions in the relational model should be explicable either within the model or, at the very least, at the same level of abstraction as the model.

To avoid complexity, the approach taken in RM/V2 is to assume that each of the operands includes a primary key, and that the DBMS has information concerning which column of that operand, simple or composite, constitutes that key. This assumption is consistent with the expected use of **T-joins** for generating schedules. After all, when scheduling activities, it is necessary to know precisely for each line in the schedule which activity is involved.

In addition to discussing the repeatable generation of orderings, it is necessary to classify the comparators as in the beginning of this section. The comparators involving ordering are called the *ordering comparators*. The two strict ordering comparators are LESS THAN and GREATER THAN, and the two non-strict ordering comparators are LESS THAN OR EQUAL TO and GREATER THAN OR EQUAL TO. The two non-ordering comparators are EQUAL TO and NOT EQUAL TO, but these two do not participate in the proposed new joins.

These new **joins** are introduced step by step in Sections 5.7.2 and 5.7.3. The sample relations S and T cited earlier are used to illustrate various points.

5.7.2 The Inner T-join

RZ-22 through RZ-25   Inner T-joins

The four new inner joins, called the **inner T-joins**, are each based on one of the four ordering comparators: LESS THAN, LESS

THAN OR EQUAL TO, GREATER THAN, or GREATER THAN OR EQUAL TO.

Suppose that the inner **T-join** is distinguished from the 10 full **inner joins** by doubling the square brackets around the comparing expression. For example,

V = S [[A < B]] T.

Let n = 22,23,24,25. Then the RZ feature with n as its number is a T-join that makes use of the comparator numbered n + 19 in the list of comparators cited in the first part of Section 5.7. An interesting property of V is that each tuple of S contributes to either no tuple at all in V or else to exactly one tuple in V. A similar remark can be made about contributions from tuples of T.

Next, **T-joins** are examined using the strict-ordering comparators LESS THAN and GREATER THAN, followed by an examination of **T-joins** using the non-strict-ordering comparators LESS THAN OR EQUAL TO and GREATER THAN OR EQUAL TO.

Strict Ordering in T-joins   The result V is formed by the DBMS in two major steps, which are described here to enable DBMS vendors and users to understand **T-joins**. Because **T-joins** are expected to be built into DBMS products, it should never be necessary for the user to program these steps.

1. Suppose that column P is the primary key of relation S, and thus its tie-breaker, while column Q is the primary key and tie-breaker of relation T. Suppose that relation S is ordered by *increasing values* of A; relation T, by *increasing values* of B. Whenever repetitions of a value are encountered in A, break the tie by selecting the corresponding rows from S in an order determined by increasing values of P. Whenever repetitions of a value are encountered in B, select the corresponding rows from T in an order determined by increasing values of Q.

2. Take the first tuple from S. This is the tuple with the least value from column A of relation S and, in case of ties, the least value of P. Note that the DBMS applies the comparator LESS THAN (<) to P *even if* there is a declaration in the catalog that < is not meaningfully applicable to the domain of P. Concatenate it with the first available tuple from T that satisfies A < B. This is the tuple with the least value from column B of T, and in case of ties, the least value of Q. Assuming one such tuple is found in T, mark that tuple in T as used and unavailable. To complete this first minor part of Step 2, contribute the concatenated tuple to V.

    Now take the second tuple from S and concatenate it with the first available tuple in T for which A < B. Assuming one such tuple is found in T, mark that tuple as used and unavailable. To complete this second minor part of Step 2, contribute the concatenated tuple to V. These minor steps are repeated until the whole of S is scanned. The availability marks are then erased from the operands.

This explanation is constructive and is intended to define the **inner T-join** based on the comparator $<$. Naturally, when the **T-join** operator is implemented within a DBMS, it is not required that this particular algorithm be used. All that is required is that, whatever operands are given, exactly the same result must be generated by the implemented algorithm and by this algorithm.

The extension of V resulting from this procedure is as follows:

V	(P	A	B	Q)
	k1	4	5	m2
	k2	6	9	m3
	k3	12	13	m5

The full **join** U could be an intermediate product in the formation of V, but U is not required to be an intermediate product. Although the **T-join** V represents a feasible schedule (assuming that properties A and B are date- or time-oriented), it is important to observe that some values of A and some of B may be omitted altogether in the result.

B = 3 can be thought of as a non-participant because it is a value of B less than every value of A. Similarly, A = 18 and A = 20 can be thought of as non-participants because they are values of A that are greater than every value of B.

The non-participants encountered so far are terminal. There may exist one or more non-terminal non-participants. In the preceding example, B = 11 is a non-terminal non-participant.

Now, let us investigate

$$W = T [[B > A]] S.$$

One might expect that W would have the same information content as V because the analogous full **joins** are equal to one another. However, this is not the case with **T-joins.**

To construct W conceptually,

■ relation S should be ordered by *decreasing values* of B;
■ relation R should be ordered by *decreasing values* of A.

Now, the same general procedure is followed as used in forming V. Relation S is ordered by *decreasing values* of A, and relation T is ordered by *decreasing values* of B. Take the first tuple from T. This is the tuple with the greatest value in column B of relation T and, in case of ties, the greatest value of Q. Note that the DBMS applies the comparator $>$ to Q *even if* there is a declaration in the catalog that $<$ is not meaningfully applicable to the domain of P. Concatenate it with the first tuple from S that satisfies $B > A$. This is the tuple with the greatest value of A. Assuming that one such tuple is found in R, mark that tuple as used and no longer available. Contribute the concatenated tuple to W. These steps are repeated until the whole of T is scanned. The availability marks are then erased from the operands.

The extension of W resulting from this procedure is as follows:

W	(Q	B	A	P)
	m6	15	12	k3
	m5	13	6	k2
	m4	11	4	k1

Suppose that column ordering is disregarded (this is quite normal in the relational model), but that the column headings are noted. Clearly, W is not identical to V in information content. In fact, *every tuple of W is different from every tuple of V* (a strong contrast not encountered in some other examples).

Moreover, the values that do not participate in W are

$A = 18, A = 20, B = 3, B = 5, B = 9.$

All of these non-participants are terminal. In contrast to V, in W there is no non-terminal non-participant. It is therefore important to take care in choosing the ordering of terms in an expression defining a **T-join;** otherwise, the meaning of an intended query may not be conveyed accurately to the DBMS.

Because the interesting case is that in which duplicate values actually occur in A, in B, or in both, this part is based on slightly altered extensions for S and T. The tuples marked with an asterisk ("*") have been added, and the two occurrences of 6 as a value of A are distinguished by the primary key values k2 and k6 in column P of relation S'.

S' (P	A)	T' (Q	B)
k1	4	m1	3
k2	6	m2	5
k6	6 *	m7	7*
k3	12	m3	9
k4	18	m4	11
k5	20	m5	13
		m6	15

Suppose as before that A and B draw their values from the same domain. One of the full **joins** is

$U' = S' [A < B] T'.$

Its extension has 17 tuples (of course, more than U):

Expository row number	U'	(P	A	B	Q)
1		k1	4	5	m2
2		k1	4	9	m3
3		k1	4	11	m4
4		k1	4	13	m5
5		k1	4	15	m6
6		k2	6	7	m7
7		k2	6	9	m3
8		k2	6	11	m4
9		k2	6	13	m5
10		k2	6	15	m6
11		k7	6	7	m7
12		k7	6	9	m3
13		k7	6	11	m4
14		k7	6	13	m5
15		k7	6	15	m6
16		k3	12	13	m5
17		k3	12	15	m6

Of course, the row number at the extreme left appears for expository purposes only.

Now consider

$$V' = S' [[A < B]] T'.$$

Its extension is as follows:

V'	(P	A	B	Q)
	k1	4	5	m2
	k2	6	7	m7
	k6	6	9	m3
	k5	12	13	m5

Note that, in this example, A = 18, A = 20, B = 3 remain terminal non-participants, while B = 11 remains a non-terminal non-participant. Moreover, if

$$W' = S' [[B > A]] R',$$

then W' remains quite different from V':

W'	(Q	B	A	P)
	m6	15	12	k3
	m5	13	6	k6
	m4	11	6	k2
	m3	9	4	k1

Clearly, W' is quite different from V' in information content. In fact, in this case every tuple of W' is different from every tuple of V'.

Non-strict Ordering in T-joins   Now, it is appropriate to consider the non-strict comparators LESS THAN OR EQUAL TO ($<$ =) and GREATER THAN OR EQUAL TO ($>$ =). The introduction of equality as part of the comparing brings with it a new problem: the possibility of *cross-ties*, in which two or more comparand values from one comparand column are not only equal to one another, but are also equal to two or more comparand values from the other comparand column. These occurrences of equality both within and between values in the comparand columns contribute at least four rows to the result of a full **join.** The question arises: In what way are certain rows selected to participate in a **T-join** result, while other rows are rejected?

In Chapter 17, "View updatability," the term *quad* is defined as a contribution of several rows to a **join** arising from a specific value that occurs at least twice in each comparand column, say m times in the first-cited comparand column and n times in the other comparand column. Such a contribution to any full **join** based on a comparator that involves equality must consist of a number of rows that is the product of the two integers m and n. Since each integer is at least 2, this product cannot be less than 4: hence, the name "quad." Clearly, a quad contribution cannot consist of 3, 5, 7, 11, or any prime number of rows. When quads can occur in **T-join** operands, the selection of cross-ties that survive in the result becomes an issue that must be handled by the DBMS (*not* the user).

The following example illustrates a quad. Suppose that relations S and T contain rows as indicated:

S (P A)		T (B Q)	
k7	13	13	m5
k5	13	13	m8
. . . .		. . . .	

Then, the full LESS THAN OR EQUAL TO join of S on A, with T on B, includes the following four rows because of the cross-ties arising from the multiple occurrences of the value 13 in both A and B:

Row label	U	(P	A	B	Q)
row t		k5	13	13	m5
row u		k5	13	13	m8
row v		k7	13	13	m5
row w		k7	13	13	m8
Other rows		. . . .			

Note that the row labels are purely expository.

In a **T-join,** each row of each operand may be used once only. This means that each of the rows < k5, 13 > and < k7, 13 > from S can be used once only, not twice as indicated in the preceding full **join.** Thus, in the **T-join** result for this example the DBMS must choose between row t and row u. The DBMS must also choose between row v and row w.

The defining algorithm for **T-joins** resolves cross-ties by selecting those two rows from any quad that contains in the primary key columns the combination of values that are greatest within the quad that remain unused in the result.

Remember that, in general, a quad contains $m \times n$ rows, where m and n are at least two.

In the example, columns P and Q are the primary-key columns. Row t contains the combination of least keys in the quad < k5, m5 >, while row w contains the combination of the greatest keys in the quad < k7, m8 >. Thus, row t and row w are selected to be the only participants in the LESS THAN OR EQUAL TO **T-join** of S on A with T on B.

This algorithm is designed to make execution of all **T-joins** repeatable in the sense that, if the operands remain unchanged, so does the result— even if access methods and representations of the operands have been changed in storage.

If the examples of S and T were those illustrated in Section 5.7.1 and the comparators were changed from strict to non-strict, the resulting relations U, V, W would be unchanged, because there were no occurrences of equality when comparing values from A with values from B. A similar remark applies to S' and T' in the preceding discussion. Therefore, relations S″ and T″ are introduced. Each of these relations has ties in the comparand columns; the pair of relations also has cross-ties:

S″ (P	A)
k1	4
k2	6
k6	6
k3	8
k4	9
k5	10

T″ (Q	B)
m1	3
m2	5
m7	6
m8	6
m3	9
m4	11
m5	13
m6	15

Consider the **T-join** V″ of S″ on A with T″ on B using the comparator LESS THAN OR EQUAL TO (<=). The defining expression for this **join** is

$$V'' = S'' [[A <= B]] T''.$$

The extension of V″ is as follows:

V″	(P	A	B	Q)
	k1	4	5	m2
	k2	6	6	m7
	k6	6	6	m8
	k3	8	9	m3
	k4	9	13	m5

Note that, in resolving cross-ties, the DBMS did not select the rows < k2, 6, 6, m8 > and < k6, 6, 6, m7 > to be members of V″.

The new problem that arises with the non-strict ordering comparators is the need to resolve cross-ties between comparand values by use of columns other than the comparand columns. The technique built into **T-joins** provides a systematic resolution.

The following practical example exhibits some of the limitations in the present version of the **T-join** operator. Suppose that students have registered for certain classes that are scheduled to run concurrently in various rooms and buildings. The relation ROOM identifies and describes each room that is available for classes. The relation CLASS identifies and describes each class.

ROOM   R#   Room serial number

⠀⠀⠀⠀⠀⠀BLDG   Building name

⠀⠀⠀⠀⠀⠀SIZE   Number of seats for students

CLASS   C#   Class identifier

⠀⠀⠀⠀⠀⠀STUDENTS   Number of students registered for a class

Assume the following extensions for these two relations:

ROOM	(R#	BLDG	SIZE)
	r1	lab	70
	r2	lab	40
	r3	lab	50
	r4	tower	85
	r5	tower	30
	r6	tower	65
	r7	tower	55

CLASS	(C#	STUDENTS)	
	c1	80	75
	c2	70	65
	c3	65	60
	c4	55	50
	c5	50	45
	c6	40	35

alternative column of data

To assign any class to a room, it is required that the room have a number of seats in excess of the number of students in the class. The **T-join** operator can be used to assign classes to rooms in two ways:

⠀⠀⠀U1 ← CLASS [[STUDENTS < SIZE]] ROOM

⠀⠀⠀U2 ← ROOM [[SIZE > STUDENTS]] CLASS.

Let us illustrate these two approaches. First, the rows of the operand CLASS are ordered by enrollment in each class, and the rows of ROOM are ordered by room size—both in *ascending* order, in preparation for the derivation of U1.

CLASS″ (C#	STUDENTS)
c6	40
c5	50
c4	55
c3	65
c2	70
c1	80

ROOM″ (R#	BLDG	SIZE)
r5	tower	30
r2	lab	40
r3	lab	50
r7	tower	55
r6	tower	65
r1	lab	70
r4	tower	85

U1 ← CLASS [[STUDENTS < SIZE]] ROOM

U1	(C#	STUDENTS	SIZE	R#	BLDG)
	c6	40	50	r3	lab
	c5	50	55	r7	tower
	c4	55	65	r6	tower
	c3	65	70	r1	lab
	c2	70	85	r4	tower

In the second attack on this problem, the rows of the operand ROOM are ordered by room size, and the rows of the operand CLASS are ordered by enrollment in each class, both in *descending* order, in preparation for the derivation of U2.

ROOM″ (R#	BLDG	SIZE)
r4	tower	85
r1	lab	70
r6	tower	65
r7	tower	55
r3	lab	50
r2	lab	40
r5	tower	30

CLASS″ (C#	STUDENTS)
c1	80
c2	70
c3	65
c4	55
c5	50
c6	40

U2 ← ROOM [[SIZE > STUDENTS]] CLASS

U2	(R#	BLDG	SIZE	STUDENTS	C#)
	r4	tower	85	80	c1
	r1	lab	70	65	c3
	r6	tower	65	55	c4
	r7	tower	55	50	c5
	r3	lab	50	40	c6

In this example, the two results U1 and U2 are different from one another. Neither of the **T-joins** using LESS THAN and GREATER THAN, respectively, assigns all of the classes to rooms. Class c1 is omitted from assignment in the first **T-join,** and class c2 in the second. However, if the comparators are changed to LESS THAN OR EQUAL TO and GREATER THAN OR EQUAL TO each one of these **T-joins** assigns all of the classes to rooms. In general, given any collection of classes and any collection of rooms, and the requirement that distinct classes be assigned to distinct rooms, there is no guarantee that each and every class can be assigned.

5.7.3 The Outer T-join

The **outer T-joins,** like the **inner T-joins** defined in Section 5.7.2, are each based on one of the four ordering comparators.

For each **inner T-join,** three kinds of **outer T-joins** are potentially useful: the **left outer T-join,** the **right outer T-join,** and the **symmetric T-join.** These **outer T-joins** are now defined in a constructive manner, but with no restriction intended on how they are implemented.

RZ-26 through RZ-37 Outer T-joins

The **outer T-join** of relations S on A with T on B consists of the **inner T-join** U of S on A with T on B, together with additional sets of tuples, called the *outer increments.* The **inner T-join** of S on A with T on B is denoted

$$V = S [[A @ B]] T,$$

where "@" stands for one of the four ordering comparators. S is called the *left operand;* T, the *right operand.*

There are two distinctly defined outer increments. To construct the *left outer increment,* collect those tuples of the left operand S that do not happen to participate in the **inner T-join;** to each of these, append a sufficient number of marked values to indicate that the value of each component of a tuple from T is missing but applicable. To construct the *right outer increment,* collect those tuples of the right operand T that do not happen to participate in the **inner T-join;** to each of these, append a sufficient number of marked values to indicate that the value of each component of a tuple from S is missing but applicable.

Each **outer T-join** is the **union** of the corresponding **inner T-join,** together with the following:

■ the left outer increment for the 4 **left outer T-joins** RZ-26 through RZ-29;

- the right outer increment for the 4 **right outer T-joins** RZ-30 through RZ-33;
- both increments for the 4 **symmetric outer T-joins** RZ-34 through RZ-37.

Suppose that the **outer joins** of S on A with T on B, using the comparator @, are denoted as follows:

Left outer T-join	VL = S [o[A @ B]] T
Right outer T-join	VR = S [[A @ B]o] T
Symmetric outer T-join	VS = S [o[A @ B]o] T

Note that the lowercase letter "o" is inserted between the left square brackets (for the **left outer join**), between the right square brackets (for the **right outer join**), or between both pairs of square brackets (for the **symmetric outer join**).

Taking the sample operands S, T presented in Section 5.2, the following results are obtained for the **outer T-joins** based on the LESS THAN comparator (<). Missing information is represented by a hyphen ("—") in these examples, and tuples from the **inner T-join** based on < are marked with an asterisk.

Left VL	(P	A	B	Q)
*	k1	4	5	m2
*	k2	6	9	m3
*	k3	12	13	m5
	k4	18	—	—
	k5	20	—	—

Right VR	(P	A	B	Q)
	—	—	3	m1
*	k1	4	5	m2
*	k2	6	9	m3
	—	—	11	m4
*	k3	12	13	m5
	—	—	15	m6

Symmetric VS	(P	A	B	Q)
	—	—	3	m1
*	k1	4	5	m2
*	k2	6	9	m3
	—	—	11	m4
*	k3	12	13	m5
	—	—	15	m6
	k4	18	—	—
	k5	20	—	—

5.7.4 Summary of T-joins

There are four simple **inner T-joins** corresponding to the following four ordering comparators:

RZ-22 LESS THAN

RZ-23 LESS THAN OR EQUAL TO

RZ-24 GREATER THAN

RZ-25 GREATER THAN OR EQUAL TO.

There are 12 simple **outer T-joins,** three for each of the four ordering comparators. The three types are the **left outer T-joins** (Features RZ-26–RZ-29), the **right outer T-joins** (Features RZ-30–RZ-33), and the **symmetric outer T-joins** (Features RZ-34–RZ-37).

In Table 5.1, which summarizes the 16 simple **T-joins,** the following notation is used:

I	Inner	3	LESS THAN
O	Outer	4	LESS THAN OR EQUAL TO
L	Left	5	GREATER THAN
R	Right	6	GREATER THAN OR EQUAL TO
S	Symmetric		
C	Comparator		

The **inner** and **outer T-joins** can be applied effectively when the values being compared happen to be (1) date intervals, time intervals, or combinations of both, or (2) loads and capacities. The 16 simple **T-joins** may also be useful in some other situations. They are not useful, however, if the comparator $<$ is declared in the catalog to be meaningfully inapplicable to the values being compared in the principal comparand columns.

The **T-joins** represent a step toward a relational operator that will probably appear in the next version of the relational model (RM/V3). This operator transforms two union-compatible relations involving a sequence of non-contiguous time intervals needed on some machines into a result that can be interpreted as a merged schedule for the two activities on those machines.

Before leaving the subject of **T-joins,** it is interesting to consider a counterpart to the **semi-theta-join,** namely the **semi-T-join.** It will be recalled from Chapter 4 that, under certain conditions, **semi-theta-join** can be useful in the efficient execution of inter-site **theta-joins** in a distributed database

---

Table 5.1 **Summary of Simple T-joins**

Feature RZ-	22	23	24	25	26	27	28	29	30	31	32	33	34	35	36	37
I or O	I	I	I	I	O	O	O	O	O	O	O	O	O	O	O	O
L, R, or S	—	—	—	—	L	L	L	L	R	R	R	R	S	S	S	S
Comparator	3	4	5	6	3	4	5	6	3	4	5	6	3	4	5	6

management system. In the same way, **semi-T-joins** can be useful in the efficient execution of inter-site **T-joins.**

5.8 ■ The User-defined Select Operator

The main reason for this operator is to introduce a more powerful version of the **select** operator than the built-in version described in Chapter 4. This operator permits the selection of rows from a specified relation based on any user-defined function that transforms one or more row-components into a truth value.

The *built-in* operator **select** with operand relation S involves comparing the values in a specified column of S (say A) with either

1. some specified constant or host variable (say x), or
2. values in a second specified column of S (say B).

In Case 2, each pair of values that are compared (an A-value and a B-value) must be drawn from the same row of S. The distinction between Cases 1 and 2 does not apply to the **user-defined select** operator.

RZ-38   User-defined Select

This operator is denoted S [i; p(A); t], where i is an initializing function (optional), p is a truth-valued function (required), and t is a terminating function (optional). The argument A of the function p denotes one or more simple columns of the relation S. However, the truth value of p(A) must be computable for each row using only the A-components of that row. If A is a collection of columns, more than one component of each row is involved.

Note that the comparators in any user-defined **select** are hidden in the function p. Therefore, there is only one Feature RZ-38.

Specifying i, t, or both can be omitted in any user-defined **select** command. If included in the command, the initializing function i is executed to completion at the very beginning of the **select,** and delivers what is called the temporary version of S. If included in the command, the terminating function t is executed at the very end of the **select,** at which point all rows that qualify to be selected from S or from its temporary version have been selected. The operand of i is the relation S. The operand of t is the relation resulting from all the rows of S (or its temporary version) that happen to be selected.

The languages in which the functions may be expressed should include one of the host languages supported by the DBMS, together with retrieval operators and the qualifier ORDER BY of the principal relational language, constrained to apply to the specified operand relation only.

The following example is intended to illustrate the practical use of the user-defined **select** operator. Suppose that a company has sales teams in various parts of the world. A database keeps track of sales by team in a relation called TEAM. Each team has an identifier TID that is unique with respect to teams. TID is the primary key of TEAM. The immediate properties of a team include year-to-date sales (all expressed in a single currency), total sales for each of the preceding five years, and number of members on that team.

Once each month, the company makes a statistical analysis of the year-to-date sales in relation to the sales of previous years. The function F is applied to measure long-term and short-term growth. F combines these two growths in some simple way to arrive at a performance rating. The function yields as its result the truth-value TRUE for about 10% of the sales teams, those that have achieved the best performance rating.

Let the relation describing each sales team be called TEAM. Suppose that TID denotes the team identifier (the primary key of TEAM). It is possible to use the function F to select the sales teams that have performed the best on a year-to-date basis:

WINNERS ← TEAM [;F(TID);].

Note that no initiating or terminating function is involved. Note also that F probably has several arguments (this fact is not shown).

5.9 ■ The User-defined Join Operator

This **join** operator is to a large extent user-defined, but not completely so. There are two main reasons for this:

1. the objective of continued support for optimization by the DBMS using techniques similar to those applicable to the built-in **joins;**
2. the objective of reducing, if not eliminating, the need for users to construct iterative programming loops.

RZ-39   User-defined Join

The user-defined join is more powerful than the built-in joins. It concatenates a row from one relation with a row from another whenever a user-defined function p transforms specified components of these rows into the truth value TRUE. If included in the command, the initializing function i is executed to completion at the very beginning of the **join,** before any rows of the first operand are concatenated with any rows of the second operand. Temporary versions of the operands are delivered as the result of executing i. If included in the command, the terminating function t is executed at the very end of the **join,** at which point all rows that are to be concatenated have been concatenated.

A **user-defined join** of relations S on A with T on B using functions i, p, t may be specified by means of the following expression:

S [i; p(A,B); t] T.

The operands for the initializing function i are S and T. One practical use of i is to generate temporary relations from S and T ordered by the values in their respective comparand columns A and B. The operand for the terminating function t is the result of the **join** up to that point. Incidentally, function p will rarely have an inverse, and an inverse is not required.

The languages in which the functions may be expressed should include one of the host languages supported by the DBMS, together with retrieval operators and the qualifier ORDER BY of the principal relational language, constrained to apply to the specified pair of operand relations only.

The following example extends the sales-analysis example cited in Section 5.8 for **user-defined select.** This extended example illustrates the practical use of the **user-defined join** operator.

Suppose that the previously described database also contains a relation CUST describing its large customers. One of the columns of CUST is the customer identifier CID—naturally, the primary key of CUST. Another property of each customer is the identifier TID of the sales team assigned to the customer. In this case TID is a foreign key. Other columns of CUST contain sales information similar to that in the TEAM relation, except that in each row the information applies to one customer only.

Suppose that another, different monthly analysis is required by the company for its large customers. The intent is to find *contra-flow situations*— that is, situations in which regional sales are increasing, while sales to one or more large customers in the region are decreasing. Let G be a function that is applied to customer sales data and team-oriented regional sales data. G yields the truth-value TRUE when growth of sales is positive for the region, but negative for a large customer. Team information such as team identifier TID and team manager TMGR, along with the customer name CNAME and customer location CLOC, is requested. This request can be expressed in terms of a **user-defined join** between the relations TEAM and CUST, followed by a projection:

CONTRA ← (TEAM [; G ;] CUST) [TID, TMGR, CNAME, CLOC].

The function G probably has several arguments (these are not shown in the request).

5.10 ■ Recursive Join

It has been asserted in a public forum that "the relational algebra is incapable of **recursive join**." In fact, such an assertion is astonishingly erroneous. The **recursive join** was introduced 10 years ago in one of my technical papers [Codd 1979].

RZ-40   Recursive Join

The **recursive join** is an operator with one operand. This operand is a relation that represents a directed graph. One of the columns of this relation plays a subordinate (SUB) role, while another plays a superior (SUP) role. Each tuple represents an edge of a directed graph, and by convention this edge is directed from the node identified by the SUP component down to the node identified by the SUB component. Because **joins** are normally applied to pairs of relations, it is convenient to think of the single operand as two identical relations. The **recursive join** acts on this pair of identical relations by matching each SUB value in one operand to a SUP value in the second operand. It yields all of the pairs of identifiers for nodes that are connected by paths in the acyclic graph, no matter what the path lengths are.

It is useful to compare the regular **equi-join** with this recursive join. Note that a regular **equi-join** of such a relation matching each SUB value in one operand to the SUP in the second operand yields all of the paths that are precisely two edges in length. The distinction between regular **equi-join** and **recursive join** should therefore be clear: regular **join** is terminated by completion of a simple scan of one of the two relations, whether real or virtual; on the other hand, recursive **join** with respect to a path of the underlying acyclic graph is terminated only when a node is encountered which has no node that is subordinate to it. An equivalent way of expressing this termination with respect to a path is that it occurs when the path ends.

There are several versions of this **recursive join** and they differ principally in the information content of the result that is delivered. The simple version described above was presented in RM/T [Codd 1979, page 427] as the CLOSE operator. A more powerful version suitable for the bill-of-materials type of application and not yet published is likely to be included in the next version (RM/V3) of the relational model.

Some relations represent directed graphs. Relation S is a *directed graph relation* if it is of degree at least two and has the following properties:

- two of its columns are defined on a common domain;
- one of these columns has a superior role, termed SUP;
- the other column has a subordinate role, termed SUB;
- no other columns have the SUP or SUB role.

An interpretation of such a relation is that there is an edge of the graph that connects from the SUP component of any row down to the SUB component of that same row. Two edges are connected if the SUB value of one (the higher of the two edges) is the SUP value of the other (the lower of the two edges).

Suppose that a directed graph includes a sequence of edges, each connected to its successor and with the property that, if the successive edges are traversed according to the directedness of the graph, the traversal returns to the same node at which it started. Then, such a graph is cyclic, and the sample sequence of edges just described is called a *cyclic path*. An *acyclic graph* has no cyclic paths whatsoever.

An example of an acyclic graph is discussed briefly here and in Section 28.4. Figure 5.1 is a diagram of an acyclic directed graph.

An acyclic path in a directed graph consists of a sequence of edges, each of which is connected to one edge lower (except the lowest edge in the path)

Figure 5.1   An Acyclic Directed Graph G1 Representing Product Structure

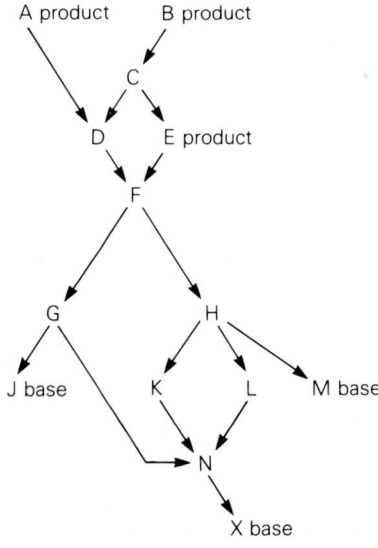

and each of which is connected to one edge higher (except the highest edge in the path). All of the paths that exist in an acyclic directed graph are acyclic. Any traversal of a path in compliance with its direction is called *downward*. Any traversal in the opposite direction is called *upward*.

Note that nothing in the definition of the acyclic directed graph concept prevents a single SUB value from being associated with more than one SUP value. In other words, nothing prevents two or more nodes from acting as superiors to a single subordinate node. A *hierarchy* is a special case of an acyclic graph in which each node may have at most one immediate superior node.

In the connectivity part of the bill-of-materials type of problem, an example of this type is the product structure graph G1, shown in Figure 5.1. In this relation, single letters are used as part serial numbers to identify parts. To save space, the acyclic graph relation AG is listed "on its side" and the immediate properties of each edge are represented by a lowercase letter:

AG	SUP	A	B	C	C	D	E	F	G	G	B	F	H	H	H	K	L	N
	SUB	D	C	D	E	F	F	G	J	N	H	H	K	L	M	N	N	X
	P	a	b	c	d	e	f	g	h	i	j	k	l	m	n	o	p	q

The graph corresponding to the relation AG appears in Figure 5.1.

Whenever product structure for two or more products is represented by a directed graph, each node represents a component and each edge represents the fact that one component is an immediate component of another. The graph in Figure 5.1 is clearly acyclic and nonhierarchic. Even if the graph of product structure begins its existence as a pure hierarchy, it is unlikely to remain that way. Thus, a general solution to the bill-of-materials problem should not assume the hierarchic structure.

There is a comprehensive solution to the general bill-of-materials problem based on the relational model. The solution is very concise, protects the user from iterative and recursive programming, and provides pertinent integrity constraints as well as manipulative capability. The **recursive join** now being described, however, is not a complete solution to this problem. (The more complete solution will be published later.)

The **recursive join** of RM/V2 has four arguments:

1. a single relation that represents an acyclic directed graph;
2. one column of node identifiers with the SUP role;
3. one column of node identifiers with the SUB role;
4. an identifier for a node from which all downward paths are to be traversed.

The result of **recursive join,** a relation that identifies every one of these downward paths, is therefore of degree three, with the columns SUB, SUP, and PI (path identifier). In each row the SUB and SUP components together uniquely identify an edge on one of the downward paths, while PI uniquely identifies that path by means of an integer generated by the DBMS. If the acyclic graph includes a total of *N* distinct paths downward from the specified node, the integers assigned to each of these paths is from the set $1, 2, \ldots, N$.

Some paths are likely to be composed of several edges. However, a particular edge may be part of two distinct paths, and may therefore occur with two distinct path identifiers. Remember that the graph is not necessarily hierarchical. The particular integer assigned to identify a path is meaningful only in the sense that it is distinct from all the other path identifiers.

A reasonable notation for **recursive join** is exhibited in the following example:

$$T \leftarrow S \, [\, SUB \mid SUP \, ; \, PI \,].$$

Note that, if this operator is to be applied to graphs that may include cycles, it must have a minor extension in its definition to avoid the peril of unending looping around the cycles. As execution proceeds, whenever the operator traverses an edge of the graph, it should temporarily mark that edge as traversed, and avoid traversing it again. RM/V2 includes only one version of **recursive join.** It works on relations that represent directed acyclic graphs. RM/V2 does not include an extended version that works on relations representing directed graphs that can have cycles in them. This extended version is a clear candidate for inclusion in RM/V3.

One interesting application of this cyclic version is that of recording contacts between criminals and suspects in a database for use by the police. In this case, contact between Person X and Person Y implies contact between Person Y and Person X, whereas the fact that Part p is an immediate component of Part q implies that Part q is *not* an immediate component of Part p.

5.11 ■ Concluding Remarks

There is no claim that the operators discussed in Chapters 4 and 5 represent all the operators that users will ever need. In fact, four more operators are introduced in Chapter 17, "View Updatability." When introducing any new operator, the reader is advised to remain within the discipline of the relational model (see Chapter 28).

Exercises

5.1   What is the **framing** operator? What are its operands and results? What is it used for? Supply an example.

5.2   What is the **extend** operator and what is it used for? If the description of S extended per T is the same as the description of S, what is true of the relations S and T?

5.3   Describe an example that illustrates **outer union,** and state how this operator is likely to be used in practice.

5.4   What are the three kinds of **outer join?** Supply an example for each kind.

5.5   Define **outer T-join** and supply an example. How is **outer T-join** likely to be used in practice?

5.6   How does **inner T-join** differ from **outer T-join?** How is **inner T-join** likely to be used in practice?

5.7   The definitions of **theta-join, semi-theta-join,** and **T-join** can be found in Chapters 4 and 5. Supply a definition of **semi-T-join.**

5.8   A need arises for an **equi-join** involving two currency columns as comparand columns. However, the values in one of the comparand columns happen to be expressed in dollars, whereas the values in the other comparand column happen to be expressed in British sterling. Explain how you would apply a **user-defined join** to solve this problem.

5.9   Describe an example that illustrates **recursive join,** and state how it is likely to be used in practice. (See also Chapter 28.)

5.10   Develop two operand relations S and T with the following properties:

- they are joinable by both **theta join** and **T-join;**
- when S and T are combined by **theta join** using the comparator GREATEST LESS THAN, the result is U, say;
- when S and T are combined by **T-join** using the comparator LESS THAN, the result is V, say;
- the relations U and V are not identical.

▪ CHAPTER 6 ▪

Naming

In this chapter, the topic of naming is discussed with respect to the management of non-distributed databases. Naming is taken up again in Chapters 24 and 25 with respect to the management of distributed databases.

When initially establishing a database, much of the naming is concerned with the database description, and hence belongs in the catalog. This naming is determined by the DBA staff who are designing the database. Later, during the interrogation and manipulation stage, much of the naming is concerned with the columns of intermediate and final results. This naming is initiated by the DBMS according to rules described in this chapter. Users must know these rules when combining several operators into one or more commands, whether these commands are executed interactively or from an application program.

In establishing or expanding a relational database, names must be assigned to domains, R-tables, columns, and functions. The features listed in the naming class (class N) make this activity reasonably systematic and in accordance with other features of the relational model—for example, protection of users from having to be aware of positioning within the database and "nextness" applied to rows and columns.

When a user attempts to insert names into the catalog, the DBMS must check whether the names are compatible with the features of class N. Because the user may be unaware of these features, the DBMS must be prepared to catch simple errors. All of the naming features discussed in this chapter apply to any single relational database, and are intended to make the database easy to understand and the interactions unambiguous.

One of the principles underlying these naming features is that, when deciding which names should be selected by the DBMS for the columns of every relation that is an intermediate or final result, interchangeability of the operands must not be reduced or in any way damaged. For example, **union** is an operator for which

$$S \cup T = T \cup S.$$

This commutativity could easily be damaged if the automatic naming of columns in the result were dependent upon which operand is cited first.

6.1 ■ Basic Naming Features

RN-1 Naming of Domains and Data Types

All domains (extended data types)—whether simple or composite, whether built-in or user-defined—must be assigned names that are distinct from one another, and distinct from the names of relations and functions.

The description of each domain must be stored in the catalog before any use is made of that domain.

RN-2 Naming of Relations and Functions

All relations, whether base or derived, and all functions, whether built-in or user-defined, must be assigned names that are distinct from one another, as well as distinct from all of the names of domains, data types, and columns.

The description of each relation and each function must be stored in the catalog before any use is made of either object.

RN-3 Naming of Columns

All columns, whether simple or composite, within any single relation must be assigned names that are distinct from one another, and distinct from the names of relations and functions.

Note that this feature does not require that all column names in the entire database be distinct from one another. Such a rule is not only unnecessary, but may also be counter-productive.

A guideline for naming that tends to make programs easier to read and understand is that the DBA and users abide by two simple rules:

1. If one considers the names of all domains, all relations, and all functions as a single collection of names, then in that collection every name is distinct from every other name.

2. Every column name is a combination of a role name and a domain name, where the role name designates in brief the purpose of the column's use of the specified domain.

For example, if the domain is QUANTITY OF PARTS (abbreviated Q) and a particular column designates the quantity-on-hand of parts, it would be appropriate to select Q as the domain name, OH as the role name, and OH__Q as the column name. Similarly, the quantity on order would be named OO__Q, and the quantity shipped would be named SHIP__Q. A DBMS that supports these guidelines should be regarded as supporting the somewhat less stringent features RN-1–RN-3.

The DBA may wish to impose the additional constraint that names of different kinds of objects should begin with a letter that designates the kind of object. For example,

Relations	R
Domains	D
Columns	C
Role prefix	P
Functions	F

While this additional constraint is not a requirement, compliance with this convention would make programs—and perhaps the database—easier to understand.

An important consequence of Features RN-2–RN-3 is that any combination of relation name and column name denotes precisely one column in the entire database, provided the column name is the name of a column within that relation. This fact is ignored in the design of the language SQL, which includes the clause SELECT . . . FROM . . . WHERE. One result is that **joins** are awkward to express in that language.

A simple syntax for such a composite name is a relation name, followed by a period, followed by the name of a column within that relation.

RN-4 Selecting Columns within
Relational Commands

The combination of relation name and column name is an unambiguous way to select a particular column in a relational database. The syntax of RL must avoid separating column names from relation names, which causes (1) difficulty in extending the language and (2) either ambiguity or needless difficulty for users in understanding relational commands.

The end user or programmer must have the option of specifying the order in which columns are to be presented in a report.

RN-5 Naming Freedom

Success of the DBMS in executing any RL command (e.g., a **join**) that involves comparing database values from distinct columns must not depend on those columns having identical column names.

At the time of this writing, the NOMAD product includes the undesirable and unnecessary constraint on **joins** cited at the end of Feature RN-5. It must be remembered that in some **joins,** both comparand columns may belong to a single relation. No pair of columns in a single relation are permitted to have the same name (Feature RN-3). Thus, a DBMS that supports this undesirable naming constraint may be unable to execute **joins** of a relation with itself using two distinct columns as comparands.

In contrast, the constraint on **joins** (see Chapter 4) that is part of the relational model—namely, that the comparand columns must draw their values from a common domain—guards against user errors in conceiving **join** commands without the adverse consequences just outlined.

6.2 ■ Naming Columns in Intermediate and
Final Results

RN-6 Names of Columns Involved in the Union
Class of Operators

In RL, when the user requests the operation R UNION S, he or she need not specify which columns of R are aligned with which columns of S, except for those columns of R and S where two or more columns of R (or two or more columns of S) draw their values from a common domain. The same applies to **intersection, difference,** and the three outer counterparts: **outer union, outer intersection,** and **outer difference.**

Of course, the language RL does permit the user to specify which columns of R are to be associated with which columns of S whenever two or more columns of R or of S draw their values from a common domain (see Chapter 3).

One reason for using domains to determine associativity of columns in the **union**-type of operator is that this reduces the burden on the user and also reduces the occurrence of errors. If the degree of either operand is N, the user would be burdened with specifying N associations. Each association is a pair of columns, one column from one operand, one column from the other operand. A second reason for using domains in this way is that they ensure that the command is meaningful.

In supporting **union,** most existing relational DBMS products check no more than basic data types. This check is inadequate to ensure meaningfulness of the **union** operation, and can easily result in incorrect data in the database.

Consider the example of two relations A1 and A2 that identify and describe customer accounts pertaining to two different services provided by a company. Suppose that A1 and A2 have identical descriptions (see Table 6.1).

Note that there are five domains (extended data types) and six columns. The two currency columns and the days-of-service column all have the same basic data type, namely, non-negative integers.

Table 6.1 **Description of Relations A1 and A2**

Columns		Domains	
A#	Account number	Account numbers	A#
CNAME	Customer name	Company names	NAME
PDATE	Date of last payment	Calendar dates	DATE
PD1	Year-to-date paid type 1	U.S. currency	U
PD2	Year-to-date paid type 2	U.S. currency	U
SERV	Days of service	Days	D

As shown in the following R-table, the five domains are

A	A# (A#	NAME CNAME	DATE PD	U		DAYS SERV)
				PD1	PD2	
	c1	Smith	88-12	500	300	60
	c2	Jones	89-01	800	0	105
	c3	Blake	88-07	400	200	55
	c4	Adams	88-10	1200	0	200
	c5	Brook	88-08	150	150	35
	c6	Field	87-12	120	200	30
	c7	Wild	88-06	200	50	45

For successful action by the **union** operator, present versions of relational DBMS products merely require those columns that are paired off to have the same *basic data type*. This means that these DBMS would accept the following pairing of columns:

A1 (A# CNAME PDATE PD1 PD2 SERV)
A2 (A# CNAME PDATE SERV PD2 PD1).

The relational model, however, requires those columns that are paired off to have the same *extended data type*. Thus, it would not allow the SERV column of A1 to be paired with either PD1 or PD2 of A2. The model would allow PD1 of A1 to be paired with either PD1 or PD2 of A2. This safety feature is one of several in the model that carry some of the meaning of the data; such features are said to be *semantic*. I avoid applying the term "semantic" to the whole model, however, because this would be making a very extravagant claim.

RN-7 Non-impairment of Commutativity

Given any one of the relational operators that happens to have two operands and to be commutative, the rule built into the DBMS for naming the columns of the result must not impair this commutativity. Similarly, this naming rule must not impair any other simple identities that apply to the operators.

An example of a commutative operator is **union,** since (as just pointed out), for any pair of relations R, S,

R ∪ S = S ∪ R.

Thus, in this case, a rule that names the columns of the result in a way that depends on whether R or S is cited first in a relational command is unacceptable.

Outer join is an example of an operator to which a simple, but different, identity applies. For any pair of relations R, S, the **left outer join** of R on A with S on B yields the same result as the **right outer join** of S on B with R on A. One simple way to ensure that the DBMS supports Feature RN-7 is to design it to choose, from any two alternative names for a column, the name that comes first alphabetically using a standard collating sequence. This choice, however, would be troublesome for users who are unaccustomed to the Roman alphabet.

RN-8 Names of Columns of Result of the Join and Division Operators

When the user requests in RL a **join** (inner or outer) or a **relational division,** if (1) any one name of any pair of column names in the result is inherited from one operand of the command, (2) the other name is inherited from the second operand of the command, and (3) the two column names happen to be identical, then that name is in each case prefixed by the name of the relation that is the source of the column.

A feature of this kind is necessitated by the fact that no two columns of the result can have the same name.

RN-9 Names of Columns of Result of a Project Operator

The column names and sequencing of such names in the result of a **project** operator are precisely those specified in the pertinent command.

RN-10 Naming the Columns whose Values are Function-generated

A column whose values are computed using a function acquires a name composed of the name of the function followed by a period followed by the name of its first argument.

If the function has only one argument, that one is treated as its first argument. If two or more columns have values that are generated by the same function, and could be assigned the same name as a result, the DBMS resolves the potential ambiguity in names by assigning in each case a sufficiently large substring of the function-invoking expression that ambiguity is resolved. Columns whose values are computed using an arithmetic expression (not an explicitly named function) are treated similarly.

Such a substring must exist; otherwise, the pertinent columns would be identical in content.

RN-11   Inheritance of Column Names

Every intermediate result and every final result of an RL command for interrogation or manipulation inherits column names from its operands (the **join** class of operators and the **union** class of operators), except for those columns covered by Feature RN-10. Such results also inherit column sequencing, except in the case of the **project** operator.

Rules for the naming by the DBMS of all columns in intermediate and final results are needed partly because of the rejection of positioning and nextness concepts in the relational model (see Chapter 1). It is worth remembering the following example: a single relational command may form the **union** of several **joins.** The user needs to know how the DBMS assigns names to columns of the **joins** (which are intermediate results) in order to be able to determine the desired alignment of columns when the **union** is executed.

6.3 ■ Naming Other Kinds of Objects

Data from a database can be archived, but only as one or more relations. Each of these relations can be base or derived. Most often, relations that are archived are derived relations. In either case, the archived relation has an *associated source relation*—that is, the relation whose name is alphabetically first of the one or more relations from which the archived relation is copied or derived.

RN-12   Naming Archived Relations

When archiving a relation, the user, normally the DBA, may choose to assign a name to it himself or herself; if not, the DBMS assigns a name. The name assigned by the DBMS is the name of the associated source relation concatenated with the eight-digit date of archiving (four-digit year first, then two-digit month, then two-digit day), followed by an integer n identifying the archived data as the nth version that day.

RN-13   Naming of Integrity Constraints

Each and every integrity constraint, regardless of its type, must be declared in the catalog and must be assigned a unique name.

This feature is necessary for the support of DBA-initiated integrity checks (see Feature RI-21 in Chapter 13). It is recommended that the naming of integrity checks be clearly distinguishable from the naming of domains, relations, functions, and columns. Note that, for a given primary key, there are likely to be many integrity constraints of the referential type. Each of these constraints must be given a distinct name.

The DBMS can make good use of these distinct names for integrity constraints when reporting on the failure of one of them. It should be remembered that a single row may contain two or more foreign keys. Thus, in the case of failure of referential integrity, it is insufficient to identify the row containing the foreign key that is giving trouble.

Frequently, a user begins his or her interaction with a database not knowing precisely what information he or she must retrieve from it. The user begins by posing some simple queries, and basing subsequent queries on information obtained from preceding ones. From time to time, it is necessary to treat results from preceding queries as operands in subsequent queries. This kind of querying is called the *detective mode* because detectives seeking information about criminal acts normally question witnesses and suspects in this way.

RN-14   Naming for the Detective Mode

A user's request for a query must include an option for the user to supply a name to be attached to the result of this query. If such a name is supplied, the DBMS checks that it does not conflict with any other names in its catalog, and, if so, stores the result of the query under the name supplied.

Exercises

6.1   Must the name of each column in the entire database be distinct from the name of every other column in the entire database? If yes, discuss why. If no, discuss why not.

6.2   Must any two columns that are to act as comparands in a relational operation be identically named? Explain your answer.

6.3   Consider an **equi-join** of S with T. Assume that one of the columns of

S has the same name as one of the columns of T. What are the implied names of columns of the result? Use a simple example to explain your answer.

6.4 Why is it useful to include the domain name as a distinctive part of a column name?

6.5 How is the domain concept used in the **union** operator (1) to make the request more meaningful and (2) to reduce the column-pairing burden on the user?

6.6 What does naming have to do with possible impairment of commutativity?

6.7 When a relation S is archived and no name is supplied for this version by the user, how is that version named by the relational model? How does this feature relate to version support (where "version" means version of the data)?

6.8 Why should each integrity constraint be distinctly named?

■ *CHAPTER 7* ■

Commands for the DBA

The main purpose of the commands discussed in this chapter is to support certain tasks that are often the responsibility of the database administrator. Examples of such tasks are finding all occurrences of values in a specified domain (see Chapter 3); introducing new kinds of information into the database; loading and unloading R-tables from various sources (e.g., virtual storage access method files); archiving and re-activating R-tables; and creating, renaming, and dropping various parts of the database description. The features presented here do not specify the syntax that might be adopted; they are intended to convey the semantics.

Use of the commands described here requires special authorization, and is normally restricted to the DBA and his or her staff. These commands are not intended to support all of the tasks that are normally within the DBA's responsibility. Among such tasks not supported by these commands, and not supported in RM/V2, are changes in storage representation and in access paths to gain improved performance on the current traffic. Such changes are likely to depend heavily upon the design of the particular DBMS product involved. It is appropriate that these differences between DBMS products exist: different vendors may use quite different storage and access techniques in attaining good performance in the execution of high-level relational commands. The relational model remains unaffected due to its high level of abstraction.

Another typical task for a DBA or a security officer is assigning appropriate authorization to users so that they may access parts of the database and possibly engage in data insertion, updating, and deletion. Support for this kind of task is included in RM/V2 (see Chapter 18, "Authorization").

Two of the commands for the DBA were introduced in Section 3.4 at the end of Chapter 3. These were the FIND commands (Features RE-1 and RE-2) for locating all occurrences of *all* active values drawn from any specified domain (FAO—AV) and locating all occurrences of *just those values* that occur both in a specified list and in a specified domain (FAO—LIST).

Of course, the term "locating" is used here in a sense that is meaningful to users of relational systems (see Chapter 3), and therefore has nothing to do with disk addresses as far as the user is concerned.

7.1 ■ Commands for Domains, Relations, and Columns

When dealing with domains and columns, it is useful to keep in mind the kinds of information declared for each one. Consider domain D; let col(D) denote the collection of all of the columns that draw their values from this domain. One aim is to include in the declaration of D every property that is shared by all of the columns in col(D). Then, the declaration of each column in col(D) need not repeat any of these common properties. It must, however, include the properties that are peculiar to that column, and these properties only.

Thus, a domain declaration normally includes the following:

- the basic data type;
- the range of values that spans the ranges permitted in all of the columns drawing their values from this domain;
- whether the comparator LESS THAN (<) is meaningfully applicable to such values.

A column declaration normally includes the following:

- an additional range constraint (if relevant) that provides a narrower range than that declared in the underlying domain;
- whether values are permitted to be missing from the column;
- whether the values in the column are all required to be distinct from one another.

For details, see Chapter 15, "The Catalog."

RE-3 The CREATE DOMAIN Command

This command establishes a new domain as an extended data type. (For more information on this topic, see Chapters 3 and 15.) The information supplied as part of the command includes the name (selected by the DBA), the basic data type (as in programming languages such as COBOL, FORTRAN, and PL/1), a range of values, and whether it is meaningful to apply the comparator $<$ to these values.

For example, it is often the case that applying the comparator $<$ to part serial numbers is meaningless. Note that, if $<$ is applicable, then so are all of the other comparators. That is the reason why only the comparator $<$ is cited in Feature RE-1. Note also that the basic data type indicates whether arithmetic operators are applicable.

RE-4 The RENAME DOMAIN Command

This command re-names an already existing domain without changing any of its characteristics. The old name and the new name are supplied as part of the command. In addition, the DBMS finds every occurrence in the catalog of a column that draws its values from the specified domain (identified by its old name), and updates the name of that domain in the column description.

Since large parts of the catalog may have to be locked during the latter process, the DBA would be well advised to make this kind of request only during periods of low activity.

References by application programs to the cited domain by its old name are not automatically updated in RM/V2, but may be in RM/V3. There should be little impairment of application programs because normally these programs do not make direct reference to any domain.

RE-5 The ALTER DOMAIN Command

A suitably authorized user can employ this command to alter an already declared domain (extended data type) in various ways. An alteration of this kind is likely to impair application programs logically. Thus, such action must be undertaken with great care, and only when absolutely necessary. The items that might be changed are the basic data type, the range of values, and the applicability of $<$.

RE-6 The DROP DOMAIN Command

This command drops an existing domain, provided no columns still exist that draw their values from this domain. If such a column still exists, an indicator is turned on to indicate that this is the case, and that the command has been aborted (see Feature RJ-7 in Chapter 11). If there is an index based on the specified domain (see Feature RE-15) and if that domain is dropped, then the index is dropped.

RE-7 The CREATE R-TABLE Command

This command stores the declaration for a base R-table or a view in the catalog. All domains cited in such a command must be already declared. Otherwise, the command is aborted and the domain-not-declared indicator is turned on (see Feature RJ-5 in Chapter 11).

The following information is supplied as part of this command.

- The name of the R-table.
- If it is a view, its definition in terms of base R-tables and other views.
- For each column, its name.
- For each column, the name of the domain from which it draws its values.
- Which combination of columns constitutes the primary key or weak identifier. (The weak identifier pertains to certain kinds of views only; see the discussion of **outer equi-join** in Chapter 5.)
- For each foreign key, which combination of columns constitute that key and which primary keys (usually only one) are the target. This item is vital for base R-tables, but less critical for views.

It would be helpful for a DBMS that uses indexes to establish a domain-based index on the domain of the primary key of the R-table being created, if such an index does not already exist. Remember that another R-table may already have a primary key on the same domain, and an index based on this domain. If the DBMS does not yet support domain-based indexes, but does support the more common type of indexes, then it would be helpful if the system created an index on the primary key. Automatic creation of indexes on the foreign keys, or corresponding expansion of existing domain-based indexes, should also be considered.

RE-8 The RENAME R-TABLE Command

This command renames an existing base R-table or a view. The DBMS then examines all view definitions and authorizations recorded in the catalog without deleting any of them. The purpose is to make changes from the old name to the new name wherever that relation is cited. The old name and the new name are supplied as part of the command.

References by application programs to the cited R-table by its old name are not automatically updated in RM/V2, although they may be in RM/V3. Of course, the catalog would have to be expanded to become more like what is usually called a *dictionary*.

The DBA would be well advised to use this command only during periods of low activity.

RE-9 The DROP R-TABLE Command

When a base R-table or a view, say S, is dropped, several parts of the database description may be affected: integrity constraints, views, and authorization constraints. It should be remembered that an integrity constraint may straddle two or more R-tables. Thus, such a constraint may involve not only the R-table S, but also one or more other R-tables. The definition of a view may also cite several R-tables, of which S is only one. It may also be necessary to drop a bundle of authorization constraints based on the R-table.

The total effect of a normal drop of a specified R-table, say S, is abandonment of three types of specifications.

1. All of the integrity constraints citing S.
2. All of the views whose definitions cite S.
3. All of the authorization constraints citing S.

Collectively, the dropping of these specifications is called the *cascading action* that is expected from the DROP request, if such action is not explicitly postponed or avoided altogether. Type 1 applies principally to base R-tables, while Types 2 and 3 apply to both base R-tables and views.

Taking all of these factors into account, dropping such a table can cause a significant impact on users of that database. This action therefore requires special authorization (see Features RA-5 and RA-6 in Chapter 18). Normally, only the DBA and his or her staff are so authorized.

Sometimes the aim of the user is to replace the dropped R-table by other tables, preserving the integrity constraints, views, and authorization constraints. The sheer bulk of these items makes them worth preserving, even if they need minor editing. For this purpose, RM/V2 provides the *catalog block* (Feature RM-7 in Chapter 12) to postpone the cascading actions. The catalog block is a sequence of commands, each of which operates on the catalog only. Certain ones of these commands may normally have a cascading effect. This cascading action is postponed. It is the catalog that is allowed to leave a state of integrity during execution of the catalog block. The postponed cascading is re-examined by the DBMS at commit time to see whether any of it must be re-executed immediately prior to the execution of the commit that terminates this catalog block.

For safety reasons, the DROP R-TABLE command is executed in three steps. However, only Step 1 is applied if the R-table is not a base relation.

In the *first step,* the DBMS checks that the table name is recorded in the catalog as either a base relation or a view. If the specified R-table happens to be only a temporary R-table, it is immediately and unconditionally dropped.

If the relation being dropped is a base R-table or a view, the DBMS checks to see whether the catalog block indicator (Feature RJ-11 in Chapter 11) is on. If it is, the DBMS drops the relation and omits any cascading action.

If RJ-11 is off, the DBMS checks to see whether there is any potential cascading action. If not, the DBMS again drops the relation. If there is potential cascading action, the user is warned of the type of such action, and notified that the cascading action can be postponed by requesting a catalog block. If the user responds "go ahead anyway," the DBMS not only drops the relation, but also takes all of the necessary cascading action. On the other hand, if the user requests that the command be aborted, the DBMS cancels its attempt to drop the specified R-table. This ends Step 1.

In the *second step,* applicable to base R-tables only, if the DBMS has decided to initiate the drop procedure, it archives the specified R-table for either a specified or a default period. This period is at least seven days (the default value). See Features RA-5 and RA-6 in Chapter 18 for the authorization aspects.

Upon expiration of the archiving period, the DBMS takes the *third and final step,* applicable only to base R-tables by deleting all rows of the data in the specified R-table. It then drops the description of that R-table from the catalog. At any time during the archiving period, the DBA can restore the R-table to its state immediately before the execution of the DROP request.

RE-10 The APPEND COLUMN Command

This command specifies the name of an existing base R-table. The DBMS appends to the description of that table in the catalog the name supplied for a new column that draws its values from an already declared domain; the name of this domain is also supplied as part of the command. Each row of that table is extended to include a value for the named column. For the time being, however, each such value is A-marked as missing, unless the VALUE qualifier RQ-13 (see Chapter 10) is specified in the command.

The VALUE qualifier is one way of handling the case in which missing values are prohibited. Another way is by utilizing Feature RI-19 (see Chapter 13).

The domain cited in the command imposes certain constraints upon the values permitted in the new column. Additional constraints for the new column may be imposed by means of column-integrity assertions. Both domain integrity and column integrity are defined and discussed in Chapter 13.

RE-11 The RENAME COLUMN Command

This command renames an existing column of some existing R-table. The name of the pertinent R-table, the old name of the column, and the new name of this column must be supplied. If an index has been created on this column, any reference within the DBMS to this column by its old name is updated.

References by application programs to the cited column by its old name are not automatically updated in RM/V2, but may be in RM/V3.

RE-12 The ALTER COLUMN Command

Occasionally, it may be necessary to make changes in the properties assigned to a column. For example, for a specific column, the DBA may decide to change from one domain to another or to alter the range of values permitted in the column.

RE-13 The DROP COLUMN Command

This command makes those component values in each row that fall in the specified column inaccessible to all users. These component values are actually removed, but at a reorganization time that is convenient for the DBMS.

Except for the special cases discussed next, this command then drops from the description of the pertinent R-table both (1) the column name and (2) the column description, including any reference therein to its domain.

If it happens that the column being dropped is part of the primary key of that R-table, the DBMS requests that a new primary key be declared. Since that and other R-tables may include numerous foreign keys drawn from the same domain as the primary key being dropped, the possibility of cascading action exists. Use of the catalog block may be appropriate in order to postpone any cascading action and to update these foreign keys.

If the column being dropped is part of a foreign key, the foreign-key declaration is dropped. If the column is simply indexed, the corresponding index is dropped. In the case of a domain-based index, only the contribution from this column is dropped.

References by application programs to the dropped column are not automatically found and reported by RM/V2, but may be by RM/V3.

7.2 ■ Commands for Indexes

Features RE-14–RE-16 apply only to relational DBMS that exploit indexes to attain good performance. The DBMS designer should remember that indexes in the relational context are tools for obtaining improved performance, and they should be used *for that purpose only*. In early releases of some relational DBMS products, uniqueness of values within a column could be accomplished, only if that column was indexed. Consequently, if the DBA dropped that index, the control over uniqueness of values was lost. Therefore, for these releases performance could not be the sole criterion for choosing whether a column is indexed. In the context of the relational model this coupling with the DBMS of semantic properties of the data with performance in making index decisions is an abuse of the index concept and a DBMS design error.

Uniqueness of values within any column should be specified as one of the properties of that column, not as a property of an index. Similarly, the kinds of marks permitted or prohibited in any column should be specified as a property of the column, not as a property of an index.

DBMS products with other kinds of performance-oriented access paths should have DBA commands similar to Features RE-14–RE-16.

RE-14 The CREATE INDEX Command

This command is intended to be designed into a relational DBMS that exploits indexes. It creates the description of an index and stores this description in the catalog. It also creates the index, although not necessarily immediately. If the DBMS receives several successive requests for indexes to be created on a single relation, it attempts to process them all in a single pass over the data. The purpose is improved performance.

RE-15 The CREATE DOMAIN-BASED INDEX Command

This command is also intended to be designed into a relational DBMS that exploits indexes. It creates an index based on the specified domain. It provides the DBMS with the storage location of each active value drawn from this domain. Such an index refers to all of the columns in the database that draw their values from the specified domain or a subset of these columns, provided such a subset can be specified conveniently by the DBA. An index of this kind may therefore straddle two or more base R-tables.

When such an index is applied to a primary domain, it yields improved performance not only on retrieval of data, including the evaluation of **joins,** but also on referential integrity. When the database is distributed and a domain-based index is created on a primary domain, that index should exist at the site or sites where the primary keys are located.

RE-16 The DROP INDEX Command

This command is also intended to be designed into a relational DBMS that exploits indexes. It drops an existing index, whose name is supplied, or reports the non-existence of an index with that name.

7.3 ■ Commands for Other Purposes

RE-17 The CREATE SNAPSHOT Command

A query is embedded in this command. The query part yields a derived R-table, whose name is supplied as part of the command. The DBMS stores this derived R-table in the database, and stores its description (including the date and time of creation) in the catalog.

Suppose that a snapshot is created from a base relation S. Unlike a view, a snapshot of S does not reflect the insertions, updates, and deletions applied to S after the snapshot was created.

This command is likely to be used heavily in the management of distributed databases. For example, if a bank has branches in several cities and a computer-managed database in each city, the planning staff at headquarters might require a weekly snapshot of the accounts data in each city. These snapshots contain data that could be as much as a week out-of-date, whereas a view would reflect all of the transactions at the branches as they occur, and therefore be much more up-to-date. Snapshots, however, are much cheaper than views, and place a much smaller load on the communications network.

RE-18   The LOAD AN R-TABLE Command

This command invokes a user-defined loading program in accordance with a name specified in the command. The function may, and very likely will, convert the data from a non-relational form into a relation.

RE-19   The EXTRACT AN R-TABLE Command

This command can unload a copy of a relation (base or derived) in whatever form the DBMS delivers the relation. Alternatively, it can invoke a user-defined unloading program by including its name. This program may (and very likely will) convert the unloaded data from a relation into some non-relational form.

If no ordering of columns is explicitly specified, it may be useful to order the columns alphabetically by column name. This procedure will improve communications between two or more DBMS, possibly at different sites, and between a relational DBMS and non-relational recipients.

The following feature would be a good option within the load utility. If supported in such a utility, it need not be supported within the DBMS itself.

RE-20   The CONTROL DUPLICATE ROWS Command

This command has as its single operand a table that may have duplicate rows in it. In other words, the operand need not be a true relation. It generates a true relation (an R-table) that contains only those rows of the operand that are distinct with respect to each other, and appended to each such row is the number of occurrences of that row in the operand. The column that contains these counts is named by the DBMS as column ZZZ or given some equally unlikely name.

Its principal use is on tables loaded from non-relational sources. Such tables are likely to contain duplicate rows.

An example of the usefulness of the CONTROL DUPLICATE ROWS command can be found in supermarkets. The customer selects a wide variety of items from the supermarket shelves and places them in a shopping cart. Then he or she pushes the cart to a check-out line to enable a cashier to accumulate the bill and complete the transaction.

The cashier takes each item one by one and draws it across a device that electronically reads the bar code on the item. For speed of execution of check-out, it is important that it be unnecessary for either the cashier or customer to have to arrange items in any specific sequence. Thus, if the customer happens to have five cans of tuna fish randomly scattered in his or her shopping cart, it is highly unlikely that these cans are drawn across the bar code reader consecutively. Thus, it requires more than a bar code reader to add up the cans of tuna fish.

Suppose the bar code readings are automatically entered into and re- corded in a computer system, partly for the purpose of adding up the bill for the complete transaction, and partly to insert this new information into a database that keeps track of inventory and, from time to time, places orders with one or more wholesale suppliers of food and housewares. Suppose also that, as the bar code for each item is entered into the computer, the computer converts it into a digital code, searches a table for descriptive properties of the item (including its price), and records the digitized bar code and properties as one more row in a table.

Such a table is bound to contain duplicate rows from time to time. For example, there are likely to be five separate rows for the five cans of tuna, but these rows are duplicates of one another and therefore not distinguish- able rows. The question arises: how can duplicate rows be avoided if the database is relational?

Resolution of this question depends on what distinctions and identifi- cations the supermarket manager deems to be useful for his or her business. One possibility is that the manager wants to keep track of what purchases are frequently coupled together in customers' habits. This requirement sug- gests that the collection of items purchased by one customer in one trans- action be kept separate from those purchased by another customer in another transaction.

Does this mean that each customer should be required to provide his or her social security number to the cashier? Certainly not: such a require- ment would be unacceptable to most customers. In addition, the manager is not likely to be interested in *identifying* each customer uniquely. Thus, the social security approach represents a serious confusion between *distinctiveness* and *identification.*

The following is one solution to this problem, and I am not claiming that it is the best. However, it does avoid corrupting a relation by storing duplicate rows within it.

What has to be maintained as a distinct collection of records or rows is the collection of items purchased in a single customer transaction. To maintain this distinctiveness does not require unique identification of each customer. Instead of placing any burden on the customer to identify himself or herself uniquely, it is the system that should bear an equivalent burden, namely that of attaching the cash register identification and time of day to each transaction.

If the system initially records each and every item of a customer's transaction in a table, then duplicate rows should be removed from this table before it is planted in the database. Of course, this removal of duplicate rows must avoid loss of information.

The transformation needed is one that counts the number of occurrences of each distinct row and develops a revised table in which each row is distinct from every other row, and each row contains the number of occurrences of its counterpart in the initially generated table. This means that the transformation needed is precisely that provided by the CONTROL DUPLICATE ROWS command.

7.4 ■ Archiving and Related Activities

From time to time data must be removed from disk storage, because it has become inactive in the database (either completely or almost completely inactive). The main reason for this is to avoid the expense of having the entire database consume too much disk storage. However, either for government reasons (e.g., tax audit) or for business reasons (e.g., internal audit), the data thus removed must normally be saved in inactive status for a certain period in an archive. Such an archive is usually supported in a storage medium with very large capacity and relatively slow access—for example, by recording the data on magnetic tape. Sometimes it is required that archived data be reactivated in a separate database for use by analysts, planners, or accident investigators.

The DBA needs to plan this archiving and reactivating of data so that it becomes a routine activity handled by the DBMS: an activity that is repeated at various intervals specified by the DBA. Some data in the database may have a very short period of activity, while other data may have a very long period of activity. For simplicity and adequate generality, RM/V2 permits *any derived relation* to be archived. Note the emphasis on any derived relation. In a relational database a derived relation may consist of any combination of rows, providing they are all of the same extended data type.

An archived relation may later be reactivated in the same database from which it came or in some other database. Alternatively, an archived relation may be dropped altogether. Reactivation in a different database is quite likely whenever a company-related accident occurs in which employees or members of the public are injured. Reactivation in a different database is also quite likely if the data reflects operations that the company requires to be regularly analyzed "off-line" for planning purposes.

In RM/V2 actions such as archiving, reactivating, and dropping may be triggered by a calendar event, by a non-calendar event, or by the expiration of a specified period of calendar days after the occurrence of some specified event. The actions and their triggering conditions are specified by the DBA as relational commands. Since these requests concern the community of users, it is inappropriate to incorporate them in an application program. Instead, the DBMS stores these commands in the catalog. Further examination of these requests and their triggering conditions must be postponed until user-defined integrity constraints are considered (see Chapter 14).

As a general rule, relational requests such as retrievals, insertions, updates, and deletions, do not touch the archived data, and are therefore unaffected by it. The following two requests, however, do involve the archived data in a very explicit way.

RE-21 The ARCHIVE Command

This command stores a specified R-table in the archive storage, and attaches to it either the specified name or, if such a name is not supplied, the name of source R-table with the present date appended (see feature RN-12 in Chapter 6). It also attaches the name or identification of the source database from which it was archived.

This command is normally applied to a derived R-table. If an R-table with the same name already exists in archive storage, it is over-written by the new version.

RE-22 The REACTIVATE Command

This command, invoked for an R-table that was previously archived, copies the specified R-table from archive storage into storage that is more readily accessible. The reactivated copy becomes part of the database specified in the REACTIVATE command. Alternatively, if the database name is omitted, it once again becomes part of the source database. If in the process an R-table with the same name (including archiving date where applicable) is encountered in the receiving database, it is over-written.

Additional commands for enabling the DBA to maintain better control over the integrity of the database are discussed in Chapter 13 (Feature RI-21) and Chapter 14 (Features RI-31, RI-32, RI-33).

Exercises

7.1 What relational objects can you create, rename, and drop using the DBA commands?

7.2 Why are the following two properties considered to be columnar, rather than domain-oriented?
1. Whether values are permitted to be missing from the pertinent column.
2. Whether all the values in the column are required to be distinct from one another.

Give examples of a type of domain, and two types of columns based on it, to support your argument.

7.3 Consider the task of appending new columns to two of the base relations. Is it necessary first to bring all the traffic to a halt? If not, explain how RM/V2 handles this problem.

7.4 Are there any commands in RM/V2 for keeping indexes consistent with whatever columns of data are indexed? Can semantic properties, such as uniqueness of values or keyhood, be associated with indexes? Explain your answer.

7.5 What is a domain-based index? How can it help improve the speed of execution of joins and of referential-integrity checks? (See also Chapter 13.)

7.6 If the occurrence of duplicate rows within a relation is banned by the relational model, why is the CONTROL DUPLICATE ROWS command needed (1) to check the existence of duplicate rows and (2) to remove the redundant duplicate rows?

7.7 What is an important reason for requiring that a user-defined function comes into effect during loading or unloading data? Does RM/V2 require such a function to be invoked when using the LOAD or EXTRACT command (Features RE-18 and RE-19), or is this optional?

CHAPTER 8

Missing Information

The purpose of this chapter is to clarify and summarize the way missing information is treated in Version 2 of the relational model. The clarification places heavy emphasis on the semantic aspects of missing information. The systematic approach of RM/V1 has been extended in RM/V2 to deal with the inapplicability of certain properties to some objects. Once again, this treatment is independent of the data type of the missing information. This extension does not invalidate any part of RM/V1.

In RM/V2 the approach to manipulating information from which values may be missing represents my current thinking about this problem. I do not feel this part of the relational model rests on such a solid theoretical foundation as the other parts. However, I do think that this approach represents a considerable improvement over the prerelational methods that amounted to leaving it up to application programmers to solve it in many different and specialized ways (even within a single installation).

8.1 ■ Introduction to Missing Information

In Section 2 of my paper on the extended model RM/T [Codd 1979], I included an account of *how* the basic relational model RM/V1 represents and handles missing information, but gave very little emphasis to *why* that approach was adopted. Included in that discussion of the manipulation of missing information was an account of the three-valued logic proposed for determining the possibilities if some of the missing information were conceptually and temporarily replaced by known values.

Criticisms have been fired at the three-valued logic approach of RM/V1. In its place, the critics propose, in effect, a return to the "good old days" when, for each column permitted to have missing information, the database administrator or some suitably authorized user is forced to select a specific value from the particular domain on which the column is defined to denote the fact that information in that column is missing.

The case for a logic having more than two truth-values is discussed in Sections 8.9 and 8.10. Criticisms are answered in Chapter 9.

In this chapter, the representation and handling of missing information are described according to the way such information is treated in RM/V2. This approach provides a stronger semantic underpinning than any nonrelational approach. One of the relatively new extensions in RM/V2 is the treatment of a property that is generally applicable to a class of objects, but inapplicable to certain members of that class. One example of such a property is the name of the spouse of each employee, when there may be a significant number of employees who are not married, and therefore have no spouse. Another example is the sales commission earned to-date in an EMPLOYEE relation, which deals with both salespeople and non-salespeople.

It is the meaning of the data that determines whether a database value is missing-but-applicable or missing-and-inapplicable. Thus, it is the database designer who should establish for each column of each relation whether missing values of each type are permitted or prohibited in that column. Sometimes a missing and inapplicable status can be derived from data found elsewhere in the database. For example, in the salesperson example, it is quite likely that the EMPLOYEE relation contains as another column the job type within the company or institution. From this datum, the DBMS can determine whether an elementary database value (db-value for brevity) is permitted or prohibited in the sales-commission column. This topic is discussed further in Chapters 13 and 14, which deal with integrity constraints.

The two types of missing information that are defined in Section 8.2 and stressed in this chapter are missing but applicable (denoted A) and missing and inapplicable (denoted I). Section 8.19 deals with operators that generate marks, and briefly discusses the relationship between (1) A and I applied to whole rows and (2) A and I applied to components of a row.

Figure 8.1 illustrates the kinds of information that can be missing. Later in this chapter, a description of how RM/V2 handles these two types of missing information, types A and I, is given.

The various technical criticisms of the RM/V1 approach to missing information that have recently come to my attention are discussed in detail in Chapter 9. That discussion includes some strong technical arguments against one proposed alternative, the scheme of "default values."

Figure 8.1 **Classification of Missing Information
in a Relational DBMS**

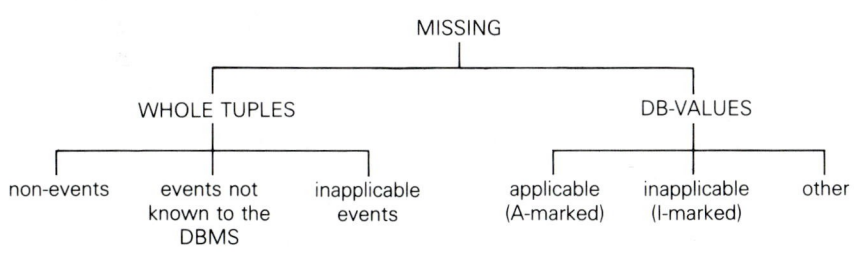

8.2 ▪ Definitions

In logic and in algebra, when the value or possible values of an item are unknown, a named variable is assigned to the item and it is usually called an *unknown*. Distinct items with unknown values are assigned variables with distinct names. Thus, a formula in logic or in algebra may involve several variables, and a common task in solving a problem is to find the values of these variables using a collection of equations.

In database management, the same approach *could* be followed. Thus, if a database contained information about employees and projects, *each occurrence* of an unknown birthdate of an employee and of an unknown start-date for a project could be recorded as a distinctly named variable.

Under certain circumstances, the DBMS might be able to deduce equality or inequality between two distinctly named variables, or to deduce certain other constraints on the variables. It would rarely be possible, however, for the DBMS to deduce the actual values of these variables. Instead, most of the unknown or missing-and-applicable items are eventually supplied by users in the form of late-arriving input or not-yet-completed calculation. On the other hand, those items marked missing-and-inapplicable behave more like unknowable items than like unknowns.

Note that in the few cases where it is conceivably possible for the DBMS to deduce actual values for missing information, the cost of such deduction is likely to be too expensive relative to the actual benefit. In the present version of the relational model, the potential complexities of using the variables of algebra or logic for missing information are avoided. Moreover, compared with pre-relational approaches, the RM/V2 approach continues to place more burden on the system and less on the application programmers and terminal users.

I have made *no* claim, now or in the past, that the relational approach to missing information places *no* burden at all on users. Any attempt, however, to put missing information on a systematic basis (i.e., an attempt that is uniformly applied to data whatever its type) will necessarily entail a learning burden. It is important that this learning burden should pay off in terms of a safer and more reliable treatment of databases, one that will strengthen the retention of database integrity.

As noted earlier, the term "elementary database value" is written as db-value for brevity. This term means any value that a single column may have in any relation. Except for certain special functions, a db-value is *atomic* in the context of the relational model. The term "datum" would have been preferred, but its plural, "data" has very broad use.

With regard to missing information, two questions seem dominant:

1. What kind of information is missing?
2. What is the main reason for its being missing?

In the relational approach, Question 1, regarding the kind of information, can be interpreted as a question concerning structural context: is the missing information a whole row, a component atomic value (a db-value) of a row, or a combination of these atomic values? There appears to be no need to consider the consequences of an entire relation being missing because a database necessarily models just a micro-world.

Moreover, the "main reason" in Question 2 can be interpreted to mean, "Is the information missing simply because its present value is unknown to the users, but that value is *applicable* and can be entered whenever it happens to be forthcoming? Or is it missing because it represents a property that is *inapplicable* to the particular object represented by the row involved?" Figure 8.1 summarizes the classification by kind (the structural context) and by reason.

In a certain row of a relation that describes the capabilities of suppliers, it may be recorded that supplier s3 is capable of supplying part p5, but the current price for this part is missing. This is an example of a missing-but-applicable value. In those rows of the EMPLOYEE relation that describe employees who are not legally married, the name of the employee's spouse is missing. This is an example of a missing-and-inapplicable value.

Note that, although there are many other ways to classify missing information, only the missing-but-applicable and missing-and-inapplicable types appear to justify general support by the DBMS at this time. In this context, "general" means independent of the particular column and of its domain or extended data type. Since DBMS users and even designers are not yet accustomed to using techniques of this generality for handling missing information, gradual introduction appears appropriate.

A basic principle of the relational approach to missing information is that of recording *the fact that a db-value is missing* by means of a *mark* (originally called a *null* or *null value*). There is nothing imprecise about a mark: a db-value is either present or absent in a column of a relation in the database.

The semantics of the fact that a db-value is missing are *not* the same as the semantics of the db-value itself. The former fact applies to any db-value, no matter what its type. The latter fact has semantics depending heavily on the domain (or extended data type) from which the column draws its values.

Like a variable, a mark is a placeholder. It does not, however, conform to the other accepted property of a variable—namely, that semantically distinct missing values are represented by distinctly named variables.

We begin with a definition of the *missing-but-applicable value mark* (for brevity, an A-mark). This mark is treated *neither* as a value *nor* as a variable by the DBMS, although it may be treated as a special kind of value by the host language. Consider an immediate property P of objects of type Z in a database. Normally P has a specific value in each and every row of that relation that provides the immediate properties of type Z objects. Suppose that, represented in the database, there is an object z of type Z and that, at this time, the value of P for this object is unknown. Then, P would be assigned an A-mark in the database, provided P is considered to be applicable to the object z. In the example introduced previously, Z is the capability of a supplier, z is the combination of supplier s3 and part p5, and P is the price that s3 charges for p5.

On the other hand, suppose that property P is inapplicable to the particular object z. Then P would be assigned an *inapplicable-value mark* (for brevity, an I-mark) in the row representing z. Thus, in the P column, each row contains a value for P *or* an A-mark *or* an I-mark. In the example cited previously, Z describes employees, z is any unmarried employee, and P is the name of the employee's spouse. Two more examples follow:

1. If an employee has a *missing-but-applicable* present salary, his or her record would have an A-mark in the salary column.

2. If an employee has an *inapplicable* sales commission (such an employee does not sell any products at this time), his or her record would have an I-mark in the commission column.

Sometimes the occurrence of an I-mark in one component of a row is based on data that occurs in other components of that row. In Example 2, both the job category and sales commission may be a component of each row of the EMPLOYEE relation. In that case, it is quite likely that inapplicability of the sales commission can be derived from the job category.

Why are these items now called "marks" rather than "values," "null values," or "nulls"? Four reasons follow:

1. The DBMS does not treat marks as if they were values.

2. There are now two kinds of marks, where there was previously just one kind of null.

3. Some host languages deal with objects called "nulls" that are quite different in meaning from database marks.

4. "Marked" and "unmarked" are better adjectives in English than are "nulled," "un-nulled," and "nullified."

To pursue the first reason, a mark in a numeric column (a column that normally has numeric values) cannot be arithmetically incremented or decremented by the DBMS, whereas the numeric values that are present can be subjected to such operators. To be more specific, if x denotes a db-value, A denotes an A-mark, and I denotes an I-mark, this is the effect of the arithmetic operator **addition:**

$$
\begin{array}{lll}
x + x = 2x & x + A = A & A + x = A \\
A + A = A & A + I = I & I + A = I \\
I + I = I & x + I = I & I + x = I
\end{array}
$$

A similar table holds for the three arithmetic operators **minus, times,** and **divide** (except that when both arguments are db-values the result is what one would expect from ordinary arithmetic). Similarly, a mark that appears in a character-string column (one that normally has character-string values) cannot have a second character-string concatenated with that mark by the DBMS, in contrast to the character-string values that are present in the database. A table similar to the one just given for addition also holds for concatenation. These remarks can be summarized as follows:

If I-marks are placed in the top class, A-marks in the second class, and all db-values in the third class, the combination (arithmetic or otherwise) of any two items is an item of whichever class is the higher of the two operands.

How, then, can these marks appear in a column that normally contains values? Present hardware is of little help: it fails to support any special treatment of marks as distinct from values. For the same reason, present host languages, such as COBOL and PL/1, are also of little help.

In the relational approach, one way to support marks by software is to assign a single extra byte to any column that is allowed to have applicable or inapplicable marks. This approach, adopted for A-marks in the IBM mainframe and mid-range relational DBMS products (DB2 and SQL/DS), appears to be fundamentally sound, although in these products some of the manipulative actions on marks should be cleaned up. Incidentally, criticisms of the way missing information is handled by SQL should not be interpreted or presented as criticisms of the relational model. Moreover, criticisms of SQL's treatment of missing information do not justify abandoning database nulls or marks.

The principal feature of RM/V2 pertaining to the way missing information is perceived by users is Feature RS-13 (see Chapter 2).

8.3 ■ Primary Keys and Foreign Keys of Base Relations

An important rule for relational databases is that, to maintain integrity, information about an unidentified (or inadequately identified) object is *never* recorded in these databases—a sharp contrast to non-relational databases. Thus, the declaration of exactly one primary key for each base relation is mandatory; it is not an optional feature. Moreover, the primary-key attribute is not permitted to include marks of either type (see Section 8.6). The pertinent RM/V2 feature is called *entity integrity* (Feature RI-3 in Chapter 13).

As an aside, the mere fact that such marks are prohibited from appearing in a column does not of itself make that column the primary-key attribute of a base relation. It is required that the catalog include an explicit declaration of the primary key of each base relation (see Feature RC-3 in Chapter 15).

A foreign key consists of one or more columns drawing its values from the domain (simple or composite), upon which at least one primary key is defined. In the case of composite foreign keys, it is possible that some, perhaps all, of the component values of a foreign key value are allowed to be A-marked (missing-but-applicable). This case needs special attention. Those *components of such a foreign key value that are unmarked should adhere to the referential-integrity constraint.* This detail is not supported in many of today's DBMS products, even when the vendors claim that their products support referential integrity.

I strongly recommend that database administrators or users consider very carefully the question of whether to permit or prohibit A-marks in foreign-key columns, and also that they document how and why that decision was made. Sometimes there will be a strong business case for prohibiting missing information altogether in foreign-key columns. However, reasons are presented in some detail in Section 4.3 for choosing to permit A-marks in these columns (see Features RB-33 and RB-34, the primary-key update operators). On the other hand, I-marks must be prohibited in all foreign-key columns in the entire database, because such a mark contradicts the foreign-key concept.

8.4 ■ Rows Containing A-marks and/or I-marks

According to Feature RI-12 in Chapter 13, any row containing nothing but A-marks and/or I-marks can and should be discarded by the DBMS from the relation in which it appears, no matter what the type of the relation. Such a row would be illegal in a *base relation,* because of the entity-integrity rule (see Section 8.6). Such a row does not bear information in any *derived relation,* whether it be a view, a query, a snapshot, or even an updated relation.

An external symbol is needed for the marks in several cases. Whenever such a symbol is needed, the following are suggested:

Type of Mark	A-mark	I-mark
External symbol	— or ??	!!

8.5 ■ Manipulation of Missing Information

Feature RM-10 in Chapter 12 is the RM/V2 feature of most importance with regard to manipulation of missing information. It calls for an approach that is uniform and systematic across the entire database. In particular, the approach is applicable to missing database values only, and must be independent of the data type of the missing information.

Features RM-11 and RM-12 in Chapter 12 specify the actions of arithmetic operators and concatenation on A-marked and I-marked values, respectively. Feature RJ-3 in Chapter 11 is an indicator that is turned on whenever a relational command encounters a missing db-value.

8.6 ■ Integrity Rules

There are two integrity rules that apply to every relational database:

1. Type E, *entity integrity*. No component of a primary key is allowed to have a missing value of any type. No component of a foreign key is allowed to have an I-marked value (missing-and-inapplicable).

2. Type R, *referential integrity*. For each distinct, unmarked foreign-key value in a relational database, there must exist in the database an equal value of a primary key from the same domain. If the foreign key is composite, those components that are themselves foreign keys and unmarked must exist in the database as components of at least one primary-key value drawn from the same domain.

A single instance of referential integrity is an example of an inclusion dependency. In the case of referential integrity, the set of distinct values in a foreign key must be a subset of the set of primary-key values drawn from the same domain. Casanova, Fagin, and Papadimitriou (1984) report interesting relationships between inclusion dependencies and functional dependencies.

It is important to observe that the entity-integrity and referential-integrity rules specify a *state* of integrity, not what *action* is to be taken by the system if an attempt is made to violate either rule. In the case of referential integrity, the DBMS should support *at least* three options:

1. refuse the command;
2. cascade the updates or deletes on the primary key values to all foreign keys defined on the same domain; **or**
3. replace each corresponding foreign-key value with an A-mark.

The DBMS rejects any attempts by users to replace each corresponding foreign-key value by an I-mark, since that would violate the second part of entity integrity.

This required choice of violation responses is the reason that the referential-integrity constraint should be supported in a general manner similar to that for user-defined integrity constraints (see Chapter 14), where a general choice of actions is also needed.

Finally, it should be possible for the DBA or any suitably authorized user to define additional special-purpose integrity constraints and the action to be taken if there is an attempted violation. These constraints are specific to the particular database involved.

If, as is usual, several columns take their values from a common domain, marks may occur in some of these columns and not in others. For example, a primary-key column is not permitted to contain any occurrences of either kind of mark, whereas (at the DBA's discretion) corresponding foreign-key columns (on the same domain) may be permitted to contain occurrences of the A-mark. Thus, declarations concerning whether a mark is permitted in or prohibited from a column should normally be associated with that column, not with the corresponding domain from which it draws its values.

8.7 ∎ Updating A-marks and I-marks

A-marks and I-marks are treated differently from one another with regard to updating. This difference stems from the fact that an A-mark indicates that a value is at present unknown, whereas an I-mark indicates that a value is in some sense unknowable, given the present state of the micro-world being modeled.

An A-mark in column C may be replaced by any db-value that complies with the domain constraints and column constraints declared for column C; this replacement may be carried out by any user authorized to make updates in column C. Similarly, any db-value in a column for which marks are permitted can be replaced by an A-mark.

An I-mark in column C may be replaced by an A-mark or by any actual value, provided that:

∎ the DBMS finds that the user has the necessary extra authorization; **and**

∎ pertinent integrity constraints are satisfied.

See Section 14.3 for more details.

In Figure 8.2, "*" means that extra authorization is needed as required by Feature RA-9 (see Chapter 18). The authorization mechanism requires that the user who replaces any database value or A-mark by the I-mark must have special authorization for this action. Such authorization is also required for any change from an I-mark in the reverse direction.

The I-mark is strictly stronger than the A-mark. Any user who is authorized to update values in a column is thereby permitted to change any active value into an A-marked value, or vice versa. However, changing any non-missing value *directly* into an I-marked value or vice versa, requires special authorization (enforced by the DBMS), because that would be a direct attempt to violate the meaning of an I-mark.

In the examples already cited, changing a price from missing-and-applicable to a specified value is no threat to the integrity of the database. On the other hand, changing an employee's sales commission from missing-but-inapplicable to a specified value could damage database integrity. Thus, an I-mark is treated as if it were an integrity constraint of a special kind—namely, one applied to selected objects rather than selected object types.

8.8 ■ Application of Equality

What does it mean to assert that one missing-but-applicable value equals another? Is it appropriate to speak of the equality of two inapplicable values? In other words, under what circumstances does equality make sense? The RM/V2 position is that there are two kinds of equality of marks to be considered: (1) *semantic equality,* in which the meaning participates heavily, and (2) *symbolic (or formal) equality,* in which the meaning is ignored.

With regard to semantic equality, a factor that must be taken into account is how applicable and inapplicable values are expected to be used. Their uses are quite different in nature. In fact, the truth-value of

A-mark = I-mark

is FALSE with respect to both types of equality.

How about equality between any two occurrences of the *same type of mark?* Since the symbol is the same in both cases, the two occurrences are symbolically equal. The question of semantic equality, however, needs more detailed investigation, and is discussed in the next section.

Figure 8.2 **State Diagram Specifying Permitted Updates**

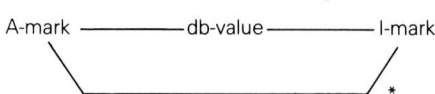

8.8.1 Missing-but-Applicable Information

Missing-but-applicable information presents the opportunity to ask what might be true if one or more missing values were to be temporarily replaced by actual values. Frequently, "what-if" databases must be developed and manipulated separately from the so-called operational databases. This occurs because the former represent *what might be the case* if certain events were to take place in the future (in the business or in its environment), while the latter represent *reality*. Accordingly, updates in the "what-if" databases must be regarded as representing conceptual actions (analytical, planning, or projecting into the future). An important advantage of the A-marks is that some of the analysis can be carried out directly on the operational data without making any conceptual updates.

Suppose a database includes information about employees, including each employee's birthdate. Suppose also that birthdate is one of the immediate, single-valued properties of an employee that is allowed to be temporarily missing for one or more employees. It is quite possible that when an employee's birthdate is unknown, the actual value of this date may (eventually) prove to be *any* date that lies within the range of employee ages permitted by law and by company policy. Such a range of dates would be specified as a formula based on a variable representing the date of the current day. This formula would be included in the catalog declarations for the specific column (quite likely) or in the catalog declarations for the domain from which this column draws its values (less likely).

In this case, the set of possible values is quite large. In general, however, *whether the set of possible values for a property is large or small,* there must be at least two possibilities—otherwise, the property's value would be known. It would therefore be a mistake to expect the value TRUE when evaluating a logical condition that involves semantically comparing either one missing-but-applicable value with another or one such missing value with a known or specified value. For example, what is the truth value of the inequality

BIRTHDATE > 66-1-1

for a missing birthdate? It is clearly neither TRUE nor FALSE. Instead, it can be said to be MAYBE (meaning maybe true and maybe false; the DBMS does not know which holds). When focusing on the domain of truth-values, the logical truth-value MAYBE can be thought of as a value-oriented counterpart for the A-mark.

When represented by A-marks, two missing values possess marks that match one another symbolically, but not necessarily semantically. As time advances, the database is subjected to commands that modify the data. Thus, users and/or programs may eventually replace these two marks by different values.

8.8.2 Inapplicable Information

A natural subsequent question is, "Must the systematic treatment of in-applicable values cause an additional extension of the underlying three-valued logic to a four-valued logic?" Such an extension is logically necessary, and it now seems appropriate to introduce it as part of the relational model.

At first glance, it appears to make sense to handle equality between two inapplicable-value marks just like equality between two actual values. Note, however, that I-marks are neither values nor placeholders for values. They mean *unknowable* rather than *unknown*. Thus, within the condition part of a relational-language statement, whenever an I-mark is equated to an actual value, an A-mark, or an I-mark, the truth-value of such a condition is always taken to be MAYBE of type INAPPLICABLE.

8.9 ■ The Three-Valued Logic of RM/V1

A database retrieval may, of course, include several conditions like BIRTH-DATE > 66-1-1, and the conditions may be combined in many different logical combinations, including the logical connectives AND, OR, NOT and the quantifiers UNIVERSAL and EXISTENTIAL. (See the explanation at the end of Section 4.2, dealing with relational division, and the works listed in the predicate logic part of the Reference section.)

Suppose, as an example, that a second immediate property recorded for each employee is the present salary of that employee. Suppose also that this column is allowed to have missing db-values. How does the DBMS deal with a query involving the combination of conditions

$$(\text{BIRTHDATE} > 66\text{-}1\text{-}1) \lor (\text{SALARY} < 20{,}000),$$

where either the birthdate condition or the salary condition or both may evaluate to MAYBE? Clearly, the DBMS must know the truth-value of MAYBE or TRUE, TRUE or MAYBE, and MAYBE or MAYBE.

From this it can be seen that *there is a clear need in any systematic treatment of missing values to extend the underlying two-valued predicate logic to at least three-valued predicate logic.*

In the following truth-tables for the three-valued logic of RM/V1, P and Q denote propositions, each of which may have any one of the following truth-values:

t for true *or* m for maybe *or* f for false.

The truth values t, m, f are actual values, and should not be confused with marked values or the MAYBE qualifiers (see Table 8.1).

In the relational model, the universal and existential quantifiers are applied over finite sets only. Thus, the universal quantifier behaves like the logic operator AND, and the existential quantifier behaves like OR. Both

Table 8.1 **The Truth Tables of Three-Valued Logic**

				Q				Q	
P	**not P**	**P $\vee$ Q**	**t**	**m**	**f**	**P $\wedge$ Q**	**t**	**m**	**f**
t	f	t	t	t	t	t	t	m	f
m	m	P m	t	m	m	P m	m	m	f
f	t	f	t	m	f	f	f	f	f

operators are extended to apply the specified condition to each and every member of the pertinent set.

When an entire condition based on three-valued, first-order predicate logic is evaluated, the result can be any one of the three possibilities TRUE, MAYBE, or FALSE. If such a condition is part of a query that does not include the MAYBE option, the result consists of all the cases in which this condition evaluates to TRUE, and no others.

If in this query the keyword MAYBE is applied to the whole condition, then the result consists of all the cases in which this condition evaluates to MAYBE, and no others. This qualifier is used only for exploring possibilities; special authorization would be necessary for a user to incorporate it in one of his or her programs or in a terminal interaction.

One problem of which DBMS designers and users should be aware is that in rare instances the condition part of a query may be a tautology. In other words, it may have the value TRUE no matter what data is in the pertinent columns and no matter what data is missing. An example is the following condition pertaining to employees (where B denotes BIRTHDATE):

$$(B < 66\text{-}1\text{-}1) \vee (B = 66\text{-}1\text{-}1) \vee (B > 66\text{-}1\text{-}1).$$

However, if the DBMS were to apply three-valued logic to each term and it encountered a marked value in the birthdate column, each of the terms in this query condition would receive the truth-value MAYBE. MAYBE OR MAYBE yields the truth-value MAYBE. Thus, the condition as a whole evaluates to MAYBE, which is incorrect, but not traumatically incorrect.

There are two options:

1. warn users not to use tautologies as conditions in their relational-language statements (tautologies waste the computer's resources);

2. develop a DBMS that examines all conditions not in excess of some clearly specified complexity, and determines whether each condition is a tautology or not.

Naturally, in this latter case, it would be necessary to place some limitation on the complexity of each and every query, because with predicate logic the general problem is unsolvable. In my opinion, option 1 is good enough for now because this is not a burning issue.

8.10 ■ The Four-Valued Logic of RM/V2

Consider an example of a combination (either by AND, or by OR) of two logical conditions used in selecting employees:

(birthdate > 50-1-1) AND/OR (commission > 1000).

Suppose that, for a particular employee, the first condition evaluates to the truth-value missing-and-applicable and the second to missing-and-inapplicable. What is the truth-value of the whole condition?

Clearly, the truth tables of four-valued logic must be examined. In the following tables (Table 8.2), t stands for true, f for false, i for *missing-and-inapplicable*, and a for *missing-and-applicable*. Note that t, a, i, f are actual values, and should not be confused with marked values.

Note that we obtain the truth tables of the three-valued logic by replacing i by m *and* a by m (where m simply stands for missing, and the reason for anything being missing is ignored). It should be clear that four-valued logic is more precise but more complicated than three-valued logic. Four-valued logic is selected as an integral part of RM/V2 (see Feature RM-10 in Chapter 12).

If a DBMS vendor feels that the extra complexity of four-valued logic is not justifiable at this time, the external specifications of its DBMS product should permit expansion at a later time from three-valued to four-valued logic support without affecting users' investment in application programming, or with only a minimal impact. If four-valued logic is built into a DBMS product initially or as an extension, either it should agree with the four-valued logic just described, or its departures should be defended in writing from a technical and practical standpoint.

Table 8.2 The Truth Tables of Four-Valued Logic

P	not P	P ∨ Q	Q t	Q a	Q i	Q f	P ∧ Q	Q t	Q a	Q i	Q f
t	f		t	t	t	t		t	a	i	f
a	a	P a	t	a	a	a	P a	a	a	i	f
i	i	i	t	a	i	i	i	i	i	i	f
f	t	f	t	a	i	f	f	f	f	f	f

A repetition of the warning about multi-valued logics that I included in [Codd 1986a, 1987a] may be appropriate here. Such logics can yield the truth-value MAYBE for an expression that happens to be TRUE because it happens to be a tautology. For example, find the employees whose birth year is 1940 or prior to 1940 or after 1940. Every employee should be assigned the value TRUE for this condition, even if his or her birth year happens to be missing! This warning applies to other multi-valued logics. It may be necessary in the future for DBMS products to be equipped with detection algorithms for simple tautologies of this kind.

8.11 ■ Selects, Equi-joins, Inequality Joins, and Relational Division

The manner in which algebraic **selects, equi-joins, inequality joins,** and **relational division** treat A-marks and I-marks is determined by the semantic treatment of equality described in Section 8.8. An **inequality join** is a special kind of join using the inequality comparator NOT EQUAL TO.

Thus, whenever an **equi-join** involves comparing two items for equality, and either just one of them is a mark or both of them are marks of the same type (both A or both I), the pertinent rows are glued together *if and only if* the MAYBE qualifier has been specified.

Suppose that a query Q does not include the MAYBE qualifier. Then, executing Q delivers only those cases in which the condition part of Q evaluates to TRUE. To obtain a result from this query that includes all the TRUE cases and all the MAYBE cases, it is necessary to apply the **union** operator: Q **union** (Q MAYBE).

8.12 ■ Ordering of Values and Marks

Ordering should be handled in a manner similar to that described for equality. There are two kinds of ordering to be considered: *semantic ordering* and *symbolic ordering*. The semantic version applies when using a less-than condition or a greater-than condition in a statement of a relational data sublanguage. The symbolic version applies when using the ORDER BY clause (e.g., to determine how a report is to be ordered). Let us consider symbolic ordering first.

The present ordering as implemented in DB2 in the ORDER BY clause of SQL involves nulls (i.e., A-marks) representing missing-and-applicable values. (The case of inapplicable values is not yet handled at all by the language SQL or by the DB2 system.) DB2 places nulls at the high end of the value-ordering scale. In order to be compatible with this ordering, A-marks are placed at the high end, immediately after values. On top of A-marks are the new I-marks. This is the *symbolic (or formal) ordering*.

Note that inapplicable information in a particular column *could* be supported in extended SQL by requiring the DBA or a suitably authorized user to declare a value from the pertinent domain as the one to represent such inapplicability for a given column. I definitely advocate, however, that this approach *not* be taken. For one thing, this approach would implicitly and potentially define as many different orderings for the missing db-values relative to the existing db-values as there are columns that are allowed to have missing db-values. Instead, I believe it is more systematic and more uniform across different data types to use a special mark (the I-mark) because these marks are not database values.

Now let us consider the *semantic ordering*. The truth-value of each of the following expressions is MAYBE (not TRUE)

$$(\text{db-value} < \text{mark}) \, , \, (\text{mark} < \text{db-value}) \, , \, (\text{mark} < \text{mark})$$

for any type of mark and any db-value. The same applies to these expressions if the symbol "<" is replaced by the symbol ">". If such an expression involves either one or two occurrences of marks, the truth-value of the expression is MAYBE.

There has been some criticism that the symbolic ordering of marks relative to values runs counter to the semantic ordering and the application of three- or four-valued logic. I fail to see any problem, however, because the use of truth-valued conditions involving ordering when applying a relational data sublanguage is at a higher level of abstraction than the use of the ordering of marks relative to values in the ORDER BY clause of a relational command (see Feature RQ-7 in Chapter 10).

8.13 ■ Joins Involving Value-ordering

Joins involving the comparators

LESS THAN OR EQUAL TO

LESS THAN

GREATER THAN OR EQUAL TO

GREATER THAN

treat applicable and inapplicable marks as determined by the usual orderings of db-values and the semantic ordering of marks defined in the immediately preceding section. If the MAYBE qualifier does not accompany the request for a **join,** then (as usual) only those items are generated for each of which the entire pertinent condition has the truth-value TRUE. On the other hand, if the MAYBE qualifier is applied to the entire condition part in the command, only those items are generated for each of which the entire pertinent condition has the truth-value MAYBE.

Consider a database that includes two relations T1 and T2 that describe events of type 1 and type 2, respectively; the description includes the date of occurrence of each event. Suppose that a request is made that involves pairing off events of type 1 with events of type 2, provided the type 1 event occurs before the type 2 event. Such a pairing activity can be expressed in terms of a **join** of T1 on the date of the type 1 event with T2 on the date of the type 2 event using the comparator $<$.

For the sake of simplicity, suppose that the extensions of T1 and T2 are as follows:

T1 (E#	EDATE	. . .	)
e1	88-02-14		
e2	86-03-22		
e3	—	(A-marked)	
e4	88-12-27		

T2 (V#	VDATE	. . .)
v1	86-03-13	
v2	89-01-27	
v3	87-08-19	

Also suppose that two requests are as follows:

T ← T1 [EDATE < VDATE] T2
T″ ← T1 [EDATE < VDATE] T2 MAYBE.

Then, the derived relations T and T″ are as follows:

T (E#	EDATE	V#	VDATE)
e1	88-02-14	v2	89-01-27
e2	86-03-22	v2	89-01-27
e2	86-03-22	v3	87-08-19
e4	88-12-27	v2	89-01-27

T″ (E#	EDATE	V#	VDATE)
e3	—	v1	86-03-13
e3	—	v2	89-01-27
e3	—	v3	87-08-19

8.14 ■ Scalar Functions Applied to Marked Arguments

In this context, a *scalar function* is a function that transforms scalar arguments into a scalar result. Consider the effect of such a function when one or more of its arguments is marked.

In general, if the strongest mark on one of its arguments is I, then the scalar result is I-marked. If, on the other hand, the strongest mark is A, then the scalar result is A-marked.

For example, let @ denote any one of the arithmetic operators $+, -, \times$, /, and let z denote an unmarked scalar argument. Then:

z @ a = a   z @ i = i   a @ z = a   i @ z = i
a @ a = a   a @ i = i   i @ a = i   i @ i = i

The functions NEGATION, OR, and AND are not exceptions to this general rule because of the distinction (noted in Section 8.9) between the truth values a and i, on the one hand, and marked truth values (A-marked and I-marked), on the other.

8.15 ■ Criticisms of Arithmetic on Marked Values

Occasionally one must be careful when asking a computer to carry out ordinary arithmetic: One should not request it to divide any number by zero. For example, if each customer can make several partial payments instead of one lump sum, one might ask a question such as "What is the average payment made by each customer?" This seemingly innocent question can cause the machine to complain every time a customer is encountered who has made no payments at all, because it is then being asked to divide zero by zero.

The same kind of remark holds for arithmetic operations upon values from columns in which the value-inapplicable mark may occur. Suppose the employee relation contains two columns:

1. the total salary earned to date;
2. the commission earned to date.

Suppose also that for some employees the commission is marked inapplicable. Consider the request "What is the total income earned to date for each employee?", where total income is equal to salary (always applicable) plus commission (if applicable). If this is carelessly expressed as salary plus commission, the answer for any employee who has an inapplicable commission is inapplicable, using the table for addition shown on page 174. What is needed in this case is that the amount added for commission should be zero when the commission is applicable.

The first reaction often heard is that, instead of the commission being marked inapplicable, it should be set to zero. One problem this action would cause is that the DBMS might not (and very probably would not) be able to distinguish between a case in which commission was inapplicable and a case in which it was applicable but the employee had actually earned zero commission to date. Moreover, in this case virtually every integrity constraint that involved the inapplicable state for a value in the commission column could not be expressed.

A second claim often heard is that the addition table is incorrect, and the entry $x + I = I$ should be replaced by $x + I = x$. While this might be appropriate for this example, consider a second example. Suppose one requested Q1, the average commission earned by employees, when one really intended to request Q2, the average commission earned by those employees entitled to earn commissions. If there do exist some employees who are entitled to earn commission, and if the cases of commission being inapplicable are each represented by the value zero, execution of Q1 delivers an incorrect result without any alarm from the computer. If, however, the cases of inapplicability are represented by I-marks, then execution of Q1 delivers an I-mark and that will alert the user to his or her folly.

8.16 ■ Application of Statistical Functions

In applying a statistical function to the db-values in one or more columns of a relation, it is desirable to be able to specify how A-marks and I-marks are to be treated by this function, if it should encounter either type of mark. A practical approach is to support two temporary replacements: one for the A-mark occurrences and another for the I-mark occurrences.

A convenient way of expressing the replacement action is by means of two separate, single-argument functions: AR (which stands for A-mark replacement) and IR (I-mark replacement). In each case, the single argument is a scalar constant or a scalar function that operates upon other component values in the row being examined and delivers a scalar value. The pertinent features of RM/V2 are RQ-4 and RQ-5 (see Chapter 10).

The function or qualifier specifying the replacement is called the *substitution qualifier*. This qualifier is applicable to every kind of statistical function. However, if the statistical function has two or more arguments and these are applied to two or more columns, the specified replacement action must apply to all of these attributes.

An example of practical use of this qualifier is the calculation of a salary budget for each department based on the present salary of each member of a department. If a few salaries are missing (and therefore A-marked), one may wish to compute the total for each department by requesting that each A-mark occurrence be replaced temporarily by the maximum salary of those persons known by the DBMS to be members of that department.

In certain special cases, the two replacements may be values equal to one another. In certain other special cases, one or both of the replacements may be a mark identical to the mark being replaced. The need for this case is determined by the default action for omitted substitution qualifiers being specified as "ignore marks of the corresponding type."

Note that the state of the database is not changed by the execution of any one of these statistical functions alone. In other words, the substitutions replacing marks by values or by marks are in effect during, and only during, the execution of the pertinent statistical function. One advantage of making these substitutions temporary is that certain kinds of possibilities can be investigated without setting up a separate "what-if" database.

If the substitution qualifier is omitted altogether from a statistical function request, the DBMS would assume that *only the unmarked values should contribute to the result*. On the other hand, if the existence of any occurrence of a mark of type q in the operand is to yield an A-mark as the result, there must be a qualifier in the command requesting that marks of type q be detected, but not modified in the temporary substitution sense (i.e., a mark of type q should be replaced by itself).

Notice that any replacement action specified in this way is a replacement of a marked *argument* of the function, not of any *result* the function might deliver. Moreover, the specified scalar replacement(s) must be values belonging to the domain from which that column draws its values, and must comply with any additional constraints that have been declared for that specific column.

Finally, any specific replacement action applies to just one of the columns cited in the retrieval or update command. Of course, several of the columns cited may be subject to replacement actions. In general, if N columns are cited in a relational command, there may be as many as $2N$ replacement actions specified in that command, two for each distinct citation.

Thus, a single pair of occurrences of replacement qualifiers (one for I-marked values, one for A-marked values) for each command is generally inadequate. It should be replaced by a pair of replacement qualifiers for each column cited in any pertinent command. The syntax must allow one pair to be specified for each statistical function cited, and unambiguously associate that pair with the pertinent function.

Little has been said about the results generated by the scalar and aggregate functions discussed in this section and Section 8.17. Feature RF-8 in Chapter 19 specifies that marked values are not generated by scalar and aggregate functions when acting upon unmarked arguments.

8.17 ■ Application of Statistical Functions to Empty Sets

This issue, raised by critics, is not directly related to the subject of missing values. Nevertheless, I touched upon it in Section 2.5 of [Codd 1986a] because SQL happens to generate null as the result of applying certain statistical functions (such as AVERAGE) to an empty set. Since the null of SQL was introduced to denote the fact that a db-value is unknown, it is an unwise choice now to mean something entirely different—namely, that an arithmetic result is undefined. This topic is clarified in more detail here, but only with respect to the relational model, not SQL.

Section 9.5 deals with the case of applying a statistical function to a collection of sets, some of which are empty and some non-empty. We must treat the extreme case where all the sets are empty (even if there is only one set in the collection of sets), and in such a way that all these cases behave in a consistent way. As a first step, an initial value of zero must be established immediately before the evaluation of the pertinent function against the specified sets.

If the empty-set qualifier is omitted from a command, each occurrence of an empty set is ignored. In addition to the value returned, however, there must be a trigger (known as the *empty trigger*) that is turned on whenever at least one set encountered in the execution of this command is empty.

Suppose that the *value* returned, whenever a statistical function is applied to a single empty set, is the initial value just cited, that is, zero. A special case needs careful attention to avoid misinterpretation of the value returned. Whenever (1) a statistical function is cited in a command, (2) this function (for example, AVERAGE) happens to require dividing by the number of elements in the pertinent set, and (3) the value returned by the function is zero for one or more of the sets, then it is normally necessary to examine each of these sets for its possible emptiness. Such an examination would distinguish the empty-set case from the case in which the statistical function happened to generate zero from elements actually encountered in the set. The reader should remember that the burden of this extra examination arises from ordinary integer arithmetic, in which dividing by zero is unacceptable. The burden of this extra examination is therefore *not* a consequence of the relational model.

Moreover, the relational model is consistent with elementary arithmetic. Every DBMS based on that model should also be consistent with elementary arithmetic.

Marks in the relational model are intended to represent the fact that information (more precisely, a db-value) is missing, and should be sharply distinguished from the case in which the value of a function (such as arithmetic division) is undefined.

8.18 ■ Removal of Duplicate Rows

Unfortunately, in many present releases of relational DBMS products, derived relations (often loosely called tables) are corrupted by leaving duplicate rows in them unless the user appends an explicit qualifier requesting that these duplicate rows be removed. A common example of this problem occurs in a corrupted projection that does not happen to include the primary key of the operand relation.

Although it is possible in SQL for the user to specify explicitly that all but one occurrence of any duplicate rows be removed, the user can choose to retain duplicate rows because he or she is unaware of the consequences. Users should not be burdened with this choice, and the DBMS optimizer should not be impaired by permitting duplicate rows under any circumstances.

If two or more rows happen to contain the same actual values and no marks (applicable or inapplicable), the removal of duplicate rows is obvious. The interesting case for this chapter is that in which some of the values are missing.

In this case, suppose that a typical pair of row components for which equality is to be tested is $< x,y >$. Then, it seems reasonable to assert that two rows are duplicates of one another, if one of the following conditions is satisfied by every pair tested:

1. x and y are actual values and x = y, **or**

2. one of the pair is marked and the other is not, **or**

3. both x and y are marked, and the marks are *symbolically equal* (i.e., both values are A-marked or both are I-marked),

and if condition 1 is satisfied by at least one tested pair of components. When duplicate rows are discovered by the DBMS, it should remove all but one occurrence of the duplicate rows.

As an example, consider a relation EMP that identifies and describes employees:

EMP	(EMP#	ENAME	DEPT#	SALARY	H_CITY	)
	E107	Rook	D12	10,000	Wimborne	
	E912	Knight	— A	12,000	Poole	
	E239	Knight	— A	12,000	Poole	
	E575	Pawn	D12	— A	Poole	
	E123	King	D01	15,000	Portland	
	E224	Bishop	— A	— A	Weymouth	

"— A" denotes a missing-and-applicable value. Suppose the relation E is derived from EMP by true projection (not the corrupted variety) onto DEPT# and SALARY:

E ← EMP [DEPT#, SALARY].

Before and after the removal of duplicate rows and empty rows, the following information is derived (the user sees only the AFTER version):

BEFORE → AFTER

E'	(DEPT#	SALARY)		E	(DEPT#	SALARY)	
	D12	10,000			D12	10,000	
*	— A	12,000			— A	12,000	#
**	— A	12,000			D12	— A	##
	D12	— A			D01	15,000	
	D01	15,000					
***	— A	— A					

The rows labeled "*" and "**" are treated as duplicates of one another because the corresponding components in these rows constitute the following:

■ pairs of equal db-values, and *there exists at least one pair of this type;*
■ pairs in which a db-value is accompanied by a missing value.

The row labeled "***" is removed because it consists of nothing but missing values. Note that the rows marked "#" and "##" are not treated as duplicates because of the lack of at least one pair of corresponding components that have equal values.

There has been some criticism of the fact that this scheme for removal of duplicate rows does not conform to the *semantic notions of equality* described in Section 8.8. I fail to see any problem, however, because the semantic notions of equality are applicable at a higher level of abstraction than the symbolic equality involved in removal of duplicate rows.

8.19 ■ Operator-generated Marks

The introduction of a new column C for a selected base relation R is achieved by appending to the catalog a description of this column. This causes the DBMS to record in R itself an A-mark in column C for each row in R. It does not make sense to record the I-mark because it is senseless to assert that every value in a column is unknowable—in that case, why have the column at all?

The operators **outer join** and **outer union** are capable of generating derived relations in which some of the columns have one or more missing db-values. Which type of mark should the DBMS generate? It seems reasonable to generate A-marks only. If a suitably authorized user believes that I-marks are needed instead, he or she will have to replace some A-marks by I-marks.

Note that A-marks are weaker than I-marks in that a user requires no special authorization beyond the usual update authorization if he or she wishes to update an A-mark into a db-value (see Section 8.7).

Moreover, it is easier for the user to delve into "what-if" kinds of interactions on the relation wherever A-marks occur, since in these cases he or she need not get special authorization beyond that for querying.

The question has been raised of why those operators that are capable of generating new marks in the result create only A-marks, never I-marks. (In this context, "new marks" mean marks not simply copied into the result from one or other of the operands.) The answer is that A-marks are preferred because they are the weaker and more flexible of the two types. Hence, they are more readily changed by users, without needing any special mark-type-change authorization.

8.20 ■ Some Necessary Language Changes

Here several minor language aspects are covered together, even though most are discussed elsewhere in this book. An example is the use of the MAYBE qualifier on a condition, whenever only those items are needed for which this condition evaluates to MAYBE. Note that, in order to support this qualifier, the DBMS must be able to handle either three-valued or four-valued logic (including the truth tables).

Moreover, if the items X are needed for which the condition K evaluates to either TRUE or MAYBE, then a command such as

(X where K) ∪ (X where K MAYBE)

should be used. Further, if the DBMS supports four-valued logic, then two additional qualifiers, MAYBE__A and MAYBE__I, are needed to specify for a given truth-valued expression which of the truth-values a and i are to replace the truth-value t as the truth-value that qualifies values to be retrieved. MAYBE__A means maybe true, maybe false, but certainly applicable, while MAYBE__I means neither true nor false, but inapplicable.

Also note that, because the MAYBE qualifiers apply to conditions that may involve negation, OR, AND, the existential quantifier, and the universal quantifier, they require that the DBMS handle four-valued logic internally, and *not* put that burden on users, as does the present version of SQL. The MAYBE qualifiers are described in Features RQ-1–RQ-3 in Chapter 10.

In the following discussion, changes in language are expressed as changes to SQL. It should be a simple matter to adapt them to any other reasonably complete, relational data sublanguage.

It is necessary to be able to refer to marks that are similar to the way SQL presently refers to nulls, except that the user should be allowed to distinguish between the two types of marks when he or she wishes to do so.

One user-friendly solution that is *not* being advocated is to introduce the clauses shown in Table 8.3 to refer to the presence and absence of an A-mark, an I-mark, or either type of mark (in case the user does not care which type of mark is involved). These clauses are not part of RM/V2 because the MAYBE__A, MAYBE__I, and MAYBE qualifiers of Features RQ-1–RQ-3 are more powerful. The SQL clauses IS NULL and IS NOT NULL should be abandoned swiftly.

Here is an example using the clauses listed in Table 8.3:

1. find the employees who are eligible to receive sales commissions; **and**
2. find the employees who are ineligible to receive sales commissions.

In many companies, query 1 is much more likely than query 2, because usually only a minority of employees are eligible for such commissions. In pseudo-SQL, appropriate statements for these queries would be as follows:

1. SELECT serial__number FROM employees
   WHERE commission IS NOT I-MARKED

2. SELECT serial__number FROM employees
   WHERE commission IS I-MARKED

Table 8.3 **Possible Clauses for Simple Conditions**

Type	Presence of Mark	Absence of Mark
A-mark	Is A-marked	Is not A-marked
I-mark	Is-I-marked	Is not I-marked
Either	Is missing	Is not missing

Additional needs are the substitution qualifiers AR and IR, when applying a statistical function to any column in which marks may occur (see Section 8.16), and the empty set qualifier ESR, when applying a statistical function to a collection of sets, some of which may be empty (see Section 9.5).

8.21 ■ Normalization

The concepts and rules of functional dependence, multi-valued dependence, and join dependence were developed without considering missing db-values. Early papers on functional dependence were [Codd 1971b and 1971c]. A comparatively recent paper on these dependencies is [Beeri, Fagin, and Howard 1977].

All the normal forms based on these dependencies were also developed without considering missing db-values. Does the possible presence of marks in some columns (each mark indicating the fact that a db-value is missing) undermine all these concepts, and theorems based on them? Fortunately, the answer is no: a mark is not itself a db-value. More specifically, a mark in column C is semantically different from the db-values in C. Thus, the normalization concepts *do not* apply and *should not* be applied globally to those combinations of columns and rows containing marks. Instead, they should be applied as follows:

■ the normalization concepts should be applied to a conceptual version of the database in which rows containing missing-but-applicable information in the pertinent columns have been removed;

■ these concepts should also be applied when any attempt is made to replace a mark by a db-value.

When an attempt is made to insert a new row into a relation and a certain component db-value is missing, it is pointless for the system to base acceptance or rejection of this row on whether the missing db-value *does meet or might meet or fails to meet* certain integrity constraints based on a dependence in which the pertinent column is involved. The proper time for the system to make this determination is when an attempt is made to replace the pertinent mark by an actual db-value.

One might be tempted to treat I-marks differently from A-marks. One or more users, however, may be authorized to replace an I-mark by a db-value. Thus, all marks should be treated alike, regardless of type, in the matter of testing any dependence constraint, whether it be functional, multi-valued, join, or inclusion. For every row that contains a mark in the column or columns being tested, the DBMS should wait until an attempt is made to replace the marked item(s) by an actual db-value.

A fully relational DBMS should have the capability of storing (in its catalog) statements defining the various kinds of dependencies—including the functional, multi-valued, join, and inclusion types of dependencies—as they apply to the particular database being managed.

A program should also be available to deduce all the dependencies that are a consequence of those supplied by the DBA or other suitably authorized users, so that, when attempting to change a mark into a db-value, no dependence that is logically implied by others is overlooked by the DBMS. Further, such a DBMS should be able to check the database against one or more of these integrity constraints whenever necessary, and without explicit invocation by an application program. In general, such checking is likely to be necessary whenever a mark is replaced by a db-value.

Exercises

8.1 Does the relational model use a specially reserved numeric value to represent the fact that a numeric database value is missing? Does it use a specially reserved character-string to represent the fact that a character-string database value is missing? Give reasons for your answers.

8.2 In RM/V2, what are the two main reasons for values being missing from a database? Is the NULL term in SQL capable of distinguishing between these reasons? If your answer is yes, explain how this would be accomplished by means of two examples.

8.3 The comment is frequently made that "nulls are a headache; who needs them?" Take a position on nulls (marked values) and three- or four-valued logic versus special values reserved by users to mean that a value is missing. Now defend that position from the viewpoints of technical soundness and usability by the community of users.

8.4 Do the three-valued logic in RM/V1 and the four-valued logic in RM/V2 preserve the commutativity of AND and OR?

8.5 Supply the truth table for four-valued logic.

8.6 The MAYBE qualifiers apply to (1) the whole condition part of a query, (2) a truth-valued expression, and (3) part of a query that refers to just a single column. Which of these represents the generality of scope most accurately? Give one example of the use of the MAY-BE_A qualifier, and one example of the use of the MAYBE_I qualifier.

8.7 Which of the three alternatives in Exercise 8.6 represents the generality of scope of the IS NULL phrase in present versions of the language SQL?

8.8 You are applying a statistical function to a column that is allowed to contain missing values. You want each missing value to be ignored. How is that accomplished?

8.9 You are applying a statistical function to a numeric column that is allowed to contain missing values. You want each A-marked value to be temporarily replaced by 399, and each I-marked value by 0. How is that accomplished?

8.10 The function AVERAGE is being applied to a numeric column in relation S. S happens to be empty. What kind of result is delivered by the relational model? By SQL?

CHAPTER 9

Response to Technical Criticisms Regarding Missing Information

There has been some justified technical criticism of the treatment of missing information in the data sublanguage SQL. Some of this criticism has been directed by mistake at the relational model [Codd 1986a, 1987c].

As explained in Chapter 1, it is important to distinguish between technical criticisms of the model, on the one hand, and of the implementations and products based on that model, on the other. With respect to the treatment of missing information, technical criticisms have strayed across the boundary without proper justification. I shall discuss criticisms that have appeared in recent technical articles, along with a counter-proposal called the *default value scheme* (for brevity, DV). I devote an entire chapter to dealing with these criticisms for two main reasons. First, the way the relational model deals with missing data appears to be one of its least understood parts. Second, discussion of these criticisms may help readers understand the approach and why it was adopted.

9.1 ■ The Value-oriented Misinterpretation

The representation in IBM relational DBMS products of *missing database values* in any column by means of an extra byte seems correct. In the IBM manuals, the corresponding marks are sometimes called *nulls* and sometimes called *null values*. Few of the ways in which these products process missing information, however, conform to Version 1 of the relational model. There are numerous cases in which the processing of nulls (more specifically,

A-marks) in the IBM product DB2 is non-systematic. These cases, however, should not be construed as criticisms of the relational model itself.

Any approach to the treatment of missing information should consider *what it means* for a db-value to be missing, including how such occurrences should be processed. A basic principle in the relational model is that the treatment of all aspects of shared data in databases is not just a representation issue. There are always other considerations which the DBMS must handle, especially the approach to manipulating the data and the preservation of database integrity.

It is quite inappropriate to leave these considerations to be handled by users in a variety of ways, and buried in a variety of application programs. This principle applies just as forcefully to missing information. Thus, *missing information is not just a representation issue.*

9.2 ■ The Alleged Counter-intuitive Nature

Consider the following examples: (1) suppliers in London and (2) suppliers not in London, where the CITY column for suppliers is allowed to have missing-but-applicable indicators (A-marks). One criticism of the relational model is that it requires the user to make the distinction between (1) "suppliers *known to the system* not to be in London" and (2) "suppliers not in London."

It has been asserted that this distinction is subtle and likely to mystify the user. Subtlety, however (like beauty), is in the eyes of the beholder. What is more important is that a user, in failing to make this very distinction, may cause serious errors, errors that could have serious consequences for the user's business.

In order to comment on the *default value scheme* (DV) [Date, 1986] for representing missing information, it is necessary to describe that approach first. In this scheme, if items of data are allowed to be missing in a column C, it is left to one or more users to declare that a particular value in C denotes the fact that a datum is missing in C. There is no constraint that all columns, in which missing values are permitted, must use the same representation of the fact that a value is missing. Moreover, the user who declares the "default value" for column C is expected to embody in his or her application program the method by which any missing values in column C are to be handled.

To return to the discussion of "suppliers known to the system not to be in London" and "suppliers not in London," this distinction may well be judged subtle by some users. However, even if the default value scheme were adopted, this would not prevent or help prevent the occurrence of the type of error in which the user fails to make this distinction.

Let us look at the example in more detail, demonstrating how the DV scheme constitutes a non-solution to the problem. Consider a relation S identifying suppliers and describing their immediate, single-valued properties. Let one of these properties be the city in which the supplier is based. A sample snapshot follows:

S	(S#	SNAME	CITY	. . .)
	s1	JONES	LONDON	. . .
	s2	SMITH	BRISTOL	. . .
	s3	DUPONT	v	. . .
	s4	EIFFEL	PARIS	. . .
	s5	GRID	v	. . .

"v" denotes a character string, declared in the catalog to be the "default value" for the column CITY in the relation S, which in the DV scheme means "unknown" or "missing" for this column only. Note that v may be *any* character string that does not represent the actual name of any existing city (e.g., "???" or "XXX").

Now consider these two queries:

Q1: Find the suppliers in London
Q2: Find the suppliers NOT in London

If these queries are represented in a relational language (such as ALPHA [Codd 1971a], SQL [IBM 1988], or QUEL [Relational Technology 1988]), ignoring the occurrences of v, and therefore ignoring the occurrences of missing db-values, the answer to Q1 would be s1. This answer is correct only if interpreted as those suppliers *known by the system* to be in London, since at any later time an occurrence of v may be updated to "LONDON." Q2 would similarly yield the set (s2, s3, s4, s5), which is *definitely incorrect* when interpreted as the suppliers known by the system not to be in London, and *potentially incorrect* when interpreted as the suppliers actually not in London.

Thus, the user of a DBMS equipped with the DV scheme *must* take into account whether a column is allowed to contain missing values, shaping the query accordingly, and differentiating in his or her thinking among (1) what is known to the system, (2) what is actually a fact, and (3) what could be the case. This requirement of the DV approach to missing information forces the user to make the very same distinctions for which the relational approach to missing information has been criticized.

The burden on the user of having to make these distinctions is not removed by having him or her formulate the query as "find the suppliers not based in London and not based in '???'. " In fact, the burden arises because the problem of dealing with missing information correctly is just not a simple problem.

The claim that the DV approach "avoids all the difficulties associated with the null value scheme" [Date, 1986] is clearly incorrect. I would characterize the DV scheme as an approach that is likely to entice the naive user and whose claimed simplicity is quite likely to trap the unwary and give rise to serious mistakes.

Finally, consider the idea that a notion should be rejected because it is "counter-intuitive." This is a type of criticism that I cannot accept as technical in nature, precisely because it is too subjective with respect to a person and the culture and era in which he or she lives. One example should suffice, although there are many.

At least 10 centuries ago, very few people were concerned with making long voyages, whether over land or sea. Most people therefore had no cause to consider that the earth might not be flat, and that the shortest distance from A to B on the surface of the earth is not a straight line, but instead an arc of a great circle. Thus, when the scientific proposal was made that the earth is spherical, most people considered the proposal extremely counter-intuitive. Today, however, it would be quite difficult to find anybody who considers this idea to be counter-intuitive. Thus, if an idea appears to be counter-intuitive, it is not necessarily wrong. Similarly, if an idea is appealingly intuitive, it is not necessarily right.

9.3 ■ The Alleged Breakdown of Normalization in the Relational Model

In attempting to show that the relational model runs into difficulties with normalization, the critics cite an example of a base relation R (A,B,C) satisfying the functional dependence A→B, for which it is not assumed that A is the primary key, so that A can be permitted to have missing db-values. The critics assert that serious problems are bound to arise if R contains a row (?,b1,c1) and an attempt is made to insert another row (?,b2,c2), where b1 and b2 are not equal, and ? denotes an A-mark. They assert that *either* the two nulls must be considered distinct from one another *or* the second row must be rejected because "it might violate the dependency" [Date, 1986] when the null is replaced by an actual value.

The critics seem to have rejected without supplying a reason a third option, which is the one adopted in the relational model. That is, whenever the A component of a row is missing (or becomes missing), the functional dependence A → B is not enforced by the DBMS for this row until an attempt is made to replace the mark (null) in column A by an actual db-value. In fact, if the proposed DV scheme were adopted, this third option would not be available, because a null or missing value is treated in the DV scheme as just another database value. Hence, in the DV scheme the functional-dependence constraint must be enforced upon first entry of the row, and this gives rise to the possibility that a row might be erroneously rejected by the DBMS.

The critics also assert that, if the second row is not rejected upon attempted entry, "we are forced to admit that we do not have a functional dependency" [Date, 1986] of B on A. This is clearly one more instance of a value-oriented misinterpretation.

The claim that the normalization procedure breaks down is false. It should be clear that, because nulls—or, as they are now called, marks—

are *not* database values, the rules of functional and multi-valued dependence do not apply to them. Instead, they apply to all unmarked db-values.

With the DV scheme, the normalization procedure does break down, precisely because missing information is treated as database values. This is one more reason why I contend that the DV scheme is not an acceptable solution to the problem of handling missing information in databases.

The following example, more practical and less symbolic, is intended to illustrate the absence of any effect of missing values on normalization. The example is a slightly modified version of one presented in [Codd 1971b].

The relation EMP identifies and describes employees. Three of its columns are shown:

E#   Employee serial number (the primary key)
D#   Department serial number
CT   Contract type

In this company, a department is assigned to exactly one type of contract. It will be convenient to refer to this as Rule 1. One consequence of Rule 1 is that the EMP relation is not in third-normal form. The following functional dependencies are applicable:

$$E\# \rightarrow D\# \rightarrow CT.$$

Note that the department D# to which an employee E# is assigned is an immediate property of an employee, while the contract type CT is an immediate property of the department. In the column CT. the values g and n appear. They denote two types of contracts, government and non-government, respectively.

EMP	(E#	. . .	D#	CT)
	e1	. . .	d5	g
	e2	. . .	??	g
	e3	. . .	d2	n
	e4	. . .	d3	n
	e5	. . .	d2	n
	e6	. . .	??	n
	e7	. . .	d8	g

In this example, the two department numbers that are missing must be distinct, because of Rule 1 and the fact that the contract types in column CT of these two rows are distinct. The problems associated with checking functional dependency where there are missing values can be avoided completely by postponing the checking of compliance of each row with the functional dependence D# → CT until the attempted update of the missing department serial number (if any) to a non-missing value.

9.4 ■ Implementation Anomalies

In general, the present state of relational DBMS products in regard to the representation and handling of missing information is far from satisfactory. For IBM products based on the language SQL, the main problem is the way missing information is handled, rather than its representation. In non-IBM products, even the representation aspects have gone astray. In several of these products, the DBMS designer has misinterpreted nulls as db-values (see Section 9.1).

In at least one well-known (and otherwise sound) DBMS product [Relational Technology 1988], zero was chosen as the value to indicate missing information in all numeric columns. I consider the number zero to be far too valuable in its normal role in all kinds of business activities—for example, as a real number representing the actual quantity of a part in stock or the actual quantity of currency owed by one or more customers. Therefore, I do not consider zero to be an acceptable value to be reserved by a DBMS for denoting a missing numeric db-value. In fact, in the context of computer-supported database management, it is unacceptable to reserve *any* specific numeric value or character-string value to denote the fact that a db-value is missing.

9.5 ■ Application of Statistical Functions

An example involving the sum of an empty set of numbers is sometimes used to show that SQL encounters difficulties by unconditionally yielding the SQL null as the result. While I agree with this example when interpreted solely as an SQL blunder, I do not agree with the use of it as an example that justifies outright rejection of the relational approach to missing information.

If the sum were to yield zero unconditionally as the result, there would be the problem that the average of an empty set of numbers would not be the sum divided by the count (the number of elements in the set). This problem arises, however, because 0/0 is normally taken to be undefined in elementary mathematics; this difficulty does *not* stem from the relational approach to missing information. When taking averages, it is necessary for programmers and users to provide special treatment for the case in which the divisor (i.e., the number of elements in the set) is zero, because zero exhibits a unique behavior when it is used as a divisor. Incidentally, I fail to see how the DV scheme provides any solution or simplification for this problem.

I consider this problem to be quite separable from the question of how to deal with missing information. Nevertheless, the approach taken to this problem in the relational model can be illustrated by taking the example of generating the total salaries earned by each department, where each total is computed as the sum of the salaries earned by each employee assigned to the pertinent department. Let us assume that a few departments exist that have zero employees assigned to them at this time.

In applying statistical functions, there are two important alternative methods of handling occurrences of empty sets.

1. Each occurrence of an empty set is ignored (i.e., passed over).
2. A value, specified by the user, is taken as the *result* for each occurrence of an empty set.

Note the difference between these two actions if the statistical function happens to be the AVERAGE, and if the value selected in the second approach is zero. The first action omits the departments that have zero members, while the second generates zero *for each such department*.

The empty set qualifier, a function ESR with a single argument, say x, causes each occurrence of an empty set to yield the result x and does not affect the result obtained from each non-empty set. Omission of this qualifier altogether causes each occurrence of an empty set to be ignored.

9.6 ■ Interface to Host Languages

Host languages do not include support specifically aimed at the semantics of the fact that information in databases may be missing. This means there is bound to be an interface problem, whatever approach is taken in the data sublanguage. If the approach taken on the database side of the interface is uniform and systematic (independent of data type), the interface is likely to be simpler than an approach like the DV scheme, which requires database users to keep inventing, column by column, their own techniques for dealing with this problem—not to mention the burden of communicating their inventions to other users of the database.

The relational approach therefore has a strong advantage in this area over the DV scheme. In this chapter and in the relational model itself, one major concession has been made to reduce user confusion about the host-language interface—namely, a change from the terms "null" and "null value" to the term "mark" for the indicator that designates the fact that a db-value is missing.

9.7 ■ Problems Encountered in the Default-Value Approach

There are six main problems with the DV approach:

1. The DV approach does not appear to provide any tools for the *handling* of missing information, but merely provides a means for *representing* the fact that something is missing.

2. The representation proposed is by means of a db-value, which forces the testing of functional dependencies and other kinds of dependencies at the time data is entered—the wrong time if a missing value is involved.

3. The representation of the fact that a db-value is missing is not only dependent on the data type of each pertinent column, but can even vary across columns having a common data type. All of this presents a severe burden in thinking and in inter-personal communication for the DBA, end users, and programmers.

4. The numerous and varied techniques for *handling* missing data will be buried in the application programs, and it is highly doubtful that they will be uniform or systematic, or even documented adequately.

5. Each missing db-value is treated as if it were just another db-value (i.e., the DV approach ignores the semantics and suffers from the value-oriented misinterpretation).

6. The DV approach is a step backward from the relational model to an ad hoc, unsystematic approach frequently adopted in the pre-relational era.

In the case of item 5, numerous specific consequences were cited earlier in this chapter, along with the ensuing penalties.

It is also important to realize that, whatever the approach, the DBA, application programmers, and end users *must cope with the semantics of the fact that some db-values for some columns may be missing.* Because the DV scheme offers no tools for handling missing information in a uniform, systematic way, users are forced to invent a variety of ad hoc, unsystematic ways, over which the DBMS cannot exert any real integrity control. Finally, research in this area is still being pursued, and I make no claim that the relational model, as it now stands, treats missing information in a way that is unsurpassable. Any replacement, however, must be shown to be technically superior.

9.8 ■ A Legitimate Use of Default Values

Suppose that a bank has a central database that includes information on all of its customer accounts. When a branch of the bank enters a new account, the information is inserted into the database from a terminal located in that branch. If the person making the entry omits the branch code (which identifies the branch), the system could assume with reasonable safety that the branch is identified by the particular terminal used for the entry.

In this example, a default value is being used for the branch code, and, during the entry of a new account, it is the system that computes an appropriate value for this code, and then inserts that code into the database along with the rest of the account information from the terminal. It is important to realize that at no time is the branch code actually missing from its database context: a record that describes a customer account in detail. Therefore, this example is clearly distinguishable from a case of information missing in the database.

Use of the word "system" in the last two paragraphs is intentionally vague. It should not be interpreted as meaning the DBMS. No specific feature of RM/V2 supports this kind of use of default values, which can be handled adequately by terminal support that is programmed by users—provided, of course, that the system, of which the DBMS is part, can make the identification of a requesting terminal available along with each request.

9.9 ■ Concluding Remarks

In the past, I have intentionally included in the relational model a systematic treatment of missing-but-applicable information (information that is temporarily unknown). In RM/V2, I am now adding similar treatment for missing-and-inapplicable information (information that is unknowable). The whole treatment of missing information is intended to remove from database administrators and users the burden of solving this problem in highly specialized, and often inadequate, ways.

I make no claim that this systematic treatment is either intuitive or counter-intuitive. Neither do I claim that users who have used the old style with non-relational DBMS will be able to avoid the burden of learning the new approach. I also do not claim that missing-but-applicable information, inapplicable information, and the derivation of deductions therefrom are thoroughly understood yet.

Finally, I do not claim that RM/V2 handles the "half-missing" case, in which a specific and precise value is unknown, but either a small range of possible values is known, or else there is a high probability that the missing value is one of a very few values. This case may not be ignored in RM/V3, but it is now more urgent for DBMS products to handle the cases for which RM/V2 provides support. In any event, it will be necessary to show that the extra machinery (hardware and/or software) needed to support the "half-missing" case is going to pay its way.

The old-style approach used values that were specially earmarked by users to represent missing information (and misrepresent the semantics). The earmarking and the invention of manipulation techniques were likely to be different for each different column and were a significant burden on database administrators and users. The reader will undoubtedly agree that the present scheme in the relational model is far more systematic than the old-style approach, and moves more of the burden of handling missing information from the users to the DBMS.

Version 1 of the relational model was defined precisely in [Codd 1968–1979]. One of the great advantages of the relational approach is the unparalleled power of its treatment of integrity. It is high time for vendors and users to place more emphasis on the introduction and retention of database integrity, and consequently invest more effort in learning the systematic treatment of missing information as described in this book.

Exercises

9.1 What is the default-value approach, and in what ways is it unsatisfactory for representing and handling the treatment of missing values? State five undesirable properties.

9.2 In what circumstances is it appropriate to store default values in a relational database? Has this anything to do with values that are missing from the database? If so, what is the connection?

9.3 Suppose that functional dependencies and multi-valued dependencies that are applicable to a certain database are stored in the catalog as DBA-defined integrity constraints. How does the relational model cope with these constraints when numerous columns are allowed to have missing values?

9.4 How does RM/V2 cope with the application of an aggregate function to an empty set? What does SQL deliver as the result? Which of these actions makes sense? Explain your answer.

9.5 Provide a legitimate case in which a default value (one not supplied by the user) should be stored in a database? Does the DV scheme support this type of default value? How is this case related to the representation and handling of missing information?

CHAPTER 10

Qualifiers

A qualifier is an expression that can be used in a command to alter some aspect of the execution of that command. In the context of this book, the commands of interest are relational commands; during execution of these commands, the focus of interest is the effect of the qualifiers on database management. Features RQ-1–RQ-13 (the 13 qualifiers) are discussed in this section.

Normally, when a truth-valued condition in a relational command is evaluated, the specified combination of target values is extracted from the database, if and only if the complete condition evaluates to TRUE (abbreviated t). The first three features, RQ-1–RQ-3, are used to change the qualifying truth-value from t to one of the MAYBE truth values (a or i) for whatever scope of the condition is embraced by the MAYBE qualifier. Table 10.1 exhibits for each pertinent feature which truth-value becomes the qualifying truth-value in place of t.

Table 10.1 **Qualifiers and Truth Values**

F		Q
	TRUE	t
RQ-1	A-MAYBE	a
RQ-2	I-MAYBE	i
RQ-3	MAYBE	both a and i

Table 10.2 Qualifiers

Feature	Qualifier	Pertinent Context
RQ-1	A-MAYBE	Condition part of any operator
RQ-2	I-MAYBE	. . . .
RQ-3	MAYBE	. . . .
RQ-4	AR(x)	Any column in any request
RQ-5	IR(x)	. . . .
RQ-6	ESR(x)	Any command
RQ-7	ORDER BY	Any retrieval command
RQ-8	ONCE ONLY	Any inner join
RQ-9	DOMAIN CHECK OVERRIDE	Any operator involving inter-column comparisons
RQ-10	EXCLUDE SIBLINGS	Operators involving PKs
RQ-11	DEGREE OF DUPLICATION	Any retrieval operator
RQ-12	SAVE	Any relational assignment
RQ-13	VALUE	Any command that can generate marked values

The absence of a TRUE or MAYBE qualifier indicates the TRUE case by default.

Features RQ-4 and RQ-5 deal with the temporary replacement of missing occurrences of values by specified values, where "temporary" means during execution of the pertinent command only. Feature RQ-4 provides for temporary replacement of A-marked values, while RQ-5 provides for temporary replacement of I-marked values. The need for these features is explained in Chapter 8.

Feature RQ-6 deals with the handling of empty sets. Feature RQ-7 imposes ordering upon the rows of the resulting relation, while RQ-8 forces each tuple from each operand to be used once if possible, or else not at all, in executing a **join.** Feature RQ-9 is the qualifier that suppresses the checking of domains when a relational command involves using one or more pairs of columns as comparands.

Feature RQ-10 pertains to controlling the propagation of certain operators (such as **update** and **delete**) to the sibling values of a given primary-key value. RQ-11 requests the DBMS to append to each row a count of the degree of *potential duplication* of that row in the result of a **projection** or **union,** if duplicate rows had not been prohibited in the relational model. RQ-12 requests the DBMS to save the relation formed as a result of executing a command. Table 10.2 provides a list of all the qualifiers and the context in which they are applicable.

10.1 ■ The 13 Qualifiers

In the context of a command that can generate marked values, RQ-13 causes a specified value to be inserted instead of these marked values. The three qualifiers in Features RQ-1–RQ-3, all based on four-valued logic, are concerned with extracting values when the condition part of a query has a truth-value other than TRUE or FALSE. A relation EMP that identifies and describes employees is used to illustrate the effect of these qualifiers:

EMP	(EMP#	ENAME	DEPT#	SALARY	BONUS)
1	E107	Rook	D12	10,000	— I
2	E912	Knight	D05	— A	2,000
3	E239	Knight	D03	12,000	1,800
4	E575	Pawn	D12	— A	— I
5	E123	King	D01	15,000	— A
6	E224	Bishop	D03	— I	2,500

"A" denotes an A-mark, and the corresponding value is missing and applicable. "I" denotes an I-mark, and the corresponding value is missing and inapplicable. The row numbers are purely expository.

The query to be applied in each case is as follows: retrieve the employees whose salary exceeds 11,000 and whose bonus is less than 4,000. This query can be expressed using the Boolean extension of the **select** operator:

$$Q \leftarrow EMP [(SALARY > 11,000) \wedge (BONUS < 4,000)].$$

Without any qualifier, query Q selects row 3 of the EMP relation.

RQ-1 The MAYBE_A Qualifier

This qualifier, based on four-valued logic, can be applied to any truth-valued expression in an RL command. The DBMS focuses on those items for which this expression has the truth-value a (which denotes MAYBE-AND-APPLICABLE). For example, if the MAYBE_A qualifier is applied to the whole condition, then the DBMS yields as the final result just those items for which the whole condition has the truth-value a.

Do not confuse the MAYBE_A qualifier with the truth-value a or with an A-marked value. The query Q qualified by MAYBE_A selects rows 2 and 5 of the EMP relation.

RQ-2 The MAYBE__I Qualifier

This qualifier, based on four-value logic, can be applied to any truth-valued expression in an RL command. The DBMS focuses on those items for which this expression has the truth-value *i* (which denotes maybe and inapplicable). For example, if the MAYBE__I qualifier is applied to the whole condition, then the DBMS yields as the final result just those items for which the whole condition has the truth-value *i*.

Do not confuse the qualifier MAYBE__I with the truth value *i* or with an I-marked value. The query Q qualified by MAYBE__I selects rows 4 and 6 of the EMP relation. It does not select row 1, since the non-missing salary is less than 11,000.

RQ-3 The MAYBE Qualifier

This qualifier, based on four-valued logic, can be applied to any truth-valued expression in an RL command. The DBMS focuses on those items for which this expression has the truth-value *a* or *i* (either applicable or inapplicable). For example, if the MAYBE qualifier is applied to the whole condition, then the DBMS yields as the final result just those items for which the whole condition has the truth-value *a* or *i*.

Do not confuse the qualifier MAYBE with the truth-values *a* or *i*, or with marked values (an A-marked value or an I-marked value). The query Q qualified by MAYBE selects rows 2, 4, 5, and 6 of the EMP relation.

If the DBMS supports features RQ-1–RQ-3 fully, it must support four-valued logic under the covers. For more details on four-valued logic, see Chapter 8.

RQ-4, RQ-5 Temporary Replacement of Missing Database Values

In applying statistical functions to database values in one or more columns of an R-table, missing occurrences of such values can be temporarily replaced (during the execution of the function only) by applying the qualifier AR(x), which replaces A-marked values by x (in the case of Feature RQ-4) or the qualifier IR(x), which replaces I-marked values by x (in the case of Feature RQ-5).

RQ-6 Temporary Replacement of Empty Relation(s)

The qualifier ESR(x) appended to an RL expression causes each empty relation encountered *as an argument* during the execution of that expression to be replaced by the set whose only element is x, provided x is type-compatible with the pertinent relation (normally, of course, x is a tuple).

10.1.1 Ordering Imposed on Retrieved Data

The ability of a DBMS to deliver derived data in any specified order that is based on values within the result should be understood from two points of view: (1) the terminal users, and (2) the application programmers.

Frequently, a terminal user must see the data retrieved from a relational database in some specific sequence. Moreover, an application programmer may be faced with the task of taking the retrieved data, an entire derived relation, and interfacing that data to a host language that, for computing reasons, is able to process no more than a single record at a time. Such a programmer is likely to require that the retrieved data be ordered in some specific sequence.

The relational model does not permit the programmer to take advantage of the sequence in which the data in the database happens to be stored. Two important reasons for this are as follows:

1. the DBA may alter the way data in the database is stored at any time to improve performance and to cope with changes in traffic on the database;

2. the program should work correctly on a system of different design (even if it is supplied by another vendor), and a different design may not support precisely the same representations of data in storage;

RQ-7 The ORDER BY Qualifier

An ORDER BY clause consists of the following:

■ the ORDER BY qualifier;

■ names for those columns of the operands whose values are to act as the ordering basis;

■ a symbol ASC or DESC indicating whether the ordering is to be by ascending values or descending values.

An ORDER BY clause can be appended to a relational command that retrieves data. The DBMS then delivers the data in the order specified.

One option available to the user is to base the ordering on the values occurring in a simple or composite column of one of the operands or of the resulting relation. If the ordering in the result is not represented (redundantly) by values in one or more columns of the result, the DBMS must warn the user of that fact (see Feature RJ-10 in Chapter 11).

If the ordering is based on character strings, a collating sequence is used that is declared by name only, if standard, or by name and extension, if non-standard.

If the comparator < is inapplicable to the extended data type of any of the columns upon which the ordering is based, the DBMS applies the comparator to the corresponding basic data type. (See Chapter 3 for the distinction between basic data type and extended data type.)

As just noted, the DBMS must warn the user when the ordering in the result is not represented (redundantly) by values in one or more columns of the result. This warning is required because a user might expect to be able to use *all* of the information in the result for further interrogation. It is important to remember that the relational operators are incapable of exploiting any information that is not represented by values in R-tables. This *incapability* is neither an accident nor an oversight. It is intended to keep the relational operators from becoming overly complicated in handling simple tasks.

Consider the example of the relation C, which identifies and describes the capabilities of suppliers. This relation is intended to provide information concerning which suppliers can supply which kinds of parts. Examples of properties that are applicable to capabilities are as follows: speed of delivery of parts ordered, the minimum package size adopted by the supplier as the unit of delivery, and the price of this unit delivered.

S#	Supplier serial number
P#	Part serial number
SPEED	Number of business days to deliver
QP	Quantity of parts
UNIT_QP	Minimum package
MONEY	U.S. currency
PRICE	Price in U.S dollars of minimum package.

There are five domains: S#, P#, TIME, QP, and MONEY.

C	(S#	P#	SPEED	UNIT_QP	PRICE)
	s1	p1	5	100	10
	s1	p2	7	100	20
	s1	p6	12	10	600
	s2	p3	5	50	37
	s2	p5	8	100	15
	s3	p6	15	10	700

s4	p2	10	100	15
s4	p5	15	5	300
s5	p6	10	5	350

Suppose there is an urgent need for fast delivery of certain parts. The following request tabulates triples consisting of the serial numbers of suppliers, the serial numbers of parts, and the speed of delivery; all the triples are ordered by part serial number (major participant) and speed (minor participant):

C[S#, P#, SPEED] ORDER BY (P#, SPEED).

Upon receipt of this request, the DBMS delivers the following result:

C	(S#	P#	SPEED)	
	s1	p1	5	p1
	s1	p2	7	p2
	s4	p2	10	p3
	s2	p3	5	
	s2	p5	8	p5
	s4	p5	15	
	s5	p6	10	
	s1	p6	12	p6
	s3	p6	15	

Note that the option of requesting the ordering to be based on values in a column of the result allows the values computed according to a specified function to be used as the ordering basis. For example, suppose that a relation EMP containing information about employees is being interrogated, and that EMP has:

- a column containing the present salary of each employee; **and**
- a column containing the department number of each employee.

Consider this query: find the department number together with the total salary earned by all employees assigned to that department. It must be possible to display the result ordered by these total salaries.

10.1.2 The ONCE Qualifier and Its Effect upon Theta-joins

The **inner** and **outer T-joins** were introduced in Section 5.7. An interesting property of the **T-joins** is that each tuple of the operands participates at most once in the result. It is entirely possible that some of the operands' tuples do not participate at all in mid-sequence—neither at the early end nor at the late end.

RQ-8 The ONCE ONLY Qualifier (abbreviated ONCE)

When attached to a request for an **inner T-join**, the qualifier ONCE converts this request into a special **inner T-join**, in which every tuple of the operands participates exactly once with few exceptions. The exceptions can occur at the early end, the late end, or both ends of the sequence, where early and late are based on values of date and/ or time in the comparand columns. Similarly, the qualifier ONCE converts an **outer T-join** into a special **outer T-join**, in which every tuple of the operands participates exactly once without exception.

How is this full participation realized? Consider the example that was introduced in Section 5.7. The sample operands are relations S and T:

S (P	A)
k1	4
k2	6
k3	12
k4	18
k5	20

T (Q	B)
m1	3
m2	5
m3	9
m4	11
m5	13
m6	15

The result of taking the **inner T-join** based on $<$ of S on A with T on B (omitting the qualifier ONCE) is the relation V, assuming that

$$V \leftarrow S [[A < B]] T.$$

V	(P	A	B	Q)
	k1	4	5	m2
	k2	6	9	m3
	k3	12	13	m5

Notice that tuples $< k4, 18 >$ and $< k5, 20 >$ of relation S and tuples $< m1, 3 >$, $< m4, 11 >$, and $< m6, 15 >$ of relation T did not participate at all in the result.

If the qualifier ONCE is attached, however, the result is generated by first sorting each relation by increasing time (S is sorted by A, T is sorted by B). The next step is to start at the tuple in S with the earliest time, namely $< k1, 4 >$. This tuple is coupled with the earliest tuple in T, namely $< m1, 3 >$. To do this and still comply with the comparand $<$, the time component of the tuple $< m1, 3 >$ from T is incremented by the least integer amount (i.e., 2) to make it satisfy the LESS THAN condition. When coupled, the resulting tuple is $< k1, 4, 5, m1 >$. Note that I have reversed the last two components for expository reasons.

The next step is to couple < k2, 6 > from S with < m2, 5 > from T by incrementing the time component of the row from T by the least amount (again, 2) to make it comply with the LESS THAN condition. The resulting tuple is < k2, 6, 7, m2 >. These steps are repeated and yield first < k3, 12, 13, m3 >, then < k4, 18, 19, m4 >, then < k5, 20, 21, m5 >, and finally the tuple < m6, 15 > from T is left as a non-participant. Notice that the necessary increments are not constant. The resulting relation is

W	(P	A	B	Q	)
	k1	4	5	m1	
	k2	6	7	m2	
	k3	12	13	m3	
	k4	18	19	m4	
	k5	20	21	m5	

If, instead of the inner T-join, the symmetric outer T-join had been used with the ONCE qualifier, the result would have been

W	(P	A	B	Q	)
	k1	4	5	m1	
	k2	6	7	m2	
	k3	12	13	m3	
	k4	18	19	m4	
	k5	20	21	m5	
	—	—	22	m6	

Note that the time component of the last tuple < m6, 15 > from T has been incremented by the least integer amount (i.e., 7) that will make it greater than the largest time component in the rest of the result.

Note that the operands S and T remain in the database unchanged. Thus, it would be incorrect to regard this operation as an update of either S or T. The user may need to bear in mind, however, that the values in the result are not necessarily drawn from the database without change. Whatever changes take place are certainly not the result of applying a simple transformation uniformly across all the values in a column.

RQ-9 The DOMAIN CHECK OVERRIDE (DCO) Qualifier

If specifically authorized, use of the qualifier DCO in a command permits values to be compared during the execution of the command that are drawn from *any pair* of distinct domains in the entire database. The qualifier may, however, be accompanied by the name of a unary relation containing a specific list of the names of domains. The effect of this list is to request the DBMS to permit comparing activity that involves pairs of distinct domains, only when the names of those domains appear in the list.

A user who is authorized to use qualifier RQ-9 across the entire database is endowed with tremendous power for doing good or evil. This is why I would recommend that the authorization for domain check override normally be confined to a short, specified list of domains only, and even then only for a short time and specific trouble analysis.

For more detail, see Features RJ-6 in Chapter 11, RM-14 in Chapter 12, and RA-9 in Chapter 18. Use of this qualifier would seldom be authorized, and then for only a short time. The principal use is for detective work in trying to determine how a portion of the database lost its integrity. For example, if the domains for a particular database happen to include a part serial number domain and a supplier serial number domain, and they happen to have identical basic data types (both character strings of length 12, say), one might wish to ask which of these semantically distinct serial numbers happens to be identical to one another when viewed simply as character strings.

RQ-10   The EXCLUDE SIBLINGS Qualifier

In some of the manipulative operators (Features RB-33–RB-34, RB-36–RB-37), the primary key of some base relation is either specified directly or is indirectly involved, and certain action is to be taken on the siblings of this primary key. This action on the siblings is thwarted if the EXCLUDE SIBLINGS qualifier is attached to the command.

See Section 4.3 for definitions and details.

RQ-11   The Appended DEGREE OF DUPLICATION (DOD) Qualifier

Assume that the DOD qualifier is appended to the projection of a single relation or to the **union** of two union-compatible relations. For each row in the result, the DBMS calculates the number of occurrences of that row if duplicate rows had been permitted in the result. This count is appended to each row in the actual result as an extra component. Thus, the result is a relation with an extra column, which is called the *DOD column* here.

This qualifier enables the DBA to grant a user access to enough information from the database for him or her to make correct statistical analysis, without granting access to some primary keys that happen to be sensitive. See Chapter 18 for further information on this topic, as well as an alternative approach that can be taken by the DBA and DBMS.

Examples of **projection** with the DOD qualifier appear next. The operand is as follows:

R	(K	A	B	C	D	. . .)
	k1	a1	b1	c1	d1	. . .
	k2	a1	b1	c1	d2	. . .
	k3	a1	b1	c1	d2	. . .
	k4	a1	b1	c2	d3	. . .
	k5	a2	b1	c1	d3	. . .
	k6	a2	b2	c2	d4	. . .

The results are as follows:

R [A	B	C] DOD
a1	b1	c1 3
a1	b1	c2 1
a2	b1	c1 1
a2	b2	c2 1

R [A	B] DOD
a1	b1 4
a2	b1 1
a2	b2 1

R [B	C] DOD
b1	c1 4
b1	c2 1
b2	c2 1

R [A] DOD
a1 4
a2 2

R [B] DOD
b1 5
b2 1

R [C] DOD
c1 4
c2 2

R [D] DOD
d1 1
d2 2
d3 2
d4 1

Clearly, any DOD **projection** of R that includes the primary key K of R will have as many rows as R does, and in each row the DOD component will be exactly one. Note also that if relation R happens to be empty, every projection of R is empty, whether or not the pertinent projection is DOD-qualified.

An example of **union** with the DOD qualifier appears next. The operands are as follows:

S (A	B	C)
a1	b1	c1
a2	b2	c2

T (A	B	C)
a2	b2	c2
a3	b2	c2

The result is as follows:

S UNION T	(A	B	C	DOD)
	a1	b1	c1	1
	a2	b2	c2	2
	a3	b2	c2	1

Note that 1 and 2 are the only two possible values for the DOD component of the DOD-qualified **union** of any two union-compatible relations. Note also that, if both operands happen to be empty, the result is empty whether the **union** is DOD-qualified or not.

Implementation of Feature RQ-11 in an index-based DBMS is quite easy and cheap—most of the code needed for RQ-11 must be developed to support the CREATE INDEX command in any case (see Feature RE-14 in Chapter 7).

Each of the statistical functions built into the DBMS should have two flavors: one that treats each row as it occurs (just once, ignoring any DOD component, if such exists); the other that treats each row as if it occurred n times, where n is the DOD component of that row (see Chapter 19 for details).

RQ-12 The SAVE Qualifier

The SAVE qualifier may be attached to any relational assignment (see Feature RB-30 in Chapter 4). Let T be the relation formed by this assignment. The SAVE qualifier requests the DBMS to store the description of T in the catalog, and to save T as if it were part of the database.

If the SAVE qualifier is omitted, and if T still exists at the end of the interactive session or after the pertinent application program is executed, then the DBMS drops T. Thus, the SAVE qualifier causes a relation to be saved for shared use. Omitting the SAVE qualifier restricts the pertinent relation to private and temporary use—as far as the DBMS is concerned. A user must have the necessary authorization to make a copy of a base or derived relation to be saved for private use (outside the control of the DBMS). He or she may then issue an EXTRACT command (see Feature RE-19 in Chapter 7).

RQ-13 The VALUE Qualifier

When this qualifier is attached along with a value v to a command or expression that (1) creates a new column in a relation (base or derived) and (2) would normally fill this column with marked values, it causes v to be inserted in this column instead of each of the marked values.

This qualifier can be used with the advanced operator RZ-2 to extend a relation per another relation or with the DBA command RE-10 to append a named column to the description and to the extension of a base relation.

Exercises

10.1 Which qualifiers in RM/V2 support the extraction of data for which the truth value of the whole condition is
1. a = unknown due to a missing-but-applicable datum?
2. i = unknown due to a missing-and-inapplicable datum, and
3. either a or i.

10.2 Describe the effect of appending the AR qualifier with 912 as its argument to a statistical function applied to a numeric column.

10.3 Describe the effect of appending the IR qualifier with the character string "??" as its argument to a statistical function applied to a character-string column.

10.4 What is the DBMS required to do if the user includes the ORDER BY qualifier in his or her request, and the ordering is not represented redundantly by values in the result?

10.5 With what kind of operators can the ONCE qualifier be attached to one or both of the operands? What is the effect of this qualifier?

10.6 How is a regular **join** on < with the ONCE qualifier related to a **T-join** on <?

10.7 Describe the domain checking that is inhibited by the domain check override.

10.8 What action is excluded on what primary keys when the EXCLUDE SIBLINGS qualifier is used?

CHAPTER 11

Indicators

An *indicator* is a side effect of executing a relational command. If turned on during the execution of a relational command, it indicates the occurrence of an exceptional condition pertaining to the relational result, an intermediate result, or one of the arguments. Note that indicators are best implemented as return codes, preferably with explanatory comments. There is likely to be a need for more indicators than the 14 listed in Table 11.1.

Each of the 14 indicators cited in Features RJ-1–RJ-14 is turned off at the beginning of the execution of each type of RL command that is capable of turning such an indicator on, so that its state at any time reflects the outcome of the most recently executed command of this type.

Of course, the language RL must permit use of these indicators as part or all of a condition expressed within an immediately following RL command. To support this, each of the 14 indicators (except RJ-11–RJ-14) comes in pairs, say u and v, because it is necessary to distinguish between the use of an indicator as an argument in a command and its use as a result of that command.

During execution of an RL command, the indicator u is used to remember the indication from the immediately previous RL command, and the indicator v is prepared to accept the indication from execution of the current RL command. During execution of the immediately following RL command, the roles of u and v are reversed. All a user must know is that, when an indicator (no matter what its type) is tested in the condition part of an RL request, it reflects the execution of the immediately preceding RL command.

Table 11.1 **Indicators**

Feature	Type	Indicator	Pertinent Features
RJ-1	Result	Empty relation	All operators
RJ-2	Argument	Empty divisor	**Relational division** (RB-27)
RJ-3	Result	Missing information	All operators
RJ-4	Argument	Non-existing argument	RE-2, RE-3, RE-5, RE-6, RE-8, RE-9, RE-12
RJ-5	Argument	Domain not declared	Drop domain (RE-4)
RJ-6	Argument	Domain check error	**Selects, joins, relational division** (RB-27)
RJ-7	Argument	Column still exists	Alter domain (RE-3)
RJ-8	Argument	Duplicate row	Loading
RJ-9	Argument	Duplicate primary key	Loading
RJ-10	Result	Non-redundant ordering	ORDER BY qualifier (RQ-7)
RJ-11	Result	Catalog block	Blocks to alter database description (RM-7)
RJ-12	Result	View not tuple-insertible	Create view
RJ-13	Result	Tuple-component not updatable	Create view
RJ-14	Result	View not tuple-deletable	Create view

The term "immediately preceding RL command" means the RL command that the DBMS encountered as the immediately preceding one from the particular terminal or program, whichever is pertinent. The terms "preceding" and "following" apply in this case to RL commands only, not to any host-language commands in between the RL commands.

As can be seen from Table 11.1, most of the indicators are *argument indicators*. This means that, when turned on, they reflect an exceptional condition that applies to one of the arguments of a command.

Two of the six result indicators (Features RJ-1 and RJ-2) are intended to relieve users of the burden of detailed (and possibly programmed) examination for emptiness in one or more relations, and for the possibility that one or more cases of missing information were encountered during the execution of the command.

11.1 ■ Indicators Other than the View-Defining Indicators

RJ-1 Empty-relation Indicator (Result Indicator)

When the result of any retrieval or manipulative command expressed in RL is generated, an *empty-relation indicator* is turned on whenever the final result happens to be (or to include) an empty relation.

RJ-2 Empty Divisor Indicator (Argument Indicator)

If (1) a command in RL is about to be executed, (2) it involves relational division, and (3) the divisor relation happens to be empty, then an empty-divisor indicator is turned on, and the result generated by the DBMS from the division is the dividend with the divisor columns removed.

The empty-divisor indicator is set to zero at the beginning of the execution of each RL command. The indicator is set to one (and remains set to one) whenever within any command a **relational division** is encountered for which the divisor is empty. Therefore, upon completion of the execution of a single command of RL, if the empty-divisor indicator is in state one, this indicates that an empty divisor was encountered in one or more of the **relational divisions** within that command. This indicator is most helpful when the divisor happens to be an intermediate result, one that exists for only a short time during the execution of a more comprehensive command.

The relation that results from a **relational division** by an empty set is just what one would expect from the corresponding expression in predicate logic involving the universal quantifier. For example, suppose the database includes an R-table indicating in each row that supplier S# *can supply* part P#. If the user is finding the suppliers, each of whom can supply every one of a list of parts, and if that list happens to be empty, then every supplier recorded in the CAN__SUPPLY relation qualifies.

RJ-3 Missing-information Indicator (Result Indicator)

Whenever, during the execution of any retrieval or manipulative command expressed in RL, the DBMS encounters a database value declared to be missing, the missing-information indicator is turned on.

RJ-4 Non-existing Argument Indicator
(Argument Indicator)

The DBMS is unable to find an argument in accordance with the name specified in the command being executed. Execution of the command is aborted.

RJ-5 Domain-not-declared Indicator
(Argument Indicator)

An attempt has been made to execute a CREATE R-TABLE command in which a column draws its values from domain D, and the DBMS finds that domain D has not been declared. Execution of the command is aborted.

RJ-6 Domain-check-error Indicator
(Argument Indicator)

An operator has been requested that involves comparing values from two columns. The DBMS discovers that (1) the columns cited do not draw their values from a common domain, and (2) the user has not specified DOMAIN-CHECK-OVERRIDE in his or her command. The domain-check-error indicator is turned on, and execution of the command is aborted.

This feature protects the database from damage by those users who happen to make errors in formulating **selects, joins,** and **divides.** Such errors are quite likely when a naive or tired user is trying to exploit a powerful relational language. For more detail, see Feature RQ-9 in Chapter 10, Feature RM-14 in Chapter 12, and Feature RA-9 in Chapter 18.

The following feature is effective when the DBA or some other suitably authorized user attempts to drop a domain from the catalog without making sure that there no longer exists in the database a column that draws its values from that domain.

RJ-7 Domain Not Droppable, Column Still
Exists Indicator (Argument Indicator)

An attempt has been made to execute a DROP DOMAIN command, but a column still exists that draws its values from that domain. When this indicator is turned on, the DBMS aborts the DROP DOMAIN command.

See Features RE-3 and RE-6 in Chapter 7 for more detail.

RJ-8 Duplicate-row Indicator (Argument Indicator)

When loading data from a non-relational source into the base R-tables of a relational database, the DBMS examines the data to see whether duplicate rows occur. If so, the duplicate-row indicator is turned on.

For both Feature RJ-8 and Feature RJ-9, it is assumed that the description of each base R-table is in the catalog before the loading is started. This applies even if the base R-table is empty before the loading. Of course, the description includes an identification of which column(s) constitute the primary key.

The duplicate-row indicator is not intended for use during any manipulative operations that are totally within the relational model. Such operations never generate duplicate rows.

RJ-9 Duplicate-primary-key Indicator (Argument Indicator)

When loading data from a non-relational source into a base R-table of a relational database, the DBMS examines the data to see whether there are duplicate occurrences of primary key values. If so, the duplicate-primary-key indicator is turned on.

Features RJ-10 and RJ-11, which follow, are also described in Section 4.3 in the context of the insert operator RB-31.

RJ-10 Non-redundant Ordering Indicator (Result Indicator)

As noted in Feature RQ-7 in Chapter 10, the ORDER BY qualifier can generate a result in which tuples are ordered according to information not included in the result. When this occurs, the non-redundant-ordering indicator (NRO) is turned on.

RJ-11   Catalog Block Indicator (Result Indicator)

This indicator indicates that a catalog block of commands is being executed. It is turned on by a BEGIN CAT command only and turned off by an END CAT command only. Thus, it stays on throughout the execution of a catalog block.

During the execution of a catalog block, the DBMS uses this indicator to suppress cascading action that would occur if the indicator had been off. See the DROP R-TABLE command (Feature RE-9 in Chapter 7) for an example of a command in which the cascading action is dependent on the state of the catalog-block indicator.

11.2 ■ The View-Defining Indicators

At the beginning of execution of a CREATE VIEW command, the indicators RJ-12, RJ-13, RJ-14 arc all turned off. The DBMS then examines the updatability of the declared view using algorithm VU-1 or some stronger algorithm (see Chapter 17). Each of the three indicators is either left off or turned on, whichever accurately reflects the extent of updatability of the view.

RJ-12   View Not Tuple-insertible

From the view definition contained in a CREATE VIEW command, the DBMS has inferred that the view is not tuple-insertible.

RJ-13   View Not Component-updatable

From the view definition contained in a CREATE VIEW command, the DBMS has inferred that at least one component of every tuple in the view is not updatable.

Of course, as part of the execution of a CREATE VIEW command, the DBMS determines for each component (virtual column) whether it is or is not updatable. This information is stored in the catalog (a bit for each component), so that it is not necessary to recompute any of it when any update is requested on this view.

RJ-14 View Not Tuple-deletable

From the view definition contained in a CREATE VIEW command, the DBMS has inferred that the view is not tuple-deletable.

For more information on view updatability, see Chapter 17.

Exercises

11.1 Describe the empty-relation indicator and the empty-divisor indicator. In what ways is each of these indicators useful?

11.2 Upon completion of the execution of an RL command, it is found that the missing-information indicator has been turned on. What does this mean?

11.3 What are the domain-oriented indicators, and what is their purpose?

11.4 A file is being loaded into a relational database from a non-relational source. Explain the two indicators that may be turned on, and indicate two distinct forms of undesirable redundancy.

11.5 A user is trying to drop a domain. The DBMS refuses, and the column still exists indicator is turned on. What does this mean?

11.6 What is the purpose of the non-redundant ordering indicator?

11.7 Consider a request for tuple insertion, component update, or tuple deletion acting on a view. Is it at request time or at view-definition time that the DBMS determines whether the request can be honored while maintaining integrity? Justify the timing adopted in the relational model.

■ *CHAPTER 12* ■

Query and Manipulation

The features described in this chapter concern the general properties and capabilities of the relational language, not its specific features, and certainly not its syntax.

12.1 ■ Power-oriented Features

RM-1 Guaranteed Access

Each and every datum (atomic value) stored in a relational database is guaranteed to be logically accessible by resorting to a combination of R-table name, primary-key value, and column name. (This feature is Rule 2 in the 1985 set.)

The access path supporting this feature cannot be canceled. Most other access paths, however, are purely performance-oriented, and can be both introduced and canceled. Both Feature RM-1 and Feature RM-3 are needed in order to support ad hoc query without pre-defined access paths.

Clearly, each datum in a relational database can be accessed in a rich variety (possibly thousands) of logically distinct ways. It is important, however, to have at least one means of access, independent of the specific relational database, that is guaranteed—because most computer-oriented concepts (such as scanning successive addresses) have been deliberately omitted from the relational model.

Note that the guaranteed-access feature represents an associative-addressing scheme that is unique to the relational model. It does not depend at all on the usual computer-oriented addressing. Moreover, like the original relational model, it does not require any associative-addressing hardware, even though the need for such hardware was once frequently claimed by opponents of the relational model.

The primary-key concept, however, is an essential part of Feature RM-1. Feature RS-8 requires each base relation to have a declared primary key (see Chapter 2). Feature RM-1 is one more reason why the primary key of each base relation should be supported by every relational DBMS, and why its declaration by the DBA should be mandatory for every base relation.

RM-2 Parsable Relational Data Sublanguage

There is at least one relational language (denoted RL in this book) supported in the DBMS (not in an optional additional software package) such that (1) RL statements must be capable of being represented as parsable character strings, and can therefore be written or typed by a programmer, (2) for each manipulative operation, each and every operand is a relation, and (3) for each manipulative operation, each generated result is a relation with the result indicators (see Chapter 11) acting as a possible source of additional information.

A few vendors strongly promote interaction by programmers based on multiple-choice questions generated by the DBMS. This is claimed to be an alternative to writing programs, but I believe that the claim is insufficiently substantiated. This unproven claim is one important reason for requiring statements that are parsable character strings. Three additional reasons for this requirement are as follows:

1. it facilitates program maintenance;
2. the language is then in a form suitable for formal analysis;
3. the language may represent a standard for interfacing the DBMS to software packages on top (e.g., application development tools and expert systems).

Interactive tools that are claimed to make written or typed programs obsolete do not yet appear to support the maintenance requirement adequately. Moreover, these tools are badly in need of a published abstract model.

RM-3 Power of the Relational Language

Excluding consideration of general logical inference, RL as a language has the full power of four-valued, first-order predicate logic [Pospesel 1976, Stoll 1961, Suppes 1967, Church 1958].

The DBMS is capable of applying this power to all the following tasks:

- retrieval (database description, contents, and audit log);
- view definition;
- insertion;
- update;
- deletion;
- handling missing information (independent of data type);
- integrity constraints and authorization constraints.

If the DBMS is claimed to be able to handle distributed data, it can handle the following task:

- Distributed database management with distribution independence, including automatic decomposition of commands by the DBMS and automatic recomposition of results by the DBMS (see Features RP-4 and RP-5 in Chapter 20).

This last task represents a target to which the DBMS should apply the relational language RL, rather than a reason to extend RL. In other words, RL is scarcely affected by the need to support the management of distributed databases.

Of course, if the DBMS is to handle all the tasks specified in Feature RM-3, it would need additional capabilities beyond predicate logic. Clearly, to take just two examples, functions and arithmetic operators may also be needed. We emphasize the *predicate logic* because it is vital as a source of power of the relational language, and will remain so until another logic as powerful and rigorous is developed, which could take another two millennia.

RM-4 High-level Insert, Update, and Delete

The relational language RL supports **retrieval, insert, update,** and **delete** at a uniformly high, set level (multiple-records-at-a-time). (This Feature is Rule 7 in the 1985 set.)

This requirement gives the system much more scope in optimizing the efficiency of its execution-time actions. It allows the system to determine which access paths to exploit to obtain the most efficient code. It can also be extremely important in obtaining efficient handling of transactions across a distributed database. In this case, users would prefer that communication costs are saved by avoiding the necessity of transmitting a separate request for each record obtained from remote sites.

If a product supports *retrieval only* at this high level, it is not a relational DBMS, but merely a system that includes a relational retrieval subsystem.

RM-5   Operational Closure

RL is mathematically closed with respect to the relational operators it supports.

This means that the retrieval and manipulative operators that can be invoked by statements in RL are incapable (and must remain incapable) of generating a result that is neither a relation nor a set of relations (although the indicators mentioned in Chapter 11 may provide additional output). The following misinterpretations are common:

- that RL *cannot* be expanded to support more operators than are currently part of the relational model;
- that an operator must *not* generate a relation that lacks a primary key.

Regarding the second misinterpretation, it is worth noting that, when a relation is generated that does not have a primary key, it always has a weak identifier. Note also that, as mentioned in Chapter 1 and elsewhere, in RM/V2 no relation, whether base or derived, is allowed to have duplicate rows.

Feature RM-5 is as necessary in database management as arithmetic closure is in accounting. When applying addition, subtraction, and multiplication to numbers, the accountant knows that the result is always a number. Therefore, it is always possible to continue the process and use a result from one activity as an argument for another. Similarly, when a user interrogates a relational database, the result is always a relation. Thus, it is always possible to continue the process and use a result from one activity as an argument for another. This feature makes it possible for users to employ interrogation in a detective style.

12.2 ▪ Blocking Commands

If a DBMS is to be more than a simple query system, it must support the transaction concept. The precise definition accepted today is due to the System R team at IBM Research. (I believe that a principal contributor to this definition was Jim Gray.)

A *transaction* is a logical unit of work that transforms a consistent state of the database into a consistent state, without necessarily preserving consistency at all intermediate points. All actions within this logical unit of work must succeed, or else none of them must succeed. This atomicity of the unit of work must be applicable even though a sequence of several commands is normally involved in specifying the work to be done within that unit.

Within the logical unit of work, the DBMS may build up numerous changes for the database: entirely new rows to be inserted, rows that have been updated, or deletions. Usually these changes are accumulated in a cache memory until a command to commit the changes (usually called COMMIT) is received. Then, all the changes are recorded in the database.

If a failure occurs in either the hardware or the software during execution of the transaction, it is the responsibility of the DBMS to ensure that none of the changes accumulated in the cache memory is recorded in the database. If the program discovers some irregularity, such as an attempt to divide by zero, it issues a ROLLBACK command to abort the transaction and cause none of the changes to be committed to the database.

Three commands are necessary (the System R terms are adopted):

1. BEGIN signals the DBMS that a transaction is about to begin.
2. COMMIT signals the DBMS that a transaction has been completed in a normal manner, and that therefore all the changes to the database generated by this transaction can be committed to the database.
3. ROLLBACK signals the DBMS that none of the changes to the database generated so far in the execution of this transaction is to be committed.

RM-6   Transaction Block

The BEGIN and COMMIT commands identify the beginning and ending of a block of commands. At least one of the commands within a block must be expressed in the relational language; the others may be expressed in either the relational language or in the host language or in both. Such a block constitutes a transaction if, during its execution, either all parts succeed or none succeeds. ROLLBACK signals the DBMS (1) to terminate this execution of the transaction requested by the program, and (2) to avoid committing to the database any of the changes already developed during this execution of the transaction."

The following practical example illustrates the need for this feature. Suppose that a customer requests a bank to transfer $1,000 from his or her checking account to his or her savings account. Such a transfer is normally programmed so that the first action is an attempted withdrawal of $1,000 from the checking account (which incidentally checks to see whether the balance in the checking account is sufficient for the withdrawal to be made). If the first action is successful, the second action is to deposit this amount in the savings account.

Suppose that immediately after the withdrawal succeeds, a hardware failure occurs and the computer is taken off-line. Then, the corresponding deposit has not been put into effect. If the withdrawal has been recorded in the database and the deposit has not been recorded, the customer has lost $1,000. Therefore, such a transfer of funds from one account to another should be treated as a logical unit of work (i.e., as a transaction) so that all of it succeeds, or none of it succeeds.

RM-7 Blocks to Simplify Altering the Database Description

An RL command—labeled CAT here—signals the DBMS that the immediately following commands are all RL commands (i.e., no host language occurs in the package) and that each of these commands deals with changes in the catalog. The sequence of commands is ended by the RL command END CAT. In executing a block of RL commands defined in this way, the DBMS postpones certain actions until the command END CAT is encountered. The postponed actions include cascading actions normally associated with dropping base R-tables and views, plus the application of certain I-timed integrity constraints. Immediately before encountering END CAT, the DBMS cancels that part of the postponed cascading of view elimination, which has become unnecessary by END CAT time. It also cancels cascading of deletion for those authorization assertions that are still meaningful. The term *I-timed* is defined on page 313.

This feature concerns reducing or eliminating cascading actions on the catalog that result from changes in the catalog requested by isolated (unblocked) RL commands. Examples of such actions follow:

- dropping every view whose definition depends on an R-table (base or view) when that table is being dropped;
- dropping all authorization commands that refer to an R-table when that table is being dropped.

In many cases, Feature RM-7 enables the DBMS to eliminate or drastically reduce cascading action (such as the dropping of all views defined on a relation R when R is dropped) that results from unblocked commands that request changes in the catalog.

The main purpose of this feature is to relieve the DBA and any other suitably authorized user from the burden of having to redefine or redeclare all the items dropped in cascading action, when it would be necessary to restore many of them by hand as soon as one or more replacement R-tables are created. A second purpose is to permit the DBMS to optimize its treatment of the block of catalog commands as a whole.

For example, the addition in the catalog of a new column to the description of a base R-table can involve a complete scan of all rows of that R-table to alter the way each row is stored. If two columns are added to a single R-table by means of two consecutive, but unblocked, catalog commands, the DBMS will make two complete scans of all rows of that R-table. On the other hand, if these two commands are placed within a catalog block, then the DBMS can handle both columns by means of just one scan. If the pertinent R-table is large, the gain in performance could be significant.

12.3 ■ Modes of Execution

RM-8 Dynamic Mode

The DBMS supports the following kinds of changes dynamically— that is, without bringing activity on the regular data to a halt, without changing the source coding of any application programs, and without any off-line recompiling of any source RL statements:

1. creating new and dropping old domains, R-tables, and columns for already-declared R-tables;
2. creating new and dropping old representations in storage for parts of the database;
3. creating and dropping performance-oriented access paths;
4. changing the authorization data in the catalog;
5. changing declarations in the catalog (e.g., data types, user-defined functions, integrity constraints).

The relational approach is intentionally highly dynamic. In contrast to non-relational DBMS, it should rarely be necessary to bring the database activity to a halt for any reason.

RM-9 Triple Mode

The same language, RL, can be used in three distinct ways. First, RL can be used interactively at terminals. Second, statements in RL can be incorporated into application programs. Third, statements in RL can be combined to specify the action to be taken in case of attempted violation of an integrity constraint (see Chapters 13 and 14).

Generally speaking, adherence to this feature enables an application programmer to develop and debug the database statements separately from the remainder of the program in which these statements occur.

12.4 ■ Manipulation of Missing Information

RM-10   Four-valued Logic: Truth Tables

The DBMS evaluates all truth-valued expressions using the four-valued logic defined by the truth tables that follow:

P	not P	P∨Q	Q				P∧Q	Q			
			t	a	i	f		t	a	i	f
t	f	t	t	t	t	t	t	t	a	i	f
a	a	a	t	a	a	a	a	a	a	i	f
i	i	i	t	a	i	i	i	i	i	i	f
f	t	f	t	a	i	f	f	f	f	f	f

In these tables, t stands for TRUE, a for MISSING AND APPLICABLE, i for MISSING AND INAPPLICABLE, and f for FALSE. Note that t, f, i, and a are actual values, and should not be regarded as marked values. Because the sets retrieved and manipulated in database management are all finite, the existential and universal quantifiers can be treated as iterated OR and iterated AND, respectively.

Evaluation of a truth-valued expression according to this logic is executed by the DBMS without assistance from the user. This does not mean that users should be unaware of four-valued logic, but they need not be continuously concerned with the details.

RM/V1 involved only three-valued logic; no distinction was made on the basis of reasons why information might be missing. Such a distinction, however, is made by RM/V2. (For details, see Chapter 8.)

RM-11   Missing Information: Manipulation

Throughout the database, missing database values are manipulated by the DBMS uniformly and systematically, and, in particular, independent of data type.

Users should be able to exploit the full expressive power of the four-valued predicate logic in RL. In particular, the MAYBE qualifier should be applicable to any truth-valued expression, whether a complete logical condition or just part of such a condition.

(This feature is part of Rule 3 in the 1985 set; see Feature RS-13 in Chapter 2 for the representation part.)

RL should permit the MAYBE qualifier to be applied either to the whole condition or to part of it. When a view is cited within a query command, the DBMS must replace the name of the view by its definition. As a result, the expanded query can contain a condition that originates partly from the original query and partly from the view definition. Exactly one of these, the command or the definition, could have a MAYBE qualifier attached to all of its condition, while the other has no such qualifier. Thus, in the expanded command, the MAYBE qualifier applies to no more than part of the condition. It is, however, appropriate to remember that any part of a condition to which the MAYBE qualifier is attached must be a truth-valued expression.

RM-12 Arithmetic Operators: Effect of Missing Values

A marked database value in a numeric column cannot be arithmetically incremented or decremented by the DBMS, whereas the unmarked values can be subjected to such operators.

If x denotes a numeric database value, A denotes an A-mark, and I denotes an I-mark,

$$x + x = 2x \quad x + A = A \quad A + x = A$$
$$A + A = A \quad A + I = I \quad I + A = I$$
$$I + I = I \quad x + I = I \quad I + x = I$$

A similar table holds for the three arithmetic operators minus, times, and divide. When both arguments are unmarked database values, however, the result is what would be expected from ordinary arithmetic.

RM-13 Concatenation: Effect of Marked Values

A marked value in a character string column cannot be subjected to concatenation with any other string by the DBMS, whereas the unmarked values can.

Let $\wedge$ denote the concatenation operator and x an unmarked character string. Using the symbols A, I as in Feature RM-12,

$$x \wedge x = xx \quad x \wedge A = A \quad A \wedge x = A$$
$$A \wedge A = A \quad A \wedge I = I \quad I \wedge A = I$$
$$I \wedge I = I \quad x \wedge I = I \quad I \wedge x = I$$

12.5 ■ Safety Features

RM-14 Domain-constrained Operators and DOMAIN CHECK OVERRIDE

Those relational operators that involve comparison of database values are normally constrained to compare pairs of values if and only if both are drawn from the same domain (and therefore have the same extended data type).

There should seldom be any need to override this constraint. However, if the need does arise, the qualifier DOMAIN CHECK OVERRIDE (or DCO) may be attached to the command or to an appropriate expression in the command.

See Feature RA-9 in Chapter 18 for the authorization required to use the DCO qualifier. See Feature RQ-9 in Chapter 10 for the DCO qualifier itself, and Feature RJ-6 in Chapter 11 for the DOMAIN CHECK ERROR indicator.

The normal mode of operation helps protect users from formulating RL commands incorrectly, but of course does not provide complete protection.

As just pointed out, those relational operators that involve comparing database values are normally constrained to compare pairs of values if and only if both values in a pair have the same extended data type (see Chapter 3). Occasionally, however, a function may be applied to one or more database values in certain columns to yield a value to be compared with database values in another column or columns. Alternatively, two functions, possibly distinct, may be applied to each pair of comparands before the comparison is carried out. Since ordinary programming languages can be used to implement the function(s) involved, and since these languages do not support the extended data types of the relational model, it is not easy to specify the extended data type of such function-generated values. The following feature should prove helpful.

RM-15 Operators Constrained by Basic Data Type

In using any operator that normally compares pairs of database values to compare a function-generated value with a database value or a function-generated value with another function-generated value, the requirement of Feature RM-14 that the values to be compared must be of the same extended data type is relaxed: they are merely required to be of the same basic data type (e.g., both character strings or both integers).

RM-16 **Prohibition of Essential Ordering**

It is never the case that an R-table, whether base or derived, contains an ordering of rows or ordering of columns, in which the ordering itself carries database information not carried by values within the R-table.

If such an ordering were permitted, the information carried in or by that ordering would *not* be retrievable using relational operators. Assuming that such an ordering is *not* permitted, it is always possible to continue using RL in order to pursue a line of investigation by requesting additional queries or manipulations on these results. An example of this feature being ignored is the CONNECT command of the ORACLE product.

RM-17 **Interface to Single-record-at-a-time Host Languages**

The programming languages FORTRAN, COBOL, and PL/1 are obvious candidates (others may be candidates also) as host languages for any relational language RL. The DBMS must therefore be able to deliver the retrieved relation a block of rows at a time, where a block can be as small as one row, but is preferably many hundreds of rows.

A cursor that traverses the retrieved relation *may be supported* by the DBMS, although it is preferable that the traversal be executed using the HL. Normally this cursor scans from block to block, touching each block only once. Note that this type of cursor does not scan data within the database, but scans retrieved data only. Such a cursor is more easily managed by programmers in a bug-free way than those cursors that scan data within the database.

If the programmer has omitted the ORDER BY clause in his or her relational request, the program should not be based on the assumption that the sequence in which rows of the result are delivered by the DBMS will remain unchanged when a similar request is executed at a later time.

RM-18 The Comprehensive Data Sublanguage

The relational language RL is comprehensive with respect to database management in supporting *all* of the following items interactively at a terminal and by program (see the triple mode feature, Feature RM-9): (1) data definition, (2) view definition, (3) data manipulation, (4) integrity constraints, (5) authorization, and (6) transaction boundaries (BEGIN, COMMIT, and ROLLBACK). (This feature is Rule 5 in the 1985 set.)

In the relational approach, most of these services require the use of four-valued, first-order predicate logic. It seems counter-productive to require users to learn several different languages to make use of this power. Therefore, it does not make sense to separate the services just listed into distinct languages.

As an aside, in the mid-1970s ANSI/SPARC generated a document advocating 42 distinct interfaces and (potentially) 42 distinct languages for database management systems. Fortunately, that idea seems to have been abandoned.

12.6 ■ Library Check-out and Return

In some installations, a database may be used as an engineering tool. It will then contain details of the engineering design of various pieces of machinery. For each piece of machinery, there may exist several versions representing successive improvements in design. Since the creation or modification of a design can take hours or days to conceive and to express in detail, an engineer is likely to spend much more time on changing the database than that required for commercial transactions. Therefore, concurrency control for engineering-type activities must be quite different in nature from that appropriate for commercial transactions. It seems essential that the DBMS provide some support for distinctly engineered versions. The library check-out and return features that follow represent a minimum level of support for those DBMS products that are intended to support computer-aided engineering.

RM-19 Library Check-out

A duly authorized user can retrieve for several hours or days a copy of part of the database representing an engineering version of a piece of machinery (hardware or software) for the purpose of making design changes and creating a new version for that piece of machinery. The DBMS marks the version from which the copy is retrieved as one that is being improved.

RM-20 Library Return

A duly authorized user can store a new version of the design of a piece of machinery in the database. The request to store this version must be accompanied by a new identifier for it. The request is rejected if this identifier already exists as a version identifier in the database.

Exercises

12.1   What is meant by navigating through the database one record at a time? Does the relational model support such navigation? State two reasons for your answer.

12.2   List 10 tasks to which the principal relational language can apply four-valued, first-order predicate logic.

12.3   What is a transaction? Is it safe for the database to lose integrity in some early portion of a transaction if it regains integrity by the end of that transaction?

12.4   What is the purpose of the CAT block? Explain how it works.

12.5   You wish to make the following changes in the database or in its description:
    1.   Rename one of the base relations.
    2.   Unload a second relation, drop it from the DBMS, reorganize the data, and reload a reorganized version of it, restoring the same name as before in the catalog.

In each case, is it necessary first to bring all of the database traffic to a halt? When the drop occurs in Case 2, is there a way to prevent all authorization data for this relation from being lost? Or to prevent all views defined on this relation from being lost? Explain.

12.6   List five kinds of activities that are supported dynamically by RM/V2 (i.e., without bringing the traffic on the database to a halt).

12.7   The triple mode feature indicates that the principal relational language can be used in three distinct ways. What are they?

12.8   List the truth values of (1) a OR f, (2) t AND i, (3) NOT i, and (4) NOT a, where t denotes TRUE, a denotes MISSING AND APPLICABLE, i denotes MISSING AND INAPPLICABLE, and f denotes FALSE.

12.9   Under what circumstances does the relational model merely require comparand columns to have the same basic data type, instead of requiring these columns to have the same extended data type? What are the reasons for this relaxation?

12.10   What six capabilities must the principal relational language have, if it is to be comprehensive?

CHAPTER 13

Integrity Constraints

Preserving the accuracy of information in a commercial database is extremely important for the organization that is maintaining that database. Such an organization is likely to rely heavily upon that accuracy. Critical business decisions may be made assuming that information extracted from the database is correct. Thus, incorrect data can lead to incorrect business decisions.

In the relational model, the approach to maintaining the accuracy and integrity of the database is preventive in nature. General methods for preventing the database from being damaged by users of all kinds are far easier to conceive than general methods for repairing the damage once it is done.

One major step toward the goal of correctness of the data is the enforcement of integrity constraints by the DBMS. Many of these constraints represent rules pertaining to the business. When enforced, these constraints require the data to be continually consistent with those rules.

Continual and dynamic enforcement is the responsibility of the DBMS itself. Enforcement is totally misplaced if it is made the responsibility of a software package added on top of the DBMS as an afterthought, because such a package can easily be bypassed.

Without doubt, the relational approach is opening up databases to many more people than any previous approach. It is no longer the case that just a few members of an organization can access the data because of the highly specialized skills and knowledge needed. Therefore, far more responsibility must be placed on the DBMS to maintain the integrity of the data. Up to the time of writing this book, DBMS vendors have failed to provide adequate support for the integrity features of the relational model.

Occasionally in this chapter and the next, the term "user-defined integrity constraints" is used. This term means integrity constraints defined by suitably authorized users. Normally, such authorization is assigned to the DBA and his or her staff only, since these are the people ultimately responsible for the correctness of the data.

Many people have the incorrect notion that integrity constraints merely amount to validation of data upon its entry into the database. Integrity constraints, however, are much broader in scope. They may be applicable upon insertion, update, or deletion of data, and the timing of applicability is normally specified as part of the pertinent declarations.

13.1 ■ Linguistic Expression of Integrity Constraints

Early in the development of non-relational DBMS (and also in the development of artificial-intelligence prototypes), the objective was often adopted of casting as much as possible of the system's behavior into data structure. This approach was thought desirable because it might simplify the programming. Actually, the programming often became much more complicated, and the systems became much harder to understand.

In the relational approach, in sharp contrast to non-relational approaches, declaration of user-defined integrity constraints is made largely *independent of the data structure* (both physical and logical) to achieve integrity independence (see Feature RP-3 in Chapter 20). Such constraints must be specified *linguistically* using the principal relational language, RL.

Features RI-25–RI-27 and RI-31 in Chapter 14, together with Features RL-10 and RL-11 in Chapter 22, help users to specify those kinds of constraints that involve inter-set relationships, such as inclusion dependence (the inclusion of one set of database values within another).

13.2 ■ The Five Types of Integrity Constraints

Information about *inadequately identified* objects is never recorded in a relational database. To be more specific, the following two integrity constraints apply to the base relations in *every* relational database, and should be enforced by the DBMS:

1. Type E, *entity integrity*. No component of a primary key is allowed to have a missing value of any type. No component of a foreign key is allowed to have an I-marked value (missing-and-inapplicable).

2. Type R, *referential integrity*. For each distinct, unmarked foreign-key value in a relational database, there must exist in the database an equal value of a primary key from the same domain. If the foreign key is composite, those components that are themselves foreign keys and unmarked must exist in the database as components of at least one primary-key value drawn from the same domain.

Note that the domain concept plays a crucial role in this and in other kinds of integrity. For convenience, the following abbreviations are adopted: PK denotes primary key; FK denotes foreign key.

Cases in which the key is a combination of columns and some (perhaps all) of the component values of a foreign key-value are allowed to be marked as "missing, need special attention." *Those components of such a foreign-key value that are unmarked should adhere to the referential-integrity constraint.* This detail is often *not* supported in today's DBMS products, even when the vendors claim that their products support referential integrity.

Of these two types of integrity, some versions or releases of relational DBMS products support entity integrity. Only a few, however, provide even partial support for referential integrity. The most important reason for this partial support or lack of support is omission of support for the domain concept. Also, support is omitted in most products for primary and foreign keys. In addition, there is failure to support features that would enhance the performance of this kind of integrity constraint, such as domain-based indexes (see Feature RD-7 in Chapter 21).

To a large extent, Version 2 (Release 1) of IBM's DB2 supports referential integrity, a substantial improvement over Version 1. The support is incomplete, however, for the following reasons.

■ It fails to include domains supported as extended data types (see Chapter 3).

■ The primary key of each base relation is optional, when it should be mandatory.

■ There is no TC timing (PK update problem).

■ There is no TT timing (cyclic key state problem).

■ A foreign key is allowed to cross-refer to only one primary key (when more than one base relation may each have a primary key based on the same domain). There is no partial check on composite FK, for which at least one component is missing and at least one is not missing.

■ The only alternative to on-the-fly checking involves use of a utility program (see Sections 13.3 and 13.6, including Feature RI-22).

Before introducing the types of integrity constraints in the relational model, it is worth noting that the terms "integrity constraint" and "violation of an integrity constraint" convey the original motivation for the concept. These terms fail, however, to convey certain important future uses of the concept. Its use is likely to grow beyond maintenance of database integrity into application-oriented actions based on specified states of data arising in the database and on date and time occurrences.

For example, for certain kinds of parts held in inventory, whenever the quantity-on-hand sinks to pre-specified levels, the DBMS may take the action of ordering certain computed or pre-specified quantities of those parts. This kind of use will probably receive more attention in RM/V3.

RI-1–RI-5 Types of Integrity Constraints

Integrity constraints are of five types: (1) D-type or domain integrity (Feature RI-1), (2) C-type or column integrity (Feature RI-2), (3) E-type or entity integrity (Feature RI-3), (4) R-type or referential integrity (Feature RI-4), and (5) U-type or user-defined integrity (Feature RI-5).

In English, an easy way to remember the five types is that the corresponding letters are those of the words CURED (the pleasing one to remember) and CRUDE. All five types must be supported by the DBMS using declarations expressed in RL. In this task the full power of RL, including but not limited to four-valued, first-order predicate logic, must be applicable.

One reason that C-type integrity is part of the relational model is that it makes it possible to avoid the needless complexities and proliferations of domains that are subsets of other domains. For example, suppose that a database contains many currency columns, all of the same currency type (all U.S. dollars, say). Then, only one currency domain need be declared. The range of values that is included in the definition of this domain is wide enough for all company uses. Each column, however, that reflects a more narrowly defined range (maximum expenditure by certain departments, say) would have an additional range constraint applied to the column: in other words, a C-type integrity constraint that the DBMS links with the D-type constraint by logical AND.

Referential integrity is defined and discussed in Section 1.8. Its definition was briefly repeated earlier in this section. User-defined integrity is discussed in Chapter 14.

13.3 ■ Timing and Response Specification

In RM/V2 each integrity constraint is assigned a timing, and there are precisely two types of timing. The timing type TC specifies that integrity-constraint checking is to be executed by the DBMS no later than the end of execution of whatever relational request (normally originating from a user or application program) is now active. The timing type TT specifies that integrity-constraint checking is to be executed by the DBMS at the end of execution of whatever transaction the relational request participates in. Of course, a request may be free of any transaction context: that is, the request does not participate in any transaction. In this case, all those integrity constraints of type TT are inapplicable.

To explain these two timing types in more detail, consider the action taken by the DBMS whenever a relational request is being executed. It is advisable to remember that the normal source of each relational request is either an application program or a user who is interacting with the database using a terminal. On the other hand, the normal source of an integrity constraint is the catalog.

The catalog is the direct source for types D, C, R, and U, whose definitions are explicitly stored in the catalog. It is the indirect source for type E through use of the declarations of all primary keys, and, of course, these declarations are stored in the catalog. The action taken by the DBMS consists of Steps 1–5 for a request that participates in a transaction, and Steps 1–3 only for a request that does not participate in any transaction.

Step 1 Some time during the execution of the request (possibly at the very beginning) the DBMS determines which of the five types of integrity constraints and which of the possibly many instances of these types are applicable to the current request.

Step 2 The DBMS inspects the timing types of each applicable integrity constraint that is not of type E. Integrity constraints of type E are always of timing type TC. Most integrity constraints of types D and C are also of timing type TC.

Step 3 Before the end of execution of the relational request, the DBMS completes the checking of those constraints that are applicable to this request and of timing type TC.

Step 4 The DBMS appends those constraints that are applicable to this request and of timing type TT to a list pertaining to the current transaction.

Step 5 Immediately before committing all changes resulting from a transaction to the database, the DBMS checks all the constraints of type TT in the list of applicable type TT constraints accumulated during the execution of that transaction.

Note that Step 3 is applicable to every manipulative request regardless of whether that request participates or does not participate in a transaction.

Of course, designers of DBMS products may choose to implement early and tuple-by-tuple execution of type TC integrity checking for performance reasons, but then the onus is on them to prove that the total support for integrity checking in their DBMS product covers all the RM/V2 requirements (see Feature RI-22).

RI-6 Timing of Testing for Types R and U

Each constraint specification of Type R or U must include a symbol specifying a timing condition. Thus, whenever the DBMS determines that a particular constraint is pertinent to a command just executed, it must also examine the timing symbol to determine whether the constraint is to be tested either (1) immediately, upon completion of execution of the command being executed (type TC), or (2) as part of the execution of a COMMIT command in attempting to complete a transaction (type TT) and immediately before committing any changes to the database.

In Case (2), it is entirely possible that the DBA may have requested the abortion of any transaction that attempts to violate a particular integrity constraint. Note that the timing types TC and TT are independent of the types D, C, E, R, U cited earlier in Features RI-1–RI-5. Use of T-timing for types D, C, or E, however, will probably be quite rare.

The on-the-fly timing of IBM's DB2 is discussed in Section 13.6.

RI-7   Response to Attempted Violation for Types R and U

Accompanying each R-type and U-type integrity constraint, there must be a *violation response* V, which defines the action to be taken by the system in case of attempted violation of the constraint. The system permits this action to be expressed in RL, in the host language, or in both. Of course, every execution of V is also subject to whatever integrity constraints are applicable to V. These constraints may be of any of the five types D, C, E, R, or U, and either of the two timings TC or TT.

ROLLBACK is an example of a command that should be permitted. It is reasonable, however, for the DBMS to prohibit use of the COMMIT command as part of the violation response, because normally a transaction is in progress (originating from an application program or interactively from a terminal), and execution of that transaction may not be completed.

RI-8   Determining Applicability of Constraints

Before completion of the execution of any RL statement, the DBMS must examine the catalog to see whether any C-timed integrity constraints must be tested. Before completion of the execution of any transaction (indeed, before committing any of the changes to the database), the DBMS must examine the catalog to see whether any T-timed integrity constraints must be tested. Whenever the DBMS finds that a constraint must be tested, it proceeds to execute the specified test.

RI-9   Retention of Constraint Definitions for Types R and U

The DBMS stores the following in the catalog: (1) the definition of the violation response for each instance of a referential-integrity constraint, along with identification by column names of the pertinent PK-FK association; (2) the definition of each user-defined integrity constraint, including its violation response.

RI-10   Activation of Constraint Testing

As a consequence of Feature RI-8, integrity constraints are directly activated by the DBMS. They are *not* activated by an explicit call from any application program, and *not* by any user at a terminal. If integrity constraints were activated in either of these ways, it would be all too easy to bypass them altogether.

There are two important reasons for Features RI-9 and RI-10. First, integrity constraints are a concern of the community of users, not just of a single application programmer. Second, the act of keeping the database in compliance with any integrity constraint should not depend on *any voluntary action whatsoever* by any user or programmer (whether it be including the code in his or her program to do the checking or including a call to invoke a checking program).

Now, relational DBMS products have been put on the market without adequate support for integrity constraints. Thus, some users have been forced to place these constraints temporarily in their application programs until the vendor supports them in the catalog, which is where they belong. Consequently, when a vendor introduces support for new types of these constraints should in no way depend on whether each constraint does or does not appear in any application program.

Users of today's relational DBMS products are advised to provide themselves with standard procedures to develop application code so that whatever integrity constraints are incorporated in applications today can be easily identified and removed, when the products are improved in their handling of all five types of integrity constraints.

RI-11   Violations of Integrity Constraints of Types D, C, and E

Violations of integrity constraints of Types D, C, and E are never permitted. If the source of an attempted violation is an application program, the DBMS returns a code indicating that it has not executed the request. Then, the programmer can choose (if appropriate) to include commands in his or her program to bring the program to a complete halt if this code is encountered. If the source is a user at a terminal, the DBMS simply denies the user's request and sends a message explaining the denial.

If a user were allowed to record in the database the immediate properties of an object without recording that object's primary-key value, serious problems would arise in trying to maintain database integrity. For example, if two rows in the R-table for employees have equality in corresponding property values (whenever these values do not happen to be missing from the database), but one or both primary-key values is missing, how can one resolve the following question: Do these two rows represent two distinct employees or just one? In such a case, the count of the number of rows may not be equal to the number of employees in the company.

In the following example of a relation EMP that identifies and describes employees, notice that, in each of the two rows for employee(s) named Knight, the primary-key value is missing. Do these two rows represent two distinct employees or just one?

EMP	(EMP#	ENAME	BIRTH_DATE	SALARY	H_CITY	BONUS)
	E107	Rook	23-08-19	10,000	Wimborne	5,500
	—A	Knight	38-11-05	12,000	Poole	—I
	—A	Knight	—A	12,000	Poole	—I
	E575	Pawn	31-04-22	11,000	Poole	3,100

"—A" denotes missing-and-applicable; "—I" denotes missing-and-inapplicable. This is a good example of a database that has lost its integrity. It is also one of the simplest of such examples.

13.4 ■ Safety Features

RI-12   User-defined Prohibition of Missing Database Values

For any column of any base R-table other than a column that is a component of the primary key of that table, the DBA can explicitly request that missing database values of specified types be prohibited. As a result, the DBMS will reject as unacceptable any execution of a single RL command that attempts to place an A-mark or an I-mark (whichever has been prohibited) in such a column.

See Feature RI-19 regarding the introduction of such a constraint. The DBMS must *not* require that, if C is a column in which missing values are prohibited, then C must be indexed, because indexes are supposed to be creatable and droppable at any time for *performance reasons only*. A prohibition of missing values of either type, of course, is quite redundant and unnecessary if the column happens to be part of or the whole of the primary key of the pertinent base R-table. In this case, the entity-integrity constraint is automatically applied (see Feature RI-3). An explicit prohibition of I-marks in any foreign-key column is redundant for the same reason.

In no way, however, does Feature RI-12 make the entity integrity feature RI-3 unnecessary. The mere fact that a column or combination of columns of a base R-table is prohibited from accepting missing database values cannot be interpreted by the DBMS as a declaration that the pertinent combination is the primary key of that base R-table.

Duplicate values are automatically prohibited from each simple or composite column that happens to be the primary key of a base relation. Occasionally, there is a need to prohibit duplicate values from occurring in simple or composite columns *other than the primary key*. The following feature provides this capability.

RI-13 User-defined Prohibition of Duplicate Values

A suitably authorized user can declare of any simple or composite column in a base relation that duplicate values are prohibited from occurring in that column.

The DBMS may either ignore or reject any attempt by the user to apply Feature RI-13 to the primary key, since such an attempt is completely unnecessary. The DBMS prohibits duplicate values from occurring in the primary key without an explicit request to do so.

It is also unnecessary to apply Feature RI-13 to the combination of all columns in a base relation in an attempt to prevent the occurrence of duplicate rows, since the DBMS performs this task without an explicit request to do so.

RI-14 Illegal Tuple

A tuple consisting of nothing but marked values is prohibited from all R-tables, whether base or derived.

Such a tuple is already prohibited from base R-tables because each such table must have exactly one primary key, none of whose component values can be missing. In derived relations, such a tuple is clearly devoid of information.

RI-15 Audit Log

The DBA can request the DBMS to maintain an audit log of at least all the changes committed to the database (both description and contents). The information recorded in this log includes at least the date, time, and identifiers of the user, the terminal, and the application program (if any such program was involved).

The information in this log need not be directly recorded in a manner seen by users as a collection of relations, but it must be dynamically translatable to such a form by a program that is part of the DBMS. The audit log thus generated can be interrogated by any suitably authorized user who makes use of RL. The translating utility can be executed with a frequency specified by the DBA (once a day and once a week must be supported as options).

The term "dynamically" in this context means without bringing the database traffic to a halt.

Most database management systems maintain a recovery log, but this log is often inadequate for auditors to trace who was responsible for each change made to the database (in terms of both description and contents), and at what date and time the changes were made. In a few products, an audit log is supported that goes beyond the requirements of Feature RI-15 by recording all querying activity as well as all manipulative activity.

RI-16 Non-subversion

Languages other than RL may be supported by the DBMS for database manipulation (the relational model does not prohibit such languages). If any of these languages is non-relational (e.g., single-record-at-a-time), there must be a rigorous proof that it is impossible for the integrity constraints expressed in RL and stored in the catalog to be bypassed by using one of these non-relational languages. (Feature RI-16 is Rule 12 in the 1985 set.)

Note that an example of inability to bypass an integrity constraint does not constitute a proof of adequate generality. The following general assertion must be proved: For all possible database requests permitted by the DBMS product, all possible transactions permitted by that product, and all possible integrity constraints permitted by that product, it is impossible to bypass any applicable integrity constraint. Also note that Feature RI-16 is extremely difficult for a system to support if the system is "evolving" from a non-relational architecture to a relational architecture; such a system already supports an interface at a lower level of abstraction than the relational language in which the integrity constraints are specified.

13.5 ▪ Creating, Executing, and Dropping Integrity Constraints

RI-17 Creating and Dropping an Integrity Constraint

RL includes a CREATE CONSTRAINT command and a DROP CONSTRAINT command. The CREATE command includes the following items: (1) a name for the constraint distinct from any constraint name currently in the catalog, (2) the type D, C, E, R, or U, (3) the constraint definition, and (4) the timing type TC or TT. Execution of this command causes this information to be stored in the catalog. The DROP command identifies the integrity constraint to be dropped by name. Its execution merely causes the named integrity constraint to be removed from the catalog.

RI-18 New Integrity Constraints Checked

When a new integrity constraint of any type (except the type covered in Feature RI-19) is introduced into the catalog, or an integrity constraint that already exists in the catalog is modified, the activity must be part of a CAT block (Feature RM-7). The DBMS immediately checks those parts of the database that are potentially affected by the new constraint in an attempt to find all violations of that constraint that already exist in the database. The user is notified of each such violation and the DBMS stops execution in the CAT block until the user responds by rectifying the violation. If no such remedial action is forthcoming within a reasonable time, the DBMS rejects the integrity constraint. After all violations of the new integrity constraint in the entire database have been detected and rectified, the DBMS accepts the integrity constraint and completes the CAT block. From then on, the DBMS enforces the constraint.

RI-19 Introducing a Column Integrity Constraint (Type C) for Disallowing Missing Database Values

When a Type C integrity constraint, which disallows the occurrence of missing values in a specified column, is introduced into the catalog, the database at that instant may be inconsistent with this constraint. That is, the pertinent column may happen to contain numerous occurrences of missing values. Enforcement of this integrity constraint in full is therefore delayed in the following sense.

Those marks that already occur in this column at the time of dec-laration of the constraint are allowed to continue to exist until each and every such mark is updated to an acceptable database value. On the other hand, the DBMS rejects any attempt to update a database value already in the pertinent column to a mark that indicates the value is now missing.

In other words, the introduction of a constraint that disallows missing database values in a specified column is enforced gradually. No new occur-rences of marks are allowed, but those that exist in the specified column are allowed to continue to exist until they are updated to database values. This kind of gradual enforcement can be applied to certain types of integrity constraints other than the prohibition of missing values. The next version of the relational model (RM/V3) is likely to include such gradual enforce-ment as an additional option on these other types.

If the column happens to be a foreign-key column, referential integrity is applied as usual to the non-missing foreign-key values only. Note that a column of a base R-table that is either the whole primary key or a component of the primary key is not allowed to have any database values missing, beginning with the creation of that R-table.

13.6 ■ Performance-oriented Features

In the following feature, the database scope of a command or transaction is discussed. This is the part of the database that could have been adversely affected by execution of the command or transaction. Note that this scope can be broader than just the part of the database that was actually touched by the command or transaction.

For example, a simple update applied to a primary-key value touches only that primary-key value, but it may damage referential integrity in several parts of the database not touched. Those foreign-key values that previously matched this primary-key value (scattered widely in the database and not touched) may be, and probably will be, adversely affected by the change in primary-key value.

RI-20 Minimal Adequate Scope of Checking

When integrity constraints must be checked dynamically either at the end of a command or at the end of a transaction, the DBMS is designed to make this check over that part of the database that could have been adversely affected by the command or by the transaction, but no more than that.

The preceding feature is applicable during DBMS-initiated dynamic checking of integrity constraints. Occasionally, the DBA must be able to initiate a *complete check* of an integrity constraint over an entire relation or over several entire relations if it is a multi-relation constraint. For example, such a check is needed soon after loading a new relation from a non-relational source.

RI-21   Each Integrity Constraint Executable as a Command

One of the commands in RL is intended for DBA-initiated execution of any designated integrity constraint that is stored in the catalog. The name of the particular constraint, not its type, is specified as part of the command to designate the operand. The result of executing the command is a complete listing of all violations of the specified integrity constraint.

This command can be applied to integrity constraints of all five types. To support this feature, it is essential that each occurrence of a particular kind of integrity constraint (e.g., referential) must be given a distinct name (see Feature RN-13 in Chapter 6). The term "occurrence" in this sentence should not be interpreted in a row-by-row sense, but instead at the relational level.

To avoid a reduction in performance when the DBMS checks referential integrity, designers of IBM's DB2 invented the on-the-fly technique. This technique is also applicable to checking other kinds of integrity constraints. As its name implies, an integrity constraint is checked piece by piece as the execution of a command proceeds to affect pieces of the database.

This technique is excellent for attaining acceptable performance, but it fails to support cases in which the execution of a command or transaction initially violates an integrity constraint, but later recovers from this violation. In fact, the transaction concept of System R was invented for this reason.

The occasional inapplicability of the on-the-fly approach is the justification of the following feature. Note that it does not adversely affect performance in those cases in which the on-the-fly technique is applicable in a correct manner.

RI-22   On-the-fly, End of Command, and End of Transaction Techniques

If the DBMS uses the on-the-fly technique as its normal technique for checking integrity constraints, it must be able to resort to an end-of-command or end-of-transaction technique in those cases when the on-the-fly technique does not work correctly.

IBM's DB2 Version 2 does not support this feature. Consequently, extreme care is necessary when a user wishes to update a primary-key value and have the corresponding foreign-key values similarly updated to conserve the matching of values that existed earlier. Using DB2 and assuming no specially favorable circumstances, neither of the following steps is valid as the first step:

1. update the primary-key value;
2. update one of the foreign-key values.

In both of these cases, the on-the-fly implementation of referential integrity fails.

Is there any way of handling this kind of update in DB2? Yes, but it is very complicated—and needlessly so, especially when a single command is adequate in the relational model (see Features RB-31 and RB-32 in Chapter 4). In the following explanation, assume that the foreign keys are those that refer to the given primary key, that x is the old primary-key value, and that y is the new primary-key value.

1. Copy a new row into the relation S with the same component values as the row whose primary key is to be updated, except for the primary-key value itself, which in the new row is set to y.
2. Update each corresponding foreign-key value from x to y.
3. Delete the row containing the old primary-key value x.

Although this algorithm may appear to be simple, its complexity is enormous. Step 1 involves using host-language commands (SQL alone is inadequate for this task). Step 2 requires the user either

■ to know all of the columns that are foreign-key columns with respect to the given primary key column (a very risky assumption due to the highly dynamic nature of relational DBMS), **or**
■ to develop a program to scan all the foreign-key declarations in the catalog and find all those that refer to the given primary key.

While this scan and all the remaining actions in Step 2 are taking place, the user of DB2 must ensure through explicit or implicit locking that no other user either introduces a new foreign-key referencing the given primary key, or deletes the row of S that has the new primary-key value.

At least one alternative algorithm handles this problem correctly in DB2, but it is also needlessly complicated. In any event, the algorithm involves multiple SQL statements instead of just one (See Feature RB-33 or RB-34), and therefore degrades performance.

With regard to the problem of updating primary keys, the complexity of DB2—from the user's standpoint and in terms of implementation—stems from the omission of a simple and cheap feature in the relational model (namely, support of domains as extended data types; see Chapter 3). When I introduced the domain concept into database management 20 years ago as part of the relational model [Codd 1971b, 1971a], it was regarded by almost all of my IBM colleagues as a purely academic exercise. It is now time for the implementors of DBMS products to recognize that the domain concept *must* be implemented as part of the DBMS if these products are to provide adequate support for database integrity. Without adequate support for database integrity, DBMS vendors are asking DBMS consumers to put their businesses at unnecessary risk.

Exercises

13.1   What are the five types of integrity in the relational model? Is recoverability from failures in hardware or software directly related to any of these five types? If so, how? Does it matter whether a vendor's DBMS supports any of these forms of integrity?

13.2   Is the relational approach to database integrity based on prevention or on cure? Why?

13.3   Are integrity constraints explicitly invoked from an application program? If not, why not, and how are these constraints invoked?

13.4   What does it mean to say that a cyclic key state exists in the description of a relational database? How does this concept relate to the transaction concept?

13.5   IBM introduced partial support for referential integrity in Version 2 (Release 1) of its DBMS product DB2. List six ways in which this release falls short of full support for referential integrity, and explain the consequences for users.

13.6   Sometimes people assert that it would be adequate if a DBMS always responded to an attempted violation of a referential integrity constraint by rejecting the user's request. Describe an example that demonstrates the need for at least one alternative reaction.

13.7   IBM's Version 2 of DB2 uses the on-the-fly technique during execution of a transaction for checking whether referential integrity is being maintained. Develop a set of necessary and sufficient conditions under which this technique is guaranteed to work correctly.

13.8   If Exercise 13.7 is solved, can the end-of-transaction timing be used by the DBMS as a fallback for checking referential integrity whenever the system discovers that the conditions for correctness of the on-the-fly technique are not in effect? What does this improved support provide in the case of row insertions when there happens to be a cyclic key state?

13.9 Can a user prohibit the occurrence of duplicate values in: (1) a simple column (2) a composite column? If so, how?

13.10 A row is generated in a derived relation, and it contains nothing but marked values.
1. What does RM/V2 do with the row?
2. Can such a row occur in a view?
3. Can such a row occur in a base relation? In each case, explain why RM/V2 behaves this way.

13.11 What are the major differences in content between a recovery log and an audit log?

13.12 Missing values were permitted in a column that has existed for some time. What problems can arise in introducing a new constraint on that column that prohibits the occurrence of missing values?

CHAPTER 14

User-defined Integrity Constraints

Integrity constraints other than those of the domain, column, entity, and referential types are needed for relational databases. There are two main reasons. First, these user-defined integrity constraints permit the database administrator to define, in a way that can be enforced by the DBMS, many of the company regulations pertaining to the company operations that are reflected in the database. Second, these constraints permit the database administrator to define, also in a way that can be enforced by the DBMS, many of the government and other regulations that apply to these company operations. Once these constraints are defined and entered into the catalog, the DBMS enforces them. Consequently, there is no need to depend on voluntary compliance by application programmers or end users.

Although the term *user-defined* is applied to these integrity constraints, any user who is attempting to define such an integrity constraint must be authorized to do so (see Chapter 18, "Authorization"). Normally, where the number of users is large and the database is production-oriented, few users are so authorized. The DBA, of course, is one such user, since he or she bears primary responsibility for the safety and accuracy of the database and its compliance with company and governmental regulations. It is likely that any other users similarly authorized would be on the DBA's staff.

As mentioned in Chapter 13, it is important to keep in mind that eventually integrity constraints, especially those of the user-defined type, will be applied not only to keep the database in an accurate state by preventing violations of these constraints, but also to trigger specified positive actions (that cannot be interpreted as responses to violations) when specified conditions arise in the database. Actually, a small class of this type (clock-triggered actions) is supported by RM/V2.

14.1 ■ Information in a User-defined Integrity Constraint

What information must a user-defined integrity constraint contain? It is easy to see that the four components named in Feature RI-23 are necessary; normally, these four should also be sufficient.

RI-23 Information in a User-defined Integrity Constraint

A user-defined integrity constraint has four components: (1) Timing type TC or TT, (2) those actions by terminal users (TU), application programs (AP), or the date-time clock that trigger the testing of the condition, (3) a specification of the condition to be tested, and (4) the name of a procedure that specifies the action to be taken in case of attempted violation. Both the user-defined integrity constraint and its violation procedure are stored in the catalog.

Let us consider each of these items in turn. The timing type, described in Chapter 13, is set to TC if the specified condition (Item 3 in the preceding list) is to be tested at the end of execution of the triggering command. It is set to TT if the condition is to be tested at the end of execution of whatever transaction includes the triggering command.

Now for those actions by application programs or terminal users that trigger the testing of the specified condition.

RI-24 Triggering Based on AP and TU Actions

The DBMS detects as actions that trigger the testing phase of user-defined integrity constraints at least the following types of encounters: (1) a retrieval from a specified relation, (2) an insertion into a specified relation, (3) an update of a specified relation and column (either not involving an I-marked value or involving an I-marked value), and (4) a deletion from a specified relation. These actions are detected by the DBMS regardless of whether they stem from application programs (AP) or from terminal users (TU).

RI-25 Triggering Based on Date and Time

The DBMS is stimulated to invoke the testing phase of user-defined integrity constraints by the advance of date and/or time to pre-specified absolute values or by the lapse of pre-specified date and/or time intervals from some specified starting date and time.

The timing types TC and TT are inapplicable to integrity constraints for which the triggering is based on date and time.

Each integrity constraint of this type has exactly one absolute date and/or time. If it is to be periodically activated, this is merely the starting time, and a date and time interval need to be specified also. Such a timing is recorded in the catalog as the triggering action of an integrity constraint. If the condition-to-be-tested component of such a constraint is omitted, or if that component is specified and happens to have the value TRUE, action is invoked and it is specified in the integrity constraint as the action-to-be-triggered component.

It is worthwhile to digress for a moment into issues related to implementation. When the DBA enters a clock-triggered integrity constraint into the catalog, the request must indicate (perhaps indirectly) an absolute date and/or time and indicate whether the activation is to be periodic with some specified interval.

The DBMS maintains a queue of date-time combinations ordered so that the earliest is at the top of the queue. This earliest combination is transmitted to the clock as the next date and time to create an alarm. At that time the alarm takes the form of an interruption of the DBMS's activities (at some convenient time, but not significantly delayed). The DBMS then finds the pertinent integrity constraint, and executes its condition part. If the constraint is to be periodically activated, the DBMS places a freshly incremented date-time combination in the queue.

14.2 ■ Condition Part of a User-defined Integrity Constraint

The third component of a user-defined integrity constraint is the specification of a condition to be tested. Such a condition is normally a truth-valued expression of the relational language. This expression must have the value TRUE if the integrity constraint is to be satisfied; the qualifier MAYBE is not permitted in such an expression.

Conditions can be imposed either on states of the database or on changes in states of the database. Consider two conditions that stem from a company's policy. One is imposed on database states; the other, on changes of state:

1. each employee's salary cannot exceed a certain limit determined by the employee's position or job in the company;

2. each salary cannot be increased by more than a certain percentage determined by the employee's position or job in the company.

The following example illustrates the practical reasons for including user-defined integrity constraints in RM/V2 and the information contained in these constraints.

EMP		
	EMP#	Employee serial number
	ENAME	Employee name
	BIRTH_DATE	Date of birth of employee
	SALARY	Present salary
	JOBCODE	Position or job within company

EMP	(EMP#	ENAME	BIRTH_DATE	SALARY	JOBCODE)
	e10	Rook	1923-08-19	17,000	j5
	e91	Knight	1938-11-05	12,000	j7
	e23	Knight	1938-11-05	14,000	j7
	e57	Pawn	1931-04-22	10,000	j9
	e01	King	1922-05-27	23,000	j1
	e34	Bishop	1930-09-17	16,500	j7

A relation called CONTROL contains for each position held by employees the maximum salary for that position:

CONTROL		
	JOBCODE	Job within company
	MAXSAL	Limit on salary for the job
	PERCENT	Limit on percentage increase in salary

CONTROL	(JOBCODE	MAXSAL	PERCENT)
	j1	30,000	20
	j2	25,000	10
	j5	20,000	10
	j7	15,000	8
	j9	15,000	8

Suppose that the salary of an employee is being raised to some new level. Clearly, this employee's row in the relation EMP must be modified. It is the new version of this row that must be checked by the DBMS before the row is committed to the database. It is quite inadequate for the DBMS to check intermediate results that are developed along the way to the new version of the pertinent row. The DBMS is responsible for ensuring that all the values being committed to the database conform to the integrity constraints.

Now, in the example under consideration, the salary increase may be entered from a terminal or may be computed. The DBMS is not responsible for monitoring how the new salary is created. After the new salary has been created and has become a component of the new row, and after this row is ready for commitment to the database and is no longer under the control of the application program or user, then the DBMS must go into action and check that the new salary complies with the pertinent integrity constraints. Regardless of how the salary increase is created, it is only a step on the way to the new salary. Checking this increase as an intermediate result is irrelevant.

That is why integrity constraint 2 in the preceding list is expressed in terms of the new and old salaries, not in terms of a salary increase that may have been generated already. Although these two versions of the increase in salary are very likely to be identical, the possibility of mathematical equality is not at issue. Instead, the question is which *occurrence* of the increase must be checked if database integrity is to be enforced.

Incidentally, the use of the prefixes "new" and "old" makes this kind of integrity constraint easier to write and more comprehensible to those who did not write it. Let the updated salary (when it is under the control of the DBMS) be denoted by new_SALARY.

Suppose that the pertinent employee has jobcode = j.

Condition 1: new_SALARY < CONTROL.MAXSAL
          where JOBCODE = j

Condition 2: (new_SALARY − old_SALARY)
          < old_SALARY × CONTROL.PERCENT
                  where JOBCODE = j

The kind of command that is to trigger the testing of these conditions is an update on the SALARY component of a row of the EMP relation. The timing type is TC.

On update of EMP.SALARY: If NOT condition 1, then REJECT

On update of EMP.SALARY: If NOT condition 2, then REJECT

For information on the REJECT command, see Section 14.9.

It is not difficult to conceive of similar examples that stem from government regulations instead of company policy. In one such example, the total year-to-date income tax withheld from each employee's salary must be within 10% of the total tax on the year-to-date salary, where that tax is defined by a formula that conforms to the pertinent law or regulation.

If the preceding condition is not satisfied, it is reasonable to say that an attempted violation of the pertinent integrity constraint has taken place. However, when specifying an appropriate user-defined integrity constraint, it is important to identify the condition when TRUE must trigger the exceptional action by the DBMS, because this is the condition that is required in that integrity constraint.

As an example of a clock-triggered constraint, consider the following command. Starting on October 8 at 3A.M. and every 7 days thereafter, archive the derived relation S consisting of all those rows of R for which the component DONE has the value 1. In a manufacturing company, R might be information about orders of parts, and DONE = 1 might mean that the ordered parts and invoice have been received, and the invoice paid. In an airline, R might be a passenger list for each flight on each day. Moreover, DONE = 1 might mean that the flight has been successfully completed. In this second case, deletion might be more appropriate as the triggered action instead of archiving.

14.3 ■ The Triggered Action

The fourth and final component of a user-defined integrity constraint is the action to be taken in the event the condition is TRUE (see Feature RI-23). This action takes the form of a simple procedure—known as the *triggered action*—encoded in some combination of the principal host language and the principal relational language. Such a procedure is stored in compiled form in the catalog and given a name.

The fourth component of a user-defined integrity constraint is the name of the triggered action procedure. For performance reasons, there might be a symbolic name table *under the covers* that would accelerate access to the code when needed.

14.4 ■ Execution of User-defined Integrity Constraints

All user-defined integrity constraints (whether of timing type TC or TT) are examined by the DBMS at the end of executing each RL command to determine which ones are applicable. If an applicable constraint is of type TC, it is executed immediately. If an applicable constraint is of type TT, the DBMS notes that this constraint must be executed at the end of this transaction. In this way, the DBMS avoids, at the end of the transaction, a burdensome exploration of the commands within the transaction to determine which integrity constraints are applicable at that time.

Execution of the condition part of a constraint of type TT must be postponed to the end of the transaction. If executed earlier, the condition could evaluate to TRUE (triggering the exceptional action), even though, if executed at the end of the transaction, the condition would evaluate to FALSE (no exceptional action necessary).

Note that it is completely unnecessary for any application program or any terminal user to invoke any integrity constraint at any time. This statement applies to all such constraints, whether user-defined or not. Once an integrity constraint has been defined and entered into the catalog, it is the sole responsibility of the DBMS to invoke it whenever it is applicable. Thus, with a relational DBMS there is no reliance on voluntary action by users in order to maintain the integrity of the database.

Consider what happens whenever a relational command is executed. Let us assume that the user-defined integrity constraints are kept in the catalog in separate tables as shown next (although the relational model does not specify such an organization).

Table	Basis of Constraints
1	Pure retrieval (i.e., no update intended, this is the least important case)
2	Insertion
3	Update
4	Deletion
5	Date and time clock

The implementor may also decide to split each of the first four tables into two by timing type (TC and TT). With either of these organizations, if it is desired to base an integrity constraint upon two of these types of commands (e.g., insertion and update), the constraint must be recorded in two tables (a table for insertions and a table for updates).

Suppose that a relational command is being executed, and that it is one of the four types: pure retrieval, insertion, update, and deletion. Suppose also that this command involves just one relation, say R. Then, at the end of execution of this command, the DBMS scans the table that corresponds to the type of command (Table 1, 2, 3, or 4). From this table, the DBMS selects only those user-defined integrity constraints (if any) that specify the relation R.

For each constraint selected, the DBMS examines the timing type. Suppose that the timing type is TC. Then, the DBMS proceeds to execute the condition part of the integrity constraint. If the result of this execution is FALSE, the DBMS proceeds to the immediately following command. If the result of this execution is TRUE, the DBMS executes the designated procedure for attempted violation. Now, this procedure may simply reject the pertinent command. If so, the DBMS aborts the entire transaction, which means that none of the changes that this transaction would have made to the database are committed.

If the timing type is TT, the DBMS merely notes that the condition part of this integrity constraint must be checked at the end of the transaction. Just before committing the transaction, the DBMS checks whether any integrity constraints have been postponed to this time. If there are several such constraints, the sequence in which they are executed must not affect the outcome. If the outcome is affected, this is most likely because of an inconsistency between integrity constraints (a DBA error)—this is a potential problem for which the DBA must maintain a careful watch. It will be some time before tools are available to simplify the discovery of inconsistencies between integrity constraints.

14.5 ■ Integrity Constraints Triggered by Date and Time

In many commercial installations certain activities need to be triggered on the basis of date and/or time only. A good example of an activity that needs to be done automatically on a routine basis is archiving of some information in the database. If such tasks are executed automatically, neither the DBA nor anyone else has to watch a calendar or clock. An assumption is that the DBMS has access to a clock within the computer system that registers both date and time, and that this clock can act as a rather sophisticated alarm.

Each integrity constraint triggered by date and time must contain a clause specifying either an absolute or a relative date and time. An example of a relative date is every seven days starting on October 8. An example of a relative time is every 24 hours starting at 3:00A.M. A combination of date and time might be every seven days at 3:00A.M. starting on January 12 at 3:00A.M. Normally, the DBMS acts as soon after the specified date and/or time as the necessary locks are released. Of course, at any time various locks may be held by commands and transactions that are already in the process of being executed.

Note that, if date d and time t are specified as a triggering event, the action to be taken when the combination d, t occurs is precisely that specified in the catalog as the triggered action procedure. As pointed out earlier, the phrases *triggering event* and *triggered action* are more appropriate in this context. Note also that in the case of actions triggered by date and time it is either the *truth* of the specified condition or the absence of such a condition that triggers the action.

14.6 ■ Integrity Constraints Relating to Missing Information

Marked values represent the fact that some information is missing from the database. How are these marked values created at data entry time and at later times? How is the choice made between an A-mark and an I-mark? These questions are answered by an insertion feature, RI-26, and an update feature, RI-27.

RI-26 Insertion Involving I-marked Values

In any tuple that is to be inserted into a database there may be component values missing. For each missing value, the DBMS must determine which of the following is appropriate: (1) a default value based on the source of the request (a terminal or work station or an application program), (2) an A-marked value, or (3) an I-marked value. If none of these is appropriate, the DBMS must reject the insertion of this tuple. Note that item (1) is a real value, and it must therefore comply with all the integrity constraints for this column. On the other hand, items (2) and (3) denote the fact that the value is actually missing.

At data entry time, one or more rows are inserted into a base relation, possibly through a view. If a component of a row is missing from the input, the DBMS examines the description in the catalog of the corresponding column and poses the following sequence of questions to the catalog:

1. Is there a default value based on the terminal or work station from which the input came (e.g., the branch identifier in the case of a bank with many branches)?
2. Which types of mark, if any, are permitted in that column?
3. Is there an integrity constraint that generates the correct type of mark?

If the answer to Step 1 is yes, the sequence terminates after Step 1: the DBMS inserts the default value and accepts the input. If the answer to Step 1 is no, the DBMS proceeds to Step 2. If the answer to Step 2 is that both types of marks are prohibited, the sequence terminates after Step 2, and the DBMS rejects the input.

If in Step 2 the DBMS finds that I-marks are prohibited (as in the case of a foreign key) but that A-marks are permitted, the DBMS terminates the sequence after Step 2, and prepares to insert an A-marked value as the pertinent datum. The actual insertion takes place only if it is in compliance with any existing integrity constraint pertaining to A-marked values in that column. In case of non-compliance, the DBMS terminates the sequence and rejects the input.

Similarly, if in Step 2 the DBMS finds that A-marks are prohibited but I-marks are permitted, the DBMS terminates the sequence after Step 2, and prepares to insert an I-marked value as the pertinent datum. The actual insertion takes place only if it is in compliance with any existing integrity constraint pertaining to I-marked values in this column. In case of non-compliance, the input is rejected.

Now, if both types of marked values are permitted, the DBMS first seeks an explicitly stated preference in the request. If a preference is stated there, the DBMS inserts the preferred type of marked value. If the system fails to find such a preference, it then searches the description of the pertinent column to see which one, A or I, is to be inserted. If a preference is stated in that part of the catalog, the DBMS honors the preference. Otherwise, the DBMS inserts an A-marked value (the default case).

An external symbol is needed for the marks in several cases. Whenever such a symbol is needed, the following are suggested:

Type of Mark	A-mark	I-mark
External symbol	??	!!

RI-27 Update Involving I-marked Values

In any tuple within the database that is to be updated, there may be an attempt to replace a database value or A-marked value by an I-marked value. The DBMS must then search the catalog to determine (1) if I-marked values are prohibited from belonging to that column or (2) if their entry is permitted, but they do not conform to some other integrity constraint. In either case a violation of some integrity constraint is being attempted, and the DBMS must invoke the appropriate violation response.

In the case of an update rather than an insertion, a concern that integrity is preserved arises if the update is an attempt to change a db-value into an I-marked value, or vice versa. The DBMS is designed to seek as a first step a DBA-defined integrity constraint in the catalog pertaining to I-marks and the column affected. If the system finds a pertinent constraint, it checks the constraint and either accepts the update (if the constraint is satisfied) or rejects it (if the constraint is not satisfied). If the DBMS fails to find a pertinent constraint, it accepts the update. In any event, of course, the user must be specially authorized to make such an update. The DBMS treats such authorization quite separately from the enforcement of integrity constraints.

14.7 ■ Examples of User-defined Integrity Constraints

In Section 14.2, the example was discussed of enforcing limits on salary increases by means of user-defined integrity constraints. Now follow some new examples.

14.7.1 Cutting Off Orders to Supplier s3

Suppose that an instruction has been issued within a company that no new orders are to be placed for parts from supplier s3, but that existing commitments to s3 will be completed. Then, user-defined integrity constraints such as the following two are needed:

On insertion into ORDER: If S# = s3, then REJECT

On update of S# in ORDER: If new__S# = s3, then REJECT

14.7.2 Re-ordering Parts Automatically

The first of the following two examples illustrates the need for responding to attempted violations of integrity constraints in more complicated ways than simply rejecting the command or the transaction. In this context, even the term "attempted violation" seems incongruous. A more appropriate term is "triggering event."

The first example involves two relations, one called PART, which identifies and describes the various kinds of parts, and one called REORDER, which provides "standard orders" for use when the quantity-on-hand of a particular kind of part falls so low that it becomes necessary to re-order that part. Suppose that the relations are as follows:

PART P#   Part serial number   Primary key
      PNAME   Part name
      SIZE   Part size
      Q   Quantity of parts
      OH__Q   Quantity of parts on hand
      OO__Q   Quantity of parts on order
      MIN__Q   Minimum quantity of parts
                of this kind to be stored

There are only four domains.

	P#	PNAME	SIZE	Q		
PART	(P#	PNAME	SIZE	OH__Q	OO__Q	MIN__Q)
	p1	shaft	10	400	300	300
	p2	wheel	20	850	0	800
	p3	radiator	5	400	200	300
	p4	chassis	12	400	0	200
	p5	bumper	6	620	150	400
	p6	lever	15	420	200	350
	p7	fan	5	500	50	400

REORDER P#   Part serial number   Primary key
         S#   Supplier serial number   Foreign key
               (preferred supplier)
         R_Q   Re-order quantity
         O_D   Date of order
         . . .   .

	P#	S#	Q	
REORDER	(P#	S#	R_Q	. . .)
	p1	s12	600	. . .
	p2	s5	1600	. . .
	p3	s5	600	. . .
	p4	s17	400	. . .
	p5	s6	800	. . .
	p6	s2	700	. . .
	p7	s8	800	. . .

. . .   .

Whenever quantities of part p are withdrawn from inventory, and the remaining quantity is less than that specified in the minimum quantity component MIN_Q of the p row of the PART relation, a DBA-defined integrity constraint causes the DBMS to extract a copy of the p row from REORDER, to update the order date to the current date, and to transmit this order to the preferred supplier. The quantity of part p that should be ordered and the preferred supplier of part p are also components of the p row of REORDER. In this context, placing an order is merely constructing a one-line order.

14.7.3 Automatic Payment for Parts

Suppose that it is current company policy to make payment for parts as soon as they are delivered. Consider the action taken at the time of receipt of the parts—namely, the insertion of a new row into the parts-received relation PR. The new row specifies the supplier and the date of receipt. This insertion must trigger generating a check and recording in the PR relation that payment has been made.

If the company policy in this example is to pay at least 21 days later and no more than 31 days later, the problem takes on a new aspect, involving an action that is triggered on a delayed basis. The delay is begun by a delay-triggering event (the receipt of parts accompanied by an invoice). The reader may wish to consider the simple extensions to RM/V2 to enable it to cope with this practical requirement. Extensions of the relational model to cope with this practical need are postponed to RM/V3.

These exercises clearly indicate the need for the host language to be usable in programming the triggered action.

14.8 ■ Simplifying Features

In the late 1960s, I decided to take a close look at how databases were being designed. At that time it was clear to me that there did not exist any engineering discipline upon which database design could be established. One result was that designers found it extremely difficult—and frequently impossible—to explain why they had chosen a particular design. The only reason that appeared meaningful to me was the attainment of acceptable performance on the first application that was developed to run on the database. Of course, this often meant that the database design was inconsistent with attaining good performance on subsequently developed applications.

Two major problems, and hence challenges, presented themselves. First, there was a complete absence of concern for the database as an object that would continue to exist and evolve independently of any collection of application programs that might exist at some instant in time. Second, there was no rational basis for database design because there were no carefully conceived concepts at a sufficiently high level of abstraction. Database design cannot be successfully pursued if the only concepts available are bits and bytes. For these reasons, I developed the first three normal forms [Codd 1971b and 1971c] and created the field of normalization of relations for database management—a field that now requires a textbook of its own to explain adequately.

Normalization was originally conceived as a systematic way (with proper theoretical foundations, of course) of ensuring that a logical design of a relational database would be free from insertion, update, and deletion anomalies. And indeed, designs that are proposed today can be defended on a rational basis! This subject is pursued further in Section 17.5.1.

In developing the logical design for a database, it is now quite usual to consider the following types of dependency: functional, multi-valued, join, and inclusion. These dependencies, however, should not be treated as if they were valuable at database design time only. All of them should remain in effect until the database is redesigned in part or completely. This means that many of these dependencies should be cast in the form of DBA-defined integrity constraints. Certain elementary constraints can be managed by the DBMS without specific instruction from the DBA.

From time to time, but not frequently, it may be necessary to change one or two of the integrity constraints that define the dependencies. Consequently, to establish these dependencies in the first place, and to modify them later, there is a need for a data model that can easily accommodate such changes without impairing the correctness of already developed application programs.

The relational model was designed to accommodate these and other kinds of changes gracefully. Going beyond this adaptability to changes in database design, there is a need for several extensions to the principal relational language: extensions that simplify the expression of these dependency constraints. Some sample features are listed in Section 14.8.1.

14.8.1 Integrity Constraints of the Database Design Type

These constraints are truth-valued expressions that are applicable whenever the pertinent data is present in the database. Each one is not applicable in those instances (tuples or rows) where any of the pertinent data happens to be missing from the database. In the following discussion, the term "column" should be interpreted as a column that may be simple or composite.

RI-28 Functional Dependency

Column B is functionally dependent on column A: R.A → R.B. For each base relation, the DBMS assumes that all columns that are not part of the primary key are functionally dependent on the primary key, unless otherwise declared.

Using this assumption, the DBA need not declare a very large number of obvious functional dependencies. A simple example is the case of a relation EMP that identifies employees by employee serial number and describes employees by their immediate properties that are of concern to the company, including the department DEPT# to which the employee is assigned. Suppose, however, that EMP also includes an immediate property of the department, namely the contract type CT for that department (incidentally, I am not advocating this step). In this case, the three pertinent functional dependencies within the EMP relation are as follows:

E# → DEPT#

E# → CT

DEPT# → CT.

Of these three functional dependencies, the DBA would need to declare only the third one.

RI-29 Multi-valued Dependency

Column B is multi-valued dependent on column A and column C is independent of B's dependency on A: R.A ➔ R.B / R.C.

The symbol ➔ is intended to distinguish this kind of dependency from the functional dependency of Feature RI-28, in which the symbol → was used.

RI-30 Join Dependency

Column A is join dependent on columns B and C: R.A = R.B * R.C.

RI-31 Inclusion Dependency

Column A is inclusion dependent on Column B. That is, the set of db-values in R.A is a subset of the db-values in R.B: R.A is-in R.B. The DBMS assumes that each declared foreign key is inclusion dependent on (1) its target primary key, if just one target is declared, or (2) the union of its target primary keys, if several happen to be drawn from the pertinent primary domain.

This assumption is justified by the fact that referential integrity must be maintained. The term "is-in" stands for "is included in." As usual, a different syntax may be adopted, but the truth-valued expressions should not be any more complicated than these. As noted earlier, the columns A, B, and C involved may be simple or composite.

This concludes the coverage of user-defined integrity constraints. This type of constraint represents an exciting opportunity for DBMS vendors to demonstrate their technical and inventive capabilities. It also presents new challenges for DBAs. In part this is due to the richness with which conditions can be expressed in the principal relational language, RL.

14.9 ■ Special Commands for Triggered Action

A few commands must be added to RL to enable the DBA to define certain kinds of responses to attempted violations of referential and user-defined integrity by application programs and terminal users. These commands make use of the awareness of the DBMS with respect to the following:

- whether the DBMS is making a C-timed check or a T-timed check;
- if it is a C-timed check, what kind of command is causing the attempted violation;
- whether a primary domain is directly involved;
- whether an application program or an interactive user is involved.

Regarding the last item, the desired response to attempted violation may be different in the case of an interactive user and an application program because the DBMS can communicate with the interactive user. For example, the system can tell the user that his or her request is denied, and supply the reason for this denial.

One of the commands in the immediately following Features RI-32, RI-33, and RI-34 is likely to prove to be what is needed in such a response. There is no requirement, however, that any one of these commands be used in any triggered action.

RI-32 The REJECT Command

If checking is C-timed, reject the command and, if that command is part of a transaction, reject the transaction also. If checking is T-timed, reject the transaction.

RI-33 The CASCADE Command

Case 1: If a primary key is being updated or deleted without using the cascade option in the command, and the CASCADE command is used in the violation response, the DBMS cascades the update or delete to all corresponding foreign keys. Case 2: Let D be a primary domain. If a foreign-key value from this domain D is being inserted in the database as a component of a row, and if there is no equal value in a primary key defined on D, then a new row is inserted into a relation whose primary key is defined on D, and the primary-key value in this row is equal to the foreign-key value just mentioned. This action takes place only if all the non-primary-key columns accept marks. If one or more of these columns does not accept marks, the DBMS executes a REJECT instead.

RI-34 The MARK Command

If the cause of attempted violation can be pinned on non-primary-key column(s) and missing values happen to be acceptable in those columns, mark the corresponding components as missing but applicable. If the marking fails, the DBMS executes a REJECT instead.

Of course, the marking can also fail because of declarations in the catalog that prohibit marks from occurring in certain columns.

Exercises

14.1 If you were a DBA, would you grant users who did not report to you permission to add new integrity constraints to the catalog? Supply reasons for your answer.

14.2 What are the three principal reasons for supporting user-defined integrity constraints? Supply a fourth that is more futuristic in nature.

14.3 What are the four main components of a user-defined integrity constraint? What does each component mean?

14.4 Are user-defined integrity constraints incorporated in application programs? If not, why not, where are they stored, and how are they invoked when they must be invoked?

14.5 What language features make it simpler to express the dependencies of database design as integrity constraints?

14.6 List three commands that must be part of the principal relational language, if that language is to support the types of violation responses that are frequently needed.

14.7 Why should the DBMS support integrity constraints based on date and time? Supply an application-oriented example that illustrates the need for this feature of RM/V2, and that does not involve archiving.

■ *CHAPTER 15* ■

Catalog

An important property of the relational model is that both the database and its description are perceived by users as a collection of relations. Thus, with very few exceptions, the same relational language that is used to interrogate and modify the database can be used to interrogate and modify the database description. No new training is needed.

Of course, as we have seen in Chapter 7, there are a few extra commands in RL that deal primarily or even solely with the catalog. These commands cannot be applied to the regular data only. A user who wishes to access the database description or any of its parts must be authorized to do so. Otherwise, the authorization mechanism will prevent the user from gaining access.

The database description is stored in the catalog, which also contains its own description.

15.1 ■ Access to the Catalog

In the relational model, the *catalog* holds the database description. In some relational DBMS products this description is also called the catalog, while in others it is called the directory. Whatever it is called, it should be carefully distinguished from a *dictionary*, which normally includes all of the information found in the catalog, but also contains a large amount of information concerning the application programs that operate on a scheduled or non-scheduled basis upon various parts of the database.

It is important that the DBMS provide very fast access to the information in the catalog, to prevent a major bottleneck. On the other hand, normally the need for speed of access is significantly less in the part of the dictionary that does not include the catalog.

RC-1 Dynamic On-line Catalog

The DBMS supports a dynamic on-line catalog based on the relational model. The database description is represented (at the logical level) just like ordinary data, allowing authorized users to apply the same relational language to the interrogation of the database description as to the regular data. (This feature is Rule 4 in the 1985 set.)

This feature is a very important tool for database administrators. When asked whether a specific piece of information is in the database under his or her supervision, a DBA can rapidly use a simple terminal or workstation to interrogate the database description and obtain the answer, even if the DBMS is on a mainframe system. Pre-relational DBMS products often failed to provide the DBA with this tool.

One consequence of Feature RC-1 is that each user, whether an application programmer or end user, needs to learn only one data model, an advantage that most non-relational systems do not offer. For example, IMS (IBM, n.d.), together with its dictionary, required the user to learn two distinct ways of structuring data. Another consequence is that authorized users can easily extend the catalog so that it becomes a full-fledged, active, relational data dictionary, whenever the DBMS vendor fails to do so.

RC-2 Concurrency

The DBMS has a sufficiently sophisticated concurrency-control mechanism that it can support multiple retrieval and manipulative activities on the catalog, on the regular data, or on both concurrently.

It is important to remember, however, that the catalog can easily become a major bottleneck, since the DBMS must access the catalog when it processes many of the accesses to the regular data, whether by application programs or by terminal users. Therefore, during hours of heavy traffic on the regular data, it is unwise to grant many users the privilege of accessing the catalog. The term "regular data" means data not in the catalog.

15.2 ■ Description of Domains, Base Relations, and Views

Domains, relations, views, integrity constraints, and user-defined functions are each described separately because, to a large extent, they are objects whose existence is mutually independent.

■ Many relations may make use of a single domain.

■ Some views cite more than one base relation in their definitions.

■ Integrity constraints often involve more than one base relation.

■ User-defined functions are most often needed in constructing various types of queries.

Domains, base relations, and views are now discussed in that order. Integrity constraints were discussed in detail in the two preceding chapters. In Section 15.3, they are discussed from the standpoint of the catalog. User-defined functions are discussed from the standpoint of the catalog in Section 15.4 and in more detail in Chapter 19.

RC-3 Description of Domains

For each distinct domain (i.e., extended data type) upon which the database is built, the catalog contains its name, its basic data type, the range of values permitted, and whether the comparator LESS THAN ($<$) is meaningfully applicable to the values drawn from this domain.

Note that, if the comparator $<$ is applicable, then all the other comparators are also applicable. For details of domain description, see Section 3.2.

RC-4 Description of Base R-tables

For each base R-table, the catalog contains at least the following items: (1) the R-table name, (2) synonyms for this name, if any (a DBA option), (3) the name of each column, (4) for each column, the name of an already-declared domain, from which the column draws its values, (5) for each column, which kinds of missing values are permitted (if any), (6) for each column, whether the values are required to be distinct within that column, (7) for each column, constraints beyond those declared for the domain, (8) for each column, the basic data type, if applicable, (9) whether the column is a component (possibly the only one) of the primary key (required for a base R-table), and (10) for each foreign key, the sequence of columns (possibly only one column) of which it is composed, and the target primary keys (possibly only one) in the database.

Regarding Item 6, it must be possible to request distinctness of values in any column without that column having to be indexed! If the DBMS requires there to be an index in this case, the design is in error in coupling a semantic property (distinctness of values) with a performance-oriented feature (an index).

Regarding Item 9, according to Feature RS-8, each base R-table is required to have exactly one primary key. Regarding Item 10, according to Feature RS-10 (see Chapter 2), each base R-table may have any number of foreign keys, including the possibility of having none at all.

Occasionally a column is encountered in which the values are constant; that is, these values should not be updated, although any value can be removed if the entire row is deleted. Instead of introducing a declaration to this effect as one more property of a column, RM/V2 leaves it to the DBA to use the authorization mechanism to withhold updating privileges on such a column.

The declaration of any composite column is optional; this decision is normally made by the DBA. Each composite column that is declared is an ordered combination of two or more simple columns, all of which belong to a single base relation.

RC-5 Description of Composite Columns

For each composite column declared, the catalog contains its name, the name of each simple component column, and an order-defining integer for each of these simple columns. The order-defining integer is one for the first component, two for the second, and so on.

RC-6 Description of Views

For each view, the catalog contains at least the following items: (1) the view name, (2) synonyms for this name, if any, (3) the name of each simple column, (4) for each column, the name of an already declared domain (unless the column is not directly derived from a single base column), (5) whether the column is a component (possibly the only one) of the primary key (if applicable) of the view, (6) the RL expression that defines the view, (7) whether insertions of new rows in the view are permitted by the DBMS, (8) whether deletions of rows from the view are permitted by the DBMS, and (9) for each column of the view, whether updating of its values is permitted by the DBMS. For more information on items 7, 8, and 9, see Feature RV-6 in Chapter 16 and the whole of Chapter 17.

The domains (extended data types) of computationally derived columns can be difficult to determine. Present-day host languages normally do not deal with this problem, although it seems necessary for both relational and host languages to deal with it. Hence, determining the domains of computationally derived columns is not a requirement at this time. The basic data type of each computationally derived column, however, should be recorded in the catalog.

15.3 ■ Integrity Constraints in the Catalog

As noted in Chapter 14, integrity constraints that are called user-defined are normally defined by the DBA or by staff reporting to the DBA. Each of these constraints represents company policy and rules, *or* government regulations, *or* database design factors that stem from the meaning of the data.

RC-7 User-defined Integrity Constraints

For each multi-variable integrity constraint of type U (user-defined), the catalog contains its complete definition. This includes its name, the triggering event, timing type, the logical condition to be tested, and the response to any attempted violation of this condition.

The DBMS fails to support this feature if it does not support user-defined integrity constraints. See Feature RI-5 in Chapter 13, and the whole of Chapter 14.

RC-8 Referential Integrity Constraints

For each integrity constraint of type R (referential), the catalog contains its complete definition. This includes its name, its triggering event, its timing type, the keys that are involved, and the response to attempted violation (relating this action to the keys involved).

The DBMS fails to support this feature if it does not support referential integrity constraints (see Feature RI-4 in chapter 13).

Features RC-7 and RC-8 are extensions of Feature RC-3.

15.4 ■ Functions in the Catalog

RC-9 User-defined Functions in the Catalog

For each user-defined function, the catalog contains its name, the source code, the compiled code, the names of relations in the database to which the function requires read-only access, whether the function has an inverse, the name of this inverse, the source code for the inverse, and the corresponding compiled code.

It is certainly permissible for the four types of code cited in this feature to reside in the regular database, especially if the host system has the performance-oriented feature that keeps any data that is frequently a bottleneck cached in fast memory.

15.5 ■ Features for Safety and Performance

RC-10 Authorization Data

The catalog contains all the data specifying which interactive users, which terminals, and which application programs are authorized to access what parts of the database for what kinds of operations and under what conditions (see Chapter 18).

In the relational model, all authorization is based on explicitly stated permission rather than explicitly stated denial. This means that users and application programs are unable to gain access to any part of the database other than those parts that they have been explicitly granted permission to access. The granting of permission must be by means of one or more GRANT commands from a user, such as the DBA, who has the pertinent authorization to grant.

RC-11 Database Statistics in the Catalog

The catalog contains all statistical information about the database that is used by the optimizer in precompiling and recompiling RL commands. This includes at least (1) the number of rows in each base R-table and (2) the number of distinct values in *every* column of *every* base R-table (not just those columns that happen to be indexed at any specific time). (See also Features RD-8 and RD-9 in Chapter 21.)

Consider two extreme cases. If the catalog contains statistical information about the database, and if the optimizer fails to use any of this information in precompiling or recompiling each RL command, the DBMS fails to support this feature. Similarly, if the catalog does not contain any statistical information at all, the DBMS fails to support this feature, whatever use the optimizer makes of its privately held statistics.

Exercises

15.1 List the major items stored in the catalog. What extra information does a dictionary contain? Which of these components, catalog or dictionary, is used by the DBMS to compile or interpret relational requests?

15.2 How many primary keys can a base relation have? Can the number of primary keys change over time?

15.3 How many foreign keys can a base relation have? Can the number of foreign keys change over time?

15.4 Supply an example of a view that does not have a primary key. Which column(s) constitute the weak identifier?

15.5 List the four items that are required in the description of a *domain*. Supply a reason for each item.

15.6 List the five items that are required in the description of a *user-defined integrity constraint*. Supply a reason for each item.

15.7 List the five items that are required in the description of a *referential integrity constraint*. Supply a reason for each item.

15.8 List the eight items that are required in the description of a *user-defined function*, if that function has an inverse. Supply a reason for each item.

15.9 Concerning statistical information about the database, what is the minimum information required by RM/V2, and where must it be kept?

■ *CHAPTER 16* ■

Views

Views are intended to insulate users, including application programmers, from the base relations, allowing (1) changes in definition to be made in the base relations, and (2) corresponding changes to be made in the view definitions, in such a way as to keep the views unchanged in content. Views also permit users to perceive the database in terms of just those derived relations that directly belong in their applications. These views can also be used to confine a user's interaction with the database by approving one or more views as the only way they are authorized to interact with the database.

16.1 ■ Definitions of Views

RV-1 View Definitions: What They Are

Views are virtual relations represented by their names and definitions only. Apart from these names and definitions, the DBMS does not retain any database information (other than DBMS-derived view-updatability information) explicitly for views. The DBMS stores view definitions in the catalog, and supports view definitions expressed in terms of the following three alternatives only: (1) base R-tables alone, (2) other views alone, or (3) mixtures of base R-tables and views.

Consider some examples of views. Suppose that the database includes relations as follows: S stands for suppliers, P stands for parts, and C stands for capabilities of suppliers in supplying parts. The relation S includes columns S# for supplier serial number, SNAME for name of the supplier, CITY for the city in which the supplier is located, and STATUS for a simple rating of the supplier. Suppose that the extension of S happens to be as follows:

S	(S#	SNAME	CITY	STATUS)
	S1	Smith	London	20
	S2	Jones	Poole	10
	S3	Blake	Poole	25
	S4	Clark	London	20
	S5	Adams	New York	15

The relation P includes columns P# for part serial number, PNAME for name of the part, SIZE for size of the part, OH_Q for quantity-on-hand, and OO_Q for quantity-on-order. Suppose that the extension of P happens to be as follows:

P	(P#	PNAME	SIZE	OH_Q	OO_Q)
	P1	nut	10	500	200
	P2	nut	20	235	150
	P3	bolt	5	39	240
	P4	screw	12	50	0
	P5	cam	6	50	8
	P6	cog	15	10	10

The capabilities relation C includes columns S# for supplier serial number, P# for part serial number, SPEED for speed of delivery expressed in business days, UNIT_Q for the quantity that represents a unit in which the part is sold, and PRICE for the cost of the unit quantity when obtained from the specified supplier. Suppose that the extension of C happens to be as follows:

C	(S#	P#	SPEED	UNIT_Q	PRICE)
	S1	P1	5	100	10
	S1	P2	5	100	20
	S1	P6	12	10	6000
	S2	P3	5	50	15
	S2	P4	5	100	15
	S3	P6	5	10	7000
	S4	P2	5	100	15
	S4	P5	15	5	3000
	S5	P6	10	5	3500

Then, an example of a view derived from a single base R-table (a so-called *single-table view*) is the relation that represents the suppliers located in London. Such a view would be represented in the catalog by a formula such as

S [CITY = London],

along with the name of the view and certain properties of the view that are discussed later in this chapter and the next.

The DBMS is designed to evaluate views as infrequently as possible and as partially as possible. If this view were fully evaluated from the base R-table S in the state just indicated, its extension would be as follows:

S	(S#	SNAME	CITY	STATUS)
	S1	Smith	London	20
	S4	Clark	London	20

An example of a more complicated view is the **equi-join** of S on S#, with C on S# represented by

S [S# = S#] C.

If this view were fully evaluated with the database in the state indicated above, the extension would be as follows:

VIEW	(S#	SNAME	CITY	S#	P#	SPEED	. . .	PRICE)
	S1	Smith	London	S1	P1	5		10
	S1	Smith	London	S1	P2	5	. . .	20
	S1	Smith	London	S1	P6	12		6000
	S2	Jones	Poole	S2	P3	5	. . .	15
	S2	Jones	Poole	S2	P4	5		15
	S3	Blake	Poole	S3	P6	5	. . .	7000
	S4	Clark	London	S4	P2	5		15
	S4	Clark	London	S4	P5	15	. . .	3000
	S5	Adams	New York	S5	P6	10		3500

The ellipses (". . .") indicate that the UNIT__Q column has been omitted to conserve space. Note that, just as with base relations, it is normally unnecessary at any time for the user to know what extension any view happens to have at that time.

RV-2   View Definitions: What They Are Not

No view definition is of a procedural nature (e.g., involving iterative loops). Also, no view definition entails knowledge of the storage representation, access paths, or access methods currently in effect for any part of the database, whether these techniques directly support relations as operands or single records as operands.

This feature makes it simple for any user to define views, whether the user happens to be a programmer or not.

RV-3 View Definitions: Retention and Interrogation

View definitions are created using RL. These definitions are retained in the catalog. They may also be queried using the same language RL used for interrogating the regular data. In both activities—view definition and interrogation of such a definition—the full power of RL, including four-valued, first-order predicate logic, must be applicable.

Retention of view definitions in the catalog is important because views are normally of concern to the community of users, not just one user or programmer.

Figure 16.1 illustrates two views derived from a single base relation. One is a projection; the other, a row selection.

16.2 ▪ Use of Views

Features RV-4–RV-6 are motivated by a desire (1) to support a powerful authorization mechanism that depends heavily on views, and (2) to protect the user's investment in application programming and in training by requiring programs and users to interact directly with views, instead of the base R-tables.

RV-4 Retrieval Using Views

Neither the DBMS nor its principal relational language, RL, makes any user-visible distinctions between base R-tables and views with respect to retrieval operations. Moreover, any query can be used to define a view by simply prefixing the query with a phrase such as CREATE VIEW.

An example of an undesirable distinction is found in Version 1 of IBM's major database management product, DB2. The operator **union** can be used

Figure 16.1 **Two Views Derived from a Single Base Relation**

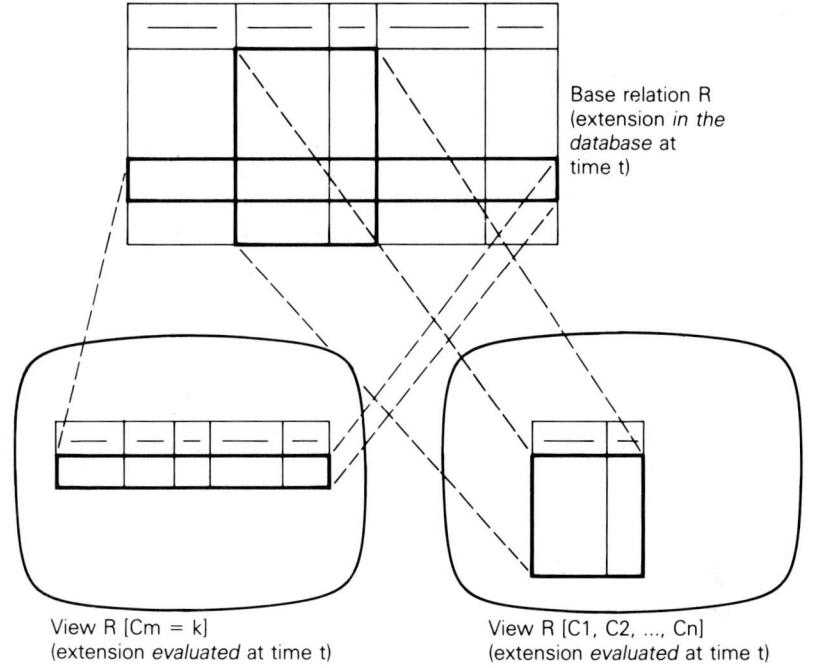

Base relation R
(extension *in the
database* at
time t)

View R [Cm = k]
(extension *evaluated* at time t)

View R [C1, C2, ..., Cn]
(extension *evaluated* at time t)

in a query on base R-tables, but cannot be used in creating a view. Such a restriction can make life difficult for companies that have similarly structured data at several different sites. Such companies frequently must create a view based on the **union** or **outer union** operator to allow headquarters staff to use the view as a source of planning data.

RV-5 Manipulation Using Views

Neither the DBMS nor its principal relational language, RL, makes any user-visible manipulative distinctions between base R-tables and views, except that (1) some views cannot accept row insertions, and/ or row deletions, and/or updates acting on certain columns (Algorithm VU-1 or some stronger algorithm fails to support such action), and (2) some views do not have primary keys and therefore will not accept those manipulative operators that require primary keys to exist in their operands.

For more information on Algorithm VU-1, see Chapter 17, "View Updatability."

RV-6 View Updating

To evaluate the updatability of views at view-definition time, the DBMS includes an implementation of Algorithm VU-1 or some stronger algorithm. Neither the DBMS nor its principal relational language, RL, makes any user-visible manipulative distinctions between base relations and views, except that:

1. some views cannot accept row insertions, and/or row deletions, and/or updates acting on certain columns because Algorithm VU-1 or some stronger algorithm fails to support such action; and

2. some views do not have primary keys (they have weak identifiers only) and therefore will not accept those manipulative operators that require primary keys to exist in their operands.

(This feature is a slightly modified version of Rule 6 in the 1985 set.)

One result of adherence by a DBMS to Feature RV-6 is that all views that are theoretically updatable by Algorithm VU-1 are also correctly updatable by the system without the DBMS having to guess the user's intent. VU-1 tackles a large class of views, including those that are frequently encountered.

Note that a view is theoretically updatable if there exists a time-independent algorithm (based on data description and data content alone) for unambiguously determining a single series of changes to the base relations that will have as their effect precisely the requested changes in the view. Unfortunately, the general problem of determining whether or not a view is theoretically updatable cannot be decided logically [Buff 1986]. Thus, Features RV-5 and RV-6 are related to Algorithm VU-1 (see Chapter 17), which I consider just a beginning in tackling this problem.

In Feature RV-6, the phrase "theoretically updatable" is intended to include insertion and deletion, as well as modification of data that is already in the database. The views handled by VU-1 are those that retain primary keys, in the case of views defined on single relations; those that retain appropriate combinations of primary and foreign keys, in the case of **join**-type views; and those that involve traceability of source, in the case of **union**-type views.

An alternative way of expressing Feature RV-6 is that, in its language(s), the DBMS must not make any manipulative distinctions between base R-tables and views, except for those views that, according to Algorithm VU-1 or a more powerful algorithm, cannot accept row insertions and/or row deletions and/or updates acting upon certain columns.

If a DBMS handles the view-updatability problem correctly for all those views supported by VU-1, and the vendor claims that its product can handle additional views, the view-updatability algorithm must be made publicly available for analysis, along with a proof that it is strictly more powerful than VU-1.

16.3 ■ Naming and Domain Features

RV-7   Names of Columns of Views

In creating a view, RL permits a user to name any column of this view differently from the way its source column (if such exists) is named. The DBMS however, retains in the catalog the name of the source column (if any), as well as the new name for the pertinent view column.

This feature is required to enable the DBMS to trace back to the base R-table and its appropriate column whenever an update is requested for this view column (see Chapter 17).

RV-8   Domains Applicable to Columns of Views

A view is created using a definition that does *not* indicate, for each column, the domain from which that column draws its values. Apart from the exception cited in the next paragraph, domain identification is deduced by the system at view-definition time, and is stored in the catalog along with the rest of the view definition. If, however, values for that column are computationally derived, then the basic data type (instead of the extended data type) is derived and stored at view-definition time.

Note that the command defining a view provides a one-to-one correspondence between the columns of the operands and the columns of the result, except in the case of computationally derived columns and certain kinds of **union**-type views.

Exercises

16.1 What is the main reason for supporting views? For now, disregard the use of functions to transform values from base relations into values that will appear in views. Does RM/V2 permit views to be defined using (1) the host language only, (2) the principal relational language only, or (3) a mixture of both? What is the answer to this question if functions are included in the view definition?

16.2 Can a view definition involve details concerning storage-representation and access methods in effect at view-definition time? Supply reasons for your answer.

16.3 Can a primary key be deduced for every RM/V2 view? If not, cite an example to support your assertion. What is the row-identifying component called that can be used as an alternative, when necessary? Why is this component bound to identify each row uniquely within any view?

16.4 A user asserts that RM/V2 requires that there should be no user-visible distinctions at all between base relations and views with respect to (1) retrieval, (2) insert, (3) update, and (4) delete. Which of these can be achieved for all views? Explain.

16.5 When a view is created, the domain of each column does not have to be declared. Under what circumstances is the DBMS unable to determine the domain for a column? What does the DBMS do in such a case? Supply one reason why the DBMS must know the domain of each column.

▪ CHAPTER 17 ▪

View Updatability

In the relational model, a view is a virtual relation represented by its defining declaration, inserted by means of a command such as CREATE VIEW. It is not represented directly by stored data. Insertions, updates, and deletions can be requested as operators upon views in a relational database management system.

Some views, however, cannot accept *some* of these operators unless the system guesses the user's intent. Such guessing is extremely dangerous unless the system checks with the user regarding his or her intent—which is not always possible and, when possible, not always convenient.

The problem discussed in this chapter is the *view-updatability problem:* how to design the DBMS so that it is able to determine whether a request for an insertion, update, or deletion can be honored without guessing the user's intent. I introduce two algorithms, VU-1 and VU-2, as a first step in solving this problem for the whole range of basic operators in the relational model.

Before proceeding, it is useful to consider two simple examples of non-updatable views to make sure that all readers understand the problem. First, suppose that the database contains a relation EMP that uniquely identifies employees by means of the primary key EMP# and provides their immediate properties:

Base: EMP (EMP# NAME BIRTH_DATE GENDER
        SALARY . . .)

Now suppose a single-table view E is created that is the projection of EMP onto two columns, neither of which is the primary key, say GENDER and SALARY. When the view is evaluated, true projection eliminates any duplicate rows. Corrupted projection (supported in some DBMS products, but not part of the relational model) does not. Regardless of whether duplicate rows are eliminated or not, suppose that a user is authorized to delete one or more rows from the view.

Such a request must be reflected in some change applied to the base relations because they are the only relations that reflect the true state of the database. Corresponding to a single row in the view E, there may be many rows in EMP. Thus, the question arises: How can the DBMS decide which row or rows in the base relations must be deleted? Should it delete all the rows in EMP that have the particular combination of gender and salary specified in the request, or should it merely delete an arbitrarily selected row in EMP that has this combination? Whatever it does, the DBMS would be guessing the user's or program's intent; such behavior is unacceptable in managing a shared database.

Now for a second example, this one involving **union** and a view based on two relations, not just one as in the first example. Suppose that two of the base relations in the database are SE and SW, where SE provides the identification and immediate properties of suppliers east of the Mississippi River, while SW provides similar information about suppliers west of the Mississippi. Suppose also that SE and SW are union-compatible and that neither SE nor SW contains a column that indicates directly by its values whether the supplier is east or west of the Mississippi.

Base: SE (S# SNAME CITY STATE . . .)
Base: SW (S# SNAME CITY STATE . . .)

Now, suppose that a view S is created as the **union** of SE and SW. Suppose also that a user is authorized to enter a new row into the view S. Such a request must be reflected in some change applied to the base relations, which are the only relations that reflect the true state of the database. How does the DBMS decide which of the two base relations SE and SW is to be the recipient of this row? Even if two of the immediate properties of suppliers recorded in SE and SW are the city and state in which each supplier is located, it is not appropriate to assume that the DBMS or the database has any knowledge about geography, and in particular about which cities and states are on which side of the river.

It is worth noting that, in this second example, the view S is actually the disjoint **union** of SE and SW, a reasonably simple case; still, however, entry of new rows into the view is not admissible. Nevertheless, whatever it does, the DBMS would be guessing the user's or program's intent, and such behavior is unacceptable in managing a shared database.

Returning to the more general aspects of view updatability, in an article published in two parts in *Computerworld* [Codd 1985], I specified 12 rules intended to help users evaluate DBMS products that are claimed to be relational. Rule R6, pertaining to the question of view updatability, asserted in its original form

All views that are theoretically updatable are also updatable by the system.

This rule was a reaction to the ad hoc nature of the design of many relational DBMS products, specifically in regard to requests for row insertion, updating, and row deletion applied to views. Part of the problem with these systems, as we shall see, was and is their incredible lack of support for primary keys, foreign keys, and domains—incredible because I made it clear to the designers well in advance that it was important not to omit these particular features.

A few months after publication of the 1985 *Computerworld* article, I received a letter from H. W. Buff [1986] of a Swiss re-insurance firm in Zurich proving that the general question of whether a view is updatable cannot be decided in the logical sense. This means that there does not exist any general algorithm to determine whether an arbitrary view is updatable or not. What, then, can be designed into the system, if it is to be reasonably systematic in its support of views, and yet avoid unreasonable overhead?

First, consider the question of whether a user is authorized to access data through a specific view, and whether he or she can cause the DBMS to take actions such as insertion, update, and deletion in accordance with this view. It is important to observe that this question can be separated completely from the topic of view updatability discussed in this chapter. In fact, the relational model *requires* these two topics to be treated separately from one another. Authorization is discussed in Chapter 18.

In the approach adopted here, as a *first step* I define an algorithm that determines for any given view whether it belongs to an elementary class of views, each of which is clearly updatable in a non-ambiguous manner. If the view is found not to belong to this class, the system merely reports it cannot handle the request, avoiding any assertion that the view is not updatable at all. In Section 17.6, I cite a reasonable change to the 1985 form of rule R6, intended to reduce the possibility that it might be misleading.

One of the reviewers for this book stated that [Dayal and Bernstein 1982] and [Keller 1986] reported independent work on view updatability that is somewhat similar to the approach I describe in this chapter. I regret that, at the time of writing this book, I was unaware of this work and still have not seen the papers.

One approach to view updatability that does not represent a solution places the burden completely on the DBA staff, in the following sense. For each view, the DBA is required to supply a program that translates each kind of action on the view into corresponding actions on one or more base relations. There may have to be an escape mechanism of this kind, but it should not be the routine mechanism for handling views.

17.1 ■ Problem-oriented Definitions

The term "tuple" is frequently used in this chapter. The reader is reminded that a tuple of a relation is a row of an R-table. In the title and in this chapter so far, the term "updatability" is used in making a general reference to the collection of operators: tuple **insertion,** tuple **deletion,** and **update** of specific components of a tuple that already exists in the database.

Now it is necessary to be more specific, clearly distinguishing among these three kinds of operators.

A view is considered *tuple-insertible by a DBMS,* if the DBMS accepts any collection of tuples (all of the same type and all compatible with the relation type) as an insertion to the view and correctly executes this insertion, provided only that the set of tuples and every one of its components meet the integrity constraints in the context of the transaction in process, and no help is needed from the user to resolve any ambiguities.

Similarly, a view is considered *tuple-deletable by a DBMS,* if the DBMS accepts and correctly executes a request to delete any subset of its tuples, provided only that such a **deletion** meets the integrity constraints in the context of the transaction in process, and, once again, that no help is needed from the user to resolve any ambiguities.

In dealing with the **update** operator, it is necessary to consider the action for each component of each of the tuples involved, and not deal with it in terms of complete tuples of a view as a whole. A column of a view is *component-updatable by a DBMS,* if the DBMS accepts and correctly executes a request to update that column, provided only that such an **update** meets the integrity constraints in the context of the transaction in process, and no help is needed from the user to resolve any ambiguities.

In each of these three cases, "correct execution" means that, for the requested action upon the view V, the DBMS determines that there is either a unique or a uniquely sensible collection of corresponding changes to be made to the base relations—changes that have as their effect upon the extension of V (a view that is not necessarily materialized) precisely those changes requested on the view. Another way of expressing this is that the changes applied to the view would hold if view V were conceptually changed into a base table.

Again, in each of these three cases, along with the phrase "meets the integrity constraints" goes the phrase "in the context of the transaction in process." This extra phrase is necessary because a single command within a multi-command transaction can validly and temporarily create a violation of any integrity constraint that has T-type timing for testing to see whether there has been an attempted violation. As explained in Feature RI-6 (see

Chapter 13), T-type timing means just before committing the changes resulting from the transaction to the database. Normally, of course, temporary violations in the middle of a transaction are removed by the end of the transaction.

17.2 ■ Assumptions

By way of introduction, a view V for a relational database is defined solely in terms of base relations, other views, or both, using a relational language. If the definition of V happens to involve other views, the occurrences of names of these views can be replaced by their definitions, and so on until the definition of V has been expanded to involve base relations only.

For brevity, the original view definition is called the *unexpanded* version, and the fully expanded definition is called the corresponding *fully expanded* version. Of course, if the definition of a view is given in terms of base relations only, then these two versions are identical.

The two algorithms are collectively called the *view updatability algorithms.* Whenever it is necessary to describe a property that is applicable to both of the algorithms VU-1 and VU-2, the term VU will be used.

It is now appropriate to consider Assumptions A1–A4 underlying both of the proposed view updatability algorithms, VU-1 and VU-2.

17.2.1 Assumption A1

The definition of a view and its consequences with respect to **insertion, deletion,** and **update** of its tuples must be understood by users. Users, however, need not know or exploit any details of the DBMS implementation or storage-representation. This includes as a special case that users need not know or exploit the ordering of tuples in base tables or any internal identifiers for specific tuples (so-called *tuple ids*).

Assumption A1 should not be interpreted as *requiring* all users to understand the view-updatability algorithms; it is absolutely necessary that only the DBA and his or her staff should understand these algorithms. Many users may not wish to concern themselves with this issue. They may prefer to think of a view as if it were a base relation, although I am not advocating this over-simplification.

17.2.2 Assumption A2

The decision regarding whether a view is tuple-insertible, tuple-deletable, or component-updatable can be made on the basis of the following:

■ the fully expanded definition of the view (not its extension);

■ the declarations of the base tables stored in the catalog;

■ integrity constraints in the catalog;

■ simple information about any statistical or aggregate functions explicitly involved in the view definition.

The simple information in the last item amounts to whether the function has an inverse, and, if so, the name and program for this inverse.

17.2.3 Assumption A3

The decision regarding whether a view V is tuple-insertible, tuple-deletable, or component-updatable is, on the one hand, dependent on parts of the database description at *view-definition time*. On the other hand, this decision is required to be independent of (1) whether any view other than V is affected by updating on V, and (2) the extension of the database at view-definition time.

This decision can therefore be made without considering as a whole the potential or actual value of that view (the so-called *extension* of that relation) or the actual value of the base relations from which that view is derived.

Thus, it is *not* necessary for algorithm VU to evaluate view V in order to make the decision regarding the updatability of view V. Assuming that the DBMS has decided that the view is updatable in one or more of the three senses cited, the system may have to examine part of the extension of the view whenever it encounters a manipulative request (a particular **insertion, deletion,** or row-component **update**) in order to handle this request correctly.

The decision making by the DBMS in Assumption A3 is concerned with determining whether or not a view is updatable and, if so, in what ways it is updatable. The process of actually applying a request for an **insertion, update,** or **deletion** to a view is entirely different. Nothing in Assumption A3 prohibits this latter request-time process from including inspection of the extension of the pertinent view or of its operands.

17.2.4 Assumption A4

The translation activity invoked at *request time* is not permitted to convert an operator of one type into an operator of a quite different type. More specifically, an **insertion** must be converted into one or more insertions, an **update** into one or more updates, and a **deletion** into one or more deletions.

For users, this constraint makes the updating of views much more comprehensible. Now let us consider the purposes served by each one of the first three assumptions.

17.2.5 Purposes of Assumptions

Assumption A1 is valuable whenever the system responds with a message to the effect that a requested **insertion, deletion,** or **update** is refused. Users can examine the problem themselves, if they so desire, because an examination does not entail use of the unavailable information.

Assumption A2 permits the decision algorithm to be independent of the implementation of any relational DBMS.

Assumption A3 enables the DBMS to determine the tuple-insertible, tuple-deletable, and component-updatable characteristics of a view at the time of entry of the view definition—when it should be done—instead of every time the view is used. Suppose that a suitably authorized user, perhaps the DBA, requests a change in the database description that might affect the updatability of one or more existing views. Now, because the view-updatability decision is made at view-definition time and is dependent on parts of the database description, the DBMS must examine what effect, if any, the requested change in database description might have upon this decision. If the DBMS finds that the decision might be altered, it must re-execute Algorithm VU exactly as if the pertinent view definition had just been entered into the catalog.

The assumptions underlying Algorithm VU-2 consist of Assumptions A1–A4, together with one additional assumption, A5.

17.2.6 Assumption A5

For any view that the DBA or any other authorized user can introduce into the catalog, *interpretation algorithms* determine the action to be taken when a request is made for an **insertion, update,** or **deletion** to be applied to this view.

17.3 ■ View-updatability Algorithms VU-1 and VU-2

These algorithms are alternatives; only one is needed to make a decision regarding view updatability. Thus, only one should be implemented in a relational DBMS. Algorithm VU-2 is intended to be strictly more capable than Algorithm VU-1. As will become apparent, however, Algorithm VU-2 depends heavily on the interpretation algorithms of Assumption A5. Also, more research is needed to ensure compliance of both algorithms with Assumption A4.

Each algorithm VU establishes the following for any given view whose definition involves only the basic relational operators:

■ whether that view is tuple-insertible,

■ whether that view is tuple-deletable, and

■ which of its columns, if any, are component-updatable.

These algorithms are intended to be invoked by the relational DBMS whenever it receives the definition of a proposed view. The results generated by either algorithm are stored in the catalog, and are therefore available to anyone who has authorization to access that part of the catalog.

Incidentally, it may happen that users need a view for retrieval purposes only. Thus, when Algorithm VU encounters the definition of a view and finds that this view is not tuple-insertible, not tuple-deletable, and not component-updatable, it is *not* appropriate for VU to reject the view request altogether. Instead, VU returns its three-fold decision both by turning on appropriate indicators (see Features RJ-12–RJ-14 in Chapter 11) and by recording these results in the catalog along with the view definition.

It is easier to understand Algorithm VU by keeping in mind that the algorithm makes its decision at view-definition time—not later, at request time, when an actual request for a **deletion, insertion,** or **update** on a view is received. It is the responsibility of the DBMS to respond to a request made at request time in a manner that is consistent with the decision made by Algorithm VU at view-definition time. Nevertheless, to explain how VU works at view-definition time, it is necessary to look at examples of the subsequent response by the DBMS at request time.

The main steps in algorithm VU are as follows:

1. Convert the fully expanded view definition from the source language (e.g., QUEL [Relational Technology 1988] or SQL) into a sequence of operations of the relational algebra, a sequence that contains no superfluous operations and no **Cartesian product.**

2. Examine each of the relational algebra operations to determine whether it generates a view that is tuple-insertible, tuple-deletable, or component-updatable, or some combination of these properties.

3. Let property P denote any one of the three properties tuple-insertible, tuple-deletable, component-updatable. Consider the collection of algebraic operations resulting from Step 1. If any one of these operations by itself yields a view that does not have property P, write in the catalog that the given view definition yields a view that does not have property P.

Step 1 was treated in [Codd 1971d] and [Klug 1982].

The remainder of this section deals with the treatment of each basic operator of the relational algebra by algorithm VU. No claim is made that either VU-1 or VU-2 is able to discover *all* the possibilities of tuple **insertion, deletion,** and **updating.** An implementor of VU within a DBMS may find it advantageous to save some of the intermediate results to help later in the actual execution stage of those **insertions, deletions,** and **updates** permitted on the pertinent view.

17.3.1 Prohibition of Duplicate Rows within a Relation

An operator of the relational algebra may have either one or two operands. No operand is permitted to have duplicate rows, and the result does not contain any duplicate rows. One of the many reasons for adhering to the prohibition of duplicate rows in any relation is that view updatability is impaired if duplicate rows are permitted at any stage (for details, see Chapter 23).

It is important to note that some of the relational languages supported by today's DBMS products are defective in permitting duplicate rows within a relation. SQL is one of these defective languages. Thus, much of what follows is applicable to an SQL environment *only if the following discipline is pursued:*

- specify one primary key for each and every base relation;
- use DISTINCT in every SQL command to which it can be applied;
- avoid use of the qualifier ALL on each and every UNION command.

The potential occurrence of duplicate tuples at any stage means that the DBMS will be unable to trace the origins of each tuple occurrence back to a particular row of the corresponding operand by means of an algorithm that is independent of the database state. Moreover, this inability to trace origins applies quite often even if duplicate tuples are eliminated as a last step in the derivation.

Therefore, let us assume that, for each of the algebraic operators considered next, each operand and each result is assumed to be devoid of duplicate tuples. Let us also assume (but only for the time being) that, for each of the algebraic operators considered next, the operands are base relations and the result is a view. Each operator is examined first with regard to tuple-insertions, then tuple-deletions, and finally updates of tuple-components.

17.3.2 Solution-oriented Definitions

When a component value of a row in a view is to be updated, or when a new row is to be inserted, it is necessary to consider which of the following cases is applicable:

- *The untransformed case:* the pertinent component is a value stored in the database;
- *The transformed case:* the pertinent component is the result of applying some function either to a single value or to several values stored in the database.

The transformed case involves finding the name of the pertinent function in the catalog, searching its description for the name of its inverse (if any exists in the database), and finding where in the database the code for the inverse is stored. This phase of the inspection is called Part 1. In this case, if no inverse exists in the database, Algorithm VU declares that the pertinent column of the view is not component-updatable, and Part 2 (specified next) is ignored.

A column of a view is *back-traceable* if one of the following conditions is applicable:

- The transformed case: an inverse function exists, and the code for this inverse is retrievable from the database;
- The untransformed case.

Both cases involve tracing the row and its components back to one or more specific rows in the operand relation(s); this task is called Part 2 of the inspection. Whenever Part 2 is successful, the view is said to be *back-traceable with respect to its rows*. Part 2 is described for each operator when dealing with the insertion of rows.

A view is *completely back-traceable* if every row and every column of that view is back-traceable. Part 1 of the inspection is successful if every column of the pertinent view is back-traceable. When Algorithm VU has determined that every column of the view is back-traceable, it proceeds to Part 2 and determines whether every row is back-traceable also. This last part of the inspection, Part 2, is described for each of the basic operators.

17.3.3 General Remarks about the Decision Problem

The view-updatability decision made by Algorithm VU is based on its finding in regard to the back-traceability of the view, as follows:

- If the view is back-traceable with respect to rows, it is tuple-deletable;
- If it is completely back-traceable (rows and all columns) it is tuple-insertible;
- If it is back-traceable with respect to rows and with respect to a specific column, then that column is component-updatable.

Some views lack normalization, even those that the DBMS decides are updatable in one or more of the three respects just cited. For example, a **join** that matches primary-key values in one relation to corresponding foreign-key values in another is not normalized. In these cases, the user or program may encounter update anomalies of the type described in [Codd 1971b].

It is the responsibility of the DBA to declare for each base relation and view whether or not it is fully normalized. The information in this declaration is saved in the catalog.

17.3.4 The Select Operator

Suppose that the view

T = SELECT R (A # x),

where R is a relation, # is one of the comparators applicable to the **select** operator, and x is a constant, a host-language variable, or the name of a second column (say, B) of relation R.

The **select** operator of the relational algebra selects complete tuples from the operand relation. Consequently, if there are no duplicate tuples in the operand, there are none in the result. Thus, the system encounters no problem relating which tuple of the result (the view) corresponds to which tuple of the operand. This view is therefore back-traceable with respect to its rows.

Accordingly, Algorithm VU declares the following for every view based on the operator **select:**

■ The view is tuple-deletable;

■ If it has nothing but back-traceable columns, then it is tuple-insertible;

■ Each column that is back-traceable is component-updatable.

Later, at request time, when a tuple is presented for insertion into the view T, the DBMS checks to see that this tuple satisfies the condition part of the view definition (A # x). If it does not, that particular insertion is rejected, and an error indicator is turned on.

One final remark on updating views: an update to a component value of a row in a view can be non-compliant with the definition of the view. It can cause the entire row to be removed from the view. For example, if a row in the view

$$T = R [A < 100]$$

happens to contain 90 as its value of A, and if a user requests that value be incremented by 25, then the DBMS updates the corresponding value of A in R to 115. The effect of this update is that the pertinent row is removed from the view T.

If the DBA would prefer the request to be rejected, he or she must *either* place an additional authorization constraint upon the user—namely, that no **update** is allowed to take a row out of the view (this is one more reason why authorization should not be based on views only) *or* make use of the *N*-person turn-key feature, Feature RA-5 (see the remarks following Feature RA-6 in Chapter 18).

17.3.5 The Project Operator

Suppose that

$$T = R [A, B, C, . . .],$$

where A, B, C denote columns of the relation R.

When executed, the **project** operator selects only those columns whose names are cited in the view-defining command. If the primary key is included in the list of columns to be selected, there is a clear one-to-one correspondence between the rows in the view and the rows in the operand. Such a view is declared by Algorithm VU to be tuple-insertible and tuple-deletable. Although Algorithm VU could make the same decision if a candidate key (and not the primary key) were included in the list of columns to be selected, it does not do this, partly because the class of updatable views would not be significantly enlarged in this way, and partly because RM/V1 and RM/V2 do not require all of the candidate keys for every base relation to be recorded in the catalog.

If, on the other hand, neither the primary key nor any candidate key is included in the list of columns to be selected, there is no guarantee that any row in the end result (a relation) corresponds to precisely one row in the operand. One way of describing this situation is that one or more rows in the result can have *ambiguity of origin*. Hence, for reasons of safety, a view based on **projection** in which the primary key is not preserved must be treated as not tuple-insertible, not tuple-deletable, and not component-updatable. Accordingly, for every view V that is based on the operator **project** and includes the primary key of the operand, Algorithm VU declares that,

■ view V is tuple-deletable;

■ if V has nothing but back-traceable columns, V is then tuple-insertible;

■ each column that is back-traceable is component-updatable.

A possible improvement over both VU-1 and VU-2 in regard to **projection** is for the DBMS to treat as tuple-deletable a projection that includes a column, all of whose values are declared in the catalog to be distinct within the column and in which it is also declared that missing information is not allowed. This is so slight an improvement, however, that it is not included in either algorithm.

It is now appropriate to consider views, each of which is based on two relations.

17.3.6 The Equi-join Operator

A simple example may help the reader to understand the problem. This example includes detailed commentary on the extension of a view, even though the aim is to have the DBMS decide whether the view is tuple-insertible, component updatable, and/or tuple-deletable at view-definition time. Think of this commentary as nothing more than an attempt to explain the problem.

It should be remembered that extensions of base relations, and therefore of views when they are evaluated, are continually changing because of the many interactions by users with the database. One reason that the updatability decision should be made by the DBMS at view-definition time is that it is quite unstable behavior for the DBMS to decide when one request is made that the view is updatable, then at an immediately following request to decide that it is not updatable, and at still another time to decide that, once again, it is now updatable.

Suppose that R and S are two base relations, each having the present extension shown next. Suppose that column B of R and column C of S draw their values from a common domain. These two columns are accordingly chosen to act as the *comparand columns* in the **equi-join** of R with S. Suppose that V is a view defined by

CREATE VIEW V ← R [B = C] S.

The extension of V is shown next, along with the operand relations R and S:

R (A	B)		S (C	D)		V (A	B	C	D)	
a1	1		1	b1		a1	1	1	b1	1
a2	2		2	b2		a2	2	2	b2	2
a3	2		3	b3		a3	2	2	b2	3
a4	3		3	b4		a4	3	3	b3	4
a5	4		4	b5		a4	3	3	b4	5
a6	4		4	b6		a5	4	4	b5	6
			4	b7		a5	4	4	b6	7
						a5	4	4	b7	8
						a6	4	4	b5	9
						a6	4	4	b6	10
						a6	4	4	b7	11

The row numbers on V are for explanatory purposes only.

Table 17.1 indicates what should take place when deletions are applied to the view V, *if* the DBMS were to decide on the acceptability of a deletion at the time a request is made. The "if" clause is for explanatory purposes only.

Deletion of any one of Rows 1–5 applied to V can be put into effect by deleting just one row in R only, in S only, or in both base relations. The effect is to delete just one row of V, exactly the one the user requested. It is worth noting that Row 1 involves matching one row of R with one row of S (the comparand value is one), while each of Rows 2 and 3 involves matching *many* rows of R to just *one* row of S (the comparand value is two), and each of Rows 4 and 5 involves matching *one* row of R to *many* rows of S (the comparand value is three).

The reason why the DBMS rejects deletion of any one of the Rows 6–11 of V is that it would be necessary for the DBMS to delete more than one row in V to maintain the view V in conformity with its definition as a **join.**

The effect of this is to delete more information than the user would anticipate, and to make the view behave differently from a base relation.

Table 17.1 **Effect of Deletions on the View V**

Row in V Deleted	Action on R	Action on S
1	Delete row 1	Delete row 1
2	Delete row 2	Nil
3	Delete row 3	Nil
4	Nil	Delete row 3
5	Nil	Delete row 4
6	Reject	Reject
7	Reject	Reject
8	Reject	Reject
9	Reject	Reject
10	Reject	Reject
11	Reject	Reject

For example, deletion of Row 7 in view V < a5, 4, 4, b6 > appears to require deletion of the row < a5, 4 > in R, and the row < 4, b6 > in S. If just these deletions are executed, the rows that disappear from the view V are Rows 6, 7, 8, and 10—three more than the user requested. It is worth noting that, in each of these cases, the relationship between rows of R and rows of T that have a common value in R.B and S.C is *many-to-many*.

It is clearly unnecessary work for the DBMS to decide view updatability each time a request is received for **insertion, update,** or **deletion.** As pointed out earlier, repeated decision making at request time makes the DBMS behave in an unstable fashion.

Furthermore, an early decision regarding view updatability at view-definition time ensures that the decision is not based on the somewhat ephemeral extension of the view. Therefore, the DBMS must know when it can depend on the continued existence of a one-to-one, many-to-one, or one-to-many relationship between those rows of R and those rows of S that have equal comparand values. In the relational model, such relationships are guaranteed, regardless of time and regardless of changes in extension, when one comparand column is a primary key and the other is either a primary key or a foreign key whose values are drawn from the same domain. Both of the algorithms VU take advantage of this fact.

Any additional time-independent relationships that are guaranteed not to be many-to-many must be peculiar to a particular database. These relationships are often represented by a declaration for column R.B that all of the values in R.B are distinct from one another and that there are no missing values in R.B. In other words, R.B is a candidate key for relation R. Then, for any column S.C that draws its values from the same domain as R.B, a one-to-many relationship exists between column R.B and S.C. Only Algorithm VU-2 takes advantage of these relationships in making its decision on view updatability.

Consider the view

$$T = R [B = C] S,$$

where B denotes a column of relation R, and C denotes a column of relation S. Suppose also that the simple or composite columns B and C whose values are being compared are as cited in Cases 1, 2, or 3.

1. The primary key of R is being compared with the primary key of S;
2. The primary key of R is being compared with a corresponding foreign key of S;
3. The primary key of S is being compared with a corresponding foreign key of R.

In each of these three cases, one should assume that the keys being compared are drawn from the same domain, since this is what is meant by the term "corresponding" in the three cases.

Now for some terminology. In any relational operation that involves comparing values between a pair of columns (simple or composite), this pair of columns must normally draw its values from a common domain. As introduced earlier, columns being compared are called the *comparand columns*. Between the values in a pair of comparand columns (say R.B, S.C), there may exist a relationship indicated in Row 1 of the table below. The **join** has a corresponding description in row 2:

Row 1	Relationship	One-to-one	One-to-many
Row 2	Join	One-to-one **join**	One-to-many **join**
Row 1	Relationship	Many-to-one	Many-to-many
Row 2	Join	Many-to-one **join**	Many-to-many **join**

Of interest are relationships such as these that are independent of time, not those that happen to exist for a short time because of the data that happens to be active in that time interval. Therefore, one can expect to encounter phrases such as the *time-independent PK-to-FK relationship,* where PK is an abbreviation for primary key and FK is an abbreviation for foreign key.

In Case 1, it makes little sense to permit R = S, since a relation is allowed to have only one primary key. On the other hand, in Cases 2 and 3 it may happen that R and S are either the same or distinct relations. It is assumed, however, that in all three cases the pairs of columns being compared are defined on the same domain; of course, the DBMS checks whether this is the case.

Case 1 is the simplest. No ambiguity of origin can arise in the result. Hence, any view defined as in Case 1 is tuple-deletable; if the view is back-traceable with respect to its columns, it is tuple-insertible also.

It is easy to see that what applies to Case 2 must also apply to Case 3, with the appropriate interchange of relations R and S in the reasoning. In Case 2, if the view is back-traceable with respect to its columns, insertion of a new tuple into the view can easily be put into effect by splitting this tuple into two parts:

1. one part (say p1) corresponding in type to relation R;
2. the other part (say p2) corresponding in type to relation S.

Let the result of appropriately back-transforming p1 and p2 be p1" and p2", respectively. If p1" does not already occur in R, it is inserted into R. If p2" does not already occur in S, it is inserted into S. If both p1" and p2" already occur in R and S, respectively, the DBMS rejects the insertion as an attempt to put a duplicate row into the view, and an error indicator is turned on.

In Case 2, deletion of a tuple that does not exist in the view is rejected, and an error indicator is turned on. Deletion of a tuple that already exists in the view can be handled in a fashion rather similar to that for insertion.

First, split the tuple to be deleted into the two parts p1 and p2 as before. Then, examine the view to see whether any tuple other than the one being deleted has p2" as its type S part. If not, delete p2" from S. Regenerate the view and check it to see whether any tuple other than the one being deleted has p1" as its type R part. If not, delete p1" from R. If no deletion is indicated in either operand, the original deletion command should be rejected as inapplicable, and an error indicator is turned on.

The term *quad* means a contribution of several rows to a **join** arising from a specific value that occurs at least twice in each comparand column (say m times in the first-cited comparand column and n times in the other comparand column). Such a contribution to the **equi-join** must consist of a number of rows that is the product of the two integers m and n. Since each integer is at least two, this product cannot be less than four: hence, the name "quad." Clearly, a quad contribution cannot consist of 3, 5, 7, 11, or any prime number of rows. The integers m, n are the parameters of any selected quad.

Quads are a phenomenon pertinent to the **join** operators when they are applied to operands that have a many-to-many relationship between the comparand columns. This phenomenon should not be confused with the phenomenon of ambiguity in origins, which is applicable to many relational operators.

Suppose that a view is the **equi-join** of two given relations. Suppose also that the comparand-column relationship is many-to-many, and hence one or more quads can exist in that **equi-join.** Then, the deletion of exactly one row that happens to belong to one of these quads generates a relation that can no longer be the **equi-join** of the given relations. The product mn reduced by one cannot be either m (n-1) or (m-1) n, because each of m and n is greater than or equal to two. Similarly, the insertion of exactly one row that happens to expand one of the quads by one row can no longer be the **equi-join** of the two given relations. Algorithm VU-1 does not conduct any searching for quads, since that could be effective only at request time. Instead, at view-definition time, the algorithm rejects any attempt to delete rows from or insert rows into any view that is a many-to-many **equi-join** (that is, an **equi-join** for which there exists a many-to-many relationship between the comparand columns).

Similar remarks apply to any deletion of several rows from (or insertion of several rows into) a many-to-many **equi-join** that leaves any quad in that **join** with a prime number of rows.

The methods of handling insertion and deletion in Cases 2 and 3 work because a PK-to-FK relationship is a time-independent, one-to-many relationship, provided the keys are drawn from a common domain. Therefore, quads cannot occur in the corresponding **join.** Hence, quads and their associated problems are not encountered in a view that is a **join** involving PK and FK columns based on a common domain.

Equi-joins according to columns other than those cited in Cases 1–3 could have quads since the time-independent relationship between the comparand columns *can be* many-to-many. In Algorithm VU, it is not assumed that either the DBA or the DBMS is aware of those cases (if any exist in the given database) in which it happens that the time-independent, non-key, comparand-column relationship is not many-to-many. Therefore, VU rejects as non-updatable all views based on **equi-join** other than those cited in Cases 1–3.

In summary, for every view T based on **equi-join,** Algorithm VU inspects the catalog to see whether Case 1, 2, or 3 applies. If one of these cases is applicable, VU declares the view T to be tuple-deletable. VU also examines every such view T to see whether it has nothing but back-traceable columns. If this additional condition is applicable, VU declares the view to be tuple-insertible. Finally, for each component that is back-traceable, VU declares that component to be updatable. If none of the Cases 1–3 applies to the view T, Algorithm VU declares T to be not tuple-deletable, not tuple-insertible, and not component-updatable.

17.3.7 Inner Joins Other than Equi-joins

Consider a view that is a **join** based on the comparator LESS THAN (<). Suppose that the relation R is joined with the relation S using column A of R and column B of S as comparand columns (A and B may both be simple or both composite). In such a **join,** each A-value occurrence is likely to be associated with many B-values.

Consider the following example:

T = R [A < B] S.

R (A C)		S (B . .)	T (C A B . .)		
2	c1	1	c1	2	3
4	c2	3	c1	2	4
5	c3	4	c1	2	7
9	c5	7	c1	2	11
13	c6	11	c2	4	7
			c2	4	11
			c3	5	7
			c3	5	11
			c5	9	11

Note that, in this example, the value 13 in column R.A and the value 1 in column S.B do not participate in the **join** based on LESS THAN. Moreover, the value 9 in column R.A and the values 3 and 4 in column S.B are the only values that occur once in the corresponding columns of the **join** T. Thus, these three values participate in their respective columns and in exactly one row each.

This once-only occurrence permits the DBMS to select a specific row of R (in the case of 9 in R.A) and of S (in the case of 3 and 4 in S.B) to be deleted when the corresponding row in the **join** T is deleted. However, the DBMS cannot make any sensible deletion in R or in S for any other row in the **join.** Since only a relatively few values at the low end in S.B and at the high end in R.A enjoy the once-only occurrence in the **join** T, it seems simplest to reject deletions of rows altogether in any view based on a LESS THAN **join.** This is precisely the action taken by Algorithm VU.

Similar remarks apply to the **inner joins,** for which the comparators are LESS THAN OR EQUAL TO, GREATER THAN, GREATER THAN OR EQUAL TO, and NOT EQUAL TO. However, the four **inner joins,** for which the comparators are limit-imposed (GREATEST LESS THAN, GREATEST LESS THAN OR EQUAL TO, LEAST GREATER THAN, and LEAST GREATER THAN OR EQUAL TO) deserve special attention.

Inner joins can be used with or without the ONCE qualifier. With the ONCE qualifier, each tuple of each operand can be used only in at most one tuple of the result. Only this case is examined here. Treatment of these **joins** is illustrated using the GREATEST LESS THAN comparator and the ONCE qualifier, first assuming that the values in R.A are distinct and that the values in S.B are also distinct.

T = R [A G< B] S ONCE

R (A	C)		S (B	. .)		T (C	A	B	. .)
2	c1		1			c1	2	3	
4	c2		3			c3	5	7	
5	c3		4			c5	9	11	
9	c5		7						
13	c6		11						

A request to delete the row $< c3,5,7 >$ from the view T can be interpreted in one of three ways:

1. delete the row containing 5 from R;
2. delete the row containing 7 from S;
3. delete both rows (5 from R and 7 from S).

Of these three versions, the third is selected by VU because it is both simple and the most symmetric (i.e., lacking in bias).

Now consider an example that is similar in all respects, except that: (1) the values in R.A are not all distinct, and (2) column C in R is explicitly illustrated to distinguish between the two rows of R that contain 5 in R.A.

Note that the result is different from the previous result with respect to the comparand columns:

R (A	C)		S (B	. .)		T (C	A	B	. .)
2	c1		1			c1	2	3	
4	c2		3			c3	5	7	
5	c3		4			c4	5	11	
5	c4		7						
9	c5		11						
13	c6								

The request to delete the row $< c3, 5, 7 >$ from the view T is interpreted by VU as a deletion of row $< 5, c3 >$ from R and the row containing 7 from S.

Accordingly, algorithm VU declares that, for every view based on one of the **inner joins** other than **equi-join,** and based on the four limit-imposed comparators with the qualifier ONCE attached:

- that view is tuple-deletable;
- if that view has nothing but back-traceable columns, it is tuple-insertible;
- each column that is back-traceable is component-updatable.

All other views based on **inner joins** (except **natural join** and **equi-join**) are not tuple-deletable, not tuple-insertible, and not component-updatable.

17.3.8 The Natural Join Operator

Both Algorithm VU-1 and Algorithm VU-2 treat views defined as natural **joins** in a way that is very similar to their treatment of views defined as **inner equi-joins.** Removal of the redundant column from the **equi-join** does not affect the action taken by these algorithms significantly.

17.3.9 The Outer Equi-join Operator

Algorithm VU handles **outer equi-joins** in the same way as the **inner equi-joins,** except for the two items that follow. Assume that, in the definition of the view T, the first-cited operand is R and the second is S. There are some differences in the dynamic handling by the DBMS at request time of insertions and deletions because of two facts:

1. The R-part of a tuple to be inserted into T may happen to have all of its component values missing, if the operator is either **right** or **symmetric outer join;**

2. The S-part of a tuple to be inserted into T may happen to have all of its component values missing, if the operator is either **left** or **symmetric outer join.**

17.3.10 The Relational Division Operator

Algorithm VU rejects tuple insertions, tuple deletions, and component updates applied to any view defined using relational division. Such changes have a major effect on the operand relations in terms of which the view is defined. In addition, appropriate interpretations of such operations are not at all clear.

17.3.11 The Union Operator

Consider a view

$$T = R \cup S,$$

where R and S are relations that are union-compatible. Normally it is impossible to deduce from the relation T alone which of its rows came from R, which from S, and which from both R and S.

Deletions of rows from a union-based view are a simple matter and are always accepted by VU. At request time, the deletion of a row from T causes the DBMS to check whether that row occurs in R, in S, or in both. If the row occurs in R, it is deleted from R. If it occurs in S, it is deleted from S.

Algorithm VU-1 on Union   Suppose that an insertion of just one row is to be made into the view T. The question arises as to whether this row should be inserted into R alone, into S alone, or into both. Normally, there is no basis for the DBMS to decide which action to take. If T happens to be the *disjoint union* of R and S at all times of integrity, however, the row inserted into T should be inserted into either R or S, but not both. Under these circumstances, how can the DBMS determine which one? One reasonable source for this information is the user-defined integrity constraints in the catalog. One of these constraints should clearly state the following:

■ that T is the disjoint union of R and S (not just any union); **and**

■ that the values in a particular simple or composite column of R identify the corresponding rows as originating from R (not S), while the values in the corresponding column of S identify the corresponding rows as originating from S (not R).

When these two catalog-based conditions are satisfied, and every column is back-traceable, Algorithm VU-1 accepts insertions into the view T. For all other views based on the **union** operator, it rejects insertions.

When these two catalog-based conditions are satisfied, each column that is back-traceable is component-updatable. Otherwise, Algorithm VU-1 rejects updating components in such a view.

Algorithm VU-2 on Union When inserting a row into a view that is a **union** of two relations R, S (not necessarily disjoint), it is possible to use a function (normally defined by the DBA) to determine whether the row should actually be inserted into R only, into S only, or into both relations. Such a function is called a *view-interpretation* function.

The DBMS treats this function just like an integrity constraint except that it is neither C-timed nor T-timed (see Feature RI-6 in Chapter 13). Instead, the DBMS examines it at *command-interpretation time* (early in the execution of an RL command); it is said to be *I-timed*.

At view-definition time, Algorithm VU-2 looks in the catalog to see whether a view-interpretation function for this view has been stored there. If so, the DBMS records in the catalog that the requested **union** view is tuple-insertible. If no interpretation function is found for this view, the DBMS resorts to making this decision according to VU-1.

Consider again the example of a **union** view cited at the beginning of this chapter. This view (R UNION S) concerned suppliers west of the Mississippi River (relation R) and those located east of the Mississippi (relation S). Using Algorithm VU-1, this view was found to be *not* tuple-insertible.

Using VU-2 and a suitable view-interpreting function, the view R **union** S can now be treated as tuple-insertible. All that this function need do is to use the city and state components of each row offered to the DBMS for insertion into the view R **union** S. By consulting an extra table stored in the database and indicating which states are west of the Mississippi and which ones are east (Minnesota and Louisiana excluded), the view-defining algorithm, and hence the DBMS, can determine which side of the river the supplier was on, and hence whether to enter the row into R or into S. (In the case of Minnesota and Louisiana, the function must examine a separate table indicating which cities in these states are on which side of the Mississippi (New Orleans straddles the river)).

Pending the development of a clearly superior algorithm, Algorithm VU-2 is being held as a candidate for insertion into RM/V3. Note that VU-2 does not require the operand relations to be disjoint.

17.3.12 The Outer Union Operator

Insertions of rows into a view based on **outer union** are treated by Algorithms VU-1 and VU-2 just as they treat such insertions in the case of **union.** Note, however, that if the row being inserted belongs in one of the operand relations, say R, and if it contains a component value that for R should be missing (since R does not include the corresponding column), that value will be dropped as the insertion into R is made. A similar constraint also applies to S.

For both operands, the DBMS turns on a warning indicator whenever a component value of an inserted row is dropped altogether upon entry into the database. Deletions of rows from a view based on **outer union** are also treated just as in **union.** To execute the **outer union** correctly, however, the DBMS must take note of the type differences between the view T and its operands R and S.

17.3.13 The Intersection Operator

Consider a view

T = R ∩ S,

where R and S are relations that are union-compatible. Then, every row of T occurs in both R and S.

If the user requests deletion of a row from the view T, the DBMS must delete it from both R and S. Algorithm VU-1 declares such a view to be tuple-deletable.

An insertion of a new row into T requires the DBMS to insert the back-transformed version of that row as follows:

■ into R if it is already present in S;

■ into S if it is already present in R;

■ into both R and S if it is present in neither.

Algorithm VU-1 therefore declares such a view to be tuple-insertable, provided every column is back-traceable. Note that, if at request time the back-transformed version of the row to be inserted is already present in both R and S, the DBMS treats the request as an attempt to create duplicate rows in T, rejects that particular request, and turns on an error indicator.

For a view based on **intersection,** each column that is back-traceable is component-updatable.

17.3.14 The Outer Intersection Operator

Deletions of rows from a view based on **outer intersection** are treated just as in the case of **intersection.** In some circumstances, however, the DBMS must take into account the type differences between the view T and its operands R and S.

Insertions of rows into a view based on **outer intersection** are also treated just as in **intersection.** Note, however, that when making corresponding insertions into the operands R and S, the DBMS must take into account the type differences between the view T and its operands R and S.

Once again, for every view based on **outer intersection,** each column that is back-traceable is component-updatable.

17.3.15 The Relational Difference Operator

Consider a view

$$T = R - S,$$

where R and S are relations that are union-compatible. Then, every row in T is required to occur in R, but must not occur in S.

The DBMS can handle requests for deletions of rows from T by simply making those deletions effective on R. The alternative—introducing the given row into S as a new row—would have the same effect on T as deleting that row from T because of the definition of the view T. This action, however, is deemed inconsistent with user expectations regarding any deletion. Users normally expect every request for a deletion to cause information to be removed from the database.

A user's request to insert a new row in T can be correctly handled by the DBMS if (1) every column in T is back-traceable and (2) the DBMS simply inserts the back-transformed version of that row into R only. As a precaution, the DBMS should check first that the back-transformed version of the row being inserted into R does not already occur in S. If the system finds that the row in question does already exist in S, it should reject the insertion and turn on an error indicator.

Thus, views based on **relational difference** are treated by VU-1 as follows:

■ as tuple-deletable;

■ as tuple-insertible, provided every column is back-traceable;

■ as component-updatable for each back-traceable column.

17.3.16 The Outer Difference Operator

For all views based on **outer difference,** the manipulative activities (deletions of rows, insertion of new rows, and updating of components) are treated just as in the case of **relational difference.** In some circumstances, however, the DBMS must take into account the type differences between the view T and the operands R and S.

17.4 ■ More Comprehensive Relational Requests

Usually a single command in a relational language based on predicate logic will require that a sequence of algebraic operators be executed. The command is decomposed into such a sequence. Then, this sequence is examined by Algorithm VU-1, one operator at a time.

Let us refer to the properties tuple-insertible, tuple-deletable, and component-updatable by the generic name *property P*. Only if three conditions are satisfied docs Algorithm VU-1 declare the whole view (defined by the pertinent command) to have property P:

1. every operator in the sequence is found to have property P;
2. at most one outer operator occurs in the view definition, and it generates the final result only;
3. there is no occurrence of any one of the MAYBE qualifiers.

One consequence of this approach is that columns such as primary-key columns that are crucial to property P in one part of a relational command cannot be discarded by projection in another part of that command. For example, the comparand columns in an updatable **join** must be retained in the ultimate result.

In what way does Algorithm VU-2 open up Pandora's box? Unless great care is taken in designing the DBMS as a host to view defining functions, database administrators will be able to use this facility to re-interpret actions on views in extremely irregular ways. For example, an insertion into a view could be re-interpreted as a deletion from that view.

On any column C that the DBA chooses, it is possible for him or her to impose two semantic constraints:

1. that all the values in column C are distinct;
2. that no values are missing from column C.

Since these two constraints are applied by the DBMS to all primary keys unconditionally, it is senseless for the DBA to attempt to impose or drop these constraints on primary keys. Suppose, therefore, that column C is not the primary key of the pertinent relation. In supporting views to which manipulative actions can be correctly applied (without any guessing by the

DBMS), these constraints appear to make column C as good as a primary key.

However, neither Algorithm VU-1 nor Algorithm VU-2 exploits constraints of this type defined by the DBA. The main reason for this "weakness" in these algorithms is that the DBA is free at any time to drop either or both of these constraints—as free as he or she is to introduce them. Such a drop could cause certain views to change drastically with regard to their updatability. Some or all of the ability to delete tuples, update tuples, and insert tuples is likely to be lost when these constraints are dropped.

17.5 ▪ Fully and Partially Normalized Views

So far, the question of view updatability has been discussed with little regard for the meaning of the insertions, updates, and deletions. The main concern has been to identify and avoid situations in which the DBMS would have to guess the user's intent because of difficulties in back-tracing from views to base relations, or because of functions that do not have inverses. Now, it is appropriate to bring into focus the fact that an updatable view may not be a fully normalized relation.

I introduced and discussed normalization of relations in 1971 [Codd 1971b and 1971c]. My main goal was to develop some theory that would be applicable to logical database design, and especially to the creation of a sound collection of base relations.

Our main concern here, however, is in the creation of views, not base relations. Now, a view, just like a base relation, may be fully normalized or not. This property holds even if the view is tuple-insertible, component-updatable, and tuple-deletable. If the view is likely to be subjected to many insertions, updates, and deletions, the DBA must examine whether it is normalized or not.

17.5.1 Normalization

Because some readers may not be familiar with the concepts involved in normalizing relations, these concepts are briefly discussed here.

One of the aims of normalizing a collection of relations is to make the insertions, updates, and deletions clear in meaning and therefore easily understandable. Normalization has little to do with pure retrieval. In fact, normalization usually involves breaking relations into relations of smaller degree (those with fewer columns); this tends to reduce performance on pure retrieval because many more **joins** must often be executed.

Every database is intended to model some micro-world. Thus, the objects to which reference is made in the following list are those found in this micro-world. The basic ideas in normalization are to organize the information in a database as follows:

- Each distinct type of object has a distinct type identifier, which becomes the name of a base relation.

- Every distinct object of a given type must have an instance identifier that is unique within the object type; this is called its primary-key value.

- Every fact in the database is a fact about the object identified by the primary key.

- Each such fact contains nothing other than the single-valued immediate properties of the object.

- Such facts are collected together in a single relation, if they are about objects of the same type. The result is a collection of facts, all of the same type.

Note that this methodology makes no distinction between abstract objects and concrete objects. Furthermore, no distinction is made between entities and relationships.

It is the coupling together of facts of different type that gives rise to problems. Such facts are likely to be independent of one another with regard to their truth in the micro-world and their existence in the database. Inserting a fact of one type does not usually require inserting a fact of another type at the same time. Deleting a fact of one type does not normally require deleting a fact of another type at the same time. As I discussed in [Codd 1971b, 1971c], the problem with relations that are not fully normalized is that insertions, updates, and deletions can create unpleasant surprises for users because of anomalies in their behavior and meaning.

Consider an example involving suppliers and simple shipments of parts. A typical fact about a supplier includes an identifier (the supplier serial number), the company name and address, a suitable contact within the company, and his or her telephone number. A typical fact about a simple shipment includes the supplier serial number, the part serial number, the quantity of parts shipped, the date of receipt at the receiving end, the amount to be paid, whether this amount has been paid, and the date of payment.

Suppose that the fact f about each supplier is coupled with the facts g1, g2, . . . gn about shipments from that supplier. Because it is then necessary to repeat f with every g, the first problem noticed is the serious level of redundancy in the relational representation. The adoption of a hierarchic structure to remove this redundancy is a backward step, one that introduces a whole new set of complexities and problems. These have been thoroughly discussed elsewhere (see [Codd 1970]).

It is now appropriate to comment on insertions, updates, and deletions applied to the unduly coupled relation.

Insertion Anomalies   Usually the suppliers from which a company acquires its parts constitute a relatively stable collection. On the other hand, fresh orders are continually being placed with each supplier, and for almost every order there will be a new shipment. Thus, there is a continual need for insertions of new facts concerning new shipments. Every time a new shipment is entered into the database using a normal insert command (see Feature RB-31 in Chapter 4), it must be accompanied by the fact pertaining to the cited supplier, even if that fact already occurs many times in the database. This is clearly an unnecessary burden to place on the users.

When a new supplier is being entered into the database, it is unfortunately necessary to enter information concerning a shipment from this supplier. It would help users if there were a concise way of asserting that the shipment information is missing from the unduly coupled tuple.

Update Anomalies   Suppose that one of the suppliers moves from one location to another. A change must be made in the supplier's address, and perhaps in other properties also. This address, however, may occur in many rows of the unduly coupled relation. Unless the user employs a command more sophisticated than the update commands described in Chapter 4 (Features RB-30–RB-32), translation of this request into correct commands is a tedious task, one in which the user must be aware of the unfortunate redundancy cited earlier.

Archiving and Deletion Anomalies   Suppose that a particular supplier has five distinct shipments recorded in the database. As just described, each recording of a distinct shipment is accompanied by a repetition of the basic fact about the supplier that is shipping the parts involved.

Suppose that when a shipment is paid for, the database fact pertaining to this shipment is either archived or deleted. With each archiving or deletion, the redundancy level of the fact pertaining to the supplier is reduced by one. It may happen that this supplier receives no fresh orders for such a long time that the level of redundancy is reduced step by step from five down to one, and finally to zero. In the range from five down to one no problem arises because the basic fact concerning the pertinent supplier is retained in the database. In the final step, however, when payment is made for the last of the five shipments, this fact is removed from the database altogether. In this example, as in others, the archiving or deletion proceeds in a regular manner until the final step. Then, and only then, is there a substantial, and probably unexpected, side effect: the total removal from the database of information about the supplier involved.

17.5.2 Relating View Updatability to Normalization

If the definition of a view includes a **join** of some kind, it will not be unusual for the DBMS to make a check to see whether referential integrity has been maintained. Such a check can cause any insert, update, or delete request to be rejected.

The DBMS (and preferably all users) must know which relations are the contributors to every view involving a **join,** allowing insertions, updates, and deletions to be intelligently requested. Thus, if a base relation T is the **outer equi-join** of two relations R and S that are more fundamental than T, but are not base relations themselves, R and S should nevertheless be described in the catalog, and T should be defined in terms of R and S. Such relations are then called *conceptual relations.*

17.5.3 New Operators for Partially Normalized Views and Base Relations

As an aid in explaining these operators, consider a quite useful example based on the **outer equi-join.** Let T denote the **right outer equi-join** of relation S on B with relation K on C:

$$T \leftarrow S [B = C \backslash] K.$$

It is adequate to consider either **left** or **right outer equi-join** only since the main concern is with T as an updatable view (not a base relation), and it has already been established that a view involving many-to-many matching of values in the comparand columns is not tuple-insertible, not component updatable, and not tuple-deletable.

In the examples of the use of the four new operators presented in Features RZ-41–RZ-44, assume that S denotes suppliers and K denotes capabilities of suppliers in supplying parts. If T happens to be a base relation, assume that S and K are declared as conceptual relations (not base, not view, and not query).

RZ-41 The Semi-insert Operator

An insertion into T of a fact f represented by a semi-tuple is requested. The DBMS examines the pertinent half of T to see whether the fact f already occurs there. If f is already in T, the DBMS rejects the request. If not, the DBMS associates the fact f with either an existing pairing fact that happens to have its other half missing or, if no such attaching point is available, creates such an attaching point by making a copy of a fact that can successfully pair with it.

Consider as an example the insertion of a capability for supplier s3 and part p15. If supplier s3 occurs at all in T with a missing capability, it must occur just once, and the DBMS updates this tuple to include the new capability. If s3 does not occur at all in T, the DBMS rejects the request. If s3 occurs in one or more supplier semi-tuples of T, but always paired with a capability semi-tuple, the DBMS copies one of these supplier semi-tuples and pairs it with the new capability.

RZ-42 The Semi-update Operator

An update is requested that is to be applied to a fact that is represented by a semi-tuple of T. If the DBMS is able to find at least one semi-tuple to which the update pertains, it proceeds to update every copy of the pertinent fact that exists in T. If the DBMS is unable to find such a semi-tuple, it rejects the request.

Consider as an example of an update to change the address of a specific supplier. Every copy of the supplier semi-tuple that exists in rows of T is similarly updated. If no semi-tuple is found for the specified supplier, the request is rejected.

RZ-43, RZ-44 The Semi-archive and Semi-delete Operators

The DBMS checks to see whether the fact to be archived or deleted occurs in more than one semi-tuple of T. If so, as Step 1, it archives or deletes all rows of T (except one row) in which the fact occurs. As Step 2, the DBMS marks as missing all components of the one remaining semi-tuple of T. If at the start the fact to be archived or deleted occurs only once, Step 1 is omitted and Step 2 is executed. If the fact to be archived or deleted does not occur at all in T, the DBMS rejects the request.

As an example of an archive or deletion, consider the deletion of the capability of supplier s3 to supply part p15. The DBMS checks to see whether supplier s3 occurs in just a single row of T. If so, it marks as missing all components of the capability semi-tuple. If s3 occurs in more than one row, the DBMS makes a simple deletion of the particular row in which the specified capability occurs. If s3 does not occur at all, the DBMS rejects the request.

17.5.4 Outer Equi-join versus Inner Equi-join as Views

Suppose that a decision has been made that facts of two different types must be combined in a single view by making use of either an **outer** or an **inner equi-join** with the primary key of one relation (containing facts of Type 1, say) matching the foreign key of the second relation (containing facts of Type 2, say). The question arises, Which is the better operator to choose?

Given a fact of Type 1, it is useful to say of a fact of Type 2 that it *matches* the Type 1 fact if the primary-key value in the Type 1 fact equals the foreign-key value (drawn from the same domain) in the Type 2 fact. The following question is crucial: Is it necessary for one or more Type 1 facts to exist in the database when there are no matching Type 2 facts, and for this to be obvious from the content of the view?

If this question is answered affirmatively, the choice is clearly **outer equi-join. Outer equi-join** permits the continued existence of Type 1 facts even when matching Type 2 facts have not been entered or have become obsolete and been archived or deleted.

17.6 ■ Conclusion

View updatability is extremely important because application programs and end users at terminals should always use views as the means of interacting with a relational database—the only way now known for application programs and end users to be able to cope with many kinds of changes in the logical database design without the need for reprogramming and retraining. This is known as *logical data independence*. Algorithms VU-1 and VU-2 are the tools by which relational DBMS products can adequately support determination by the DBMS of view updatability at view-definition time.

The original version of Rule R6 in the 1985 set was stronger than theoretically achievable. In Version 2 of the relational model, Rule R6 has become Feature RV-6 (repeated here).

RV-6   View Updating

To evaluate the updatability of views at view definition time, the DBMS includes an implementation of Algorithm VU-1 or some stronger algorithm. Neither the DBMS nor its principal relational language, RL, makes any user-visible manipulative distinctions between base relations and views, except that

1. some views cannot accept row insertions, and/or row deletions, and/or updates acting on certain columns because Algorithm VU-1 or some stronger algorithm fails to support such action;

2. some views do not have primary keys (they have weak identifiers only) and therefore will not accept those manipulative operators that require primary keys to exist in their operands.

Why do present versions of relational DBMS products handle the updating of views in such an ad hoc, severely limited, and ill-conceived manner?

Performance is not the reason. Perhaps one reason is that, for some time, very few people have been aware that view updatability is a major factor in attaining logical data independence.

Furthermore, if the columns that constitute the primary key are not explicitly declared to be the primary key for *at least* each base relation, then it will be extremely difficult, if not impossible, for the DBMS to determine at view-definition time whether or not that view is tuple-insertible or tuple-deletable, and which of its tuple-components are updatable (if any).

The development of algorithms that, when compared with Algorithms VU-1 and VU-2, are more efficient or more thorough (or both) can be expected. The situation is very similar to that which came about after I completed development of the first three normal forms for database organization [Codd 1971b]. I named them normal forms 1, 2, and 3 to encourage researchers to create additional normal forms—which they did.

Exercises

17.1 What are the four assumptions upon which both of the view-updatability algorithms are founded in RM/V2? What is the fifth assumption on which VU-2 only is based?

17.2 Suppose that a view is defined as a projection on a base relation and does not include the primary key of that relation. Discuss whether view-updatability Algorithm VU-1 would accept or reject the insertion of rows into the view.

17.3 Are all of the views that are definable by RM/V2

■ Tuple-insertible by RM/V2?

■ Tuple-deletable by RM/V2?

■ Component updatable by RM/V2?

If not, why not? Supply one example for each case.

17.4 Supply a brief description of Algorithm VU-1. What are the main improvements in VU-2?

17.5 Suppose that a view is defined as the **equi-join** of two base relations, and this **join** does not involve the primary key of either relation as one of the comparand columns. Discuss whether view-updatability Algorithm VU-1 would accept or reject the insertion of rows into the view.

17.6 As the security chief for a database, you have been asked to make available to a user certain columns of a relation, but these do not include the primary key of that relation. You have also been asked to grant that user the privileges of inserting and deleting rows in the pertinent projection. Should you grant all of these privileges? If not, what are the problems?

17.7 As the DBA of a database, a user has requested you to define a **union** of two base relations as an updatable view. Upon examining the pertinent base relations, you find that they are union-compatible, but that their intersection is either non-empty or not guaranteed to remain empty. Can you grant the user's request, assuming your DBMS supports view-updating Algorithm VU-1? Explain your answer. Can VU-1 be improved to enable the request to be granted? If so, how?

■ *CHAPTER 18* ■

Authorization

To quote from Chapter 13,

> Preserving the accuracy of information in a commercial database is
> extremely important for the organization that is maintaining that
> database.

A major step cited in Chapter 13 concerned the preservation of integrity.
In this chapter a second major step is discussed, namely, controlling who
has access to what parts of the database and for what purposes.

Because of its ease of use, the relational approach to database management is without doubt opening up databases to many more people than did
any previous approach. No longer can just a few members of an organization
with highly specialized skills and knowledge access data. Therefore, far more
responsibility must be placed on the DBA, and on the DBMS, to protect
the data from damage by people who lack adequate knowledge of the
pertinent company operations, procedures, and policies.

Many of those who are authorized to access the data should be permitted
by the DBA and DBMS to read the data, but not to modify it. Even when
restricted to no more than reading data, such users may be authorized to
read only specified parts of the database.

Consider the example of a production database (one that is supposed
to reflect the reality of company operations) and a user who is a member
of the planning staff. Suppose that this planner must investigate various
"what-if" types of questions. He or she may want to make some changes

in the database that reflect possible future changes, either within the company or in its environment, such as changes in the marketplace. Generally, such changes cannot be permitted on data in a production database because that database would no longer reflect the reality of present company operations. A useful approach to this problem is to request the DBMS to deliver to planning staff workstations, with some specified regularity (e.g., once a week), snapshots or summaries of parts of the production database.

The responsibility of the DBA with regard to authorization is to enter into the catalog a collection of statements that specify who is to access what information, for what operational purposes, and under what time constraints. Continual and dynamic enforcement is the responsibility of the DBMS itself. Because there can be millions of accesses every day, it would not be practical to require the DBA to adjudicate every access. Enforcement by software, however, is totally misplaced if it is made the responsibility of a software package added as an afterthought on top of the DBMS. Such a package can easily be bypassed.

It is quite normal in companies and government institutions for a significant variety of kinds of information to be present in a database. Some of this data, perhaps much of it, is not intended to be spread around within the organization (e.g., employees' salaries). Generally, the information should be available to individuals to the extent required by their job and responsibilities. This basis for the availability of information is sometimes called the *need to know*.

Institutions of different kinds often establish quite different procedures intended to safeguard the security of their information. The approach to security and authorization that is incorporated in the relational model is sufficiently flexibile that these institutions can maintain the procedures they are accustomed to using, either without any changes, or, at worst, with only minor changes.

Availability of the information must be distinguished from authorization to modify the information, whether by (1) insertion of new data, (2) update of existing data, (3) archiving of old data, or (4) deletion of obsolete data. For any given part of the database, these four distinct kinds of activities should be separately authorizable. Normally, even fewer people are authorized to engage in these activities than those who are merely authorized to access the information on a read-only basis.

In present relational DBMS products, there is a strong coupling between views and authorization, an idea that probably had its origins in IBM's System R prototype [Chamberlin et al. 1981]. One benefit of this approach to authorization is that it avoids needless complexity in the implementation. The consequences of this coupling, however, must be examined. One major consequence is examined here. Some minor ones are considered later in this chapter.

If one or more programs or users are authorized to manipulate certain rows or columns of a relation, then the scope of this authorization must be expressed in terms of a view containing just those rows and columns. Such a view must therefore be defined to put such authorization into effect. One consequence is that numerous views are defined for authorization reasons. This means that the capability of the DBMS in terms of view updatability must be strong. Unfortunately, as noted in the preceding chapter, the DBMS products available today are quite weak in this respect.

18.1 ■ Some Basic Features

RA-1 Affirmative Basis

All authorization is granted on an affirmative basis: this means that users are explicitly *granted permission* to access parts of the database and parts of its description instead of explicitly being *denied access.*

In non-relational DBMS, the approach to authorization was (and is) often negative—that is, based on explicit denial of access. In a relational DBMS, if user A grants authorization to user B, user A specifies what B *can* do, not what B *cannot* do. As a consequence, the introduction of new kinds of data into the database does not require urgent examination of any access denials to see how these denials should be extended. Instead, access approvals can be introduced quite safely and gradually as they are conceived and found to be in line with company policies or government regulations.

RA-2 Granting Authorization: Space-time Scope

In granting authorization, the full power of RL (including four-valued, first-order predicate logic) must be applicable in defining (1) the parts of the database and its description accessible for specified purposes (retrieving, inserting, or updating database values, archiving or deleting, or any combination of these activities), and (2) at what time access is permitted (using the date and time functions of RL).

If the applicability of the full power of RL in supporting authorization is achieved through views (the usual method in relational DBMS products today), then Features RV-4 and RV-5, relating to retrieval and manipulating power on views (see Chapters 16 and 17), must be fully supported in the DBMS in a systematic (not ad hoc) fashion.

When a DBMS is designed to support Feature RA-2, the usual approach taken with regard to allocating parts of the database to each user or program is flawed. Access control of this kind is achieved by exploiting views as the *sole tool*. To exploit views as a tool is fine because it leads to a simple design for the authorization mechanism. To exploit views as the *sole tool* for this aspect of authorization, however, leads to serious difficulties. The following example illustrates the problem.

Suppose that one of the base relations is the usual employee relation EMP, with employee serial number as the primary key. Suppose also that two of the immediate properties of employees included as columns in EMP are the present job title and the present salary. One possible requirement is that a particular user be allowed access to the entire job title and salary columns for the purpose of analyzing the correspondence between these two factors.

Further, in order to keep the salaries of individuals from becoming public knowledge, suppose that the DBA denies this user access to the primary key by omitting that column from the pertinent view that this user is authorized to access. This is the DBA action that is required by the DBMS that exploits views as the *sole tool* for authorizing what parts of the database can be accessed by each user.

In this particular example, the view to be defined must include the job title and salary columns, and exclude the primary-key column; in other words, the view must be a projection of EMP onto these two columns only. Assuming that the DBMS supports true **projection** and not a corrupted version of this operator, duplicate rows do not appear in the result of projecting the base relation EMP onto job title and salary only, even though there may be duplicates of these pairs of values in the EMP relation. Thus, statistical functions applied to the projection are likely to yield answers that are different from those that would be obtained from the job title and salary columns of the EMP relation itself. Given the intent of the user, the answers obtained from the non-key **projection** are simply wrong.

Does this mean that the definition of **projection** should be altered to permit duplicate rows to be retained in the result? The answer is definitely no, given the seriously adverse consequences of permitting duplicate rows (see Chapter 23).

There is a better solution to the problem. It involves imposing the database space-time constraints on the pertinent user *partly* through a view (in this case, a **projection** that includes the primary key) and *partly* through an additional mechanism that blocks this user from seeing any values in the primary key column.

It is clear that this design of the authorization mechanism is not as simple as the one that exploits views as the *sole tool* but at least it is not obviously wrong in its actions. However, if adopting the use of views as the *sole tool* requires permitting duplicate rows, then the overall simplicity of the DBMS design is significantly reduced by adding this small complexity to the authorization mechanism. Even more important, simplicity for users is achieved (see Chapter 23).

A reasonable question to ask concerning the example just described is, "How does the user distinguish between (1) a view that is a key-based **projection** with the key hidden, and (2) a view that is non-key-based and is a corrupted **projection** (one in which duplicate rows are permitted)?"

The answer is that there is no difference from the standpoint of interrogation and insertion. There could be a difference, however, from the standpoint of update and deletion. I am not advocating that the view-updatability Algorithm VU-1 (see Chapter 17) be extended to handle the case of hidden keys. The main advantage of using an approach based on view 1 rather than view 2 is that no user, not even the DBA, can create a relation that contains duplicate rows, along with all of the headaches that result therefrom.

The next obvious question is, "In requesting authorization from the DBA, how does the user distinguish between the need for (1) a view that is a key-based **projection** with the key hidden, and (2) a view that is a true **projection** on the non-key columns (one in which duplicate rows are not permitted)?"

Under this scheme, both of these requests are legitimate, and they are quite distinct from one another in meaning. A user who is carrying out statistical analysis and who is not allowed to see primary-key values is likely to want view 1. The main distinction is whether the primary key participates at all in the view. The DBA can already select participation by the primary key in a view. What is new here is that the DBA has the additional option of hiding or not hiding all of the primary-key values.

RA-3 Hiding Selected Columns in Views

A suitably authorized user such as the DBA can not only define what parts of the database a user is authorized to access by means of views, but he or she can also select columns of each view that are to be blocked from that user's access.

Suppose that a user is authorized to access a view V and apply the update operator to column A. An update to the A-component of a row w in a view can make w non-compliant with the definition of the view, causing row w to be removed from the view.

For example, if a row in the view

$$V = R [A < 100]$$

happens to contain 90 as its value of A, and if a user requests that value be incremented by 25, then the DBMS can update the corresponding value of A in R to 115. The effect of this update is that the pertinent row is removed from the view V. If the DBA prefers that the request be rejected, he or she must place an additional authorization constraint upon the user, namely, that no update is allowed to take a row out of the view. This is one more reason why authorization should not be based on views only.

RA-4 Blocking Updates That Remove Rows From a View

Suppose that a user is authorized to access a view V and to update a column A in V. The DBA has the choice of providing or denying this user the additional authorization to apply those updates to values in column A that take the corresponding row out of the view.

A company can become critically dependent on some database. If a disgruntled or careless employee is authorized to use the DROP RELATION command, he or she could issue numerous commands of this type and cause a complete or near-complete loss of the database. The following two features are aimed at protecting companies and institutions from this serious problem.

RA-5 N-person Turn-key

In those DBMS installations at which the continued existence and integrity of the database are critical to the company or institution, the DBMS must support an N-person turn-key in order for certain selected activities to be requested by a user successfully (N > 1).

A simple use of this feature is to require that both the DBA and his or her manager approve the following:

■ any execution of the DROP RELATION command;
■ any execution of the DELETE command;
■ any change in the delay period cited in Feature RA-6, following.

Feature RA-6 delays the execution of drops and large-scale deletions (possibly all deletions) by archiving the data for a specified number of days or weeks. The DBMS executes these commands in two steps:

1. archive the data immediately;
2. delete the data later.

This delay gives the installation time to react and fully recover from the damage, whether intended or not.

RA-6   Delayed Deletions of Data and Drops By Archiving

Execution of the command DROP RELATION results in the specified relation being archived for a period of at least seven days. Execution of large-scale deletions (possibly all deletions) is delayed by archiving in a similar fashion. Seven days is the default value if no longer period is specified.

Together, Features RA-5 and RA-6 provide the fundamental security that a company needs if it depends heavily on the continued existence and accuracy of its databases. A possible additional use for the *N*-person turnkey is applicable to the type of updates called *exporting updates* in distributed databases. When executed, these updates cause the DBMS to move one or more rows from a relation at one site into a relation at another site. The user or application program at the FROM site would have to be authorized to update beyond the range permitted at that site. The DBA in control of the receiving site might have to authorize reception at that site of the updated information as an insertion (see Section 24.6.2).

A quite different concern in some installations is that the private use of storage for preserving the results of queries is escalating at an alarming rate. Two approaches to limiting this questionable consumption of resources appear useful.

In the first approach, a feature is introduced into RM/V2 that blocks execution of any query for which the result exceeds the quota of storage assigned to a user or group of users, either on a per-query basis or with respect to a specified total.

The second approach requires each result of a query that the user requests the DBMS to store to be transmitted to his or her personal computer or to some storage unit that is specifically assigned to that user. For the time being, no feature of RM/V2 is proposed to handle this requirement.

18.2 ■ Authorizable Actions

RA-7 Authorizable Database-control Activities

There are at least 13 database-control activities that must be separately authorizable and authorizable in combination.

The 13 such database-control activities are as follows:

1. creating and dropping a domain;
2. creating and dropping a base R-table;

3. creating and dropping a column of an existing base R-table;

4. creating and dropping a view;

5. creating and dropping an integrity constraint by type;

6. creating and dropping a user-defined function;

7. creating and dropping a performance-oriented access path (such as an index);

8. creating a foreign key in one R-table referencing a primary key in another R-table (possibly the same R-table);

9. requesting that a specific authorization be granted or discontinued;

10. requesting a snapshot;

11. requesting that an audit log be maintained or discontinued (see Feature RI-15 in Chapter 13);

12. establishing a condition for archiving with a new label;

13. establishing the UP or DOWN mode for "rounding" pseudo-dates (e.g., February 30 or March 32).

RA-8 Authorizable Query and Manipulative Activities

At least seven database query and manipulation activities must be separately authorizable and authorizable in combination. The seven such activities are as follows:

1. retrieving on specific R-tables (base or view);

2. inserting into specific R-tables (base or view);

3. updating specific components of rows in specific R-tables (base or view);

4. updating the primary key of a specific R-table;

5. archiving rows from specific R-tables (base or view);

6. deleting rows from specific R-tables (base or view);

7. updating an I-marked value to either an A-marked value or a database value, and vice versa (see Chapter 8).

The granting of any of these operations, except the second one, may be not only confined to specific R-tables, but may also be value-dependent.

RA-9 Authorizable Qualifiers

Use of all qualifiers must be separately authorizable and authorizable in combination (see Chapter 10). The thirteen qualifiers are as follows:

Feature	Qualifier
RQ-1	A-MAYBE
RQ-2	I-MAYBE
RQ-3	MAYBE
RQ-4	AR(x)
RQ-5	IR(x)
RQ-6	ESR(x)
RQ-7	ORDER BY
RQ-8	ONCE ONLY
RQ-9	DOMAIN CHECK OVERRIDE
RQ-10	EXCLUDE SIBLINGS
RQ-11	DEGREE OF DUPLICATION
RQ-12	SAVE
RQ-13	VALUE

Other activities that should be subject to special authorization are the use of various functions recorded in the catalog, as well as the use of the date-conversion functions (see Item 14, following Feature RT-4 in Chapter 3). Although support within a DBMS product for this special kind of authorization is optional at this time, such a product should be at least designed to accept this extension later.

RA-10 Granting and Revoking Authorization

Authorization to access or modify parts of the database may be assigned to a user or to an already-declared user group and, at a later time, withdrawn from the user or from the group by using statements in the relational language RL. Cycles in which user A makes a grant directly or indirectly to user B, and user B makes a grant directly or indirectly to A, are prohibited.

When two or more users independently grant another user two or more authorizations to access parts of the database (the DBMS certainly supports this), these authorizations may overlap each other in space–time scope either partially or completely. Later withdrawal of any one of these leaves the others in effect.

Relational DBMS products on the market in the early 1980s often failed to support user groups in their authorization mechanisms. This failure meant that at least one authorization declaration was needed for each individual user, a severe burden on those responsible for this task.

RA-11   Passing on Authority to Grant

Suppose that a user authorizes another user or user group to access part of the database and to execute specified database operations. Suppose also that the grantor is authorized to pass on to other users the granting option. Then, the grantor has the option of granting to or witholding from the recipient permission to make further grants of part or all of this authorization.

This feature is compatible with government-type security, in which a few distinct classes of clearance are set up (e.g., top secret, secret, confidential). Few institutions, however, want to adopt this government-type security, which is relatively rigid and forces the DBA or security officer to establish a class structure on all users.

Therefore, the authorization class of features in RM/V2 has been designed to permit the adoption of many different approaches to database security, ranging from strongly centralized to strongly decentralized.

RA-12   Cascading Revocation

Consider three distinct users A, B, C. If user A grants specific authorization to user B, and if user B passes on part or all of this authorization to user C, revocation of the grant from A to B causes the DBMS to revoke the corresponding grant from B to C. If user U receives identical authorization from two or more sources, then U retains the pertinent authorization until every one of the sources has revoked the authorization.

18.3 ▪ Authorization Subject to Date, Time, Resource Consumption, and Terminal

RA-13   Date and Time Conditions

Authorization can be conditioned by day of the month, by day of the week, by a time interval during the day, or by a combination of these.

RA-14 Resource Consumption (Anticipated or Actual)

Authorization can be conditioned by either (1) the system's estimated resource consumption to complete the execution of any request submitted by the user (the system must make this estimate in any case as part of the optimization), or (2) limits on the resource consumption permitted for any request from the user. In the latter case, the request is started unconditionally but is aborted if the specified limits are exceeded.

Of these two options, the first one is preferred, provided the system's estimate of resource consumption is reasonably accurate. Even then, Option 2 is a good additional safety precaution.

RA-15 Choice of Terminal

Authorization can be conditioned by the particular terminal or workstation from which a user is operating.

RA-16 Assigning Authorization

For each user who interacts with a relational database, there must be at least one declaration in the catalog that he or she is authorized to engage in activities (A) within a specified space-time scope (S). Normally very few users would be authorized to pass on to another user part or all of the authorization they possess. This process of passing on authorization is called *granting*.

Occasionally it is necessary nevertheless for someone who does not have authorization with space-time scope (S) and activities (A) to be able to assign that authorization to another user. This action is called *assigning authorization*. Very few users would be authorized to assign authorization.

Thus, when a user assigns authorization to some other user or users, the assignor is granting an authorization whose scope and permitted actions are not within the range of what is owned by the assignor. It is usually the DBA and some of the DBA's staff that need to be able to assign authorization.

It is the DBA staff that is normally responsible for authorizing users to access and, in some cases, modify specified parts of the database. How would the DBA or the DBA staff then cope with a company policy that requires these people NOT to be able to access data in a relation they created? The answer is that after the DBA or staff create ANY relation, the DBMS does not automatically give the creators the right to be able to access and modify whatever data is entered into that relation. Instead, the DBA can assign user privileges to other users without having those privileges himself or herself.

Exercises

18.1 Is the scope of what a user is allowed to interrogate limited to a DBA-specified list of columns in a single relation? If not, what can the scope be, and how is it specified?

18.2 Should the authorization mechanism in a DBMS be designed so that the power of the relational language in limiting the space-time scope that is authorized for each user is totally and exclusively dependent on applying that power to defining views? Explain your position.

18.3 What are the N-person turn-key and seven-day archiving features? Why should both of these features be supported within a relational DBMS?

18.4 List the seven "create and drop" capabilities that should be separately authorizable and authorizable in combination.

18.5 Why should user groups as well as individual users be supported in regard to authorization?

18.6 Cycles are prohibited in the granting of authorization. Describe the kind of cycles that are prohibited. Explain how cascaded revocation is related to this prohibition.

18.7 What authorization features of RM/V2 enable a DBA to permit a certain amount of ad hoc query to accompany a significant load of production-oriented transactions?

■ *CHAPTER 19* ■

Functions

A query expressed as a relational command indicates what types of items are to be retrieved by listing a sequence of pairs of names. Each pair consists of a relation name followed by a column name; this is called the *target list*. A relational command of the query type also indicates the condition to be satisfied by the particular items that are to be extracted; this is called the *condition*. The condition is expressed in four-valued, first-order predicate logic.

Suppose that a database contains information about shipments within a relation named SHIP. Suppose further that for each shipment this information includes the supplier serial number s#, the part serial number p#, and the date of the shipment. An example of a query is as follows: Obtain all of the part serial numbers and dates of shipment for parts shipped after January 31, 1988. A simple relational command for this request is as follows:

get SHIP.p#, SHIP.ship—date where ship—date > 88-1-31.

The target list in this command is SHIP.p#, SHIP.shipdate. The condition is that part of the query that follows the word "where," namely, "shipdate > 88-1-31."

Functions are needed in database management for two purposes. The first purpose is to transform target database values within a query or view definition. The function is then part of the expression for the target list.

Consider as an example the database just cited. Suppose that the primary key of SHIP is the combination of supplier serial number s# and part serial number p#. Suppose that both shipdate and quantity of parts shipped are immediate properties included as columns in the relation SHIP. Someone must know the number of shipments of part p2 after January 31, 1988. Suppose also that the DBMS supports the COUNT function. Then, an appropriate query is as follows:

get COUNT(SHIP.s#, SHIP.p#) where ship__date > 88-1-31.

Note that the function COUNT occurs in the target list.

The second purpose of including functions in database management is to determine the condition to be satisfied by the target database values in retrieval and in data manipulation. The function is then part of the expression for the condition.

Consider as an example the same database, but a different query: Find the serial numbers of only those parts for which the number of shipments recorded in the database exceeds 10. An appropriate query is as follows:

get SHIP.p# where COUNT (SHIP.s#, SHIP.p#) > 10.

Note that the function COUNT occurs in the condition. Note also that this query could not be expressed as simply in SQL.

19.1 ■ Scalar and Aggregate Functions

The two types of functions discussed in this chapter are scalar functions and aggregate functions. Each type of function can be used in both of the ways just described.

A *scalar function* transforms a scalar into a scalar. An example of such a function is a currency-exchange function, which transforms an amount of money expressed in one currency into a corresponding amount expressed in some other currency.

An *aggregate function* transforms a set of scalars or a set of tuples into a scalar. An example of such a function is the COUNT function just mentioned. Another example is the SUM function, which scans a collection of numbers in a column of some relation (such as amounts that are all expressed in some common currency) and computes their sum.

RF-1 Built-in Aggregate Functions

The DBMS provides at least the five aggregate functions—COUNT, SUM, AVERAGE, MAXIMUM, MINIMUM—as built-in functions for use either in transforming target database values within a query or view-defining command, or in determining the condition to be satisfied by the target database values in retrieval and in data manipulation.

Note that an aggregate function in this context normally transforms many scalar values into a single scalar value. The usual source of the many scalar values is a simple or composite column. When an aggregate function is applied to a column that happens to contain duplicate values, all occurrences of those values participate in the action.

For example, if the SUM function is applied to a currency column C in relation R, the result obtained is the sum of *every value occurrence* in C, which is normally not the same as the sum of every distinct value in C.

Consider the example of a relation EMP that identifies employees and records their immediate properties. The SALARY and BONUS components of each row have as their values the year-to-date salary and commission earned by the employee described in that row:

EMP	(EMP#	ENAME	DEPT#	SALARY	BONUS)
	E10	Rook	D12	12,000	15,800
	E91	Knight	D12	10,000	6,700
	E23	Knight	D05	13,000	13,000
	E57	Pawn	D02	7,000	3,100

The following queries illustrate the built-in functions:

How many employees are there?   get COUNT (EMP)

What is the total bonus earned?   get SUM (EMP.BONUS)

What is the average bonus earned?   get AVERAGE (EMP.BONUS)

What is the maximum salary earned?   get MAXIMUM (EMP.SALARY)

What is the minimum bonus earned?   get MINIMUM (EMP.BONUS)

There is a simple way to obtain the sum or the count of the distinct values in a simple or composite column C, if that is what is needed: take the **projection** (uncorrupted, of course) of the relation R onto column C, and then apply the SUM or COUNT function to the result. This method takes advantage of the fact that true **projection** eliminates duplicate rows from the result.

The following query is based on the same EMP relation: What is the number of distinct salaries? get COUNT (EMP [SALARY])

A good measure of the degree of duplication of values in column C is obtained by taking the count of rows in the relation containing C and dividing that count by the count of distinct values in C. In a relation that provides the immediate properties of employees, it is likely that the degree of duplication in the gender column (which has only two values, male and female) would be very high, while the degree of duplication in the last-name column would be very low.

The abbreviation DOD stands for DEGREE OF DUPLICATION. Suppose that the values in a simple or composite column C are the intended arguments of a statistical function f. Then, for each row containing the DOD component n, the contribution of the C-component of that row is n times the value of that C-component.

RF-2   The DOD Versions of Built-in Statistical Functions

For each statistical function built into the DBMS (including SUM and AVERAGE as required by Feature RF-1), there is also a DOD version built into the DBMS. (See Feature RQ-11 in Chapter 10 for details concerning the DOD qualifier.)

RF-3   Built-in Scalar Functions

The DBMS supports at least the following arithmetic scalar functions as built-in functions and expressions in RL: addition, subtraction, multiplication, division, and exponentiation. The DBMS also supports at least the following string scalar functions as built-in functions and expressions in RL: concatenation, substring directly specified, and substring by pattern-directed search.

These functions are for use either in transforming target database values within a query or view-defining command, or in determining the condition to be satisfied by the target database values in retrieval and in data manipulation.

Note that a scalar function in this context has a fixed number of arguments (usually one or two, seldom more), that each argument is a scalar, and that the function transforms each of its arguments into a scalar result.

19.2 ■ User-defined Functions

Clearly, the number of functions supplied by the DBMS vendor as part of the DBMS is small, and therefore is not likely to satisfy all DBMS users. There must be a means by which users can add functions suited to their own businesses or institutional activities. Feature RF-4 provides the means. Subsequent features provide additional support or constraints.

RF-4 User-defined Functions: Their Use

Users can define their own functions. The DBMS can then record such functions (scalar, aggregate, or other types) in the catalog together with their names and types. The system then supports use of such functions in access targeting, in access conditioning, or in both. Use is more generally determined by the orthogonality feature, Feature RL-7 (see Chapter 22). If the function that is required happens to be statistical in nature, users can define a non-DOD version, a DOD version, or both.

Note that the non-DOD version ignores the degree-of-duplication column, if one occurs in the operand relation. On the other hand, the DOD version causes each row that has n as its DOD component to provide a contribution to f that is equal to that from n occurrences of the value in the contributing column.

RF-5 Inverse Function Required, If It Exists

Together with each user-defined function recorded in the catalog, a symbol is entered that indicates whether this function has an inverse. If so, the name of this inverse, together with the code for the inverse, is also recorded in the catalog.

Rarely is it the case that an aggregate function has an inverse.

Some functions are expected to be used in defining some columns of views. If such a function happens to have an inverse, there is a chance that the pertinent column of the view will be updatable, since in such a case the DBMS can compute from any new value in that column of the view the corresponding value (simple or composite) that it should enter into appropriate column(s) of the base R-tables.

RF-6 User-defined Functions: Compiled Form Required

The DBMS requires that each user-defined function and its inverse (if any) be written in one of the host languages, and compiled before the function is stored in the catalog.

Note that, when a user programs a user-defined function and incorporates it into a DBMS, he or she need not know anything about the internal coding or internal structure of the DBMS. The term "host language" is used to identify any one of the so-called general-purpose programming languages such as FORTRAN, COBOL, and PL/1. The relational model supports at least these three as languages with which the principal relational language can communicate.

RF-7 User-defined Functions Can Access the Database

The DBMS is capable of handling user-defined functions that make use of data extracted from the database at the time of execution of these functions.

An example of the need for this feature is found in transactions that involve currency exchange between various currencies. It is then quite likely that the database will contain a relation (say EX) that reflects the exchange rates currently in effect. Four of the columns of EX would be as follows: (1) identification of the FROM currency (primary key); (2) identification of the TO currency (primary key); (3) an amount of the FROM currency expressed in that currency; and (4) the corresponding amount expressed in the TO currency. An exchange function would have to access this relation EX with three arguments:

1. the type of currency from which the exchange is to be made;
2. the type of currency to which the exchange is to be made;
3. the number of units of the FROM currency to be exchanged.

19.3 ■ Safety and Interface Features

RF-8 Non-generation of Marked Values by Functions

The application of a scalar function to unmarked arguments and of an aggregate function to a set of unmarked database values (even if the set is empty) never yields a marked result.

In IBM's DB2, the application of the AVERAGE function to an empty set yields the NULL of SQL—a mistake because this is a case of the result being undefined, and not a case of a value missing from the database. The mistake probably resulted from a confusion about two kinds of facts:

1. The fact that a database value might be missing (represented by the NULL of SQL).

2. The fact that, for some arguments, a function may not have a defined result.

In this example, the average of zero elements is normally taken to be undefined. Whenever an empty set is encountered as an argument to the AVERAGE function, the relational model supports the options of (1) signaling this undefined state, and (2) executing user-defined action if needed (see Feature RQ-6 in Chapter 10).

Note that the outer operators (see Chapter 5) almost always generate marked values, even if the arguments contain no marked values. The addition of a new column to a base R-table also generates marks within that column. Thus, it is not intended that these operators be perceived as functions when interpreting Feature RF-8.

The power and usefulness of a relational database is increased if the following three steps are taken:

1. Columns are permitted to contain names of invokable functions, as well as the usual kinds of value-oriented data.

2. Columns are permitted to contain names of arguments, as well as the usual kinds of value-oriented data.

3. Both the relational language and the host language have the capability of invoking a function for which the name and the values of its arguments can all be obtained, either directly from the database, by use of argument names in the database, or partly from the database and partly from the host-language program and its data.

The following two features make it less likely that the user will feel that he or she is becoming more and more isolated from the outside world as interrogation of the database proceeds.

RF-9 Domains and Columns Containing Names of Functions

One of the domains (extended data types) that is built into the DBMS is that of function names. Such names can be stored in a column (possibly in several columns) of a relation by declaring that the column(s) draw their values from the domain of function names. Both RL and the host programming language support the assemblage of the arguments together with the function name, followed by the invocation of that function to transform the assembled arguments.

RF-10 Domains and Columns Containing Names of Arguments

One of the domains (extended data types) that is built into the DBMS is that of argument names. Such names can be stored in a column (possibly in several columns) of a relation by declaring that the column(s) draw their values from the domain of argument names. These arguments have values that can be retrieved either from the database or from storage associated with a program expressed in the HL.

Features RF-9 and RF-10 are very likely to be useful in making extensions to the relational model that involve user-defined functions. Therefore, more is said about them in Chapter 28.

Exercises

19.1   In the relational model, each value in a column of a relation is required to be atomic with respect to the DBMS. Under what circumstances, if any, are such values not atomic? Give examples that illustrate the use of database values in a non-atomic role.

19.2   What are scalar and aggregate functions? List the five aggregate functions that should be built into the DBMS.

19.3   For each user-defined function, which of the following is required to be stored in the catalog?

■ The source code.

■ The compiled code.

■ Both the source and compiled code.

19.4   Identify those items that are also stored in the catalog for each user-defined function, and that facilitate the updating of certain kinds of views. Explain the items you selected and why you chose them.

19.5   In certain kinds of manufacturing, the production of most products involves the use of several machines, each of which has an associated minimum interval of use and a distinct cost-of-use function. Describe a feature of RM/V2 that is essential if the computation of total cost is to be incorporated in the retrieval of data from the database.

■ *CHAPTER 20* ■

Protection of Investment

When a company or institution acquires a database management system, the immediate investment consists of the cost of the hardware and software. However, there is a longer-term investment, that may be even larger than the initial one: the investment in the development of application programs and in the training of users, both programmers and end users. The total investment is quite heavy, and the purchaser of a DBMS needs some assurance that the risk is slight.

This chapter deals with features of the relational model designed to protect the user's total investment. In particular, these features enable application programs to continue to run correctly when a variety of changes are made in the database, including changes in the physical representation of data, the logical representation, the integrity constraints, and the distribution of data between a given collection of sites.

20.1 ■ Physical Protection

RP-1 Physical Data Independence

The DBMS permits a suitably authorized user to make changes in storage representation, in access method, or in both—for example, for performance reasons. Application programs and terminal activities remain logically unimpaired whenever any such changes are made. (This feature is Rule 8 in the 1985 set.)

To handle physical data independence, the DBMS must support a clear, sharp boundary between the logical and semantic aspects, on the one hand, and the physical and performance aspects of the base R-tables, on the other; application programs and terminal users must deal with the logical and semantic aspects only. Relational DBMS can and should support this feature totally. Non-relational DBMS rarely provide complete support for this feature (in fact, I know of none that do).

20.2 ■ Logical Protection

RP-2 Logical Data Independence

Application programs and terminal activities remain logically un-impaired when information-preserving changes are made to the base R-tables, provided these changes are of the kind that permit un-impairment, either according to Algorithm VU-1 or according to a strictly stronger algorithm. (This feature is Rule 9 in the 1985 set.)

Three examples of information-preserving changes are listed below.

1. Partitioning an R-table into two or more tables by rows using row content.

2. Splitting an R-table into two tables by columns using column names, provided the original primary key is preserved in each result.

3. Combining two R-tables into one by means of a non-loss **join.** (Note that many authors now call non-loss **joins** "lossless.")

To provide this service whenever possible, the DBMS must be capable of handling insertions, updates, and deletions on all views that are updatable in accordance with Algorithm VU-1 (see Feature RV-5 in Chapter 16, as well as Chapter 17). Features RP-1 and RP-2 permit logical database design to be tackled with a high degree of independence from physical database design. Feature RP-2 also permits the logical design to be dynamically changed if necessary for any reason, without damaging the user's investment in application programs.

The physical and logical data-independence features permit database designers for relational DBMS to make mistakes in their designs without the heavy penalties levied by non-relational DBMS. In turn, this means that it is much easier to get started with a relational DBMS, because not nearly as much performance-oriented planning is needed before putting the database into operation.

20.3 ■ Integrity Protection

RP-3 Integrity Independence

Integrity constraints specific to a particular relational database must be definable in the relational data sublanguage RL, and storable in the catalog. Application programs and terminal activities remain logically unimpaired when changes are made in these integrity constraints, provided such changes theoretically permit unimpairment (where "theoretically" means at a level of abstraction for which all DBMS implementation details are set aside). (This feature is Rule 10 in the 1985 set.)

Safe control of database integrity cannot be guaranteed if these constraints are included in the application programs only.

In addition to the two general integrity constraints—entity integrity and referential integrity—which apply to each and every relational database, there is a clear need to be able to specify additional integrity constraints of the domain type, column type, and the user-defined type. Such constraints usually reflect business policies, and/or government regulations, and/or the principal types of well-understood semantic dependencies (functional, multivalued, join, and inclusion).

If, as sometimes happens, either business policies or government regulations change, it is probably necessary to change the user-defined integrity constraints. Normally, this can be accomplished in a fully relational DBMS by changing one or more integrity statements stored in the catalog. The DBMS is designed not to require any changes in the application programs or in the terminal activities, unless such changes are unavoidable. Nonrelational DBMS rarely support this feature as part of the DBMS (where it belongs). Instead, they depend on a dictionary package or application generator (which may or may not be present, and can readily be bypassed).

20.4 ■ Re-distribution Protection

RP-4 Distribution Independence

A relational DBMS has a data sublanguage RL, which enables application programs and terminal activities to remain logically unimpaired under two circumstances:

- ■ When data distribution is first introduced (this may occur because the DBMS originally installed manages non-distributed data only);
- ■ When data is redistributed (if the DBMS manages distributed data)—the redistribution may involve an entirely different decomposition of the totality of data.

(This feature is Rule 11 in the 1985 set.)

The DBMS property defined in Feature RP-4 is called *distribution independence*. This definition is carefully worded so that both a distributed and a non-distributed DBMS *can* fully support Feature RP-4. Whether a DBMS product provides such support is primarily resolved by examining the data sublanguage(s) that the product supports. Is at least one of these languages at a sufficiently high level to support both of the situations just stated, and has this been demonstrated (e.g., by a prototype)? I believe that the relational level is essential. Certainly, no non-relational approach has been published that has proved its success in supporting Feature RP-4.

Some examples of DBMS products in the marketplace that fully support Feature RP-4 are SQL/DS and DB2 of IBM, INGRES of Relational Technology, and NonStop SQL of Tandem (in their current releases). Other vendors are rapidly entering the distributed database management market. Except for distribution independence and decomposition and recomposition (see Feature RP-5), the features that appear necessary for a DBMS to excel in distributed-database management are discussed separately (see Chapters 24 and 25).

Support of Feature RP-4 by the IBM systems has been demonstrated as follows: SQL programs written to operate on non-distributed data, using System R, run correctly on distributed versions of that data using System R*, the IBM San Jose Research prototype of a distributed database management system [Williams et al. 1981]. The distributed INGRES project has shown a similar capability for the QUEL language of INGRES [Stonebraker 1986].

Distribution independence is a more serious requirement than mere location independence. The former concept permits not only all the data at any one site to be moved to another, but also a completely different decomposition of the totality of data at all sites into fragments to be deployed at the various sites.

It is important to distinguish among (1) distributed processing, (2) networking, and (3) distributed data. In the first case, application programs are transmitted to the data. In the second case, messages can be sent from a processing unit at any site to a processing unit at another. In the third case, data is derived from possibly multiple sites (the derivation being executed at whatever sites the optimizer selects for efficiency) and directed to the requesting program or terminal. Many non-relational DBMS support distributed processing, but not the management of distributed databases. Support for distributed database management—in which all the data, whether stored locally or remotely, appears to be local—has been demonstrated by relational DBMS prototypes. Whether it can be supported by any other kind of DBMS remains to be seen.

In the case of distributed relational DBMS, a single transaction may straddle several remote sites. Such straddling is managed entirely under the covers—the system may have to execute recovery at multiple sites. Each program or terminal activity treats the totality of data as if it were all local to the site where the application program or terminal activity is being executed.

A fully relational DBMS that does *not* support distributed databases has the capability of being extended to provide that support, while leaving application programs and terminal activities logically unimpaired, both at the time of initial distribution and whenever later re-distribution is made. There are four important reasons why relational DBMS enjoy this advantage.

1. *Decomposition flexibility* in deciding how to deploy the data.
2. *Recomposition power* of the relational operators when combining the results of sub-transactions executed at different sites.
3. *Economy of transmission* resulting from the fact that the DBMS has multiple-record-at-a-time capability. Thus, there need not be a request message sent for each record to be retrieved from any remote site, or a reply message for each result record to be transmitted back.
4. *Analyzability of intent* (due to the very high level of relational languages) for vastly improved automatic optimization of execution—and, when necessary, automatic re-optimization.

RP-5 Distributed Database Management: Decomposition and Recomposition

If the DBMS supports distributed database management, it uses the full power of RL (including four-valued, first-order predicate logic) to decompose each RL statement into simpler RL statements, each of which is capable of being executed at a single site. Such a DBMS also uses this full power to recombine the results from the subrequests to yield a coherent and correct response to the whole request.

Note that Feature RP-5 is not applicable if the DBMS is not claimed to support distributed database management.

20.5 ■ Summary of the Practical Reasons for Features RP-1–RP-5

Features RP-1–RP-4 represent *four different types of independence* aimed at protecting users' investment in application programs, terminal activities, and training. Features RP-1 and RP-2—physical and logical data independence— have been widely discussed for many years. Nevertheless, today there still exist DBMS products that fail to support these features. Features RP-2, RP-3, and RP-4—logical data independence, integrity independence, and distribution independence—have received inadequate attention to date, but are likely to become as important as Feature RP-1. There is no claim that these four types of independence are easily implemented in a DBMS. Feature RP-5 may help the reader understand (1) the complexity of the problem, and (2) the fact that the relational model has the capability of solving it.

Exercises

20.1 What are the four main types of investment protection that are obtainable from a fully relational DBMS?

20.2 If at its inception a database is properly designed logically and physically, why should it ever be necessary to change that design (1) logically and/or (2) physically?

20.3 Why should it ever be necessary to change integrity constraints?

20.4 If integrity constraints are changed, why be concerned about having to change a few application programs, especially if the programs are written in a "fourth generation language"?

20.5 Someone asserts that determining how data should be distributed to various sites is a design problem that occurs just once (at installation time), and concludes that distribution independence is a feature of no value. Is there any merit in this argument?

CHAPTER 21

Principles of DBMS Design

The relational model is based on the fundamental laws discussed in Chapter 29. It is intended that implementations of the model are to be based on the design principles described in this chapter. The main motivation for formulating these principles in explicit terms was the numerous blunders that have been made in various DBMS implementations.

In the next chapter, design principles for relational languages are discussed. I recommend to DBMS vendors that they use the principles in both chapters to get the designers of their DBMS products back on track.

RD-1 Non-violation of any Fundamental Law of Mathematics

The DBMS and its relational language(s) do not violate any of the fundamental laws of mathematics.

At first glance, this appears to be a completely unnecessary feature. In examining a database management system in 1969, however, I discovered that, under certain conditions, it failed to support the commutativity of logical AND. More specifically, suppose that X and Y are correctly formulated truth-valued expressions, and that Q1, Q2 are two identical queries except that Q1 has the condition X AND Y, while Q2 has the condition Y AND X. Under the special conditions, Q1 and Q2 failed to yield the same result on identical databases. This fact was not disclosed in the manuals supplied to users. Fortunately, this DBMS product failed in the marketplace.

The reader may imagine that such a blunder could have happened only in the 1960s. Unfortunately, a recent release of a well-known relational DBMS product, marketed by a vendor with an excellent reputation, fails under certain conditions to yield x from the expression x + y − y when x happens to be a date and y happens to be a date interval, even though x and y are correctly formulated. The error in the result can be as much as three days.

In my opinion, both examples illustrate the appalling lack of real concern for the quality of their products by the workers and managers in software, and an astonishing lack of concern for the very large number of institutions that are likely to be adversely affected by such sloppy work. The examples also illustrate an apparent lack of understanding of basic user requirements and basic mathematics.

RD-2   Under-the-covers Representation and Access

The DBMS may employ any storage representations and any access methods for data, provided these are implemented "under the covers"—that is, they must not be exposed to users (with the possible exception of giving the DBA a few types of commands to create and drop performance-oriented structures and access methods). Once these structures are created, the responsibility for maintaining them during insertion, update, and deletion activities belongs to the DBMS, not to users and not to the DBA.

RD-3   Sharp Boundary

The DBMS makes a sharp separation between two aspects: (1) performance-oriented features (such as indexes), and (2) semantic and logical features (such as the uniqueness of values in a column or combination of columns, the exclusion of missing values, the primary-key property, and the foreign-key property).

In general, most users should be protected from having to deal with the first item altogether. In particular, if the DBA drops an index (for example), there should be no loss of semantic features, such as those cited in the second item. Some existing DBMS products fail in this respect because they require an index to exist on any column whose values must all be distinct from one another. Distinctness of values is a semantic feature, while an index is a performance-oriented feature.

Should application programmers or end users be burdened by concern for the logical aspects of concurrency control? This question deserves special consideration.

Two types of concurrency must be supported by a relational DBMS:

1. *intra-command concurrency* consists of treating various portions of a single relational command as independent tasks, and executing these tasks concurrently;

2. *inter-command concurrency* consists of executing two or more relational commands concurrently.

RD-4 Concurrency Independence

Application programs and activities by end users at terminals must be logically independent of whether the DBMS supports intra-command concurrency, inter-command concurrency, neither, or both. Application programs and activities must also be independent of the controls (usually locking) that protect any one action A from interfering with or damaging any other action that happens to be concurrent with A.

A relational DBMS never requires the user or application program to make an explicit request for some kind of lock. Such an action would be oriented too heavily to a particular implementation. An interrogative or manipulative request, however, may represent an implicit request for some kind of lock.

Some requests cause the DBMS to impose long-term locking. An example is the updating of several primary-key values, each of which triggers corresponding updating of foreign-key values scattered in various parts of the database.

Occasionally, a terminal user makes a request that requires the DBMS to lock a large quantity of data. Then the user may leave the terminal, absent-mindedly signing off before completing whatever action would release the locks. The DBMS must protect other users and programs from unauthorized long-term locking.

RD-5 Protection Against Unauthorized
Long-term Locking

The DBA can specify a time block T permitted on every locking action caused by any request from a terminal user or application program. For each user and program, the DBA can also specify a locking quota expressed in multiples of T. Whenever one block is consumed, the DBMS checks the authorization data to see whether the quota, for which the user or application program is authorized, has been consumed. If the quota has been consumed, the DBMS aborts the request. If not, the DBMS reduces the quota by one, and proceeds with the transaction.

Whenever a terminal user is involved, each time a time block is consumed, the DBMS should check that the user is still at his or her terminal. This can easily be done by requesting the user to press a certain key if he or she wants the action to continue and wants the locks held for one more time block.

RD-6 Orthogonality in DBMS Design

Any coupling of one feature with another in the design of a DBMS must be justified by some clearly stated, unemotional, logically defensible reason.

Feature RD-6 should not be confused with Feature RL-7 (see Chapter 22). Two examples of unjustified coupling of features in a very prominent relational DBMS may clarify the intent behind Feature RD-6. Both examples involve indexes, and it should be understood that, from the standpoint of the relational model, an index is purely a performance-oriented concept, one that should be kept hidden from all users except possibly the few who are authorized to create and drop indexes.

In the first example, the relational DBMS requires that any column in which the values are constrained to be distinct from one another (a frequently encountered semantic constraint) must be indexed. Unfortunately, this means that such an index cannot be dropped purely for performance reasons.

In the second example, the relational DBMS maintains statistics for use by the optimizer to deliver improved performance. This is a good performance-oriented feature that should be independent of whatever columns happen to be indexed at any time. The statistics consist chiefly of the number of distinct values in each column. The relational DBMS, however, maintains these statistics only for those columns that are indexed—the simplest task for the implementors. As a result, it is easy to construct examples of SQL commands for which the relational DBMS will give unnecessarily poor performance. Perhaps the designers failed to realize that statistics normally do not change rapidly, and therefore need not be (and should not be) updated every time any part of the database content is changed.

In each of these examples, there is an unjustified coupling of two independent features—in the first case, a semantic feature coupled with a performance-oriented feature; in the second case, one performance-oriented feature with another quite distinct and independent one.

RD-7 Domain-based Index

For those DBMS that are based primarily on software, the DBMS supports the creation and dropping of domain-based indexes by suitably authorized users. This may also provide advantages in performance for hardware-based DBMS.

A domain-based index is a single index on the combination of columns defined on the specified domain (normally all of those columns are involved, but a suitably authorized user may select only those columns that will prove advantageous). Such an index will usually be a multi-table index. It facilitates the efficient execution of referential integrity (if the domain is a primary domain) and other occurrences of inclusion dependence. So far, the only relational DBMS I have encountered with a domain-based index is one developed at the University of Nice.

RD-8 Database Statistics

In the catalog, the DBMS stores statistics of the data (see Feature RC-11 in Chapter 15). This information is used by the optimizer to select the most efficient method of handling each retrieval and manipulative command. The DBMS updates these statistics only occasionally—certainly not upon every insert, delete, or update. The updating of statistics is executed by the DBMS with a frequency and at times requested by the DBA or any suitably authorized user.

The DBMS fails to provide full support for this feature if it either (1) supports no database statistics at all or (2) supports statistics for only those columns that happen to be indexed or happen to have some other performance-oriented property.

RD-9 Interrogation of Statistics

The DBMS statistics cited in RD-3 may be interrogated by use of RL by the DBA or by any suitably authorized user.

RD-10 Changing Storage Representation and Access Options

Commands must be available to the DBA for dynamically changing the storage representation and access method in use for any base relation *without causing logical impairment of any transaction in source code form* (whether already compiled or not), or any noticeable delays in the execution of the transactions in progress or of transactions waiting to be processed.

If transactions are normally compiled before their first execution, and if the change in storage representation or access method necessitates re-compilation, then this feature requires that the re-compilation must be automatically called into action by the DBMS without manual intervention by the DBA or by any user.

RD-11   Automatic Protection in Case of Malfunction

In case of a malfunction that causes one or more transactions to fail to complete, the DBMS must protect the database from the effects of the failed transactions.

RD-12   Automatic Recovery in Case of Malfunction

In case of a malfunction that causes one or more transactions to fail to complete, the DBMS must be able—without user intervention— to recover immediately after the cause of the malfunction has been repaired. Recovery can be deemed effective when the aborted and delayed transactions have been successfully re-executed using the state of the database effective at re-execution time.

The DBMS maintains a recovery log for this purpose. This feature is included because it is considered an essential requirement of any DBMS, whether relational or not.

RD-13   Atomic Execution of Relational Commands

Each relational command is executed in its entirety without breaks or stoppages because of restrictions on the size of operands or the size of results imposed by the DBMS implementation, or any other reason except malfunction.

A few DBMS products discontinue the processing of an RL command after processing a fixed number of rows (50,000 in one case) from any one R-table; the number is a DBMS implementation constraint. This could be an unpleasant surprise for the many users who must process much larger tables, involving in some cases millions of rows.

Sometimes programmers using a relational DBMS must apply an update across a relation that has a million rows. It is good practice to avoid tackling such an update on a global, single-commit basis, because of the possibility of a massive rollback if anything goes wrong in the later stages. The other extreme consists of processing the updates on a row-by-row basis (single-record-at-a-time); this is likely to detract from performance. An efficient solution involves tackling the update in batches of several thousand rows each at a time. Every time such a batch is successfully completed, the corresponding updates are committed to the database. Support for this progressive, batch-by-batch activity is needed in relational languages, and can be expected in RM/V3.

RD-14   Automatic Archiving

The DBMS supports the automatic archiving of data when it reaches an age specified by the DBA. The frequency of archiving is also specified by the DBA (e.g., once every quarter of a year). It must be possible to re-activate any relational snapshot that has been archived.

RD-15   Avoiding Cartesian Product

During the execution of any single RL command, the DBMS avoids generating the **Cartesian product** of two R-tables as an intermediate result, and never generates the **Cartesian product** as the final result of an RL command, except possibly in the case of a **join** being requested without any **join** condition. In this case, the DBMS issues a warning message.

The **Cartesian product** is wasteful in terms of memory space, channel time, and processing-unit cycles. Thus, if it is requested as a final result, the user should be aware that it is expensive and contains no more information than its factors.

RD-16 Responsibility for Encryption and Decryption

It is the sole responsibility of the DBMS to invoke programs for encrypting data immediately before storing it in the database, and for decrypting data upon retrieval.

The DBA must enforce this feature until an acceptable way is found for the DBMS to enforce it. Clearly, if programmers are allowed to include encrypting and decrypting functions in their own programs, the DBMS and the DBA have abandoned the maintenance of integrity in at least the encrypted data, and possibly in closely related data also.

The design principles introduced in this chapter are aimed at cleanliness of design and ease of use by the whole community of users. They are *not* aimed at reducing either the creative originality of individual implementors or the degree of competition among their respective companies.

- RD-1 Non-violation of any fundamental law of mathematics
- RD-2 Under-the-covers representation and access
- RD-3 Sharp boundary between performance-oriented features
- RD-4 Concurrency independence
- RD-5 Protection against unauthorized locking
- RD-6 Orthogonality in DBMS design
- RD-7 Domain-based index
- RD-8 Database statistics
- RD-9 Interrogation of statistics
- RD-10 Changing storage representation and access options
- RD-11 Automatic protection in case of malfunction
- RD-12 Automatic recovery in case of malfunction
- RD-13 Atomic execution of relational commands
- RD-14 Automatic archiving
- RD-15 Avoiding cartesian product
- RD-16 DBMS responsible for all encryption and decryption of data

Exercises

21.1 A designer who helped design a DBMS product says, "Who cares about any violations of mathematics? Mathematics is a subject strictly for mathematicians, whereas our DBMS is concerned with the real world." Decide whether this is a defensible position or an untenable position. Explain.

21.2 Is it required that the relations of the relational model be represented as tables in storage? If not, what are the only constraints on this representation?

21.3 A DBMS designer says, "In the old days, we never bothered about separating storage representation and access methods, on the one hand, from the logical representation, on the other hand. I fail to see why such sharp separation is necessary." Try to provide this designer with some insight regarding the need for this separation.

21.4 Supply the names and definitions of the two types of concurrency in database management. Which of these would be more advantageous if your workload involved:
1. many complex requests?
2. many simple requests?

21.5 What is a domain-based index, and what is it good for?

21.6 Can skilled application programmers develop code that runs more efficiently on a pre-relational single-record-at-a-time DBMS than on a relational DBMS that has a well-designed optimizer? Give reasons for your position. (See Chapter 26.)

21.7 Will the code described in Exercise 21.6 continue to run more efficiently (if it does) in spite of changes in the business and hence in the traffic on the database? How readily can this code be adapted to the new traffic? Explain.

21.8 A fully relational DBMS provides the following:
■ protection from hardware malfunction;
■ continuation of those processes that have not been damaged by the hardware malfunction;
■ recovery without loss of information or commands after the hardware malfunction has been repaired.

State which of these services are supported by RM/V2.

21.9 Why should **Cartesian product** be avoided in:
1. designing a relational DBMS product?
2. in using a relational DBMS that happens to support this operator?

CHAPTER 22

Principles of Design for Relational Languages

The question has often been asked, "Why not extend a relational language to become a general-purpose programming language?" More recently, often the following is asked: "What are you going to do about image data and the large numeric arrays that are common in science and engineering?"

Early in my work on database management, I decided not to try to modify any of the well-established programming languages, such as FOR-TRAN, COBOL, and PL/1, to include the kind of statements needed in database management. Experience in dealing with the standards committees for these languages had convinced me that the members were not very interested in technical issues of any depth. Thus, I concentrated on database-oriented sublanguages, languages intended for every aspect of database management only. The term "sublanguage" clearly indicates that the language is specialized, and is not intended to support the computation of all computable functions.

This direction has proved to be sound. It was subsequently pursued with great success by the developers of text editing on micro-computers. After all, how many secretaries would now be using text editors if they had to learn COBOL or PL/1 first?

Programming languages such as PL/1 and ADA have reached a total complexity that is staggering. Therefore, it seems reasonable to predict that there will be continued growth in specialized sublanguages, each capable of being used interactively alone, and of communicating with programming languages of a more general nature in order to participate in application programs.

The processing of image data and large numeric arrays, especially matrices, involves many specialized operators and functions. Two examples of specialized operators are the inversion and transposition of matrices, while the computation of their determinants involves a specialized function.

As a user option, it should be possible to embed the corresponding retrieval expressions and functions in the target part or the condition part of a request in a relational language. It should not be necessary, however, for a commercial or industrial user to learn about these separable concepts unless he or she needs them on the job. Thus, a relational language should be designed to *accommodate* a wide variety of specialized operators and functions, not all of which can be anticipated at the time the language is designed.

In Features RL-1–RL-17, following, the abbreviation RL continues to denote whatever relational language is the principal one supported by a relational DBMS.

RL-1 Data Sublanguage: Variety of Users

RL is a data sublanguage intended to support users of all types, including both programmers and non-programmers, in all logical aspects of managing databases. RL contains no commands for branching, looping, manipulating pointers, or manipulating indexes.

The reasoning behind this feature is that the introduction of commands of this type would convert RL into an overly complicated language usable by programmers, but by hardly anyone else.

RL-2 Compiling and Re-compiling

RL commands must be compilable separately from the host-language context in which they may appear. The DBMS must support the compilation of RL commands, even if it also supports interpreting them. Moreover, the DBMS must support automatic re-compilation of RL commands whenever any change in access paths, access methods, or indexing invalidates the code developed by a previous compilation.[1]

RL-3 Intermixability of Relational- and Host-language Statements

In application programs, statements in RL can be freely intermixed with statements in the host language.

[1]This feature of RM/V2 is based on work done by Raymond Lorie while he was a member of the System R team in IBM Research, San Jose.

RL-4 Principal Relational Language Is Dynamically Executable

Any request expressed as an RL command can be pieced together as a character string using RL and/or HL. This character string can then be compiled and executed either immediately or later (user's choice) as if it were a command that has been entered from a terminal.

RL-5 RL Both a Source and a Target Language

RL is designed for two modes of use, as a source language and as a target language. In the first mode, statements must be easy for human beings to conceive correctly. In the second mode, statements must be easy for a computer-based system to generate.

Frequently, a language is designed as a source language only. However, almost every source language in the computing field becomes a target language for software packages on top. This is particularly true for relational languages because many services must make use of the information in relational databases.

RL-6 Simple Rule for Scope Within an RL Command

The scope of operators, comparators, functions, logical connectives, qualifiers, and indicators within any single RL expression or command must conform to a simple and readily comprehensible rule.

RL-7 Explicit BEGIN and END for Multi-command Blocks

The scope of multi-command blocks such as the transaction block and the catalog block (see Feature RM-7 in Chapter 12) must be explicitly stated by a BEGIN type command and an END type command—except where the intended extent of the block is a single command, in which case both the BEGIN and the END are omitted. Each of the commands BEGIN and END includes some identification of the type of block.

The SQL of prototype System R [Chamberlin et al. 1981] had both an explicit BEGIN and an explicit END for transactions. The IBM product DB2 fails to support the BEGIN command; this means that it is difficult to pin down the scope of a transaction block.

RL-8   Orthogonality in Language Design

The features of RL are expressed orthogonally. When a semantic feature is supported in one context, it should be supported in every RL context in which it can be interpreted sensibly and unambiguously. No single semantic feature is expressed in two or more distinct ways with the choice of expression being context-dependent. Wherever a constant can appear, an expression can replace it, provided it yields a value that is type-compatible with the type needed in the given context.

This feature means that there is no unnecessary coupling of one feature with another. Moreover, to take an example violated by SQL, the mode of expressing the removal of duplicate rows from the result of an operation should not be dependent upon whether the operation is **projection** or **union.** In the case of **projection,** SQL requires the presence of the qualifier DISTINCT. In the case of **union,** SQL requires the omission of the qualifier ALL. Of course, duplicate rows should not have been supported as an option in the first place.

RL-9   Predicate Logic versus Relational Algebra

RL is more closely related to the relational calculus of the language ALPHA [Codd 1971a] than to the relational algebra. The purpose is to encourage users to express their requests in as few RL commands as possible, and hence improve the optimizability of these RL commands taken one at a time.

To support this feature, RL must include **join** terms as in ALPHA [Codd 1971a]. RL must also include a simple way of expressing the universal quantifier. This avoids the kind of circumlocutions and circumconceptions that require the user to translate

FOR__ALL x Px

into

NOT THERE__EXISTS x NOT Px.

Such a translation must be made by users of the SQL of IBM's current release of DB2, which lacks a simple way to express relational division.

RL-10 Set-oriented Operators and Comparators

RL includes certain set-oriented operators such as **set union, set intersection,** and **set difference.** These operators are subject, of course, to the usual constraints of the relational model that the operands and the results must be relations that are type-compatible with one another. RL also includes set comparators such as SET INCLUSION. These set operators and set comparators must be defined, at least in technical papers available to the public, in terms of the predicate logic supported in RL.

The requirement for definitions in terms of the predicate logic within RL is based on the following reasons:

■ to simplify the interface between the DBMS and inferential systems designed to operate on top of the DBMS;
■ to simplify the DBMS optimizer by making it easy, as a first step, to convert any query or integrity constraint into a canonical form.

The second reason is important in attaining good performance no matter how the user chooses to express his or her needs. In this way, the burden of gaining good performance is transferred from the user to the DBMS, where it belongs.

RL-11 Set Constants and Nesting of Queries Within Queries

RL includes certain relation or set constants, such as the empty set. It may also include, but is not required to include, the nesting of subqueries within queries, as in SQL. However, unlike the present SQL of either ANSI or IBM, if nesting is supported, it must be defined in terms of simple basic expressions of predicate logic, and it must be an optional way of expressing the request, not a required way under any circumstance.

The last two sentences in Feature RL-11 are vital to ensure effective optimization that gives the best performance regardless of the way any condition is expressed. They also simplify the task of software vendors developing software based on the DBMS as a platform. For example, such vendors may want to develop inferential packages, such as expert systems, that must interface with the DBMS using RL.

The introduction of set-oriented operators and comparators, plus set constants and nesting, frequently makes complex logical conditions easier to express, and therefore supports user productivity. On the other hand, one of the penalties of this introduction is that a given condition can now be expressed by the user in several different ways. In this case, it is extremely undesirable to burden users or software (on top of the DBMS) with the task of selecting a specific one of these ways so as to obtain the best performance with respect to the database traffic, storage representations, access paths, and access methods currently in effect.

RL-12 Canonical Form for Every Request

There must be a single canonical form for every request expressed in RL, whether interrogative or manipulative. Thus, no matter how a user chooses to express a query or manipulative action, the first step taken by the DBMS is to convert the source request into this canonical form.

This is another feature intended to enable the DBMS to assume the whole burden of finding the most efficient way to handle the request. The programmer or interactive user is then left with the sole task of determining how to express his or her logical and semantic needs.

RL-13 Global Optimization

RL statements are compiled or interpreted into target machine language. The optimization is carried out entirely within the DBMS. It is not split into a sequence of local suboptimizations such that the total sequence is less optimal than a corresponding single global optimization.

This global optimization includes at least the following:

- determining the alternative sequences in which the relational operations can be correctly executed;

- for each such sequence, selecting access paths that yield the least possible use of resources for that sequence, given the access paths currently in effect;

- finally, selecting that combination of a sequence of operations and pertinent access paths—a combination that yields overall the least possible use of resources.

In some products, optimization is implemented partly in the DBMS and partly in separate, additional software packages. As a consequence, performance suffers. Usually, a sequence of two or more local optimizations is not as good as a single global optimization.

RL-14 Uniform Optimization

For any query or data manipulation, whenever RL permits that activity to be expressed in two or more alternative (but logically equivalent) RL statements, the optimizer converts them to a canonical form, thereby ensuring that these alternatives yield target codings that are either identical or equally efficient.

This feature is intended to relieve users of the burden of selecting detailed source coding in RL for performance reasons. If not removed, such a burden would significantly reduce the adaptability of the relational approach to changes in storage representation and access paths resulting from changes in the total database traffic or from changes in the statistics of data in the database.

This feature also applies to distributed database management (see Chapters 24 and 25).

RL-15 Constants, Variables, and Functions Interchangeable

Wherever a constant can occur in an RL command, it can be replaced by an RL or host-language variable of a type suited to the context. Wherever an RL or host-language variable can occur, it can be replaced by an expression invoking a function (either built-in or user-defined), provided that function yields a result of a type suited to the context. In both cases, the substitution must yield a clearly meaningful and unambiguous command.

Regarding user-defined functions, see Chapter 19.

RL-16 Expressing Time-oriented Conditions

Time-oriented conditions can be included in any condition specified in an RL command, along with any other conditions that may be specified and oriented toward database content.

For example, RL would handle the requirement that a particular authorization be in effect for some specified interval of the day by attaching a time-oriented condition to the authorization command. See Feature RA-13 in Chapter 18, "Authorization."

RL-17 Flexible Role for Operators

In a relational command, any one of the basic operators can yield either an intermediate or a final result. More specifically, no basic operator is excluded from use in either of the following roles: (1) subordinate within an RL command to any other basic operator, or (2) superordinate within an RL command to any other basic operator.

SQL does not conform to this requirement because **union** cannot be used in a subordinate role to a **join,** although **join** can be subordinate to **union.** In other words, within a single SQL command the **union** of two or more **joins** can be requested. The **join** of two or more **unions** cannot be requested. This kind of complexity places an unnecessary load on the user's memory and makes SQL a frustrating tool to use.

In the design of a relational language, it is clearly desirable to make as few distinctions as possible between the interactive use of that language at a terminal and its use as a language for application programming. An example of a departure from this principle is the asterisk of SQL which is trouble-free when used interactively, but not trouble-free when used in application programs.

In SQL an asterisk can be used to denote all columns of a specified relation. This asterisk is intended to alleviate the burden of naming every column whenever the need arises for all columns to be involved in a query or manipulative command.

Interactive use of this feature of SQL at a terminal appears to present no special problem. Incorporation of an SQL asterisk in an application program is, however, another matter entirely. The asterisk damages the immunity of the program to such changes as the addition of new columns to the relation and the dropping of columns that already participate in that relation. This difficulty stems largely from the need to interface relational DBMS to old, single-record-at-a-time, host languages such as FORTRAN, COBOL, and PL/1. These languages deal with record structure in a rather inflexible way.

The 17 design principles introduced in this chapter are aimed at cleanliness of design and ease of use by the whole community of users. They are *not* aimed at reducing either the creative originality of individual implementors or the degree of competition among their respective companies.

- RL-1　Data sublanguage: variety of users
- RL-2　Compiling and re-compiling
- RL-3　Intermixability of RL and host-language statements
- RL-4　Principal relational language is dynamically executable
- RL-5　RL is a source language and a target language
- RL-6　Simple rule for scope within an RL command
- RL-7　Explicit BEGIN and END for multi-command blocks
- RL-8　Orthogonality in language design
- RL-9　Predicate logic versus relational algebra
- RL-10　Set-oriented operators and comparators
- RL-11　Set constants and nesting of queries within queries
- RL-12　Canonical form
- RL-13　Global optimization
- RL-14　Uniform optimization
- RL-15　Constants, variables, and functions are interchangeable
- RL-16　Expressing time-oriented conditions
- RL-17　Intermediate result from any basic operator

Exercises

22.1　Why does the relational model treat the language aspect of database management as a separate sublanguage, instead of promoting the advancement of programming languages to include database management?

22.2　What does it mean for a sublanguage to be able to communicate well with a host language?

22.3　The features in a well-designed language are orthogonal with respect to each other. Give three examples, each illustrating a distinct and serious lack of orthogonality in SQL.

22.4　What are multi-command blocks, and how are their boundaries made explicit?

22.5　Which is preferable, a data sublanguage based on the relational algebra, or one based on predicate logic? Why?

22.6　Of two sublanguages based on predicate logic, which is preferable, one that uses tuple variables, or one that uses domain variables? Why?

■ *CHAPTER 23* ■

Serious Flaws in SQL

Most of the database management systems now being introduced as products on the world market are based on the relational model. Each of these products supports the Structured Query Language (SQL) [IBM], or, more accurately, some version of this language. Very few of these versions, and possibly no two of them, are identical. In the early 1980s, the American National Standards Institute (ANSI) rapidly adopted their own version of SQL as a standard.

It appears that all present versions share the following three flaws:

1. they permit duplicate rows to exist in relations;
2. they fail to separate psychological features from logical features;
3. they fail to provide adequate support for the use of either three-valued or four-valued logic (i.e., logics with truth-values in addition to TRUE and FALSE).

The devastating consequences of these three properties are explained in this chapter. The following kinds of steps are suggested:

■ steps that vendors should take to remedy the problems;

■ precautionary steps that users can take to avoid severe difficulties before vendors take action; **and**

■ steps to avoid compatibility problems when vendors make the necessary changes in SQL.

These remarks have no effect on the relational model, since SQL is not part of that model. Nevertheless, a discussion of SQL's major flaws may help the reader acquire an improved understanding of the relational model.

23.1 ■ Introduction to the Flaws

The criticisms of SQL in this chapter are certainly not intended to be interpreted as criticisms of the relational approach to database management. SQL departs significantly from the relational model, and where it does, it is clearly SQL that falls short. Neither are the criticisms intended to be interpreted as wholesale criticism of IBM's relational DBMS products DB2 and SQL/DS. Although both of these products support SQL, they are good products when compared with other products on the market today. The flaws are serious enough to justify immediate action by vendors to remove them, and by users to avoid the consequences of the flaws as far as possible.

What, then, are the flaws in SQL that have such grave consequences? We shall describe just three:

1. SQL permits duplicate rows in relations;
2. it supports an inadequately defined kind of nesting of a query within a query;
3. it does not adequately support three-valued logic, let alone four-valued logic.

My position on these three "features" is as follows:

1. duplicate rows within relations ought to be prohibited;
2. even though I am not totally opposed to nesting, it requires precise definition and extensive investigation *before being included in a relational language,* so that a canonical form can be established for all requests;
3. four-valued logic should be fully supported within the DBMS and its language.

Criticisms of SQL have been plentiful; many are cited in this book. See, for example, [Date 1987], in which 20 or more serious errors are listed. Date's article, however, does not deal with the three most serious flaws, which are the main focus of this chapter.

23.2 ■ The First Flaw: Duplicate Rows and Corrupted Relations

When the idea was introduced that relations could be perceived as flat files or tables, the converse notion was adopted by numerous people as a true statement—namely, that any flat file or table can be perceived as a relation. This converse is totally incorrect. The flat files and tables of the past were highly undisciplined structures. Frequently, not all of the rows (or records) were required to have the same type, and duplicate rows were permitted. Design of relations became corrupted by this false idea.

Relations in the relational model and in mathematics do not have duplicate rows. There may, of course, be duplicate values within a column. I shall refer to relations in which duplicate rows are permitted as *corrupted relations*.

At first glance, permitting relations to have duplicate rows appears to be a disarmingly simple and harmless extension. When this extension was conceived, I indicated that, before any such extension was made, it would be necessary to investigate the effect of duplicate rows on the definitions of each and every relational operator, as well as on the mutual interaction of these operators. It is worth noting that I originally defined the relational operators and their mutual interaction assuming that relations had no duplicate rows (as in mathematics). In all of my subsequent technical papers on database management, I have continued to take this position.

Research into the effects of duplicate rows was simply not done by any prototype- or product-development group. Moreover, the problem was not addressed by the ANSI committee X3H2. It is now clear that the consequences are devastating.

23.2.1 The Semantic Problem

The *first and perhaps most important concern* is a semantic one: the fact that, when hundreds (possibly thousands) of users are sharing a common database, it is essential that they share a common meaning for all of the data therein that they are authorized to access. *There does not exist a precise, accepted, context-independent interpretation of duplicate rows in a relation.*

The contention that the DBMS must permit duplicate rows if its statistical functions (such as SUM and AVERAGE) are to deliver correct answers is quite incorrect. Clearly, duplicate values must be permitted within columns. For example, it is impossible to rule out the following possibilities:

■ two values of currency happen to be the same (for example, the cost of two distinct investments);

■ two employees happen to have the same birthdate;

■ two employees happen to have the same gender (male or female);

■ the inventory levels for two distinct kinds of parts happen to be identical.

Consider two or more rows in some corrupted relation that happen to be duplicates of each other. One may well ask what the meaning of each occurrence of these duplicate rows is. If they represent distinct objects (abstract or concrete), why is their distinctiveness not represented by distinct values in at least one component of the row (the primary key component) as required by the relational model?

If they do not represent distinct objects, what purpose do they serve? A fact is a fact, and in a computer its truth is adequately claimed by one assertion: the claim of its truth is not enhanced by repeated assertions. In database management, repetition of a fact merely adds complexity, and, in the case of duplicate rows within a relation, uncontrolled redundancy.

Consider how data in a database should be interpreted by users. The main reason for establishing any database is that it is an organized (and hopefully systematic) way of sharing data amongst many users (perhaps hundreds, perhaps thousands). To make such sharing successful, it is necessary for all users to understand exactly one common meaning of all of the data they are authorized to access. "*Common*" in this context means common to all users, and shared by all of them. Now, if an operand or a result contains duplicate rows, there is no standard conception of what the duplicate rows mean. There may be some private (unshared) conception, but that is just not good enough for the successful management of shared data.

23.2.2 Application of Statistical Functions

A *second concern* is the correct application of statistical functions. It is often claimed that projection should not eliminate duplicate rows. To support this claim, an example may be cited in which information about employees is stored in a relation called EMP, and this relation has a SALARY column that contains the present salary of each employee. To provide an analyst with details of present salaries, but not the items that identify employees, the projection of EMP onto SALARY is claimed to be necessary as the first step. It is also claimed that, in this projection, duplicate salaries must not be eliminated, since then the analyst is likely to deduce wrong answers to those queries of a statistical nature.

Statistical functions in relational DBMS can and should operate in the context of relations that do not have duplicate rows. This means that the relation name as well as the column name are arguments for a statistical function applied to that column.

Each of the statistical functions built into the DBMS should have two flavors: one that treats each row as it occurs (just once) ignoring any degree-of-duplication component (if such exists); the other that treats each row as if it occurred n times, where n is the degree-of-duplication component of that row (see Section 23.2.4 and Chapter 19).

23.2.3 Ordering of the Relational Operators

A *third concern* is the interchangeability in ordering of the relational operators. When manipulating non-corrupted relations (duplicate rows *not* permitted) using the relational operators of the relational model, there is a high degree of immunity to the specific ordering chosen for executing these operators. To illustrate, let us consider the operators **projection** and **equi-join.** Suppose that the **projection** does not discard any of the columns whose values are compared in the **join.** Then, provided no duplicate rows are allowed, the same result is generated whether the **projection** is executed first and then the **join,** or the **join** is executed first and then the **projection.**

Note that, if as usual the projection cites the columns to be saved (instead of those to be dropped), there must be a change of this list of columns depending on whether the **projection** preceded or followed the **join.** If, however, the **projection** cites the columns to be discarded, there need be no change in the list of these columns. Both forms of **projection** are useful.

This degree of immunity to the sequence of operators is lost when duplicate rows are permitted within relations. Consider an example involving **join** and **projection.** Suppose that duplicate rows are allowed in the result of **projection,** but not in the result of **join.** In SQL this means that the qualifier DISTINCT is used in the **join** command only.

R (A	B	C)
a1	1	c1
a2	1	c1
a3	1	c2
a4	2	c2
a5	2	c1

S (D	E)
d1	1
d2	1
d3	2

Taking the **projection** R [B,C] first and retaining duplicate rows, we obtain the following result. Then let us take the **equi-join** of this relation, with S comparing column B with column E, permitting duplicate rows in the operands, but not in the result.

R [B,C] (B	C)
1	c1
1	c1
1	c2
2	c2
2	c1

R [B,C][B = E] S (B	C	D	E)
1	c1	d1	1
1	c1	d2	1
1	c2	d1	1
1	c2	d2	1
2	c2	d3	2
2	c1	d3	2

The final result has just six rows and no duplicate rows.

Now let us reverse the sequence of operators, executing the **equi-join** first to generate relation T, and then executing the **projection** of T onto B,C,D,E.

R [B = E] S (A	B	C	D	E)
a1	1	c1	d1	1
a2	1	c1	d1	1
a3	1	c2	d1	1
a1	1	c1	d2	1
a2	1	c1	d2	1
a3	1	c2	d2	1
a4	2	c2	d3	2
a5	2	c1	d3	2

T (B	C	D	E)
1	c1	d1	1
1	c1	d1	1
1	c2	d1	1
1	c1	d2	1
1	c1	d2	1
1	c2	d2	1
2	c2	d3	2
2	c1	d3	2

The final result has eight rows, including two cases of duplicate rows. Clearly, when duplicate rows are permitted, the result obtained by executing the **projection** first and then the **join** is different from that obtained by executing the **join** first and then the **projection.** If duplicate rows had not been permitted, the results would have been identical, whichever sequence of relational operations was adopted. (The reader may wish to check this himself or herself.) What this example shows is that changing the sequence in which relational operations are executed can yield different results if the DBMS permits duplicate rows within a relation.

It is useless for an advocate of duplicate rows to dismiss the difference between these results as nothing more than two rows being duplicated— that suggests that duplicate rows are meaningless to the DBMS and to users. If duplicate rows have no meaning (Case 1), they should certainly be prohibited by the DBMS. If they have a meaning (Case 2), then this is surely a private (unshared) meaning, applicable only in some special context. There is no general meaning for duplicate rows that is accepted. Thus, once again, duplicate rows should be prohibited by the DBMS.

Another possible argument from the advocates of duplicate rows is, "Why not express the **projection** and **join** combined into a single SQL command? Then it will be impossible to use the qualifier DISTINCT on one of the operators without it becoming effective on the other."

A first reply to this is that one operator may define a view and the other a query on that view, and two users may have defined these items independently of one another. When executing such a query, it is the DBMS (and not a user) that combines the view definition with the query definition to make the query effective on base relations. A second reply is that the DBMS undoubtedly does not prevent a programmer from expressing these operators in separate SQL statements, whether one of the statements is a view definition or not.

It is worth noting here that, if the DBMS permits duplicate rows in results, it must also permit duplicate rows in operands because of the operational closure feature of relational database management systems: "The principal relational language is mathematically closed with respect to the operators it supports" (see Feature RM-5 in Chapter 12). This means that, in the principal relational language, the results of manipulative operations must always be legal as operands. If corrupted relations are permitted as results, then they must also be permitted as operands. This closure feature is intended to make it possible for users to make investigative inquiries in which it is occasionally necessary to use as operands the results of previous queries.

In case the reader thinks this is just an isolated example, let us look at a quite different one (communicated to me by Nathan Goodman) involving three simple relations, each concerned with employees—first their names, second their qualifications, and third their ages:

E1 (E# ENAME)   E2 (E# QUAL)   E3 (E# AGE).

As usual, E# stands for employee serial number. Using SQL, we can find the names of employees who have the degree Ph.D. or whose age is at least 50 (or who satisfy both conditions). One of the distinct ways in which this query can be expressed in SQL involves using logical OR. Another way involves using **union** on the serial numbers for employees that satisfy each of the conditions. *These two approaches should always yield the same result— but do they?*

The answer is that, if SQL is used, it depends on when and in what context the user requests that duplicate rows be retained or eliminated. If **union** ALL is used in this context, the result contains the names of employees duplicated whenever each employee satisfies *both* conditions (that is, he or she has the Ph.D. degree and is at least 50 years old).

The reduction in interchangeability of the sequence in which relational operations are executed can adversely affect both the DBMS and users of the DBMS. As we shall see, it damages the production by the DBMS of efficient target code (this process is usually called optimization) and substantially increases the user's burden in determining the sequence of relational commands, when the user chooses to make this sequence explicit.

Application programmers tell me they find it a confusing phenomenon that some **joins** yield duplicate rows, while others do not. They also tell me that for their applications it is both necessary and difficult to eliminate duplicate rows efficiently.

Optimization by the DBMS   A relational command usually consists of a collection of basic relational operators. Part of the optimizer's job is to examine the various alternative sequences in which these basic operations can be executed. For each such sequence it determines the most efficient way of exploiting the existing access paths. Finally, it determines which of the alternative sequences consumes the least resources. Clearly, then, any reduction in the interchangeability of ordering of the basic relational operations will reduce the alternatives which can be explored by the DBMS, and this in turn can be expected to reduce the overall performance and efficiency attainable by the DBMS.

User's Burden in Choosing an Ordering of Commands   Occasionally, the user may (for various reasons) express in two or more relational commands what could have been expressed in just one. For example, he may decide to express a projection in one command and a join in another command. Because the sequence of these commands can affect the ultimate result when duplicate rows are permitted, the user must give the matter much more careful thought than would have been necessary if duplicate rows had not been permitted. One consequence will be a proliferation of unnecessary bugs in programs and terminal activities.

The extra thinking and the extra bugs will undoubtedly cause an unnecessary reduction in the productivity of users. A far more serious consequence is that undiscovered bugs may lead to poor business decisions.

Violation of the Fundamental Law #1   As discussed in Chapter 29, the relational model is based on at least twenty fundamental laws. One of them is as follows: each object about which information is stored in the database must be uniquely identified, and thereby distinguished from every other object. This fundamental law is violated if duplicate rows are permitted in base relations. This is an important part of the job of maintaining the database in a state of integrity. The DBMS must help the DBA in this responsibility.

23.2.4 The Alleged Security Problem

It has been alleged that duplicate rows are needed to support correct statistical analysis of data in a relation that has a sensitive primary key— that is, a key that cannot be made available to the analyst. There are two ways in which this alleged need for duplicate rows can be avoided.

The first approach is by use of the degree-of-duplication (DOD) qualifier, which the DBMS should support. This qualifier enables the DBA to grant a user access to enough information from the database and enough computed information (appended to each row, a count of the number of occurrences of precisely similar rows) to enable him or her to make correct statistical analysis without access to some primary keys that happen to be sensitive. See Feature RQ-11 in Chapter 10 for more detail.

Each of the statistical functions built into the DBMS should have two flavors: one that treats each row as it occurs (just once), ignoring any DOD component (if such exists), the other that treats each row as if it occurred n times, where n is the DOD component of that row (see Chapter 19, "Functions").

In the second approach, the DBMS vendor changes the authorization mechanism in the database management system. Suppose that a view is defined as a suitable projection that includes the primary-key column(s). The user is authorized to access all of the columns in this view, except the primary-key column(s) that are blocked by the DBMS. See Chapter 18 for further information on this topic, and on the approach the DBA and DBMS can take, if this feature is supported.

23.2.5 The Supermarket Check-out Problem

In 1988 I published my contention [Codd 1988b] that duplicate rows should be avoided altogether in a relational database management system. Shortly thereafter, attempted rebuttals began to appear. In one of these attempts [Beech 1989], the example of checking out a customer at a cash register in a supermarket was described. In this example, the customer had picked up five cans of cat food, and the cashier registered each one separately and not consecutively, a common occurrence in supermarkets.

In this supermarket all the cash registers were connected to a computer with a database management system, so that all purchases were recorded in the database. The rebuttal claimed that the purchase of the five cans of cat food would have to be stored as five separate rows in the database, and that these five rows would be duplicates of one another.

What Beech and others seem to have overlooked is that part of the design of databases and rules concerning their use depends quite heavily on what the business managers consider worth recording. In particular, some semantic distinctions are beneficial to the business, while others are not. In the supermarket example, the manager of the supermarket is not likely to be interested in distinguishing one can of cat food from another if they are of the same brand. That same manager is, however, likely to be interested in determining the average number of cans of a particular brand purchased by individual customers, because he or she can then determine how much shelf space to allot to each brand. For this distinction it is necessary to distinguish each customer check-out from every other customer check-out.

Does this distinction require that the customer present a unique identification (such as a Social Security number) to the cashier? Certainly not. Does it require that each can be distinctly labelled even if it is of the same brand? Certainly not. The distinction can be made if each brand is distinctly labelled, and if each customer transaction (the purchase of all items by a particular customer) is somehow distinguished from every other customer transaction. This distinctiveness is easily achieved for transactions by means of the following steps:

1. The cash register must send its identifier automatically into the computer at the beginning of each transaction.

2. At this point, the computer must append the date and time.

3. When each item is entered by the cashier, the system must examine whether an identically identified item has been entered at some time before within the current transaction—if it has, the count of items of that brand is increased by one in the row pertaining to that brand; if it has not, a new row is recorded in the appropriate relation.

It is useful to refer to this kind of analysis as the *analysis of semantic distinctiveness*. This is an aspect of the meaning of the data that is strongly supported by the relational model. I have yet to encounter any other approach to database management that supports this aspect adequately.

Considering all the adverse consequences and incorrect allegations just cited, I still find that duplicate rows in any relation are unacceptable.

23.3 ■ The Second Flaw: The Psychological Mix-up

23.3.1 The Problem

As used here, the term "psychological" refers to what is often called the human-factors aspects of a language. The term "logical" refers to the logical power of a language, especially the power achievable without resorting to the usual programming tricks, such as iterative loops.

Normally, if proper relations are employed, a manipulative command or query expressed in terms of nesting and using the term IN can be re-expressed in terms of an **equi-join.** Let us look, however, at an example involving corrupted relations. Suppose we are given the relations EMP and WAREHOUSE:

EMP (E#	ECITY)		WAREHOUSE (WNAME	WCITY)
E1	A		W1	A
E2	B		W1	A
E3	C		W2	D
			W3	C
			W4	E

In this example, EMP is intended to list all the employees by employee serial number and city in which the employee lives; WAREHOUSE is intended to list all warehouses by serial number and city where located. Suppose we wish to find each employee name and the city in which he or she lives whenever that city is one in which the company has a warehouse. One might reasonably expect that this query could be handled equally well either by an **equi-join** or by a nesting that uses the IN term as follows:

Equi-join	**Nesting**
SELECT E#, ECITY	SELECT E#, ECITY
FROM EMP, WAREHOUSE	FROM EMP
WHERE ECITY = WCITY	WHERE ECITY IN
	(SELECT WCITY
	FROM WAREHOUSE)

The results, however, are not identical:

Equi-join Result		**Nesting Result**	
E#	ECITY	E#	ECITY
E1	A	E1	A
E1	A	E3	C
E3	C		

Once again, we have a problem that arises in part from permitting duplicate rows. This case, however, is somewhat more complicated than the ones considered earlier. Whenever the DBMS encounters a query in nested form, it must transform such a query into a non-nested form in order to simplify the task of the optimizer. Some excellent work on this transformation has been done [Kim 1982, Ganski and Wong 1987].

There appear, however, to be two major omissions from the works just cited and from other related work. First, the question of duplicate rows is not discussed. Second, even if duplicate rows were prohibited, the remaining question is whether the coverage in the work is complete with respect to *all nested versions permitted* in SQL.

My position on the nesting of SQL is that, when conceived in the early 1970s, it was an attractive idea, but one that needed careful scrutiny and investigation. This nesting was advocated by its proponents as: (1) a replacement for predicate logic in the relational world, and (2) a more user-friendly language than the preceding relational database sublanguage ALPHA [Codd 1971a].

The first-cited reason is simply not true. As time has elapsed, it has been found necessary to incorporate bits of predicate logic in the language, although errors have been made in this activity. The second-cited reason has some credibility, but would turn SQL into a curious mixture of the logical and the psychological aspects of a relational language. There are two reasons why these two kinds of aspects should be kept separate from one another:

1. a relational language must be effective both as a source language and as a target language because of the myriad of subsystems expected on top (e.g., application development systems, database design systems, expert systems and natural-language subsystems);

2. the relational approach is intended to serve a great variety of users, and therefore different users may have entirely different education, training, and background—this means that just one approach to psychological support is very unlikely to be adequate.

Accordingly, all of the statements in each of the several distinct languages providing *psychological support* should be translatable into the single language providing *logical support*. Until that translatability is demonstrated for SQL by means of a rigorous proof, serious problems in using that language will continue to arise.

Even when the translatability problem is solved, published, and implemented, there is the danger that a feature will be added to the nested queries that will introduce non-translatability. Theoretical investigation is sorely needed in this aspect of language definition.

While on the subject of nesting queries within queries, there are two features of IBM's SQL that I feel drastically reduce both the comprehensibility and the usability of that language. Let us illustrate these features by making small modifications to the examples concerning employees and warehouses (introduced earlier in this section).

Some city names occur several times in the United States, but only once in any selected state. For example, Portland occurs both in Maine and in Oregon. Suppose that to each relation, EMP and WAREHOUSE, we add a column pertaining to the state in which the city is located. Then let us try the following query:

```
SELECT E#, ECITY, ESTATE
FROM EMP
WHERE (ECITY, ESTATE) IN
    (SELECT (WCITY, WSTATE) FROM WAREHOUSE)
```

The DBMS refuses to handle this query, even though it is just like the original, except that in this case the IN clause involves a combination of columns instead of a single column. To a user, this seems totally inappropriate behavior for a DBMS. The ability of DB2 to concatenate the name of a city with the name of a state can be used to alter this query into one that can be executed. However, this is neither a general nor a natural solution to the problem.

Returning to the original relations, suppose that the query is altered to elicit more columns of data:

```
SELECT E#, ECITY, WNAME, WCITY
FROM EMP, WAREHOUSE
WHERE ECITY IN
    (SELECT WCITY FROM WAREHOUSE)
```

This time, the DBMS yields the **Cartesian product** of EMP with WAREHOUSE, except that rows that contain the cities that fail to qualify are excluded. This result is clearly not what was requested. Like the previous example, this kind of surprise is the hallmark of a poorly designed language.

23.3.2 Adverse Consequences

Optimization by the DBMS   When the prototype System R [Chamberlin et al. 1981] was passed from IBM Research to the product developers, the question of whether SQL could be translated from a nested query to a non-nested version had not been investigated. Subsequently, when the IBM products DB2 and SQL/DS were built, the problem was found too difficult to handle in the optimizer. As a result, the first three releases of DB2 perform poorly on nested queries compared with non-nested queries. This is truly ironic, because SQL had been sold to IBM's management on the basis of its alleged ease of use and power due to the nesting feature.

User's Burden in Choosing Nested versus Non-nested   The difference in performance between nested and non-nested versions of the same query puts an unnecessary performance-oriented burden on users, one that will not disappear until nesting is prohibited, or the translatability problem is completely solved and incorporated into DBMS optimizers. In nested as in non-nested queries, duplicate rows must be prohibited to avoid the additional burden of unexpected discrepancies in the results.

23.4 ■ The Third Flaw: Inadequate Support for Three- and Four-Valued Logic

DB2 is one of the few relational DBMS products that *represents* missing information independently of the type of the data that is missing—a requirement of the relational model and a requirement for ease of use. DB2 uses an extra byte for any column in which missing values are permitted, and one bit of this byte tells the system whether the associated value should be taken seriously or whether that value is actually missing.

DB2, however, completely fails to meet one more requirement of the relational model—namely, that missing information should be *handled* in a manner that is independent of the type of the information that is missing, and that the user should be relieved of the burden of devising three-valued logic. Representation of missing information is one thing, but handling it is quite another [Codd 1986a and 1987c]. Actually, three-valued logic is built into DB2, but is used only to pass over values for which the condition evaluates to MAYBE (neither true nor false). Thus, only one of the many uses of the fact that a value is missing is supported by DB2. This is mainly due to the weak treatment of missing values in SQL.

23.4.1 The Problem

How to Support Three-Valued Logic Usually the occurrence of cases of missing information in a practical database is unavoidable—it is a fact of life. I believe that, when interrogating a database for information, users prefer the DBMS as its normal behavior to take a conservative position and to avoid guessing the correct answer. Whenever the system does not know some requested fact or condition, it should admit a lack of knowledge.

The DBMS should also support, as exceptional behavior explicitly requested, the extraction of all the items that could satisfy a request if unknown values were replaced by information that yielded as many values as possible in the target list of the query.

A database retrieval may, of course, include several conditions like

DATE > 66-12-31,

where the DATE column has values of extended data type DATE, and

AMOUNT < 20,000,

where the AMOUNT column has values of extended data type U.S. CURRENCY. The conditions may be combined in many different logical combinations (including the logical connectives AND, OR, and NOT and the quantifiers UNIVERSAL and EXISTENTIAL). Suppose, as an example, that both expressions just noted participate in some condition. Also suppose that both columns are allowed to have missing database values. How does the DBMS deal with a query involving the following combination of conditions,

$$(\text{DATE} > 66\text{-}12\text{-}31) \text{ OR } (\text{AMOUNT} < 20{,}000),$$

where the date condition, the amount condition, or both may evaluate to MAYBE? Clearly, the DBMS must know the truth-value of such combinations as MAYBE OR TRUE, TRUE OR MAYBE, and MAYBE OR MAYBE. This means that the DBMS must support at least three-valued logic. If not, then the user must do the following:

1. request the primary-key values of those orders for which the DATE > 66-12-31 is TRUE;

2. request the primary-key values of those orders for which the AMOUNT < 20,000 is TRUE; **and**

3. request the **union** of the two sets generated by Steps 1 and 2.

In the case of AND instead of OR, the user would have to request in Step 3 the **intersection** of the two sets of primary keys. Users are liable to make numerous mistakes if they are forced to support three-valued logic mentally because the DBMS provides inadequate support. Who knows what crucial business decisions might be made incorrectly as a consequence?

From this, it can be seen that, in any systematic treatment by the DBMS of missing values, there is a clear need to extend the underlying two-valued predicate logic to at least a three-valued predicate logic.

In the following truth tables for the three-valued logic [Codd 1979] of the relational model RM/V1, the symbols P and Q denote propositions, each of which may have any one of the following truth values: t for TRUE *or* m for MAYBE *or* f for FALSE.

P	NOT P	P OR Q		Q		P AND Q		Q	
			t	m	f		t	m	f
t	f		t	t	t		t	m	f
m	m	P m	t	m	m	P m	m	m	f
f	t		t	m	f		f	f	f

In the relational model, the universal and existential quantifiers are applied over finite sets only. Thus, the universal quantifier behaves like the logic operator AND, and the existential quantifier behaves like OR, both operators being extended to apply the specified condition to each and every member of the pertinent set.

When an entire condition based on three-valued, first-order predicate logic is evaluated, the result can be any one of the three truth-values TRUE, MAYBE, or FALSE. If such a condition is part of a query that does not include the MAYBE qualifier, the result consists of all the cases in which the complete condition evaluates to TRUE, and no other cases.

If to the entire condition part of this query we add the keyword MAYBE, then the result consists of all the cases in which this condition evaluates to MAYBE, and no other cases. The MAYBE qualifier is used only for exploring possibilities. Special authorization would be necessary if a user is to incorporate it in a program or a terminal interaction.

Actually, the relational model calls for the DBMS to support the attachment of the MAYBE qualifier to any truth-valued expression, since a view is normally defined not using this qualifier, while a query on the view may involve it. The normal action of the DBMS is to combine the view condition with the query condition using logical AND. This action, of course, would give rise to a more comprehensive condition involving the MAYBE qualifier attached to just one truth-valued expression within that condition.

One problem of which DBMS designers and users should be aware is that, in rare instances, the condition part of a query may be a tautology. In other words, it may have the value TRUE no matter what data is in the pertinent columns and no matter what data is missing. An example would be the following condition pertaining to employees (where B denotes a DATE):

$$(B < 66\text{-}12\text{-}31)\ OR\ (B = 66\text{-}12\text{-}31)\ OR\ (B > 66\text{-}12\text{-}31).$$

If the DBMS were to apply three-valued logic to each term and it encountered a marked value (i.e., a value marked as missing) in the date column, each of the terms in this query condition would receive the truth value MAYBE. However, MAYBE OR MAYBE yields the truth-value MAYBE. Thus, the condition as a whole evaluates to MAYBE, which is incorrect, but not traumatically incorrect.

To avoid this type of error, there are two options:

1. warn users not to use tautologies as conditions in their relational language statements (tautologies are a waste of the computer's resources);
2. develop a DBMS that examines all conditions not in excess of some clearly specified complexity, and determines whether each condition is a tautology or not.

Naturally, in the latter case, it would be necessary to place some limitation on the complexity of each and every query, because with predicate logic the general problem is unsolvable. It is my opinion that Option 1 is good enough for now, because this is not a burning issue.

Treatment of Missing Values in SQL   The only concession in SQL commands to the existence of missing values is the clause IS NULL, which enables the user to pick up from any column those cases in which there are missing values. Flexible use of three-valued logic (let alone four-valued) is not supported. An example of inflexibility is the action of DB2 when the condition part of a query is evaluated as unknown. It simply does not retrieve the corresponding instances of the target data. Although in practice this is one of the options that users need, they also need others. One such option is the temporary replacement of missing values by user-specified values, where "temporary" means just for the execution of the pertinent command.

Other DBMS products that fail to go beyond present SQL, whether it be the IBM or the ANSI version, are unable to provide adequate support of three-valued logic. As a result, we can expect users to make many errors, some of which are bound to go undetected.

A somewhat separate problem is the effect of missing values on aggregate functions. The relational model supports the following options: request the missing items to be ignored, or temporarily replace each missing item by a specified value, where "temporarily" again means just for the execution of the pertinent command. SQL appears to support only one of these options: it always ignores the missing items.

23.4.2 Adverse Consequences

Overall, the SQL approach to handling missing values is quite disorganized and weak. This will lead to disorganized thinking on the part of users, an increased burden for them to bear, and many unnecessary errors. Errors that are not discovered can lead to incorrect business decisions based on incorrectly extracted data.

The SQL approach also causes some users to wish for the old approaches like "default values" that were at least familiar, even if more disorganized. Of course, the old approaches are completely out of place in any DBMS based on the relational model.

In some cases of inadequate handling of missing information, the problem is incorrectly perceived to be a problem of the relational model. In fact, the problem stems from the inadequacies of SQL and its non-conformance to the relational model.

23.5 ■ Corrective Steps for DBMS Vendors

Let us discuss the three problems in turn. First, consider the problem of duplicate rows.

23.5.1 Corrective Steps for Duplicate Rows

This correction should be handled in three stages:

1. warn users that support for duplicate rows is going to be phased out in about two years' time;

2. within the first year, install in some new release a "two-position switch" (i.e., a DBA-controlled bit) that permits the DBMS to operate in two

modes with respect to duplicate rows: (1) accepting them and (2) rejecting them;

3. drop the support for duplicate rows within a relation altogether, and improve the optimizer accordingly.

With regard to loss of integrity from databases, it is well-known that prevention is much better than cure. For this reason, the DBMS should check that duplicate rows are not being generated whenever an operator is executed that could generate duplicate rows. Three of the operators that are defined to remove duplicate rows are **projection, union,** and **appending** rows to a relation, including initial loading. Most DBMS products today fail to conform to the definitions of these operators.

To provide assistance in the loading of data into relations from tables that may contain duplicate rows, the command CONTROL DUPLICATE ROWS was introduced as Feature RE–20 in Chapter 7. Using this command, the duplicate rows are removed without loss of information.

23.5.2 Corrective Steps for the Psychological Mix-up

The most recent version of IBM's SQL (even if the duplicate row concept has been removed) should be treated as a language that stands or falls on its psychological or ease-of-use properties. A new relational language should be created with features that are highly orthogonal to one another. The language should be readily extensible, include all of the logical properties necessary to manage a relational database, be readily compilable, and be convenient to use as a target language by all the software packages that interface on top of the DBMS.

23.5.3 Corrective Steps in Supporting Multi-Valued Logic

DBMS vendors should start the work required to introduce support for four-valued logic [Codd 1986a and 1987c]. The three-valued logic just cited is a sublogic of the four-valued logic. Implementing the four-valued logic is not noticeably more difficult or time-consuming than implementing the three-valued. The four-valued logic treats information that is missing for a second reason—namely, that a particular property happens to be inapplicable to certain objects represented in the pertinent relation. With adequate support for three or four-valued logic, the IS NULL clause in SQL becomes redundant and should be phased out.

23.6 ■ Precautionary Steps for Users

While these three flaws are being corrected by the DBMS vendors, there are several steps users can take to protect their databases and hence their business. The *first step* is to avoid duplicate rows within relations at all times by insisting on continued adherence to the programming and interactive discipline:

■ exactly one primary key must be specified for each base relation;

■ the DISTINCT qualifier must immediately follow the keyword SELECT in every SQL command that includes SELECT;

■ the ALL qualifier must never accompany any **union.**

The *second step* is to avoid nested versions of SQL statements whenever there exists a non-nested version. The *third step* is to take extra care in manipulating relations that have columns that may contain missing values, and as far as possible separate the handling of missing information into easily identifiable pieces of code that can be readily replaced later.

23.7 ■ Concluding Remarks

Is it too extreme to call these SQL blunders serious flaws? I do not think so, in view of the fact that more and more business and government institutions are becoming dependent on relational DBMS products for the continued success of their operations. In my view, the three flaws described in this chapter *must* be repaired, even though the repair may cause some users to have to change some SQL portions of their programs.

DBMS vendors should immediately begin putting the corrective steps outlined in Section 23.5 into effect. Such action could easily give them a substantial competitive advantage in the eyes of their prospective customers.

The proposed changes in SQL described in this chapter also represent a great opportunity for ANSI to take the lead.

Users are strongly advised to take the precautionary steps outlined in Section 23.6. Then, the changes in subsequent releases of their DBMS will prove to be far less traumatic.

How did SQL reach the undesirable state described in this chapter? I believe that the reason can be traced to inadequate theoretical investigation.

Exercises

23.1 At first glance, SQL offers an attractive feature: the capability of nesting a query within a query. What are the problems arising from this feature of SQL?

23.2 Most, but not all, relational DBMS products violate the very basic property of the relational model that a relation, whether base or derived, must not have duplicate rows. Why, and in what ways, does this violation give rise to serious problems?

23.3 Consider the language SQL. It contains a feature called GROUP BY. Treat SQL, with this feature dropped as SQLx. Are there any queries expressible in SQL that are *not* expressible in SQLX? If your answer is yes, supply two examples. If your answer is no, supply a proof.

23.4 SQL has a nesting feature that permits a query to be nested within another query. Treat SQL with this feature dropped as SQLZ. Are there any queries expressible in SQL that are *not* expressible in SQLZ? If your answer is yes, supply two examples. If your answer is no, supply a proof.

■ CHAPTER 24 ■

Distributed Database Management

24.1 ■ Requirements

For many reasons, it is necessary to understand distributed database management clearly. Very few database management systems will survive in the 21st century if they are not capable of managing distributed databases with the extensive capabilities described in this chapter and the next.

The first necessity is to be able to distinguish clearly *distributed database management* from *distributed processing*. Some vendors claim support for distributed database management, when their products actually support nothing more than distributed processing. The relational model addresses many of the problems associated with the management of distributed databases, but offers very little help in distributed processing.

A simple, but superficial, way of distinguishing these two services is as follows. Distributed database management is the coordinated management of data distributed in various separate but interconnected computer systems. Distributed processing, which is based on a collection of programs that are distributed in various separate but interconnected computer systems, permits a program at any site to invoke a program at any other site in the network as if it were a locally resident subprogram.

There is no claim that it is a simple task to implement the level of support for distributed database management in RM/V2. Such implementation, although quite a challenge, closely represents what users need. A distributed database satisfies at least the following four conditions:

1. The database consists of data dispersed at two or more sites;

2. the sites are linked by a communications network that may be as modest as a local area network, as impressive as a satellite-based network, or anything in between;

3. at any site X, the users and programs can treat the totality of the data as if it were a *single global database* residing at X;

4. all of the data residing at any site X and participating in the global database can be treated by the users at site X in exactly the same way as if it were a local database isolated from the rest of the network.

Normally, these sites are geographically dispersed, and the communications network includes the telephone lines of at least one telephone company. For convenience, the term *network* will often be applied to the total collection of sites in a distributed database. In a widely dispersed situation, the databases are located in different countries, possibly on different continents. At the other extreme, the database sites may all happen to be located within a single city or even within a single building. It is worthwhile to observe here that more and more companies are becoming trans-nationals (the United Nations term for multi-nationals).

Condition 4 in the preceding list is required because some vendors have DBMS products that support Condition 3 but violate Condition 4. To understand this, suppose that R is one of the relations in the global database, that F is a fragment of R, and that F is allocated to one of the sites, while the remaining parts of R are stored at other sites. In the products that violate Condition 4, but not Condition 3, fragment F is permitted to be a non-relation, even though it is a table. More specifically, F consists of some of the columns of R, but does not include the primary key of R, and, as a result of the corrupted version of **projection** being used, F can contain duplicate rows. The corrupted version of **projection** fails to eliminate duplicate rows. The penalties for permitting duplicate rows were described in Chapter 23.

It is reasonable to consider the chief responsibilities of the systems that manage a distributed database. Perhaps the single most important responsibility of such systems is support for *distribution independence* [Codd 1985]. This term means that a program developed to handle data that is distributed in one way should continue to operate correctly without change when the data is re-distributed. In an extreme case covered by this definition, a program is developed to run successfully on data that is initially located completely at one site (i.e., not distributed at all). Such a program must continue to operate correctly without change when the data is dispersed to multiple sites. This is an important step in protecting the investment by DBMS customers in the development of application programs.

To support distribution independence, a necessary but not sufficient condition is that it must be possible to retrieve data without referring to any location or locations in which it may reside. This is sometimes called *location independence* and sometimes *location transparency*, although I much prefer the former phrase.This subject is dealt with in more detail in Sections 24.4 through 24.8.

For performance, fault tolerance, or other reasons, some of the data may be duplicated at different sites. If so, end users and programs must be insulated from this redundancy. This is sometimes called *replication independence*. This topic is discussed in more detail in Section 24.4.5.

A third requirement for adequate support of distribution independence is that it must be possible for a *single relational command* to operate on data located at two or more sites. This falls naturally within the scope of relational DBMS, since the optimizer breaks down each command into basic relational operators even if the data is not distributed. Note that this requirement is more stringent than merely supporting any single *transaction* operating upon data located at two or more sites.

RX-1 Multi-site Action from a Single Relational Command

In a distributed database, a single relational command, whether query or manipulative, can operate on data located at two or more sites.

Some of the older pre-relational DBMS products that were claimed by their vendors to support the management of distributed databases could transmit a transaction to a remotely located site, but the whole transaction had to be executable at that site on data located entirely at that site. This capability is called *transaction routing*, and is, of course, far less than what is needed for supporting distribution independence. In fact, the present situation is that the *only* prototypes and products that have been able to demonstrate the capability of supporting distribution independence are relational DBMS.

24.2 ■ The Optimizer in a Distributed DBMS

As we have seen, within a relational DBMS there is a component called the *optimizer*. This component is responsible for translating the high-level relational commands into the most efficient target code. Now, an optimizer may be adequate for managing local databases, but, if that is its only capability, it is likely to be quite inadequate for managing distributed databases.

Nevertheless, it is a simple task to extend a local-only optimizer to handle the distributed case. Whether a database is totally local or distributed, managing it efficiently entails finding an ordering of the basic operators within whatever relational command is to be executed (an ordering that may include concurrent execution of these operators), together with access paths for each operator, so as to develop efficient target code.

In managing local databases only, the goal is minimal use of processing power, on the one hand, and of input-output devices, on the other hand. In managing distributed databases, the consumption of inter-site communication power is a third factor that must be considered, because it may be quite significant. In fact, when the sites are far apart, this third factor is likely to be dominant.

There is likely to be a wide variation between the requirements of any two companies or institutions using a distributed DBMS. For this reason, the usual approach in DBMS products is to request the DBA at each site to insert three coefficients: one for the local processing load, one for the local input-output load, and one for the inter-site communication load. The optimizer can then calculate a single rating for each combination of a sequencing of operations and access paths.

24.3 ■ A DBMS at Each Site

One of the goals in managing distributed data is to promote *local autonomy* to the extent that is compatible with distribution independence and with the necessary inter-site integrity constraints. When one or more sites are experiencing malfunction of the hardware or software, the other sites must be able to continue to execute all of their workloads, except those portions that involve the sites that are temporarily out of action.

Why is the adjective "necessary" used to qualify the phrase "inter-site integrity constraints" in the preceding paragraph? One reason is that, even if the initial deployment of data across sites does not require such constraints, the deployment will undoubtedly evolve and require a growing number of such constraints as it evolves. A second reason is that the options in re-deployment would be severely restricted if all integrity constraints had to affect local data only.

RX-2 Local Autonomy

In distributed database management, whenever the DBMS at any site goes down, each site X that is still functioning must be capable of continuing to operate successfully and in a relational mode on data at each and every site that is still functioning, including X, provided X is still in communication with that site.

One clear consequence of Feature RX-2 is that there is no reliance on a single site in a distributed relational DBMS, whether that site be labeled "central" or not.

One aspect of this feature is that the system must support continued access to all of the data at site A by users at site A, even if the inter-site communications network is either completely or partially out of action. A more precise phrase for this subgoal is *local management of local data.*

To attain local management of local data by means of a relational DBMS, the first requirement is that, at every site, all of the data stored at that site must be perceived by end users and application programmers as a *relational database*—that is, a collection of proper relations of assorted degrees. As indicated in Chapter 1, a proper relation is one that has no duplicate rows. This requirement corresponds to Condition 4 cited earlier.

The second requirement is that there be a *relational database management system* at each and every site. During most of this chapter, the homogeneous case is assumed for simplicity—that is, at each site there is the same hardware and software, including the DBMS software. At the end of this chapter, a few remarks are made about the difficulties encountered in the heterogeneous case. The optimizing capability in a distributed DBMS should itself be distributed. Every site must be capable of controlling every request entered at that site, so that there is no reliance on a central coordinator. Every site has to be capable of (1) global planning and optimization; and (2) local planning and optimization.

An important factor in organizing the distribution of data over several sites is that the communication channels between sites be sufficiently redundant that the failure of one or two channels does not reduce all sites to managing locally resident data only. When the channel organization avoids this catastrophic behavior, it is called *fault-tolerant.* A channel organization, of course, can exhibit a high degree of fault tolerance, a modest degree, or none at all.

For example, if there were eight sites and the communication channels were unidirectional only, then the channel organization shown in Figure 24.1(a) would not be fault-tolerant at all. On the other hand, if the channels were bidirectional, this organization would be fault tolerant to a small degree. The organization shown in Figure 24.1(b) is fault-tolerant to a much higher degree, assuming that the channels continue to be bidirectional.

24.4 ■ The Relational Approach to Distributing Data

There are several widespread but false notions concerning the initial planning of how to distribute data. One false notion is that a collection of relational databases that already exist in diverse locations can simply be inter-connected by means of communications lines, and that the result is a distributed database. Unfortunately, there is more to this problem than meets the eye. An example of a potentially serious problem that is quite likely to arise is the case in which two columns, one from one relation, and one from a second, are homographs having a different meaning. See Section 6.2 for more detail.

Figure 24.1   (a) **Simple Network with Eight Sites. (b) More Stable Network with Eight Sites**

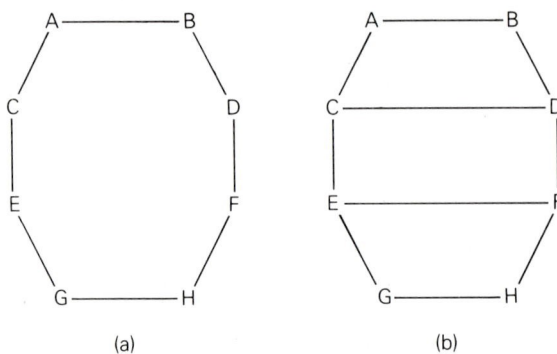

(a)   (b)

Another false notion is that, once the initial plan is put in place, re-distribution of the data will never be necessary.

When deciding how to distribute data between various sites, it is con-venient to think of the totality of data initially—and, as a matter of fact, at all later times also—as a single collection Z of relations. This totality is called the *global database*. It is the importance of this concept that strongly suggests employing a global database administrator (GDBA), who is re-sponsible for the global database, as well as a local database administrator (LDBA) for each site.

Since the global database is really a virtual database (an abstract con-cept), it could be said that the GDBA has a "virtual job," but I doubt whether he or she would appreciate such a comment because of the multiple meanings attached to the English word "virtual." Nevertheless, this job might well be one of the most important positions in any company or institution. The title "chief information officer" seems quite appropriate.

In any distributed relational network, the GDBA needs as a tool for his or her job a description of the entire global database. Such a description is contained in what I call the *global catalog*. This catalog is, of course, distinct from the on-line catalogs at each site, and more comprehensive, since the local on-line catalogs tend to concentrate on local data only. One of the reasons for having a global catalog is that it is a vital tool in conceiving and declaring integrity constraints, views, and authorization that straddle sites.

RX-3   Global Database and Global Catalog

Associated with each distributed database is the concept of a *global database* that covers all the data stored at each site. Associated with the global database is the *global catalog*. This catalog contains three parts:

GC1 The declarations for every domain, every base relation, every column, every view, every integrity constraint, every authorization constraint, and every function in the global database *as it is actually distributed,* including the sites at which they are stored.

GC2 A concise description of this totality of information as if it were a single, non-distributed database cast in *conceptual normal form* i.e., fifth normal form with minimal partitioning.

GC3 Expressions for each relation located at each site defining how that relation is defined in terms of the relations declared in GC2.

It is more useful to call GC1 the *composite global catalog* and GC2 the *normalized global catalog*.

The source code of application programs can contain local names, but these are converted by the DBMS at bind time into global names as found in GC2. It is this *globalized source code* that is retained in the system and remains unaffected by redeployment of the data, partly because it contains no local names.

RX-4   N Copies of Global Catalog (*N* > 1)

The network contains N copies ($N > 1$) of the global catalog, in the form of N small databases at N distinct sites to avoid too much reliance on whichever site is normally used by the global database administrator. These N sites can also be N of the sites in the network for regular data and the corresponding local catalogs. At these sites (at least two of them), the power supply should be mutually independent; that is, failure of electric power at one site does not normally mean failure at the other.

In a distributed relational database and, in particular, in its global database Z, it is necessary to have names for domains, relations, columns, views, integrity constraints, and functions that (1) conform to the standard naming rules for relational databases (see Chapter 6), and (2) apply to the totality of data in the network as if it were a single database. These names are called *global names* to distinguish them from any names in use locally at each of the sites. Names that are continued in local use are called *local names*.

RX-5 Synonym Relation in Each Local Catalog

To support the continued use at each site of names local to that site, each local catalog should include a synonym relation containing each local name, the type of object named by it, and the correspondence between the local name and the global database (see RX-7).

The job of interpreting global names used in relational commands is not the sole responsibility of the *N* global catalogs, because they would then become major bottlenecks. That job is dispersed throughout the network by means of the birth-site concept, which is discussed here and also in Section 24.8. This concept is due to Bruce Lindsay [1981] of the System R* team of IBM Research [Williams et al. 1981]. One of the advantages of the birth-site concept is that it does not require a centralized dispenser of names that are unique within the network. However, this concept is not a complete solution to the problem of decentralizing all resolution of names. Frequently, redeployment is not confined to simple movement of entire relations from one site to another. Redeployment can include decomposing some relations and recombining others. Then, the name of a relation on which a program operates may have to be transformed into a relation-valued expression.

Each DBMS in the network has the responsibility of keeping its portion of the global catalog consistent with the global catalog itself. The many DBA sites, each of which contains a copy of the global catalog, must send a message to whatever sites are affected whenever the GDBA makes a change in the global catalog. These messages are requests to the sites to bring their catalogs up-to-date and consistent with the global catalog. The sending of these messages can be, and should be, automatically triggered by the DBMS at the GDBA site.

Ideally, of course, any changes made by the GDBA in the global catalog should be wholeheartedly supported by the local database administrators. Similarly, any changes made by a LDBA should be wholeheartedly approved by the GDBA.

Therefore, the DBMS must support changes in a database at a specific site that are initiated by the DBA at that site, assuming he or she has been granted that privilege. Such changes cause the local DBMS to send a message immediately to the global catalog to make it consistent with these changes, along with a confirming message to the GDBA.

24.4.1 Naming Rules

Although there is every reason to believe that the naming rules introduced here actually work and would satisfy most users' needs, a distributed database management system can support alternative features, provided it can be shown that these features are at least as powerful, flexible, and comprehensible. The first and most obvious feature follows.

RX-6 Unique Names for Sites

Whenever an object is created—whether it be a domain, base relation, view, integrity constraint, or function—it is asigned a five-part name:

1. the name or identification of the user creating that object;
2. the name of the object as if it was a local object;
3. the name of the site at which the object was created (called its *birth site*);
4. the formula or command that translates from the global database to the local object;
5. the inverse formula or command (see RX-8).

The next feature is explained partly below and partly in Section 24.8, which deals with the distributed catalog.

RX-7 Naming Objects in a Distributed Database

Whenever an object is created—whether it be a domain, base relation, view, or function—it is assigned a three-part name: (1) the name or identification of the user creating that object, (2) the name of the object as if it were a local object, and (3) the name of the site at which the object was created, called the object's *birth site*.

If the object is a domain, considerable care should be taken to determine whether that domain already exists somewhere in the network. Even if exactly the same domain does not exist elsewhere, it may be possible, and is probably preferable, to expand the range of some existing domain to cover the one now needed, and introduce some column constraints that will keep the old definition applicable to those columns already existing.

Of course, an object created at a site X may at some later time be moved to site Y. Later still, it may be moved again to site Z. Therefore, there is one more name associated with each object—namely, the name of the site at which that object is residing at present. The association of this sixth name component with the first five is maintained by the DBMS at the birth site, and by the N copies of the global catalog at the GDBA sites. The goal is to protect users, programmers, and application programs from having to know this sixth name component.

In establishing a distributed database, the starting point may be several databases that have been operated independently up to that time. Then, the first step is to take a copy of the description of each database from its catalog, and examine the consequences of putting all these descriptions together as the description of one global database. This examination should include the complete naming scheme, about which the following questions should be asked:

■ Is it devoid of the kind of duplication of names that would give rise to ambiguity? (For example, is the name CAP at one site given to a relation that represents the capabilities of suppliers in supplying parts, while at another site that same name is used for a relation with an entirely different meaning—say, for actual shipments made by suppliers?)

■ Are there any instances of an object, such as a domain or a relation, common to two or more sites, and having two or more distinct names? (For example, is a relation that describes shipments at one site given a different name at another site, even though the two relations have the same meaning and are union-compatible?)

The DBMS provides considerable help in resolving these naming problems by supporting in the catalog at each site (as noted earlier) a synonym relation that contains global names or relation-valued expressions as synonyms for all the local names. This facility must be applicable to at least the names of domains, base relations, columns, views, integrity constraints, and functions.

After naming problems are resolved, the following question arises: are the databases that are being coalesced into a single global database inter-related? This problem was discussed in Section 3.1, but not in the context of distributed database. However, the approach was based on the use of domains by relations, and this is clearly applicable without change to the global database Z. If any one of the databases being coalesced is not inter-related by domains to any of the other databases, one may reasonably question the reason for coalescing—perhaps there is a plan to add new relations to one or more sites in order to inter-relate the databases at these sites, where previously they were not.

The information in the global database Z is to be distributed in some way to a collection of sites, with a collection of relations at each site. Thus, at first glance, it appears necessary to consider as candidate relations all of the relations derivable from the given collection using the relational operators.

The class of all derivable relations, however, is quite large; for a large commercial database, it may run into the millions. Thus, it is necessary to find some sensible means of reducing the options. Fortunately, there are two important concerns that quickly narrow down the options to be considered.

Perhaps the most obvious concern is that data should be distributed according to the frequency of its use. To express it another way, data should be local with respect to the users who need to access it most frequently and with the shortest response time.

For example, consider a bank that has branches in several cities, and customers who execute most of their transactions with the bank at a particular branch selected by each customer. When establishing a distributed DBMS, the usual decision by the bank is to require the data stored in each major city to be precisely that which reflects the customer accounts established in the branches of the bank in that city.

A second concern is *reversibility* of the transformations applied to the global database Z (the totality of data at all sites) in determining which of these relations (or, alternatively, which of the relations derivable from them by means of the relational operators only) are stored at which sites. This reversibility is in many ways similar to that used in deciding the ways in which a view can be updated (see Chapter 17). As shown in the discussion of decomposition in Section 24.4.3, this second requirement can also narrow down the options significantly.

As far as users are concerned, reversibility is needed primarily to facilitate re-distribution of data at some later time. DBMS vendors are advised to make this a requirement in distributing data because it simplifies the design of the optimizer. Even then, however, there is no claim that designing the optimizer is easy.

RX-8 Reversibility and Redistribution

In assigning part of the global database Z to a particular site, each relation assigned to that site must be derivable from the relations in Z by a combination of relational operators that has an inverse. In other words, each relation at each site is reversibly derivable from Z.

It is quite common for managers of data processing and information system to claim that, if the job is done correctly when first introducing a distributed DBMS, there will be no need to redistribute the data. This can be true only if the business or institution remains unchanged forever! However, there is one thing in life that is inevitable for everyone, and that is change.

24.4.2 Assignment of Relations from the Global Database Z

The most elementary distribution is to assign some of the relations in Z without any transformation to site A, to assign other relations in Z without any transformation to site B, and so on until all the relations have been assigned to sites. In some cases of database distribution, this simple approach may be adequate, but in other cases it will not be adequate. In the next two sections, other options in distributing data are considered.

24.4.3 Decomposition of Relations from the Global Database Z

Notice that, in the simple distribution just discussed, no relation in Z is decomposed into two or more pieces, and the pieces then scattered to two or more distinct sites. It is this step of decomposition that now must be discussed.

When a relation is decomposed into pieces for distribution of the pieces to various sites, the term *fragmentation* is often applied. I shall not use this term, however, because it is often used and interpreted as the breaking up of a table by rows and columns, without concern as to whether the objects resulting from this break-up are proper or corrupted relations. At least two distinct distributed DBMS prototypes—IBM's R* and Relational Technology's INGRES STAR—and one distributed DBMS product—Tandem's NonStop SQL—support vertical fragmentation of any kind, without concern regarding whether each fragment is a proper relation or not. To paraphrase Woody Allen, this bug is as big as a Buick!

In applying relational technology to the management of a distributed database, it is essential that only the relational operators be used to decompose relations in the global database into relations for the various sites. One important reason is the goal of preserving the correctness of programs when the data is re-distributed.

Consider the example of a relation R with columns A1, A2, A3, A4. Suppose that the primary key of R is A1. The fragmentation approach would permit R to be split into two tables S and T, where S has the columns A1 and A2 of R, and T has the columns A3 and A4 of R. It is assumed here that, from the standpoint of the values found in R, the columns are preserved intact. Notice that the primary key of R (i.e., A1) is now a column in S, and that this very column is now the primary key of S. Therefore, the rows of S are all distinct and S is a proper relation. The same cannot be said of T. Because the primary key of R has *not* been preserved in T, there is no guarantee that the rows of T are all distinct. Thus, T may be a corrupted relation. The difficulties stemming from this kind of table are described in Chapter 23.

What kind of column-oriented decomposition is considered correct according to the relational model? The relational operator to apply is **project.** Each projection to be stored at some site, possibly remote, must include the primary key of the relation from which the projection is made. Then, each and every projection is a proper relation with no duplicate rows, and it will be managed at the pertinent site by the DBMS at that site. Thus, the relation R just examined could be split into two or three projections, each of which includes column A1. The three-fold split would be as follows:

S (A1 A2)   T (A1 A3)   U (A1 A4)
at site B   at site C   at site D

Note that, at any time, the original relation R can be recovered from relations S, T, and U by using **equi-join** with respect to the primary keys of the relations being joined. For each relation in this example, the primary key is A1. This recovery capability permits the relation R to be re-distributed in an entirely different way at some later time, without causing any application program to be damaged logically.

There are bound to be complaints about the duplication of keys across sites that stems from the preservation of the primary key at each site that receives a projection. This duplication is a small price to pay for the power from retaining keys (e.g., non-traumatic re-distribution of the data when needed). The power is especially cheap because primary keys are seldom updated.

RX-9 Decomposition by Columns for Distributing Data

When some columns of a relation R in the global database Z are assigned to one site, and some to one or more other sites, the pertinent operator is **project** (as defined in Section 4.2), and the primary key of R *must be included* in each and every projection.

An alternative or additional decomposition is by rows. Here again, however, the selection of rows cannot be arbitrary—such as, store the first 50 at site B, the next 50 at site C, and so on. Relational DBMS are intentionally not aware of the meaning of "the first 50" and "the next 50." These concepts are leftovers from the days of file-management systems and early pre-relational DBMS products, in which the user's perception of the data was very close to the way the data happened to be stored.

A selection of rows must be made using the **select** operator. For example, one may store at site B those rows of relation R whose numeric values in column A3 range from 557722 to 999999. Another, quite distinct, example is the selection of those rows of R whose alphanumeric values in column A4 range from HHH12JJ to NNN11KK as a relation to be stored at site C. It may be worth noting that alphanumeric ordering must be based on either a declared or a standard collating sequence such as ASCII or EBCDIC.

When a relation R is partitioned by rows into several subrelations, each to be stored at distinct sites, it is possible to recover the original relation R by means of the operator **union.** The **union** ALL of sQL is not usable in this context because it is a non-relational operator, one that generates a result that may contain duplicate rows.

If, as is usually the case and as is recommended, relation R is partitioned into several *disjoint* subrelations (i.e., no pair of subrelations has any rows in common), then it will not be necessary to update the mutually redundant rows at two or more sites (because there will be no such rows) whenever an update is requested on one row.

***

RX-10 Decomposition by Rows
for Distributing Data

When some rows of a relation R in the global database Z are assigned to one site, and other rows to other sites, the pertinent operator is **select** (see Section 4.2), using ranges of values applied to a simple or composite column of R. The ranges should not overlap, which means that no row is assigned to more than one site.

***

Why is the capability of recovering the original relation important? This recovery is needed if at some later time a decision is made to re-distribute the data in a different way, possibly using different decompositions and/or different combinations. For example, the initial distribution of the sample relation might be by rows based on values in column A3. Later a re-distribution might be necessary; it might be by rows, but based on values in column A4. Still later, it might be by columns instead of by rows.

24.4.4 Combination of Relations from the Global Database Z

While the **project** and **select** operators can be used to split a single relation from Z into several relations, the **join, union, relational intersection, relational difference,** and **relational divide** operators can be used to combine several relations from Z into one relation. Clearly, if the transformations performed on relations from Z are to be reversible, these operators must be applied with considerable care. For example, just as every **projection** of relation R must include the primary key of R, so every **join** should involve the following in the comparand columns:

■ the primary key on domain D (say) of one relation; **and**
■ either a primary key on domain D of the other relation, or a foreign key on domain D of the other relation.

***

RX-11 General Transformation
for Distributing Data

Any combination of relational operators (whether of the decomposing or the combining type) is applicable to determining how the data should be distributed, provided that the total transformation is reversible.

***

24.4.5 Replicas and Snapshots

Sometimes, two or more sites need frequent access to common information in certain relations in the global database, and the GDBA may be tempted to assign copies of these relations to these sites. The type of copy that is kept up-to-date by the distributed DBMS whenever any modification (insertion, update, or deletion) is executed on one of the copies is called a *replica*. The type of copy that is not kept in such a high state of accuracy, but is merely refreshed from time to time (either by a specific DBA request or by a DBA request to refresh at specified time intervals), is called a *snapshot*. An example of a DBA command for this purpose is

CREATE SNAPSHOT R REFRESH EVERY 7 DAYS

where R denotes an expression that evaluates to a relation (including the simple special case that it is the name of a base relation).

The GDBA should decide whether a copy is to be held as a replica or a snapshot. This decision should be made with great care because replicas are significantly more expensive than snapshots in terms of performance. If only two sites are involved in the decision, and one is oriented toward production and the other is oriented toward planning, the choice is clear: accurate on-line data for the production site and snapshots for the planning site; no replicas are needed. Then, the GDBA must decide how frequently these snapshots must be refreshed.

RX-12 Replicas and Snapshots

The DBMS must support all declared replicas by dynamically maintaining them in an up-to-date state. End users and application programs can operate independently of whether these replicas exist and how many there are. The DBMS also supports snapshots that are updated to conform to the distributed database with a frequency declared by the DBA.

Why are replicas significantly more expensive in performance than snapshots? The root of the performance problem with replicas is that application programs must be protected from the burden of explicitly modifying all replicas of a given relation. This protection is necessary in order to achieve replication independence. In other words, these application programs must continue to be logically correct when a new replica of an old relation is introduced or when an old replica is discontinued. The programs must therefore modify just one copy, and the DBMS must assume responsibility for modifying the remaining copies of the pertinent relation in exactly the same way.

24.5 ■ Distributed Integrity Constraints

One more reason to perceive the totality of distributed data as a single global database is to establish all the integrity constraints that happen to be appropriate. Since certain types of integrity constraints are subject to change over the years (especially those that are DBA-defined), there must be a GDBA—a database administrator who maintains the global perspective and is responsible for the global database.

Some of the integrity constraints in a distributed database can be enforced completely at just one site, but many will straddle the data at multiple sites. These straddlers require inter-site cooperation of two kinds:

1. between DBAs to establish appropriate declarations;
2. between DBMS at the various sites for their enforcement.

RX-13   Integrity Constraints that Straddle Two or More Sites

The DBMS must support both referential integrity and user-defined integrity constraints when they happen to straddle two or more sites. Inter-site cooperation for enforcement must not involve any special action by users, but rather must be built into the DBMS at each site. The support for integrity constraints that straddle sites must protect users from having to be aware of the straddling in any way, even after one or more redeployments of the data.

24.6 ■ Distributed Views

One more reason to perceive the totality of distributed data as a single global database is to establish all of the views needed by application programmers and terminal users. Views are still defined in terms of the base relations and other views, but some of these relations may be located at distinct sites. In addition, the actual views that are needed may change over the years. Thus, once again a database administrator (the GDBA) who maintains the global perspective, and who is responsible for the global database, is needed.

All view definitions applicable to the entire database are stored in each of the global databases for use by the DBA. However, this collection of definitions is not used by the DBMS at individual sites to handle each relational request successfully.

To avoid the global databases becoming a traffic bottleneck, view definitions are scattered around the sites with whatever degree of duplication is necessary to provide good performance. One possibility is to store at each site X only those views that refer to one or more relations stored at X. Such definitions can, of course, refer to relations at sites other than site X also.

Full support of views that straddle the data at multiple sites requires inter-site cooperation of two kinds:

1. between people to establish appropriate declarations;
2. between DBMS at the various sites.

The second kind of inter-site cooperation is required due to the fact that *it is not normally true* that the view definitions for the entire distributed database are stored in each and every catalog.

RX-14   Views that Straddle Two or More Sites

The DBMS must support views when they happen to straddle two or more sites. Inter-site cooperation for this support must not involve any special action by users. It must be built into the DBMS at each site. The support for views that straddle sites must protect users from having to be aware of the straddling in any way, even after one or more redeployments of the data.

Support of inter-site views is essential to full support of distribution independence.

24.7 ■ Distributed Authorization

One more reason to perceive the totality of distributed data as a single global database is to establish all of the authorization needed by application programmers and terminal users. Authorization is still defined in terms of the base relations and views, but some of these relations may be located at different sites. In addition, the authorization that is needed may change over the years. Thus, once again there needs to be a database administrator (the GDBA) who maintains the global perspective, and who is responsible for the global database.

All declarations of authorization for the entire database are stored in each of the global databases for use by the global DBA. However, this collection of definitions is not used by the DBMS at individual sites to handle each relational request successfully.

To avoid the global databases becoming a traffic bottleneck, declarations of authorization are scattered around the sites with whatever degree of duplication is necessary to provide good performance. One possibility is to store at each site X only those declarations that refer to one or more relations stored at site X.

Full support of declarations of authorization that straddle the data at multiple sites requires inter-site cooperation of two kinds:

1. between people to establish appropriate declarations;
2. between DBMS at the various sites.

The second kind of inter-site cooperation is required due to the fact that *it is not true that* every declaration of authorization for the entire distributed database is stored in each and every catalog.

RX-15 Authorization that Straddles Two or More Sites

The DBMS must support declarations of authorization when they happen to straddle two or more sites. Inter-site cooperation for this support must not involve any special action by users. It must be built into the DBMS at each site. The support for authorization constraints that straddle sites must protect users from having to be aware of the straddling in any way, even after one or more redeployments of the data.

Support of authorization that straddles two or more sites is essential to full support of distribution independence.

24.8 ■ The Distributed Catalog

Every site has its own relational DBMS. Therefore, every site has its own catalog. What does this catalog contain in the case of a distributed database?

At each site, there must be a catalog that includes at least the description of all of the data stored at that site. If nothing more is done, then, when any DBMS at one site attempts to find data located at other sites, this may entail searching the catalog at each and every site. This task is unnecessarily burdensome for both the particular DBMS, which does the searching, and for the network, which must support a heavy amount of inter-site communication.

One solution that is unacceptable is to store the complete description of the global database Z at just one central site, and use this description to determine which sites are involved for every reference to data in the network. If this solution were adopted and the central site goes down, then the entire distributed database network would become inoperable. Further, the catalog at this central site would be a continual bottleneck in all database activities. Thus, there can be no dynamic dependence upon a single site that happens to have a catalog that describes the global database Z and indicates at which site each part of Z is stored.

At the other extreme, however, the catalog at each and every site would contain the description of the entire global database Z. In this case, there is a very high degree of redundancy between the catalogs. Any change in the database at just one site would involve making changes in the catalog at each and every site. These changes would have to be coordinated so that all the catalogs remained at all times consistent with one another and with respect to each transaction. This consistency would probably entail locking up all catalogs until any requested catalog change had been received by each and every site, and completed by each and every DBMS. This, in turn, means that virtually all the other traffic on the network would have to be stopped for however long would be required to get these catalogs into synchronism with the global catalog.

A compromise between the two extremes was invented by the R* team, then located at the IBM research laboratory in San Jose (most team members are now located at the IBM Almaden Research Center). Suppose that a relation is created at site X. Then, site X is called its *birth site*. From the user's perspective, the name of the relation has only two parts: the local name at the time of creation, and the name of the birth site. Although the local name alone is temporarily adequate for any interactive user who happens to be at the site where the relation is stored, one fact of life must be faced: the pertinent relation might at some future time be moved from its birth site to some other site; then, the local name is inadequate.

In contrast, there is a significant advantage to combining the local name with the name of the birth site to form the global name; this combined name permanently identifies the relation uniquely, no matter at what site the relation happens to be stored. Consequently, to develop application programs that need not be changed whenever a relation is moved from one site to another, it is necessary to use the global name for each relation.

RX-16 Name Resolution with a Distributed Catalog

Each base relation stored at each site has a global name that is a combination of its local name at that site, together with the name of its birth site. The catalog at its birth site includes the name of the site at which it may now be found.

An inexpensive tool for gaining improved performance is a *global-name cache* at each site. This cache can be conceived as an extension of the synonym relation described in Section 24.4. For items in the global database that are not stored at site X, but are frequently accessed from site X, the synonym relation at site X is extended to include the global name of each such item, along with the identification of the site where the corresponding object is now located.

24.8.1 Inter-site Move of a Relation

When a relation is moved from one site to another, the user making such a request must be appropriately authorized. Such a user is likely to be the global DBA or someone on his or her staff. Four sites are involved in such a move: the FROM site, the TO site, the BIRTH site, and the GDBA site. Of course, either the FROM site or the TO site (but not both) may be identical to the BIRTH site, and the GDBA site may be identical with any one of the other three sites.

Thus, when an inter-site move of a relation is requested, four sites are normally involved, each of which makes changes to its catalog contents. These changes reflect not only the fact that one or more relations have been moved, but also the changes in local and inter-site integrity constraints that result from that move. Normally, in the case of the global catalog, there are no resulting changes in integrity constraints.

The DBMS at the birth site of the pertinent relation (say R) is responsible for ensuring that its catalog contains identification of the present site of R along with its birth site. Thus, using the global name of the relation R enables any DBMS in the network that happens to be the source of a request on R to ask of its birth site where that relation is now located. The DBMS at any site can find every relation in the network by querying the catalog at exactly one or two sites: one site only if the relation happens to have remained at its birth site; otherwise, two sites.

RX-17 Inter-site Move of a Relation

A user who moves a relation from one site to another must be authorized to do so, or else the authorization mechanism will not permit the move to be executed. In the MOVE command, the user must specify the global name. By this means the DBMS at the birth site can and does update its catalog to record the new site for this relation.

24.8.2 Inter-site Move of One or More Rows of a Relation

As indicated in Section 24.8.1, a relation in the global database can be dispersed to several sites by rows using the range of values in a simple or composite column. As an example, consider a relation R that has a column drawing its values from the currency domain. Suppose that the rows of R are distributed by assigning to sites A, B, C those rows that have values in this currency column within the following ranges:

Site A:	0 to	999
Site B:	1,000 to	9,999
Site C:	10,000 to	99,999

Suppose that a suitably authorized user at some site requests an update on a row of R that happens to be located at site A, because it happens to have a currency value in the range 0 to 999. Suppose also that this update is an increment that takes the currency value into the range for site B (i.e., 1,000 to 9,999). Then, this row is automatically moved from site A to site B, and the initiative for this action is taken by the DBMS at site A.

RX-18   Inter-site Moves of Rows of a Relation

Suppose that rows of a relation R are distributed according to the range of values in some simple or composite column of R, and that an update is applied to this column of a row at site X1. Suppose also that this update takes the value out of the range of values pertaining to site X1, and into the range pertaining to site X2. Then, if an indicator in the catalog signals that moving a row can be triggered by such an update, the DBMS automatically moves the row from site X1 to site X2. A single updating relational command may result in zero, one, two or more inter-site moves of rows of a relation.

In one sense, inter-site moves of rows are simpler for the DBMS to handle than inter-site moves of relations. No changes are necessary in any catalog. Authorization for inter-site moves triggered by updates can be handled by means of the N-person turn-key Feature RA-5 (see the remarks following Feature RA-6 in Chapter 18).

24.8.3 More Complicated Re-distribution

Now, it is reasonable to ask, "What if a re-distribution of data is more complicated than the move of an entire relation from one site to another? What if a relation in the global database Z is decomposed or combined with some other relation in a new way—by using different operators, by using different columns as comparand columns, or by both means?"

Clearly, the one object that remains constant in such a change is the global database Z. Therefore, to protect application programs from damage under these circumstances, they should be developed to operate upon data in the global database or upon views that are defined on that database, making use of the information in the global catalog. The burden of using global names can be assumed to a large degree by the DBMS if it supports globalization of the source code as defined shortly after Feature RX-3. Local names can be used by end users when interacting at terminals with a local database. In all other cases, however, local names should not be used.

24.8.4 Dropping Relations and Creating New Relations

What if the global database changes because some kinds of data in the network have been dropped entirely? This type of change is similar to the dropping of information from a non-distributed database. Those application programs that make use of the dropped information are very likely to become inoperable unless some changes in them are made. The other application programs will remain unaffected. The global catalog must be contracted so that it no longer includes any mention of the kinds of items that have been removed. Those local catalogs that are affected by the drop must also be changed to be consistent with the global catalog.

RX-19   Dropping a Relation from a Site

When a suitably authorized user drops a relation R stored at site X, the following catalogs are adjusted to reflect the loss of information from the entire distributed database: (1) the local catalog at site X, (2) all copies of the global catalog, and (3) the birth-site catalog. The only application programs adversely affected are those that use the data in R.

Now, suppose that instead of dropping certain kinds of data, new kinds of data are added to one or more sites in the network. The description of the global database must be enlarged to cover the new domains, new relations, new columns, new views, new integrity constraints, new authorization constraints, and any new functions. All the application programs developed before these new additions should be capable of operating correctly without any changes whatsoever. Once again, those local catalogs that are affected by the new items introduced must also be changed to be consistent with the global catalog.

RX-20   Creating a New Relation

When a suitably authorized user creates a new relation R at site X, the following catalogs are adjusted to reflect the new information in the network: (1) the local catalog (X is declared to be the birth site), and (2) all copies of the global catalog.

24.9 ■ Abandoning an Old Site

Occasionally, because of business or institutional conditions, one of the sites managed by a distributed database system must be either abandoned, or detached from the network. Two cases must be considered. In the simpler case, all of the data at that site is to be abandoned or detached also. In the more complicated one, some or all of the data at that site is to be retained in the network, but moved to other sites in that network.

24.9.1 Abandoning the Data as Well as an Old Site

Suppose that site X is being abandoned, along with all the data stored there now. In this case, the GDBA must remove from the N copies of the global catalog all references to the relations at site X, except references to X as the birth site of any relation that happens to be located now at some site other than X. These references must remain viable if application programs are to remain as logically correct as possible.

A site other than X—one that is surviving in the network—must be chosen by the GDBA to act as if it were the birth site X. This places a responsibility on the chosen site to behave as if it were (1) the birth site of relations created at that site, and (2) the birth site of relations actually created at site X. Each DBMS at each site in the network must have the capability of assuming this kind of additional responsibility.

24.9.2 Retaining the Data at Surviving Sites

Together with the local database administrators, the GDBA must determine how the data now stored at site X (the site being abandoned) is to be re-distributed. In the simplest case of re-distribution, each relation currently stored at X is moved in its entirety to some new site. Several sites may be involved as recipients. The more complicated case of re-distribution involves the following:

■ decomposition of relations presently stored at X; or

■ combination of these relations with others in the network; **or**

■ both decomposition and combination.

This task is similar to that of establishing the distributed database in the first place. When this is done, the GDBA must select one of the surviving sites to act as the virtual birth site X for all of the relations created at X that are still in the network. (This process was discussed in more detail in the previous section.)

RX-21 Abandoning an Old Site and Perhaps Its Data

A suitably authorized user (usually the global database administra-tor) may detach a site X completely from the network, and also abandon the data stored at that site. Some other site must be designated to carry on the duties of X in keeping track of the present whereabouts of relations created at X (birth site = X), but already moved from X to some other sites. If some or all of the data is to be retained at other sites, then the GDBA should be involved, and the N copies of the global catalog and the local catalogs at receiving sites must be adjusted to reflect the re-distribution of the data formerly at site X.

In both the cases discussed in Section 24.9 and this section, application programs remain logically correct, except if they refer to data that has been abandoned or detached altogether from the network.

24.10 ■ Introducing a New Site

It must be possible to introduce a new site without adversely affecting the logical correctness of any of the application programs. The tasks for the GDBA and the local DBA for the newly introduced site are similar to those involved in establishing the distributed database in the first place.

Suppose that the new site is site X. If there is no DBMS at site X, one must be selected and installed. Care must be taken in selecting it to ensure that it is compatible with the rest of the network. Today's advertisements by DBMS vendors contain many false claims concerning compatibility.

If there is no database at site X, it will be necessary to create some domains and relations there; data may be re-distributed from other sites. As these domains and relations are created, the local catalog at site X is kept up-to-date by the DBMS at that site. Changes will also be necessary in all N copies of the global catalog and these changes are made by DBMS.

RX-22 **Introducing a New Site**

A suitably authorized user, usually the GDBA, can attach a new site X, to the network. The GDBA must decide whether data that is already in the network is now to be moved to X, or what new data is to be stored at X. The N copies of the global catalog, together with the local catalog at site X and possibly the local catalogs at other sites also, must be adjusted to reflect these decisions. Introduction of a new site does not adversely affect any existing application programs.

Occasionally, local DBAs and the global DBA may have to make a combination of changes in their catalogs. This is facilitated by the following feature.

RX-23 Deactivating and Reactivating Items in the Catalog

A suitably authorized user can deactivate any selected items in the catalog under his or her control. Later, and possibly within the same CAT block, this user can reactivate the deactivated items.

For details concerning the CAT block, see Feature RM-7 in Chapter 12.

Exercises

24.1 What is the optimizer supposed to do in a non-distributed DBMS? State three stages. What additional action is expected if the DBMS is claimed to manage distributed databases? (See Chapter 25.)

24.2 A distributed database has been in operation for a while. Assume that the data is distributed according to RM/V2. Because of changes in the business, it is now necessary to discontinue some sites, introduce others, and generally redistribute the data in a non-loss way. Will it be necessary to change the application programs in order to ensure that these programs operate correctly on the redistributed data? Provide reasons for your answer.

24.3 Assume you have a distributed DBMS that supports replication independence. In determining how data should be distributed to various sites, what is the problem in deciding whether some data should be replicated at two or more sites? What are the alternatives to replicas?

24.4 In distributed database management, suppose that you are determining how data should be deployed to the various sites, and that you have decided to use decomposition by rows based on specified ranges of values in some column. Why is it desirable to ensure that the range of values for any one site does not overlap the range of values applicable to any other site?

24.5 Consider the reversibility condition applied by RM/V2 to whatever transformations are used on the global database in planning the deployment of data in a distributed database. Consider also the reversibility condition applied in defining views that are intended to be updatable. Are these two conditions identical? If not, what are the differences and why? All parts of your answer should be precise. (See Chapter 17.)

24.6 A single relational command happens to refer to data located in several sites. Assume that it has not been compiled yet. Supply a list of three inter-site activities that the DBMS must support if the pre-execution stage is to be completed correctly. Make no special assumptions about the command.

24.7 Supply one or more reasons why is it important that the DBMS retain the source code for every relational request in distributed database management. These reasons must not include those applicable to non-distributed data.

■ CHAPTER 25 ■

More on Distributed
Database Management

25.1 ■ Optimization in Distributed
Database Management

To provide high performance on a variety of query and manipulative commands, the optimizer is an important component, even in a non-distributed
version of a relational database management system. The optimizer is even
more important in a distributed version. In fact, I would describe it as a
sine qua non.

It is not hard for a user to devise tests that show how good an optimizer
is in any given relational DBMS product. The basic idea is as follows. A
query is created that makes use of several of the basic relational operators:
for example, one or two **joins,** a **union,** a **selection,** and one or two **projections.**
Using the relational language supported by the product, the query is cast in
at least two distinct forms, which can be expected to give markedly different
performance if the optimizer is not doing its job.

These forms differ primarily in the ordering of terms within them. If
the DBMS yields quite different performance on these two forms, then it is
not executing the first important step in optimization—namely, converting
each query into a single canonical form so that the performance attained
does not depend on how the user expressed the request in the relational
language.

A question that arises is: Why is the optimizer so important in handling
distributed databases? The following example should answer this question.
It demonstrates the radical difference in performance that can be achieved
depending on the quality of the optimizer in a distributed database management system.

25.1.1 A Financial Company Example

Consider a sample distributed database that includes relations concerning customers, investments that are offered by the company, and investments held by the customers:

CUSTOMER C (stored at site X)

    C#   Customer serial number

    CN   Customer name

    CC   Customer city

    CS   Customer state

CUSTOMER-INVESTMENT CI (stored at site Y)

    C#   Customer serial number

    I#   Investment serial number

    CV   Value in U.S. dollars

INVESTMENT I (stored at site Y)

    I#   Investment serial number

    IT   Investment type

    IU   Unit of investment

Suppose that the following assumptions hold:

- 100,000 customers in relation C.
- 2,000 distinct types of investments in relation I.
- 200,000 customer-investments in relation CI.
- 2,000 bits per row (in any relation).
- 10,000 bits per second over the communications links, a rate equivalent to five rows per second.
- 1-second delay in gaining access to the communications links.
- 10 type-G investments.
- 4,000 customers in Illinois.

Consider a sample query, to be expressed in SQL: find the identifiers and names of customers in the state of Illinois who have investments of type G. One way of expressing this in SQL is as follows:

```
SELECT   C#, CN
FROM     C, CI, I
WHERE    C.CS = 'Illinois'
AND      C.C# = CI.C#
AND      CI.I# = I.I#
AND      IT = 'G'
```

There are at least six alternative methods that can be used in executing this SQL command; only these six are presented. In what follows, only the load on the inter-site communications lines is computed for each case, since this is likely to be the dominant factor. An adequate optimizer would, of course, go further and calculate processing loads at each site and input-output loads at each site.

Method 1: Move C to site Y
100K rows @ 5 per sec = 20K seconds
= 5 hours 33 mins 20 secs

Method 2: Move CI and I to site X
202K rows @ 5 per sec = 11 hours
→ GREATEST COMMUNICATION TIME

Method 3: Execute (CI * I)[IT = 'G'] at site Y,
where * denotes **natural join** using I# as the comparand
For each row, check site X to see if customer state = 'Illinois'
2 messages for each type-G investment held
= 200 messages at 1 sec delay and 0.2 sec transmission
= 240 secs = 4 minutes

Method 4: Execute C[CS = 'Illinois'] at site X
For each row, check site Y to see if customer has investment of type G
2 messages for each Illinois customer
= 8K messages at 1 sec delay,
and 0.2 sec transmission
= 9600 secs = 160 minutes
= 2 hours 40 mins

Method 5: Execute (CI * I)[CT = 'G'][C#, I#] at site Y,
where * denotes **natural join** using I# as the comparand
Move result to site X to complete the query
1 row for each type G investment held
= 100 × 0.2 secs
(ignoring single delay of 1 sec)
= 20 secs → LEAST COMMUNICATION TIME

Method 6: Execute C [CS = 'Illinois'] at site X
Move result to site Y
1 row for each Illinois customer
= 4000 × 0.2 secs = 800 secs
(ignoring single delay of 1 sec)
= 13 mins 20 secs

Of these six methods, Method 2 consumes the most communication time—11 hours—while Method 5 uses up the least—20 seconds. A high-quality optimizer, together with adequate statistics on the database, would select Method 5.

Exercise 25.2 at the end of this chapter requests the reader to (1) construct a sample database that is distributed to only two sites, (2) construct a sample query that requires information be retrieved from both sites and combined by means of a join, and (3) show that the longest time in communication across the network is N days and the shortest time is N seconds.

This exercise is not particularly difficult and demonstrates the importance of designing a high-quality optimizer in each DBMS of a distributed database management system. Such an optimizer normally selects the approach with the least communication time, since this time dominates the loading on all resources when a command happens to involve two or more sites. If the communication happens to be trans-Atlantic or trans-Pacific, the differences in communication time mean very large differences in communication cost.

These examples suggest that, if the optimizer in a distributed database management system is either weak or missing entirely, there is a serious risk that certain commands will consume an unacceptable time on the communication lines and will also make the costs of communication too heavy. In other words, a distributed relational DBMS with a weak or non-existing optimizer is a DBA's nightmare.

The examples also suggest the following question: What is an adequate collection of statistics about the database? The DBMS should occasionally generate, and use in every optimization, at least a minimal collection of statistics. This collection consists of the number of rows in each base relation, together with the number of distinct values in every column of every base relation. From these statistics and the assumption that within every column the distribution of values is uniform, the DBMS can calculate for every column the expected number of occurrences of each distinct value within that column.

It is important to realize that statistics about a database do not normally change significantly whenever a single insertion, deletion, or update is executed. Therefore, the DBMS need not modify the statistics whenever an insertion, deletion, or update is executed. There would be a severe loss of performance if the DBMS attempted to keep the statistics as up-to-date as that. In many situations, it is quite adequate if the DBMS (1) generates statistics about a base table when that table is created and loaded, and (2) updates the statistics either once every week, or only when they have changed significantly.

It is known that the usual assumption of uniform distribution within each column of the distinct values in that column is quite often far from the actual distribution. Adoption of this assumption, however, is a significant step in the right direction.

RX-24 Minimum Standard for Statistics

The DBMS must maintain at least simple statistics for every relation and every distinct column stored in a distributed database. The statistics should include the number of rows in each relation and the number of distinct values in each column, whether or not that column happens to be indexed.

In early versions of relational DB2 products, statistics were generated for only those columns that happened to be indexed. Thus, statistics on non-indexed columns were simply not available to the optimizer. This serious design flaw was corrected in later versions.

To appreciate the seriousness of this flaw, suppose that one is given the description of a distributed database, including which columns of the base relations are indexed. It is then possible to conceive sample queries whose performance is heavily dependent on statistics being available concerning non-indexed columns. This exercise demonstrates the total inadequacy of a DBMS that does not maintain statistics on *every column*, and whose optimizer fails to make full use of these statistics.

25.1.2 More on Optimization in the Distributed Case

Assume that the DBMS is receiving query and manipulative commands expressed in a relational language in a logic-based style. Optimization involves the following five steps.

1. Convert the given command into a canonical form based on first-order predicate logic.

2. Convert the command into a sequence of relational operators, a sequence that is simply and directly related to the canonical form.

3. Examine all the ways in which this sequence can be altered without altering the final result of the command.

4. Deduce, for each viable sequence of operators,

   a. which of the operators can be concurrently executed at different sites, and

   b. which access paths provide the shortest execution time for each operator.

5. Calculate for each viable sequence of operators, in combination with the best access paths for that sequence, the consumption of resources using a linear combination of processing load at each site involved, input-output load at each site involved, and communication load on the network. The coefficients in this linear combination are those established (and seldom changed) by the DBA.

RX-25 Minimum Standard for the Optimizer

The optimizer in a distributed DBMS must be capable of estimating the resources consumed in executing a relational command in a variety of ways. To generate the most effective target code, the optimizer must combine the three main components (processor time, input-output time, and time on the communication system) using a linear function in which these times appear with coefficients selected initially by the system, but alterable by the DBA.

It should be noted that relational algebra plays a significant role in the second step in optimization. My work in the period 1968–1972 [Codd 1969–1971d], during which I developed both the algebra and the logic (and, incidentally, their inter-relatedness) for querying and manipulating relations of arbitrary degree, lays the foundation for this step.

The **semi-theta-join** operator was described in Section 5.2.2. This operator can prove useful in efficiently executing **joins** between relations that happen to be stored at different sites, but it is not always the most efficient technique, because in some cases it can involve an increased amount of inter-site communication. This fact, however, should not discourage DBMS vendors from incorporating **semi-theta-join** into their designs. At present, I do not know of any distributed DBMS product that uses it.

A final note on performance distinguishes the site at which a relational request is entered from the site or sites at which it is executed. The following feature was suggested by Professor Michael Stonebraker of the University of California at Berkeley.

RX-26 Performance Independence in Distributed Database Management

In a distributed relational DBMS, the performance of a relational request is to a large extent independent of the site at which the request is entered.

25.2 ■ Other Implementation Considerations

Two types of concurrency must be supported by a relational DBMS. The first kind, called *intra-command concurrency,* consists of treating various portions of a single relational command as independent tasks, and executing these tasks concurrently. The second kind, called *inter-command concurrency,* consists of executing two or more relational commands concurrently.

RX-27 Concurrency Independence in Distributed Database Management

The DBMS supports concurrency of execution of relational operators between all of the sites in the network. Application programs
and activities by end users at terminals must be logically independent
of this inter-site concurrency, whether the DBMS supports intra-
command concurrency or inter-command concurrency or both. These
programs and activities must also be independent of the controls
(usually locking) that protect any one action from interfering with
or damaging any concurrent execution.

As previously mentioned, execution of a *single relational command* can
involve activity at multiple sites. Therefore, the execution of a *single transaction* can certainly involve activity at multiple sites. Aborting such a transaction would therefore involve recovery at multiple sites.

RX-28 Recovery at Multiple Sites

If it is claimed that the DBMS provides full support for distributed
database management, then without user intervention the DBMS
must support and coordinate recovery involving multiple sites whenever it has been necessary to abort a transaction at multiple sites.
Application programs and activities by end users at terminals must
be independent of this inter-site recovery.

The locking scheme implemented in the DBMS must detect deadlocks
that may occur between actions at distinct sites. These are often called *global
deadlocks,* but a better term is *inter-site deadlocks.*

RX-29 Locking in Distributed Database Management

The DBMS detects inter-site deadlocks, selects one of the contend-
ing activities, backs it out to break the cycle of contention, and
forces it to wait until a fresh occurrence of the deadlock is avoided
as a result of one contender completing or absorbing its transaction.
Relational languages contain no features specifically for the handling
of deadlocks.

For further information on the intricate controls needed to support the management of distributed data safely and reliably, see [Williams et al. 1981].

25.3 ■ Heterogeneous Distributed Database Management

Today, many companies make use of several computer systems in their business. It is quite likely that these systems were acquired from different vendors, and that each is operated independently of the others. There is a growing demand for software that supports the sharing of data across these systems.

In database terms, the software needed is called a *heterogeneous distributed database management system*. Ideally, such a system should be able to support all the user-oriented features of the homogeneous case. This means that the system must be able to translate correctly, and in a single uniform way, any statements expressed in a single relational language, with the following additional kinds of independence:

■ hardware independence;

■ operating-system independence;

■ network independence;

■ DBMS independence; **and**

■ catalog independence.

Today, there exists a great diversity in the hardware and software of the various vendors, in spite of all the effort that has gone into creating information processing standards. For example, no two versions of SQL from different vendors are completely compatible. Sometimes this is even true of any two versions from a single vendor. Another example: no two versions of the DBMS catalog from different vendors are compatible with one another.

The lack of appropriate and enforced standards, and the non-conformity of products with respect to existing standards, make the heterogeneous distributed DBMS an extremely ambitious goal. Except in quite simple cases of heterogeneity, the products that emerge are likely to have an extremely large number of cases of user-unfriendly exceptions, which make some of them impractical and unacceptable.

As an aside, the occurrence of duplicate rows within a relation in either the homogeneous or heterogeneous case presents a quite unnecessary additional problem.

Occasionally, one hears that a non-relational DBMS, such as IMS, is to be in the same network as a relational DBMS. Unless the non-relational DBMS is very simple, the problems encountered in trying to make this work are enormous [Date 1984].

25.4 ■ Step by Step Introduction of New Kinds of Data

There are several ways in which new kinds of data can be introduced into a distributed database. The following example stresses initiative at a particular site (site X), and how that initiative can be introduced step by step into the network using the features that have been described in Chapters 24 and 25.

In this example new kinds of data are introduced in a sequence of six steps. The abbreviations I, V, A mean integrity constraints, view definitions, and authorization constraints respectively.

The six steps for introducing new kinds of data into site X are:

1. create the necessary domains and relations—an addition to the local catalog at site X;
2. load some test data in these relations;
3. create whatever I,V,A in the local catalog are needed for purely local use, principally for testing, and make the tests;
4. obtain clearance from the global DBA for some users at site X to make read-only use of data in the network to participate in conditions for relational requests that confine their modifying activities to the new data only;
5. load regular (non-test) data into the new relations;
6. negotiate with the global DBA the introduction of these new relations into the network as site X participants.

The negotiation in Step 6 can be broken down into five parts:

6.1 examine whether any new domains created at site X can be identified as domains that already exist on the network—if so, use the global domain name and definition;

6.2 determine the correspondence between the local names newly introduced at site X and the existing collection of global names;

6.3 define necessary views ⎤ these may straddle
6.4 define integrity constraints ⎬ new and old data and
6.5 define authorization constraints ⎦ possibly several sites

25.5 ■ Concluding Remarks

The relational model represents the best existing technology for supporting distributed database management. So far, it is the only approach that supports a language of adequate level, a language in which the user is able to issue a request without dictating to the system how it is to be carried out. To quote Dr. Bruce Lindsay of IBM Almaden Research Center, San Jose:

Single-record-at-a-time DBMS products (the old approach) in which the user or programmer has to navigate his way through the database are the kiss of death in managing distributed databases.

The level of language is more than a matter of how many records or rows can be retrieved using a single command. It is also more than the complexity of the logical condition that can be expressed in a single command to determine which pieces of information are to be retrieved. Comprehensibility of statements expressed in that language represents an extremely important concern. This applies not only to end users, who may be nonprogrammers, but also to application programmers, who often must maintain programs written by people other than themselves. In such a task, comprehensibility of the statements in those programs is a *sine qua non*.

Here are some more specific reasons why the relational model lends itself to the management of distributed data. The first reason, *decomposition flexibility,* is applicable to two important tasks: (1) the task of distributing a large database to multiple sites (discussed at length in Section 24.4), and (2) the task of decomposing logically expressed relational commands into sequences of operators of the relational algebra.

From the discussion in Section 24.4, it should be obvious that the relational operators provide an extremely flexible tool for carving up the information for distribution purposes. A single relational command can touch many columns scattered over many relations. Such a command can be decomposed into the basic relational operators that are involved. The power of decomposition of relational commands should also be obvious from the discussion of optimization in Section 25.1.

The second reason why the relational model lends itself to the management of distributed data is *recomposition power.* After a relational command has been decomposed into basic relational operators acting on data at various sites, these sites return data in the form of derived relations to the requesting site. This site now has the task of recombining these returned relations into the single relation that is the overall result that was requested. All the relational operators are available for specifying this recombining activity.

The third reason is *economy of transmission.* As discussed earlier, upon receipt of a relational command, a distributed DBMS decomposes it into several basic relational operators that can be applied to the relations stored at various sites. These operators, expressed as simple relational commands, are sent as messages to the appropriate sites. Each command may involve the processing of hundreds, thousands, or possibly millions of rows in relations. If the DBMS had been an old single-record-at-a-time product, a message across the network would have been necessary for each one of the hundreds, thousands, or millions of records involved. Thus, a relational distributed database management system can be orders of magnitude cheaper than a non-relational DBMS in terms of inter-site communication costs, as well as orders of magnitude faster.

The fourth reason is *analyzability of intent* and *optimizability*. A query or manipulative command expressed in a relational language tells the DBMS what kinds of information the user wants and under what conditions, but does not specify how the system is to find and extract this information. It is therefore reasonable to say that (1) such a command expresses the user's intent, and (2) the methods used by the system to satisfy this intent are left entirely up to the system. These facts give the DBMS a very wide choice of methods from which to make a selection.

Thus, the scope for optimization is significantly wider than that of any other approach known today. In turn, this means that, with respect to the management of distributed data, it is very difficult for any non-relational DBMS to compete in combination of cost and performance with a relational DBMS that is equipped with a well-designed optimizer. Note that it is essential for an optimizer to be able to re-optimize commands in a transaction that touches parts of the database where the statistics have changed significantly. Then the DBA can feel confident that the system is really helping him or her to meet the DBA's responsibilities.

The fifth reason, *distribution independence,* was explained in Chapter 20 as one of the means by which a user's investment is protected if a relational DBMS is acquired. First of all, application programs can be developed for a non-distributed version of a relational DBMS. A distributed version of that same DBMS (if it is completely language-compatible with the non-distributed version) can then be installed. The database can be distributed to multiple sites that are geographically separated. The application programs that were originally developed for the non-distributed version will, without change, run correctly on the distributed version.

Also, the data may be re-distributed across these sites and possibly others. Once again, application programs will continue to run correctly, without changing them. This ease of redistribution is an important requirement for every company that acquires a distributed database management system, a requirement that companies often overlook.

It has been proved that distribution independence is supportable by the relational model by means of prototype relational database management systems, such as System R (non-distributed) and System R* (distributed) [Williams et al. 1981]. Not one of the non-relational database management systems has been proven to be effective in this respect. The principal reasons for this superiority in the relational approach are (1) the very high level of relational languages, and (2) the sharp separation between the user's perception and manipulation of the data, on the one hand, and the storage representation and access methods used by the DBMS, on the other.

To recapitulate, the five reasons why the relational approach lends itself to the interrogation, manipulation, and control of distributed data are as follows:

1. decomposition flexibility;
2. recomposition power;

3. economy of transmission;
4. analyzability of intent; **and**
5. distribution independence.

Exercises

25.1 Why does a DBMS need any statistics about the database? Why does a DBMS need statistics about each column of each relation in the database? Why is it insufficient for the DBMS to have statistics about indexed columns only? What are the minimum statistics required by RM/V2, and where are they stored?

25.2 Construct a sample database which is simple (three relations are adequate) and which is distributed to only two sites (two of the relations at one site, one at the other site). Construct a sample query that requires information be retrieved from both sites and then combined by means of a **join.** Select a set of realistic parameters for the communication rate across the network, the time to access the network for each message, and the number of bits per row of a relation. For some integer N of your own choosing, show that:
   1. If the optimizer does a bad job, the time spent in communication across the network is approximately N days.
   2. If the optimizer does a good job, the communication time is approximately N seconds.

   Hints:
   1. The three relations can be the usual suppliers S, parts P, and capabilities C.
   2. S and C can be stored in site # 1, and P in site # 2.
   3. Consider the query: Which suppliers are based in London and can supply instruments for airplanes?
   4. An example of parameters and their values that may be assumed:
      ■ Network access time for each message = 1 second.
      ■ Transmission speed = 10,000 bits per second.
      ■ Each record consists of 10,000 bits.
      Note that there are 86,400 seconds in a 24-hour day.

25.3 What does it mean to assert that application programs and terminal activities must be independent of inter-site concurrency?

25.4 Suppose that a transaction T straddles two or more sites. Consider the following five assertions:
   1. T must involve retrieval only;
   2. T must involve insertion only;
   3. T must involve update only;

4. T must involve deletion only;
5. T can involve any combination of retrieval, insertion, update, and deletion commands.

Which of these five assertions is true, and which is false? Which of the currently available relational DBMS products supports such multi-site execution of a transaction?

25.5 Is it possible for the execution of a single relational command to straddle two or more sites? Supply an example showing the need for this. Which of the currently available DBMS products supports such multi-site execution of a single command? Are there any constraints on the type of command?

CHAPTER 26

Advantages of the
Relational Approach

The advantages of the relational approach over other approaches to database management are so numerous that I do not claim that the 15 advantages discussed in this chapter constitute a complete list. My opinion regarding the various pre-relational approaches is that the only advantage they enjoy is that some large-scale users have a very large investment in those systems— not only in the form of large quantities of company data represented in a way peculiar to the pertinent DBMS, but also in the form of application programs that appear to work correctly against that data. Such programs are very difficult to translate into the corresponding programs needed on a relational database, a difficulty largely due to the lack of a discipline in the design and use of pre-relational DBMS products.

Even though the conversion from pre-relational to relational DBMS products is very labor-intensive and costly, I believe that users should start now to plan such a conversion, and execute the plan step by step. In this way, users can realize at an earlier time the benefits in cost, efficiency, and integrity of managing their databases by means of a more modern, relational DBMS.

When a company postpones conversion to a relational DBMS, it incurs the cost of conversion sometime in the future, when the cost will be significantly higher because of the labor-intensive nature of conversion. During the period of delay, the company also loses the productivity, safety, and security of the relational approach.

26.1 ■ Power

The relational approach is very powerful and flexible in access to information (by means of ad hoc queries from terminals) and in inter-relating information without resorting to programming concepts (e.g., iterative loops and recursion). The power stems from the fact that the relational model is based on four-valued, first-order predicate logic.

26.2 ■ Adaptability

Errors are often made in both logical and physical database design. When a database is created, it is virtually impossible to predict all the uses that will be made of it. With regard to changes in use of the data and changes in the database traffic, the relational approach is much more forgiving than any other approach. (There is no claim, of course, that it is totally forgiving.)

The features that make the relational approach more capable of accommodating change are the immunity of the application programs and terminal activities to the following types of changes:

1. the storage-representation and access methods;
2. the logical design of base relations;
3. integrity constraints;
4. the deployment of data at various sites.

Database design is still necessary. When it becomes necessary to change either the logical or the physical design, however, a relational database is much more adaptive to the changes because of these four features.

26.3 ■ Safety of Investment

How safe is an investment in a relational DBMS? Will the relational approach be replaced by some new, incompatible approach in the near future?

Many people attach considerable importance to the fact that the relational model has a sound theoretical foundation. It is based on predicate logic and the theory of relations, parts of mathematics that have taken about two thousand years to develop. Thus, it is highly unlikely that the theoretical foundation will be replaced overnight. This observation makes the relational approach a reasonably safe investment on the part of DBMS vendors and DBMS users.

Furthermore, the relational approach is the only one to offer the four important investment-protection features cited in Chapter 20: (1) physical data independence, (2) logical data independence, (3) integrity independence, and (4) distribution independence. The kinds of investments protected by these features include investments in the development of application programs and in the training of the programmers and end users. In acquiring any new DBMS product—whether relational or not, and whether hardware, software, or both are involved—a company is likely to invest more money in application programming and training than in actually purchasing the DBMS product.

26.4 ■ Productivity

Early users of relational DBMS products report a substantial increase in the productivity of their application programmers. This advantage can be traced to several facts:

- Application programs developed to run on top of a relational DBMS contain significantly fewer database statements than corresponding application programs developed to run on a non-relational DBMS.

- These statements convey intent, and are therefore easier to understand by people responsible for the maintenance of the programs, who may not be the original developers.

- The database statements are clearly separate from the non-database statements, and can be separately developed and speedily debugged using terminals.

- The burden of achieving the best performance is largely removed from the application programmer and interactive user, and is instead assumed by the DBMS.

These early users also report that end users on their systems are able to make extensive use of the information in relational databases (including the generation of requested reports) without requiring help from application programming staff. This is mainly because, in constructing the relational model, I rejected the need for users to have programming skills in retrieving and modifying data in the database (skills such as designing iterative and recursive loops and creating I/O channel commands).

This ability of end users to make direct use of information in relational databases without assistance is undoubtedly the primary reason why the relational DBMS market has expanded so quickly. In just a few years, it has overtaken the market for all its predecessors. One of the many reasons that users need substantially increased productivity is that it enables them to plan and launch new products much more rapidly.

26.5 ■ Round-the-Clock Operation

The relational approach is designed for round-the-clock operation of the database management system. Pre-relational DBMS products often required the traffic on the database to be brought to a halt if changes were to be made in the access methods or access paths, or in any aspect of the database description (e.g., the record types in the database).

In a relational DBMS, this interruption of service is unnecessary for the following reasons:

- the sophisticated nature of the locking scheme;
- the automatic recompiling of just those database manipulation commands adversely affected by any changes in the database description;
- the inclusion of both data-definition commands and data-manipulation commands within any relational language.

Indexes may therefore be dynamically created and dropped. New columns may be introduced dynamically into a base relation. Old columns may be dynamically dropped. Authorization may be dynamically granted and dynamically revoked. Domains, views, integrity constraints, and functions may be dynamically created and dropped.

26.6 ■ Person-to-Person Communicability

One of the many problems with pre-relational DBMS products was that the application programmers had to have extensive training of a very narrow kind, training oriented toward the particular DBMS installed. This meant that it was virtually impossible for a company executive to find out for himself or herself what kind of information was stored in the database. To do so, the executive had to ask a database specialist to interrogate either the system or manually prepared documents related to the particular database, and then translate his or her discovery into terms comprehensible to the executive.

With the relational approach, an executive can have a terminal on his or her desk from which answers to questions can be readily obtained. He or she can readily communicate with colleagues about the information stored in the database because that information is perceived by users in such a simple way. The simplicity of the relational model is intended to end the company's dependence on a small, narrowly trained, and highly paid group of employees.

It is important to note that, if the relational approach is being used, end users and application programmers can at last talk to one another about both the content of the database (because of its simple structure) and database actions (because end users and application programmers employ a common database sublanguage).

26.7 ■ Database Controllability

The relational model was designed to provide much stronger machinery than any pre-relational DBMS for maintaining the integrity of the database. The motivation was that many companies store in their databases information that is vital to the continued success of the company. The accuracy of this information is therefore of great concern. Now, it is well-known that preventing the loss of accuracy or integrity is much more readily mechanized than is the cure of such loss.

As explained in Chapters 13 and 14, the relational model not only supports the two types of integrity (entity integrity and referential integrity) that apply to every relational database, but also supports domain integrity, column integrity, and user-defined integrity. In this last category, the model provides the power of four-valued, first-order predicate logic in the creation by users (principally the database administrator, of course) of integrity constraints that chiefly reflect the company policy, governmental regulations, and certain semantic aspects of the data used in designing the database.

The environment in which the company operates is bound to change as time passes. Therefore, it is unrealistic to expect that company policy, government regulations, and the semantics of data will somehow remain unchanged. For this reason, the relational model supports integrity independence, which permits integrity constraints to be changed without changing application programs. This integrity independence makes it much less costly to implement changes in integrity constraints, and therefore makes the company much more adaptable to environmental changes.

Of course, in many of the relational DBMS products on the market today, support for the integrity features of the relational model is quite weak. This weakness reflects irresponsibility on the part of DBMS vendors.

26.8 ■ Richer Variety of Views

Pre-relational DBMS products were quite weak in their support of views. For example, the CODASYL-proposed DBTG standard[1] of the 1970s supported nothing more than those views that just one of the relational operators **project** can generate. The relational model, on the other hand, supports the full power of four-valued, first-order predicate logic in defining views.

Unfortunately, the relational DBMS products available today do not yet possess the strength of the relational model in regard to defining views. Within the next decade or two, however, we can expect the necessary product improvements.

26.9 ■ Flexible Authorization

Pre-relational DBMS products were embarrassingly weak in their support for permitting or denying access to parts of the database. Usually the access control was based on explicit denial of access by specified users to specified

[1]From the Report of Data Base Task Group of CODASYL Programming Language Committee, April 1971. Available from ACM, BCS, and IAG.

record types or specified fields. Usually these DBMS products also failed to support access control that is dependent on values encountered in the database.

The relational model, on the other hand, uses view definitions based on four-valued, first-order predicate logic to determine the portions of the database to which access will be permitted; these portions can easily be defined to be value-dependent. A user is then permitted by the system to access one or more specified views only, and to use certain specified relational operators only on each view.

26.10 ■ Integratability

On top of a DBMS, a user is likely to need products such as application development aids, report generation support, terminal screen painting support, graphics support, support for the creation and manipulation of business forms, and support for logical inference. Pre-relational DBMS products offered nothing more than a low-level, single-record-at-a-time interface to such products.

Relational DBMS products, on the other hand, offer a powerful, multiple-record-at-a-time language for this purpose, making it significantly easier to develop the products on top. As a result, we can expect to see a vast proliferation of products that interface with relational DBMS products and make use of the data supported in the databases.

Those products that support logical inference (e.g., a few of the so-called *expert systems*) can easily exploit the relational language interface, since a language for logical inference must be closely related to predicate logic, which is the most powerful known tool for making precise logical inferences.

26.11 ■ Distributability

Now that vendors have discovered the relational approach to database management, numerous systems capable of managing distributed databases are beginning to appear on the market. One DBMS product supports not only retrieval from remote sites, but also insertion, update, and deletion at remote sites, as well as full-scale transactions, each of which may straddle multiple remote sites without the user being aware of which sites were involved.

In Chapter 25, I discussed five principal reasons why the relational approach has been far more successful than any non-relational approach in managing distributed databases:

1. decomposition flexibility;
2. recomposition power;
3. economy of transmission;

4. analyzability of intent; **and**

5. distribution independence.

26.12 ■ Optimizability

The ability of a DBMS to assume a large portion of the burden of achieving good performance on all database interactions depends on its ability to generate the best quality target code from the source code in which the user expresses these interactions. This translation from source code to efficient target code is usually called the *optimization problem.*

Although present relational DBMS products differ significantly in their abilities to handle the optimization problem, almost all of them have far superior capabilities in this area when compared with pre-relational DBMS products. This is because of both (1) the high level of relational languages and (2) the sharp separation of the user's perception of the data from the representation of this data in storage and from the access methods presently in effect.

There are several reasons why companies should avoid depending on their application programmers, however skilled, for obtaining good perform-ance from the DBMS for their application programs. Even the most highly skilled programmers sometimes find it difficult to concentrate on the job at hand. In addition, the DBMS is in a far better position than the programmer to keep track of DBMS performance, and know when it is necessary to make changes in access methods and access paths and to recompile certain relational commands to cope efficiently with these changes.

These remarks apply whether the database is distributed or not. In the distributed case, however, the DBMS can provide an additional service. It can help determine at appropriate times whether and how the database should be re-distributed. I do not know of any current product that provides this service. Perhaps the problem will be a good subject for one or more doctoral dissertations.

26.13 ■ Concurrent Action by Multiple Processing Units to Achieve Superior Performance

For many years, people in the computer field have been aware of the vast difference in speeds of processing units, on the one hand, and secondary storage such as disks, on the other. There have been suggestions that what was needed in commercial data processing was a high-level language for input and output, but no such proposal has been forthcoming. Now, the relational approach to database management offers vast new opportunities to exploit concurrent action by multiple processing units—not just 2, 4, or 6 units, but 50, 100, or more. For example, Tandem has shown that, by adding processing units, it is possible to obtain an improvement in speed of the whole system that is linear with cost.

Tandem's NonStop SQL is more powerful in speed than any non-relational DBMS products because automatic concurrent actions are made possible by the relational approach, and Tandem exploits this concurrency opportunity to the hilt. By "automatic," I mean that the concurrency is not programmed by either the user or the application programmer.

Incidentally, Tandem's announcement and the audited benchmark finally laid to rest the ill-conceived notion that the relational approach would never be accepted because it "performed poorly." No other architectural approach is known for achieving very high performance on database management: for example, over 1000 simple transactions per second, coupled with fast response (e.g., less than 2 seconds per transaction). The IBM product IMS Fastpath, once considered a leader in performance among database management systems, has been overtaken by Tandem's NonStop SQL coupled with Tandem's NonStop architecture. Moreover, IMS and IMS Fastpath cannot catch up in this race, since they are single-record-at-a-time systems, in which opportunities for concurrent action are quite limited.

It is worthwhile to distinguish between two types of concurrency:

1. inter-command concurrency—concurrency between the execution of distinct relational commands;

2. intra-command concurrency—concurrency between tasks that are part of a single relational command.

The present release of Tandem's NonStop SQL concentrates on the first type, while the Teradata DBMS product concentrates on the second type of concurrency.

26.14 ■ Concurrent Action by Multiple Processing Units to Achieve Fault Tolerance

Today, as more and more companies become international in scope, they must operate effectively in multiple time zones. Such companies tend to need continuous, round-the-clock operation of their complete systems. Thus, if a processing unit, channel, or disk unit fails, the system as a whole should continue to function, even though its performance may be reduced.

Tandem Corporation has shown that this fault tolerance can be achieved in data processing through its NonStop architecture (hardware and software), and in database management through its NonStop SQL (software). Thus, it is clear that one advantage of the relational approach is that it lends itself to a high degree of concurrent action, which, with an appropriate architecture, in turn leads to a high degree of fault tolerance.

In scientific computing, arrays and matrices offer significant opportunities for concurrent execution; this has been exploited to obtain performance improvements. In commercial data processing, relations offer similar opportunities. The need in commercial data processing is greater, however, in that not only must performance improvements be obtained, but also significant improvements in fault tolerance must be achieved.

26.15 ■ Ease of Conversion

If and when the relational approach to database management becomes obsolete, it will be much easier to convert to whatever approach replaces the relational model. There are two chief reasons:

1. all information in a relational database is perceived in the form of values;
2. the language used in creating and manipulating a relational database is much higher in level than the languages used in pre-relational database management.

26.16 ■ Summary of Advantages of the Relational Approach

To recapitulate, the relational approach is the leading approach to database management today because of its sound theoretical foundation plus the following 15 major advantages it has over other approaches.

1. powerful approach;
2. adaptability;
3. safety of investment;
4. productivity;
5. round-the-clock operation:
   - dynamic tuning
   - dynamic change of database description;
6. person-to-person communicability;
7. control capability, especially integrity constraints;
8. richer variety of views;
9. flexible authorization;
10. integratability;
11. distributability;
12. optimizability;
13. radically increased opportunities for concurrent action by multiple processing units to achieve better performance;

14. radically increased opportunities for concurrent action by multiple processing units to achieve fault tolerance; **and**

15. ease of conversion to any new approach.

Exercises

26.1 The introduction of relations into the management of large databases has spurred the development of commercial computer systems with large numbers of processing units capable of executing many commands concurrently. Identify two types of concurrency, and give two practical reasons why the multiplicity of processing units means improved service to users.

26.2 A designer of DBMS products wrote a lengthy memorandum in the mid-1970s asserting that data models were a waste of time. He asserted that all that any vendor needed to supply were access methods. Take a position on this and compare:

  ■ the old access methods (SAM, ISAM, PAM, DAM, etc.);

  ■ the old database management systems (IMS, IDMS, ADABAS);

  ■ the relational model.

26.3 Cite four ways in which RM/V2 is adaptable to change.

26.4 Cite four reasons why a relational DBMS yields substantial increases in productivity.

26.5 What capabilities does RM/V2 provide to help the DBA keep the database well-controlled and accurate?

26.6 Cite five reasons for expecting the relational model to be more capable in managing distributed databases than any single-record-at-a-time DBMS.

26.7 Why were pre-relational DBMS products unable to support optimizing as part of the translation from source language into efficient target language?

■ CHAPTER 27 ■

Present Products
and Future
Improvements

The extent of support of the relational model (even Version 1) in present DBMS products is disappointingly low. In Chapter 27 we discuss the major errors of omission and errors of commission in these products. These errors have a negative impact not only on the DBMS products themselves, but also on products developed to run on top of these DBMS products. We will discuss the future of these products on top from two viewpoints:

1. The future if logically based.
2. What is to be expected.

The next subject to be discussed is the relatively new area of exploiting the many opportunities for concurrency offered by the relational approach in order to achieve top performance and fault tolerance. The last topic is the ability to communicate between machines of different architectures, including IBM's SAA (Systems Application Architecture) strategy.

27.1 ■ Features: the Present Situation

Present relational DBMS products and languages, including the language SQL, support at most only half of the relational model, and consequently fail to provide some of the significant benefits of the relational approach. I have encountered among the staff of vendors a curious tendency to continue supporting obsolete methods because they are familiar. To some, familiarity appears more important than technical progress.

441

27.1.1 Errors of Omission

The most important errors of omission in present versions and releases are domains as extended data types, primary keys, and foreign keys. The IBM product DB2 is one of the few that provides partial support for the keys. DB2, however, still fails to require exactly one primary key for each base R-table on a mandatory basis. It does not support the existence in the entire database of two or more primary keys on a single primary domain. These keys, of course, would necessarily occur in distinct R-tables. One consequence of two or more primary keys on a common domain is that a given foreign key may have two or more target primary keys.

Finally, updating a primary key with the same update being applied to all corresponding foreign keys (1) requires the participation of the host language, (2) is far too complicated, and (3) depends on some application programmer knowing on an up-to-the-millisecond basis the state of the foreign keys for a given primary key. If the DBMS is relational, only the system can hold such knowledge.

Additional features that are not supported in present versions of most relational DBMS products include referential integrity (although this is partially supported in DB2 Version 2), user-defined integrity constraints, and user-defined functions.

Because of the inextricably interwoven features of the relational model, each of these omissions negatively impacts numerous benefits of relational DBMS. In particular, since domains are part of many features of the model, none of these features can be fully supported without first supporting domains. To cite just three examples:

1. The DBMS should require that each foreign key be subjected to referential integrity with respect to all of the primary keys with the same domain as the foreign key. To manage this on a highly dynamic basis, the system must know all the keys that draw their values from a common domain, and this knowledge must be current on a millisecond basis.

2. Each pair of comparand columns in **joins, relational division,** and certain **selects** should be based on a common domain. The DBMS should always check this safety feature, unless the user requests the rarely used DOMAIN CHECK OVERRIDE.

3. A DBMS should check whether a requested **union** is meaningful or not. To do this, the system must be able to check the domains of all columns involved in the **union.** The same applies, of course, to **relational difference** and **intersection.**

Finally, view updatability in present products is extremely weak and inadequately investigated. Consequently, logical data independence is hardly supported at all.

27.1.2 Errors of Commission

In present DBMS products, there are not only numerous errors of omission, but also significant errors of commission, only three of which are discussed here. Among the errors of this type, SQL allows duplicate rows within a relation, whether base or derived. (See Chapter 23 for the resulting penalties.) Apparently, many vendors and ANSI have not noticed this and other flaws in SQL.

A second major flaw in SQL is the inadequately investigated nesting of queries within queries. It should always be possible for the DBMS to translate a nested version into a non-nested version. One important reason is that the optimizer can then do an equally good job, no matter which version is presented by the user. Failure in this regard places a major part of the performance burden right back in the user's lap, just as in pre-relational DBMS products—and this is *not* what I intended. Clearly, there must exist a canonical form into which all relational requests can be cast.

A third major flaw lies in the way that present DBMS represent and treat missing database values. In RM/V2, both the representation of the fact that a database value is missing and the treatment of each missing value are independent of the type of value that is missing (see Chapter 8). Several relational DBMS products fail the representation requirement by representing the fact that a numeric value is missing differently from the fact that a character-string value is missing. A few relational DBMS products satisfy the representation requirement, but fail the treatment requirement.

The only feature in SQL related to the treatment question is the clause IS NULL. This feature is clearly inadequate. Moreover, four-valued logic should be provided under the covers in any relational DBMS product; the logic supported by most relational products today is not even three-valued.

27.2 ■ Products Needed on Top of the Relational DBMS

It is clear that the rapidly expanding market for relational DBMS products opens up a substantial market for products that operate on top of these systems. Such products must interface with relational DBMS; they do so by using whatever relational language the relational DBMS supports, usually SQL. Thus, in recent years vendors, especially software vendors, have announced many new products that operate on top of the more popular relational DBMS products.

Examples of such products follow:

dictionaries	forms support
database design aids	screen painting
application development aids	graphics support
expert-system shells	natural-language support

computer-assisted software   re-engineering tools
  engineering (CASE) tools

27.3 ■ Features of the Relational DBMS and Products on Top Assuming that the Future is Logically Based

If a relational DBMS is to provide all of the benefits of the Relational Model, it is important that the errors of omission and commission be fixed first. This is the only way to avoid giving these errors a permanence that results from the substantial investment users make on the assumption that the features of a system will continue to exist.

Then, it will be possible for both vendors and users to proceed on a secure foundation with (1) all the products on top and (2) distributed relational DBMS products.

27.4 ■ Features of Relational DBMS and Products on Top, Assuming that Vendors Continue to Take a Very Short-term View

Vendors, however, are forging ahead with both products on top and distributed relational DBMS products, disregarding errors in present relational DBMS products. All the evidence indicates that they will continue to do so.

An inevitable result is that existing errors will become more difficult to fix, because more products and more users will be affected. Over time, the defects and deficiencies in the present versions of SQL will become totally embedded in relational DBMS products.

It is important to be aware that, *first, the language SQL is not part of the relational model. Second, the defects and deficiencies in SQL correspond closely to the various departures of SQL from the relational model.*

27.5 ■ Performance and Fault Tolerance

Many relational DBMS products offer excellent performance; some can outperform non-relational DBMS products. Improvements in performance are being introduced rapidly as each new version or release comes to market.

Today's leader in general fault tolerance, including DBMS fault tolerance, is Tandem, with its NonStop architecture and NonStop SQL. Moreover, the adaptable performance of the NonStop architecture will prove attractive to many companies. If a user's workload grows, he or she can cope with the growth by adding onto the installed system several closely coupled processing units and additional disk-storage units. The user need not replace the entire installed system with a completely new, higher-performance system.

27.6 ▪ Performance and Fault Tolerance Assuming that the Future Is Logically Based

As more and more companies become international and operate in multiple time zones, there is a greater need for improved fault tolerance. There is also a growing need for very high transaction rates. Therefore, DBMS vendors can be expected to recognize the growing market for increased DBMS performance and fault tolerance. Eventually, they will also recognize that relational DBMS, coupled with architecture that exploits concurrency, can exceed the performance and fault tolerance of non-relational DBMS by a wide margin.

It would be reasonable for each DBMS vendor eventually to exploit both inter-command and intra-command concurrency in its DBMS products (see Section 26.13 for an explanation of these terms).

27.7 ▪ Performance and Fault Tolerance Assuming that the Vendors Continue to Take a Very Short-term View

Why can we expect a logically based future in performance and fault tolerance? Competition will force this, and vendors seem more comfortable in competing in this arena than in any questions related to the services provided by their products.

Relational DBMS vendors will gradually see the advantages of exploiting the concurrency opportunities offered by the relational approach—specifically, performance (usually measured in simple transactions per second), performance adaptability, and fault tolerance.

27.8 ▪ Communication between Machines of Different Architectures

It is not easy to design effective communication links between machines of different architectures. Two major problems are (1) the concise representation of control messages and (2) the representation of large blocks of data. Clearly, standards are needed in both areas. Some work has been done on the first, but it appears that no attention is being given by standards committees to the second.

The relational model offers a partial solution to the representation of large blocks of data—namely, how those blocks should be organized and structured. In addition, however, we need standards dealing with the bit-level representation of the various types of atomic data. I believe that the standards committees should have considered the communication of large blocks of data before trying to standardize on the relational language SQL.

IBM has introduced a much-needed standard for its own systems of different architectures. The IBM term is the *systems application architecture* (abbreviated SAA). A major part of this IBM standard is communication between databases managed on these different architectures. This communication involves relational commands and relational blocks of data, an approach I advocated in 1970 in an internal memorandum addressed to a senior IBM manager in Poughkeepsie, New York.

Communication concerning databases between machines acquired from different vendors involves numerous problems of substantial difficulty. Nevertheless, some software vendors are beginning to work on these problems. If they are successful in solving them, the market for their products will be very substantial. The relational approach to database management appears to be the cornerstone of every current attempt to solve this communication problem.

Exercises

27.1 Present relational DBMS products fail to support numerous features of the relational model. List six such features. For each omitted feature, cite two benefits that users lose as a result.

27.2 Many relational DBMS products violate a very fundamental feature in the relational model (a part of that model from its conception 20 years ago). What is this feature, and what harm does this violation create?

27.3 Why will vendors probably be slow to correct the infidelities to the relational model in their products, but will improve their architectures rapidly to support concurrent processing of data from databases?

27.4 What kinds of products are needed on top of a relational DBMS? In what ways is SQL an inadequate database-oriented language for these products to use in communicating with the DBMS?

■ *CHAPTER 28* ■

Extending the
Relational Model

28.1 ■ Requested Extensions

I am frequently asked how the relational model can be extended to handle
(1) very large quantities of image data, (2) very large quantities of text, and
(3) computer-aided engineering design.

These kinds of data appear to require specialized user-perceived representation and specialized kinds of retrieval capability. In other words, the
representation and retrieval are different from those of the relational model.
At present, I believe that the details of handling these kinds of data should
not be explicitly incorporated in the relational model, because (at present
and in the foreseeable future) only a minority of businesses and other
institutions are concerned with these three kinds of data.

Note, however, that the version support required in computer-aided
engineering is provided to a limited degree by the library check-out and
return features, Features RM-19 and RM-20 (see Chapter 12).

Instead of expanding the relational model to handle every specialized
need, the interfacing features of the relational model should be exploited
so that the usual kinds of data handled by the model can be enriched by
developing specialized invokable functions. It then becomes unnecessary to
introduce new, specialized features into the model. With respect to the
relational language, this means the ability to incorporate data extracted from
image bases, text bases, or design bases into the target part, the condition
part, or both of a relational query. Note also that each image base, text
base, and engineering base is likely to have descriptive data associated with
it that is relational in character.

What are these interfacing features? First, Features RF-4–RF-7 in Chapter 19 support user-defined functions that can be exploited in both the target part and the condition part of a relational request. Second, if necessary, the names of these functions, the names of the built-in functions, the names of their arguments, and the values of the arguments can all be stored as regular data in a relational database. Numerous other features of the model are user-defined. Two of the most important are user-defined integrity constraints and user-defined extended data types.

Incidentally, the term "user" in "user-defined" includes database administrators and even hardware and software vendors. Such vendors are quite likely to offer a package of functions for use with a relational DBMS in accessing image data.

28.2 ■ General Rules in Making Extensions

Now let us discuss the introduction of new features into the relational model. When extending the representation, manipulative, or integrity aspects of either a DBMS or a relational language beyond the capabilities of RM/V2, I strongly recommend that the problem be examined first at the level of abstraction of the relational model. This means treating the relational model, together with any necessary and relevant extensions, as a tool for solving the problem.

This approach is recommended because it is more likely to yield an extension that is minimal in complexity with respect to (1) user comprehension and (2) implementation. It is also more likely to yield an elegant solution that avoids an unwarranted number of exceptions, each of which must be handled by additional pieces of code in the DBMS, and many of which burden users with exceptions that must be remembered. Such exceptions require different cases to be handled in quite different ways.

Suppose that a simple extension to the relational model (e.g., adding a new authorization feature) will suffice. Then, the extension should be made unless in its present form it runs counter to other features of the relational model. If and when this inconsistency is discovered, a revised version should be created that is not inconsistent.

When examining the usefulness of the model together with any necessary extensions for more complicated types of applications, the following 15 questions should be answered:

1. What is a precise statement of the general problem?
2. What mathematical tools are known to be relevant, and, using examples, how can these tools be used?
3. Does any collection of these tools solve the whole problem without the need for programming skill?
4. Is a collection of relations of the relational model an *adequate, simple* representation tool for the problem?

5. Can a combination of relations, relational operators, and functions solve the manipulative aspects of the problem, while avoiding programming concepts such as pointers and iterative loops? Are any new operators needed? If so, which ones?

6. Even though the functions may have to be coded by a programmer in one of the host languages, can the interface between the functions, their arguments, and the relational language protect the user from programming concepts?

7. Is there any need for the names of invokable functions to be part of the database? Can Feature RF-9 in Chapter 19 (repeated next) be helpful?

RF-9 Domains and Columns Containing Names of Functions

One of the domains (extended data types) that is built into the DBMS is that of function names. Such names can be stored in a column (possibly in several columns) of a relation by declaring that the column(s) draw their values from the domain of function names. Both RL and the host programming language support the assemblage of the arguments together with the function name, followed by the invocation of that function to transform the assembled arguments.

8. Is there any need for the names of arguments for these functions to be part of the database? Can Feature RF-10 in Chapter 19 (repeated next) be helpful?

RF-10 Domains and Columns Containing Names of Arguments

One of the domains (extended data types) that is built into the DBMS is that of argument names. Such names can be stored in a column (possibly in several columns) of a relation by declaring that the column(s) draw their values from the domain of argument names. These arguments have values that can be retrieved either from the database or from storage associated with a program expressed in the HL.

9. Which integrity constraints must be supported?

10. Can a combination of relations, relational operators, and functions solve the integrity aspects of the problem, while avoiding programming concepts such as pointers and iterative loops? Are any new operators needed? If so, which ones?

11. From the standpoint of (a) end users, (b) application programmers, and (c) the DBA, what are the advantages and disadvantages of the relational approach?

12. From each of these standpoints, what are both the manipulative and integrity aspects of the problem?

13. How does this approach compare with other approaches (e.g., hierarchic and network-structured approaches)?

14. Does a relational language that includes the extensions to support DBA-defined integrity constraints (described in Chapter 14) require even more extensions? If so, what are these extensions, and can programming concepts such as iterative loops be avoided?

15. From the standpoint of the DBA, what are the advantages and disadvantages of the relational approach to solving the integrity aspects of the problem when compared with other approaches?

With regard to Question 6, it is neither necessary nor desirable to require that any functions that are involved be coded entirely in the relational language. Such a requirement would necessitate extending the relational language to become just another programming language that supports the coding of all computable functions. The functions can be coded in the host language, in the RL, or a combination.

In executing these steps, it is very important to use proper relations (e.g., no duplicate rows), and to avoid the ordering of rows in any relation whenever the ordering represents information that is not also represented by values in the operand or result relations. It is also important to make sure that the extensions comply with the mathematical closure feature, Feature RM-5 (see Chapter 12). If any one of these recommendations is ignored, the extensions will be incompatible with the relational model.

In this chapter, a bill-of-materials (BoM for brevity) type of problem is used from time to time as an example. This problem is of significant scope because it is a problem of wide ranging application. It is also a good example to use as an illustration of how the model can be extended because there is a very large market for a sound solution, and hence the extensions described for this example are very likely to be made.

In 1987, I developed extensions of the relational model to handle the BoM-type of problem, both from the manipulative point of view and from the integrity preservation point of view. In 1988, I prepared a rather complete technical paper on this subject. One of my motivations for this work was that many people were glibly and falsely claiming that the relational model was incapable of solving this kind of problem. Although I have solved the BoM problem within the relational approach, the emphasis here is not on the solution, but instead on the method by which the solution was created. (The solution will be published elsewhere at a more appropriate time.)

In tackling the BoM problem, I bring to bear the powerful tools of the relational model and propose extensions to this model, especially additional manipulative techniques and integrity-preservation operators. It should be noted that the relational model requires that at least three aspects be covered: structural, manipulative, and integrity. These aspects are now discussed in turn.

28.3 ■ Introduction to the Bill-of-Materials Problem

In dealing with the BoM problem and similar problems, it is necessary to establish a precise theoretical foundation, allowing the methods developed to be handled correctly by computers. Therefore, relevant mathematical tools should be selected, such as graphs, matrices, and relations, along with their various operators.

The main purpose of using these tools is to understand the problem and then invent commands to solve it. However, such commands should be usable by people who do not understand either regular programming or the underlying mathematics.

As in Chapter 5, the terms "graph" and "network" are used to denote a set of points (called *nodes*) together with lines (called *edges*) that connect pairs of these points. When every edge of the graph has an associated direction, the graph is called a *directed graph* (or *digraph,* for brevity). It is then possible to speak of the *starting node* of each edge and the *terminating node* of that same edge. In the bill-of-materials problem, it is appropriate to make the following assumptions:

■ No edge has a single node that is both the starting node and the terminating node of that edge.

■ The number of edges that start at any selected node and provide an immediate link to any other single node is either zero or one (no other number is either necessary or acceptable).

A principal aim is to extend the relational model so that it can manage a database that happens to contain (but not necessarily exclusively) the kind of information to which the BoM-type of problem can be applied. Of the tools just mentioned, if software packages for presentation purposes are ignored, users will continue to see relations only. Graphs and matrices are used to explain the relational operators and the integrity constraints, as well as to show that implementation is feasible and potentially very efficient.

28.4 ■ Constructing Examples

To attack the problem and later to explain the solution, it is necessary to devise one or more examples that are simple enough to be readily understood, but sufficiently complicated to contain the most serious problems encountered in finding the solution. Even when, for explanatory reasons, the examples are relatively simple, the methods described should be applicable to very large relations such as would pertain in the industrial world.

In the connectivity part of the BoM type of problem, an example of this type is the product-structure graph shown in Figure 28.1. This acyclic graph represents the structure of several products by showing which parts are components of which. For the sake of simplicity, single letters are used as identifiers of distinct kinds of parts as they are assembled (including final products). An edge of the graph indicates that a certain part is an immediate component of some other part. The nodes labeled "product" represent products that are constructed within the company and then shipped out to customers. The nodes labeled "base" represent parts that are *not* constructed in the company. Base parts are likely to be purchased from outside sources and shipped in.

Whenever product structure for two or more products is represented by a directed graph, each node represents a component and each edge represents the fact that one component is an immediate component of another. That graph is certainly acyclic, but it is very unlikely to be hierarchic. Even in the unlikely case that it begins life as a pure hierarchy, it is unlikely to remain that way. Thus, *a general solution to the bill-of-materials problem should not assume the hierarchic structure.*

I claim to have a solution to the general bill-of-materials problem, one

---

Figure 28.1 **The Structure of Several Products**

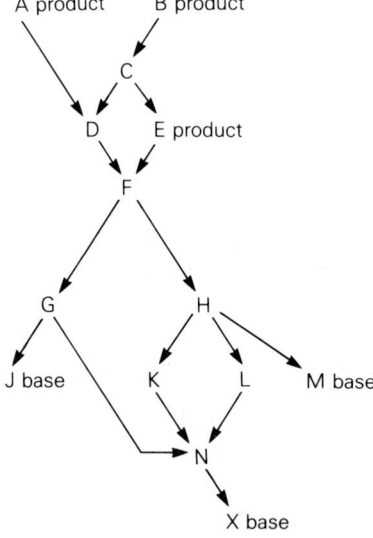

that is very concise, that protects the user from iterative and recursive programming, and that provides pertinent integrity constraints as well as manipulative power. However, the **recursive join** described in Chapter 5 is *not* a complete solution to this problem. (The more complete solution will, of course, be published later.)

28.5 ■ Representation Aspects

The problem should be carefully examined to determine if the relations of the relational model are adequate as a representation tool. If a hierarchy or network is involved in the problem, it is not necessarily true that a hierarchic or network data structure is essential, or even necessarily best.

In the BoM problem, the representation issue is how to represent product structure; such structure is often treated as if it were a pure hierarchy. Many observers draw the immediate conclusion that a DBMS is needed that exposes hierarchically structured data to users. Each hierarchic link would represent the fact that one type of part is an immediate component of another. Recent proposals to ANSI are clear evidence of this.

A hierarchy may be an adequate representation in a few manufacturing environments, but in many—probably most—it is not adequate. In these latter environments, a particular type of part may be an immediate component of several types of parts, not just one. A second, all-too-rapid conclusion is that a DBMS is needed that exposes network-structured data to users.

In fact, in 1970 I presented [Codd 1970] an extremely simple representation of product structure in the relational model by means of the COMPONENT relation:

COMPONENT (SUB_P# SUP_P# Q1 Q2 ... Qn),

where SUB_P# denotes subordinate part number, SUP_P# denotes superior part number, and Q1, Q2, ..., Qn denote immediate properties of each particular subordination.

Note that the columns SUB_P# and SUP_P# draw their values from the same domain, that of part numbers. Incidentally, if (p1, p2, q1, q2, ..., qn) is a row of the COMPONENT relation, then part p1 is an *immediate* component of part p2. The fact that part p is a non-immediate component of a part p7 (say) is not directly represented in the COMPONENT relation. A fact of this type can be easily derived by the **recursive join** operator (see Feature RZ-40 in Chapter 5 and [Codd 1979]).

The following relational representation of product structure represents the structure illustrated in Figure 28.1. To save space, the COMPONENT relation is abbreviated AG (for acyclic graph), the relation is listed "on its side," and the immediate properties of each edge are represented by a single lowercase letter.

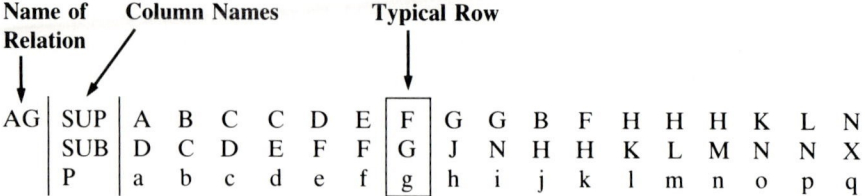

Name of Relation   **Column Names**   **Typical Row**

AG	SUP	A	B	C	C	D	E	F	G	G	B	F	H	H	H	K	L	N
	SUB	D	C	D	E	F	F	G	J	N	H	H	K	L	M	N	N	X
	P	a	b	c	d	e	f	g	h	i	j	k	l	m	n	o	p	q

In a computer-oriented sense, this kind of representation in a relation is adequate for all kinds of networks, whether they happen to be pure hierarchies, acyclic nets, or nets in which cycles may occur. It is also a very simple representation for a computer to manage. For the product-structure network, the acyclic net is adequately general.

In the preceding paragraph, I use the term "computer-oriented sense" because the relational representation is probably not the best for use by human beings, for whom graphs drawn as pictures appear to be more comprehensible and suitable. However, that subject can be discussed separately, and handled by separate code, when presenting data to people in a form more consumable by people (e.g., the formatting of reports)—it has very little relevance to mechanizing the management of data.

28.6 ■ Manipulative Aspects

It was clear at least 10 years ago [Codd 1979] that extensions to the relational model would be required to handle the manipulative and integrity aspects of the BoM application. This application involves manipulating relations that represent acyclic directed graphs. Such manipulations usually involve *transitive closure*. In the context of relations, transitive closure is expressed in the form of **recursive join.** Feature RZ-40 in Chapter 5 is a simple version of this type of **join.**

A slightly more complicated version of **recursive join** is needed for the BoM application. This is because this application has a connectivity aspect that deals with the path finding, and a computational aspect that deals with machine times, personnel times, and costs of assembling each batch of superior parts from a batch of subordinate parts. These two aspects should be handled together in as few passes as possible over the COMPONENT relation and other relations.

Whatever new operators are introduced, they should have relations as both their operands and their results, in compliance with the operational closure feature, Feature RM-5 (see Chapter 12). The attempt by the Oracle Corporation to extend SQL to handle the BoM application is quite inadequate in that the total effort is represented by the CONNECT command. This command not only violates the closure feature, RM-5, but also fails to handle many aspects of the BoM problem, including the integrity aspects. Finally, in early releases the CONNECT command failed to work on views.

28.7 ■ Integrity Checks

Normally, it is necessary to establish the kinds of integrity constraints that are pertinent to the problem at hand. If these integrity constraints cannot be expressed in terms of those types already supported in RM/V2, it becomes necessary to invent extensions of RL and algorithms to support these extensions under the covers of the DBMS.

In the case of the BoM example, RL extensions are needed, along with sample algorithms for supporting these extensions. When a database contains one or more relations, each of which happens to represent an acyclic graph, certain types of integrity checking are needed. Three of these types are discussed here: maintaining the acyclic constraint, checking for isolated subgraphs, and, when applicable, checking hierarchic structure. However, the discussion does not include the RM/V2 extensions or sample algorithms.

28.7.1 Checking for Unintended Cycles

If, as a result of insertions or modifications, a relation that represents an acyclic graph changes in such a way as to reflect a cycle in the graph, this indicates that one part p is a component (not necessarily immediate) of another q, and that q is at the same time a component (not necessarily immediate) of p. This condition is normally deemed unacceptable.

Hence, an overall method of checking the whole relation is needed to see whether it is acyclic. Furthermore, it is desirable to have a more localized method of establishing incrementally that any insertion into or modification of an acyclic relation does not introduce a cycle. In this way, the DBMS can efficiently ensure that a graph that is initially acyclic remains acyclic.

28.7.2 Isolated Subgraphs

Let us take the following definition: a subgraph of a graph G is any collection of edges all of which occur in the graph G. In the relational representation of graph G, each and every subset of that relation represents a subgraph of G.

The two extremes are the largest subgraph (i.e., G itself) and the smallest subgraph (i.e., the empty graph with no edges). If g and G are graphs, then the complement of g in G is the set of edges in G but not in g; it is denoted G - g. Note that G - g is a subgraph of G.

An isolated subgraph of G is any subgraph g of G that has no edges connecting it to the complement of g in G, namely, G - g. Therefore, in this case, the graphs g and G - g have no nodes in common. Clearly, an isolated subgraph may itself contain an isolated subgraph. Hence, one may sensibly speak of decomposing any given graph into a collection of minimal isolated subgraphs, each of which has no isolated subgraph itself. Two kinds of programs are needed: one intended merely to detect whether any subgraph of G is isolated, and a second that identifies all the isolated subgraphs of G.

Actually, when a graph G has an isolated subgraph g, then G has at least two isolated subgraphs: g and its complement with respect to G. In practice, from a purely logical standpoint, it may not be necessary to separate the isolated subgraphs by casting them into distinct relations. However, such separation may yield a noticeable performance advantage if large amounts of data are involved.

28.7.3 Strict Hierarchy

A *strict hierarchy* is not only free from cycles, but also has the property that each node has exactly one parent, except for the topmost node which has no parent at all. Occasionally, it may be necessary to check whether the strict hierarchic structure has been maintained.

28.8 ■ Computational Aspects

A general requirement is that a user be able to supply some of the arguments, that the database supplies the others, and that the DBMS invokes the appropriate DBA-defined functions. It should be possible to execute this activity by the user, together with the development of function definitions by the DBA, without programming tricks such as loops. This can be achieved within relational operators that scan graphs, whether these graphs are acyclic or not.

The main requirement in the BoM application is to compute the cost, the time, or both for manufacturing one quantum of the kind of part at the terminating node, where a quantum is the smallest number of such parts built in a single run. The result should be a relation that indicates not only the previously cited cost, time, or both, but also the contribution to these amounts from each of the edges that must be traversed in manufacturing the pertinent part at node k. Then, the cost or time for N quanta can be computed by a simple final computation.

Since each edge in the product structure graph is represented by a single row in the COMPONENT relation, it is easy to arrange for appropriate functions and arguments to be available for the edge-based computations by including as columns in this relation the names of pertinent functions, together with the names and/or values of arguments for these functions. This represents an exploitation of Features RF-9 and RF-10 (re-introduced in Section 28.2).

It may also be necessary to exploit node-based functions and their arguments. This can be arranged similarly by including as columns in a PART relation the names of pertinent functions, together with the names and/or values of arguments for these functions. The PART relation has part number P# as its primary key. This column contains at least all of the distinct part numbers that occur in the COMPONENT relation.

28.9 ■ Concluding Remarks

Once again, there has been *no* attempt in this chapter to give a full account of the extensions of the relational model planned for the bill-of-materials application. Instead, the focus was on the general task of making extensions, using the BoM as an example.

To make sensible and acceptable extensions of the relational model, it is necessary to be thoroughly familiar with the model. It is also necessary to make a thorough mathematical investigation of the problem that these extensions are designed to solve. One purpose of such an investigation is to determine whether any extensions are needed at all. Thus, it should be clear that, if a brilliant idea concerning an extension suddenly comes to mind, there remains a substantial piece of work before an extension should be proposed.

Exercises

28.1 What are the 15 questions that should be answered when extending the relational model to handle a particular type of problem?

28.2 Discuss whether conserving the mathematical closure of the relational operators is (1) crucial, (2) fairly important, or (3) of no concern whatsoever.

28.3 It has been claimed that the bill-of-materials problem involves the processing of purely hierarchic data, and that therefore a hierarchic DBMS (such as IBM's IMS) is ideally suited to the problem. Take a position on this and defend it.

28.4 In what specific way does the CONNECT command of the Oracle Corporation fail to satisfy the operational closure feature, Feature RM-5? In what additional respect is the Oracle approach to solving the bill-of-materials problem inadequate?

28.5 Supply two reasons why mathematical tools other than relations should be explored whenever a significant extension of the relational model is being contemplated.

CHAPTER 29

Fundamental Laws
of Database Management

This chapter could be regarded as summarizing in a new framework what has been presented earlier. Actually, however, it is an attempt to generalize upon the relational approach by stating concisely some 20 principles with which *any* new approach to database management should comply. My development of these principles was motivated by various object-oriented approaches to database management.

What impressed me the most in these proposals was the clear lack of knowlege of the relational model on the part of their authors. In any attempt to invent an approach that is superior to the relational model, the first step must be to learn about that model. Moreover, one should not assume that the relational DBMS products of today or the corresponding manuals fairly represent the model. As a corollary, it is highly unlikely that anyone who has learned to use a relational DBMS solely from the vendor's manual really knows how to use it.

The fundamental laws outlined in this chapter are principles to which the relational model adheres. Any new approach to database management intended to compete with the relational model should adhere to these principles. It appears unlikely that any competitor will seriously challenge the dominant position of the relational model today, because the model is based on first-order predicate logic. Predicate logic took 2,000 years to develop, beginning with the ancient Greeks who discovered that the subject of logic could be intelligently discussed separately from the subject to which it might be applied, a major step in applying levels of abstraction.

This chapter attempts to discourage the outrageous claims that have been made regarding "semantic data models." It is also an attempt to encourage researchers to direct their attention to the overall problem of database management, instead of considering only one small part, such as data structures.

The fundamental laws are as follows:

1. object identification;
2. objects identified in one way;
3. unrelated portions of a database;
4. community issues;
5. three levels of concepts;
6. same logical level of abstraction for all users;
7. self-contained logical level of abstraction;
8. sharp separation;
9. no iterative or recursive loops;
10. parts of the database inter-related by value-comparing;
11. dynamic approach;
12. extent to which data should be typed;
13. creating and dropping performance-oriented structures;
14. adjustments in the content of performance-oriented structures;
15. re-executable commands;
16. prohibition of cursors *within the database;*
17. protection against integrity loss;
18. recovery of integrity;
19. re-distribution of data without damaging application programs;
20. semantic distinctiveness.

Now, let us consider each of these laws in turn.

1. **Object identification**

   A database models a micro-world. Each object about which information is stored in the database must be uniquely identified, and thereby distinguished from every other object. The DBMS must enforce this law.

The unique identifier in the relational model is the combination of the relation name and the primary-key value.

2. **Objects identified in one way**

   Both programming and non-programming users perceive all objects to be identified in exactly one way, whether these objects are abstract or concrete and whether they are so-called entities or relationships.

So far, no one has come forward with definitions for the concepts in the "whether" clauses that are reasonable, objective, precise, non-overlapping, and unambiguous. It is extremely doubtful that the task is worthwhile pursuing. In the relational model, such distinctions are avoided altogether.

3. **Unrelated portions of the database**

   If the database can be theoretically split into two or more mutually unrelated parts without loss of information, whether stored or derived, there exists a simple and general algorithm, independent of access paths, to make this split.

The database-splitting algorithm that is part of the relational model was described in Chapter 3. It is heavily based on the domain concept.

4. **Community issues**

   All database issues of concern to the community of users (except, for the time being, performance goals and advice) should be:

   a. Removed from application programs, if incorporated therein;

   b. openly and explicitly declared in the catalog or in some part of the database to which all suitably authorized users have access; **and**

   c. managed by the DBMS. Such management includes enforcement in the case of integrity constraints and authorization.

Much of the relational model is based on Fundamental Law 4. Such support is clearly visible in the techniques used for the retention of database integrity and in the authorization mechanism.

5. **Three levels of concepts**

   Three levels of concepts must be distinguished: (1) psychological (the user's level), (2) logical and semantic (the logical level), and (3) storage-oriented and access-method (the physical level).

   A data model should address the requirements of the logical level first and foremost. Any attempt to define Level 1 or Level 3 must be accompanied by transformations of concepts, structure, data, and actions upon data from Level 2 to and from whatever level is added to Level 2. For a single logical Level 2, there may be many instances of psychological Level 1 and many instances of physical Level 3. Levels 1 and 2 do not represent different levels of abstraction.

   The relational model specifies the properties required at the logical level (Level 2), and in such a way as to leave to the DBMS vendors how to treat the physical level (Level 3) and the psychological level (Level 1). This model defines the boundaries between the three levels very sharply; and it may be the only existing approach that does this.

6. **Same logical level of abstraction for all users**

   The level of abstraction supported by the DBMS for end users must be the same as that supported for application programmers.

This law runs counter to the practices of the past, when end users were offered query products that were defined separately and packaged separately from the DBMS. The designers of these query products tried to offer end users a higher level of abstraction than the DBMS offered to application programmers.

7. **Self-contained logical level of abstraction**

   The logical level must be sufficiently complete that there is no need to proceed to a lower level of abstraction to explain how a command at the logical level works.

An example of an unsuccessful departure from this law was a DBMS product that required those users with the responsibility of defining views to know how the information was represented at a lower level of abstraction. In effect, the product limited the defining of views to the DBA staff. While these people should have the specialized skills for this job, they would rapidly become overloaded with work that users should be able to do for themselves.

8. **Sharp separation**

   In the services offered by the DBMS, there must be a sharp separation between aspects of Type 1 (the logical and semantic aspects), and those of Type 2 (the storage-representation and performance aspects, including access methods).

It is this sharp separation that makes the relational model a standard that vendors can live with, while not restricting their freedom and inventiveness to design competitive products. This separation is also of great value to users since it protects their investment in training and in the development of application programs.

9. **No iterative or recursive loops**

   In order to extract any information whatsoever in the database, neither an application programmer nor a non-programming user needs to develop any iterative or recursive loops.

This law significantly reduces the occurrences of bugs in programs, and sharply improves the productivity of application programmers and end users. Great care has been taken to uphold this law in developing the relational model, more than in any other approach.

10. **Parts of the database inter-related by value comparing**

   All inter-relating is achieved by means of comparisons of values, whether these values identify objects in the real world or indicate properties of those objects. A pair of values may be *meaningfully compared* if and only if these values are of the same extended data type. Inter-relating parts of the database is *not* achieved by means of pointers visible to users.

It is safe to assume that all kinds of users understand the act of comparing values, but that relatively few understand the complexities of pointers. The relational model is based on this fundamental principle. Note also that the manipulation of pointers is more bug-prone than is the act of comparing values, even if the user happens to understand the complexities of pointers.

11. **Dynamic approach**

Performance-oriented structures can be created and dropped dynamically, which means without bringing traffic on the database to a halt. Automatic locking by the DBMS permits such activities without damage to the information content of the database and without impairing any transactions.

With pre-relational DBMS products, there was a significant dependence on utilities—programs that changed the performance-oriented structures and access methods, but that could be executed in the off-line mode only. In other words, execution of any one of these utilities required that the database traffic be brought to a complete halt. In contrast, the relational approach, which is highly dynamic, can support the kind of concurrency architecture designed to cope with non-stop traffic on the database and provide various degrees of fault tolerance.

12. **Extent to which data should be typed**

The types of data seen by users should be strict enough to capture some of the meaning of the data, but not so strict as to make the initially planned uses and applications the only viable ones.

When a new database is created or when new kinds of information are incorporated into an already existing database, the creator is almost always unable to foresee all the uses to which the new kinds of data will be applied. While suited to the development of programs, the object-oriented approach probably imposes too many restrictions on the use of data through its typing of data.

13. **Creating and dropping performance-oriented structures**

Performance-oriented structures, such as indexes, must be capable of being created and dropped by either the DBA or the DBMS without adversely affecting the semantic information, all of which should be in the database or in the catalog.

At some time in the future, probably early in the next century, even the DBA will be eliminated from this law as an acceptable agent for creating and dropping performance-oriented structures. DBMS vendors will have invented ways in which performance-oriented structures can be automatically adjusted to support changes in the database traffic, changes that last for a reasonable time.

14. Adjustments in the content of performance-oriented structures

When data is inserted into a database, updated, or deleted from a database by a user, it must not be necessary for that user or any other user to make corresponding changes in the information content of performance-oriented structures. It is the responsibility of the DBMS to make these adjustments dynamically.

Most existing index-based relational DBMS products comply with this law by adjusting the content of their indexes automatically whenever an **insert, update,** or **delete** occurs on the data in the database.

15. Re-executable commands

Every command at the logical level of abstraction must be re- executable and yield exactly the same results, provided the data operated upon by the command remains unchanged in information content (i.e., unchanged at the logical level). This means that results must be independent of the data organization and access methods that are in effect at lower levels of abstraction.

Most of the relational operators comply with this law. None of them is affected in its results by the data organization and access methods that are in effect at the time of execution.

16. Prohibition of cursors within the database

At the logical and psychological levels, users are not required to manipulate cursors that traverse data *within the database*. However, cursors that traverse data extracted from the database are acceptable as a means of providing an interface to single-record-at-a-time host languages.

Cursors within the database, a nightmare in the CODASYL approach to database management, are the source of severe bugs that are very hard to track down. In the debate in 1974 [Codd 1974], I used an example developed by members of the CODASYL DBTG committee that was intended by them to show off their approach. I demonstrated how the manipulative activity in this example could be reduced from eight pages of DBTG and COBOL code to just one statement in a relational language. It is interesting to note that, five years later, someone discovered that there were two bugs in the CODASYL program that were directly related to cursor manipulation.

Cursors that traverse data extracted from a relational database are much easier to manage correctly. Such cursors are supported in several DBMS products to enable single-record-at-a-time host languages such as FORTRAN, COBOL, and PL/1 to interface with relational DBMS. However, these cursors are troublesome in the management of distributed databases. The file is a more promising package for a relational DBMS to use in delivering data to programs written in these languages.

17. **Protection against integrity loss**

   With the help of the DBA, the DBMS must provide strong protection against loss of data integrity.

18. **Recovery of integrity**

   The support provided for *correction* of any integrity loss actually experienced must include an audit log that is readily transformable into a database of the same kind as that handled by the pertinent approach.

Laws 17 and 18 reflect the fact that it is easier to prevent loss of database integrity than to correct such loss. Even with an audit log, trying to correct loss of integrity is often a painful task. Without such a log, it is an impossible task in most cases. Much of the emphasis in the relational model is on prevention of such loss.

19. **Re-distribution of data without damaging application programs**

   In a DBMS capable of managing distributed data, it should be possible to re-distribute the data in a highly flexible manner without affecting the logical correctness of any application programs.

The relational model appears to be the only approach known today that is capable of supporting this law. For details, see Chapters 24 and 25.

20. **Semantic distinctiveness**

   Semantically distinct observations, whether derived or not, must be represented distinctly to the users. In any database, all of the data redundancy *that is made visible to the users* must be both introducible and removable by those users who are authorized to do so, without affecting the logical correctness of any application programs and the training of interactive users.

In all base and derived relations of the relational model, duplicate rows are prohibited. Note that data may superficially appear to be redundant, but still not be redundant. The crucial question is: If the data were removed, would information be lost?

   By now, the reader should be in a good position to counter the frequently held opinion that the relational model is nothing more than its structures, and that these structures are merely tables. How could the single concept of tables comply with all 20 of the principles just outlined? A thorough reading of the preceding 28 chapters should enable the reader to determine exactly how the relational model adheres to each and every one of these laws.

Exercises

29.1 Taking each of the 20 fundamental laws in turn, list the features of RM/V2 that ensure compliance with the law.

29.2 Choose any approach to database management other than the relational model. Repeat the same 20 exercises for the approach selected. Then compare this approach with the relational model.

CHAPTER 30

Claimed Alternatives
to the Relational Model

After the publication of my papers on Version 1 of the relational model in the period 1969–1973, numerous articles began to appear proposing new approaches to database management. Frequently, the articles began with the false claim that the relational model contains no features for representing the meaning of the data.

Often these new approaches were no more than new kinds of data structure or data typing—often new to the database management field only. In other words, the authors overlooked the need to specify query and manipulative operators, integrity constraints, authorization, commands for the DBA, a counterpart to the catalog, distributed database management, user-defined data types, and user-defined functions. That is why I call each of them an "approach," and avoid using the term "data model."

Occasionally, mistakes of the past are revisited, apparently by authors who have no knowledge of the DBMS products of the past. Examples of such mistakes are repeating groups and representing information in many distinct ways. These mistakes add complexity but not generality.

In this chapter, only five kinds of approaches are discussed:

1. the universal relation approach (UR);
2. the binary relation approach (BR);
3. the entity-relationship approaches (ER);
4. the semantic data approaches (SD);
5. the object-oriented approaches (OO).

The main objective of this chapter is to improve understanding of the relational model, and especially to indicate why the relational model is the way it is. A lesser objective is to review these approaches as replacements for or alternatives to the relational model. The purpose is not to dismiss all the ideas contained in these approaches. Each one, except ER, contains some good ideas, some of which are quite eligible to be attached to the relational model.

My comments about UR and BR tend to be quite precise because these approaches are precisely defined. On the other hand, my comments about ER, SD, and OO tend to be quite imprecise because at present these approaches are imprecisely defined with respect to database management.

30.1 ■ The Universal Relation and Binary Relations

These two approaches to database design and management represent opposite extremes. UR takes all the relations in a regular relational database and glues them together by means of one operator (e.g., **natural join** based on primary and foreign keys) to form a single relation of very high degree that is claimed to contain all the information in the given database. BR splits every relation into a collection of binary relations (i.e., relations of degree two). Thus, the universal relation can be regarded as a "macro" approach; the collection of binary relations, as a "micro" approach.

Both approaches are examined with the principal aim of shedding more light on why the relational model is based on a middle-of-the-road approach—namely, a collection of relations of assorted degrees. This means that any base or derived relation of the relational model can be of *any* degree n, where n is a strictly positive integer ($n > 0$).

In contrast to the relational model, UR requires just one relation of a very large degree (the degree must be large enough to accommodate all of the information in the database). BR requires relations, each of which is of degree one or two only.

As is apparent from the referenced papers (and perhaps this chapter), it is questionable whether either UR or BR is really comprehensive enough in tackling the total problem of database management to be treated as a data model. In the case of UR, it is also questionable whether the approach deserves the label "universal."

In what follows, I point out claims that are clearly false. In doing so, my aim is not to discourage university researchers from pursuing their lines of investigation, but rather to clarify these approaches and their relationship to the relational model.

30.2 ■ Why the Universal Relation Will Not Replace the Relational Model

The "universal relation" is just one of the very many views supported by the relational model. For detailed information, see [Maier, Ullman, and

Vardi 1984]. The assertion has been made [Vardi 1988]—and the very title
of [Maier, Ullman, and Vardi 1984] makes this same claim—that the universal relation can replace the entire relational model. This assertion is quite
preposterous. I now present eight solid reasons for stating this.

In [Vardi 1988], the author complains about the need for users to
"navigate" through the logical parts of a relational database, and proposes
the Stanford University "universal relation" as a means of protecting users
from this burden. The "universal relation" fails completely to provide an
alternative to the relational model. I am not arguing, however, that Stanford
University should never have undertaken research into the "universal relation"; there may be some useful by-products of this research. Nevertheless,
I do think that the term "universal" is a complete misnomer—the reason
why it is enclosed in quotation marks in this chapter.

In [Codd 1971d], I proved that collectively the algebraic operators of
the relational model are as powerful as first-order predicate logic in retrieving
information from a relational database. Indeed, if the several relations in a
relational database are transformed into a single relation, the resulting
relation, together with operators that can interrogate a single relation only,
is not as powerful as the relational model. In the following subsections, eight
reasons are presented for asserting that UR will not replace the relational
model.

30.2.1 The Operators

First, let us look at an ordinary relational database containing several
relations, and consider how it might be transformed into a single "universal
relation." Vardi and others suggest the use of either **natural join** or **equi-
join** (it does not matter which is chosen) as the "connecting function." This
function is presumably key-based—in other words, it joins by comparing a
primary key with a foreign key. Immediately, we are struck with the notion
that there are 10 distinct kinds of **theta-joins** based on the following 10
comparators:

1. EQUAL TO
2. NOT EQUAL TO
3. LESS THAN
4. LESS THAN OR EQUAL TO
5. GREATER THAN
6. GREATER THAN OR EQUAL TO
7. GREATEST LESS THAN
8. GREATEST LESS THAN OR EQUAL TO
9. LEAST GREATER THAN
10. LEAST GREATER THAN OR EQUAL TO

In constructing the "universal relation" using **equi-join,** what happened to the nine other kinds of **theta-joins?** Moreover, what happened to **relational division,** the algebraic counterpart of the universal quantifier?

30.2.2 Joins Based on Keys

The construction of a "universal relation" from a given relational database involves the repeated application of either **natural join** or **equi-join** based on the keys of the relational model. The "universal relation" is based on the false assumption that two classes of entities (e.g., suppliers and types of parts) have only one relationship between them. This assumption is proved false by citing just one counter-example: each supplier can be related to each type of part by its capability of supplying that part; each supplier can also be related to each type of part by its possibly several, actual deliveries of that part in response to a sequence of orders for the part.

30.2.3 Joins Based on Non-keys

If only key-based joins are used in constructing the "universal relation," then it is possible that hundreds of **joins** that are not based on keys have been overlooked. An example would be the query: "Find the employees who reside in a city in which the company owns one or more warehouses." Assume that this query is applied to a frequently encountered database in which city is not a primary key because of the company's lack of interest in cities as objects whose properties need to be recorded. In the relational model, this query then involves an **equi-join** based on a non-key. I fail to see how a user would make this request against a "universal relation" without applying **equi-join** as an operator to two parts of the allegedly "universal relation."

Vardi claims the "universal relation" reduces the burden on users of choosing which operators to apply, and choosing the relations and attributes to which these operators should be applied. This claim may be true when only one operator is involved and it happens to match the one used in constructing the "universal relation." However, when there may be several operators involved in a single query and at least one of them does not match the construction operator, the user is faced with significantly more complexity than with the relational model.

30.2.4 Cyclic Key States

It is not at all clear how the "universal relation" copes with what are often called *cyclic key states.* Suppose that a relation R1 has a primary key PK1, while a relation R2 has a foreign key FK1 drawing its values from the same domain as PK1. Suppose also that the primary key of R2 is PK2, and that R1 contains a foreign key FK2 drawing its values from the same domain as

PK2. Then, R1 and R2 participate in a cyclic key state, in which the cycle is of size two.

An example may clarify this situation. Suppose that we are using the relational model and we have the following two relations:

EMP (E# . . . DEPT# . . .),

with primary key E#, and

DEPT (DEPT# . . . MGR# . . .),

with primary key DEPT#. EMP identifies and describes employees, E# is the employee serial number, DEPT# is the department identifier, DEPT identifies and describes departments, and MGR# is the employee serial number of the department manager.

Suppose that (1) DEPT# in EMP is a foreign key with respect to the primary key DEPT# of the DEPT relation, and that (2) MGR# in DEPT is a foreign key with respect to the primary key E# of the EMP relation. Then, these two relations have a two-step cyclic key state.

Clearly, such cycles can be of size greater than two. Cycles are not only possible, they occur rather frequently. Any solution to this problem in the context of the "universal relation," which requires data to be repeated in different parts of such a relation, is unacceptable as a confusing and unnecessary form of redundancy.

30.2.5 Insertion, Deletion, and Updating

As a vehicle for inserting information, deleting, and updating, the "universal relation" is replete with problems. It is a relation that is not even in third normal form, let alone fifth. One can therefore expect to encounter update anomalies galore [Codd 1971b]. If the connecting function used in constructing the "universal relation" were other than a key-based **join,** there would be the serious possibility that it could not be updated at all.

30.2.6 Coping with Change

The ability of a data model to cope with change must be taken into account. Nothing is as certain as change in requirements as time goes on. A particular relation in the relational model may become obsolete through lack of use or for other reasons (perhaps it is going to be replaced by two or more new relations with different descriptions).

The relation may then be simply dropped, and all remaining users of that relation warned of the drop. Unless that relation happens to be a boundary member of the "universal relation"—which is improbable—the data will have to be extracted from some non-boundary position of the "universal relation" and it will be necessary to reconstruct this relation completely. A similar remark applies to the counterpart in the "universal relation" of a newly introduced relation in the relational model. In either case, does this reorganization impair the application programs?

30.2.7 No Comprehensive Data Model

No data model has been published for the UR approach. To be comprehensive, such a data model must support all of the well-known requirements of database management. Until this occurs, companies intending to acquire a DBMS product should be concerned about the risk of investing in the "universal relational" approach.

As an aside, Vardi's use of the term "access path" is a complete departure from the usual use of this term. Usually, it can be assumed that, when two or more alternative access paths can be used to extract certain data from a database, the only difference between those access paths is performance. There is no semantic distinction between the paths. In a relational DBMS, it is the optimizer that selects access paths with the objective of good performance. Vardi's "access paths" are quite different because distinct paths yield distinct results (all of the paths to which he refers are semantically distinct).

30.2.8 UR Not Essential for Natural Language

The allegation in [Vardi 1988, page 85] that a "universal relation" is essential as a natural-language interface is quite incorrect. Curiously, advocates of the binary relational approach make the same claim. Certainly, at least one of the claims must be incorrect. It is my belief that both are incorrect.

During the period 1974–1977, I led the development of a prototype translator from English to a relational language, and from the relational language back into precise English. This two-way translator was accompanied by a third component that supported clarification dialogue. Incidentally, I believe that it is very risky to use a natural-language package with any kind of database unless the package supports (1) clarification dialogue, and (2) before database access, a routine check by the system that it understands the user's request by telling the user in the same natural language precisely its interpretation of the user's request.

All three components were based on the relational model and on predicate logic. The prototype, called Rendezvous [Codd 1978], was successfully tested in 1977 against 30 subjects with wide variations in their knowledge of computers and of English. Some subjects tried as hard as they could to beat the system, but failed. This evidence suggests that the natural-language claims of both the UR and the BR approaches are false.

30.2.9 Concluding Remarks Regarding UR

In conclusion, I would not rule out the "universal relation" as one of the many views that should be supported in a relational DBMS, but I consider it incapable of replacing the relational model. I also believe that for many purposes it is too complicated as a relational view, and it is not likely to be popular even in that restricted role. The question remains: What does the 'universal relation' accomplish that simpler views in the relational model do not?

30.3 ■ Why the Binary Relation Approach Will Not Replace the Relational Model

In Chapter 1, a false claim found in many mathematical textbooks was briefly discussed—namely, the assertion that every problem expressed in terms of relations of degree higher than two can be reduced to an equivalent problem in which the relations are of degree either one or two. This false idea has appealed to several people doing research in database management. Why not perceive and manipulate the information in the database as a collection of unary and binary relations?

I believe that this approach was first proposed in the IBM Hursley Laboratory in England; a prototype [Titman 1974] was built there about 1973. The approach recently re-surfaced at the University of Maryland [Mark 1988]. One attractive feature is that it is easy to get a prototype into operational state because relatively few operators must be implemented, and these few are quite simple to implement.

Users are faced with serious problems, however, if the approach is applied to the kind of large-scale databases encountered in the commercial and industrial world. If the binary relations are perceived as tables, they are two-column tables.

In what follows, nine reasons are discussed for the assertion that the binary-relation approach cannot replace the relational model. For this purpose, it is useful to have two examples, each representing just a portion of a database.

Consider a simple example: if an insurance-policy relation in the relational model has a single-column primary key (usually the policy number), together with 100 columns each containing a simple immediate property of the policy, then in the binary relationship approach there will be 100 tables each with two columns. Each table carries the policy number to identify the policy, together with just one simple immediate property.

Now consider a more complicated example: in a suppliers and parts database, suppose that there is a capability relation indicating in each row that a specified supplier can supply a specified quantum of a specified kind of part within a specified time at a specified cost. Note that the primary key of this relation is composite. It consists of the combination of supplier serial number and part serial number.

To represent this *n*-ary relation in terms of binary relations, the simple approach adopted in the insurance-policy case (i.e., repetition of the primary key along with each of the simple immediate properties) is no longer viable because each of those relations would be ternary (i.e., of degree three). One solution, perhaps the simplest, is to introduce an extra (artificial) single-column primary key in the *n*-ary version, and then convert that relation into a collection of binary relations, just as in the insurance case. Unfortunately the users will have to know about this artificial primary key in order to manipulate these binary relations properly.

30.3.1 Normalization Cannot Be Forgotten

In [Mark 1988], the author claims,

> "The model [he is referring to the BR approach] seems to be easy for non-technical people because it avoids normalization and because schemata defined in terms of the model can be read almost like natural language."

In database design, normalization can certainly be relegated to an analytical or checking stage, but it cannot be avoided altogether if surprising anomalies in insertions, updates, and deletions are to be avoided when use of the database begins. **Join** dependencies, difficult to discover even in the regular relational model, are even more difficult to discover in BR.

Corresponding to any given *n*-ary relational version of a database, there is clearly a binary relational counterpart. Consider two *n*-ary versions of a common conceptual database, one thoroughly normalized (say B1), and the other incompletely normalized (say B2). Each of these databases has a binary relational counterpart (say b1 and b2, respectively).

Unfortunately, in the binary relational form it is extremely difficult to see that b2 is effectively incompletely normalized, and that under certain conditions insert, update, and delete anomalies will occur. Thus, the claim that "normalization of *n*-ary relations can be forgotten" [Mark 1988] is false. Moreover, it is harder to cope with this aspect if the database designer is constrained to think in terms of binary relations only.

30.3.2 Much Decomposition upon Input

When information about an insurance policy is entered into the insurance database, a good proportion is entered in a single operation. Otherwise, questions such as, "To whom does this policy belong?," "Does the policy-holder satisfy our minimum requirements for this kind of policy?," and

"How frequently does the policyholder have to be billed?" could arise and be unanswerable.

If users are to perceive this policy information as part of a collection of binary relations, it is likely that the DBMS, either once upon entry or else many times, whenever the information is manipulated, must decompose the policy information into small pieces to fit into the large collection of binary relations. Even the policyholder's home address and work address each must be decomposed into at least six separate items: (1) apartment or suite number within a building, (2) building number within a street, (3) street name within a city, (4) city name within a state, (5) name of state, and (6) zip code. Presumably this task of decomposition is a burden on the DBMS, not the user. However, no matter where the burden falls such decomposition is completely unnecessary.

An important part of the difficulties encountered with the BR approach is the fact that composite domains, composite columns, composite primary keys, and composite foreign keys all must be abandoned (see Section 30.3.5). From the user's point of view, the units of information that are atomic with respect to a DBMS based on the BR approach are frequently too small to support concise and clear thinking.

30.3.3 Extra Storage Space and Channel Time

DBMS prototypes of the BR type tend to store the data in the form of a two-column table for each binary relation. The net result is that the storage space consumed for a BR database is about double what would be required for a regular relational database.

The extra bits have to be transmitted to and from the processing units across channels. Therefore, the channel load will be significantly greater than that experienced if the structure and operators of the relational model were used.

30.3.4 Much Recomposition upon Output

For obvious reasons, business and government reports are rarely, if ever, presented as a collection of two-column tables. Thus, the development of reports and replies to queries by any DBMS based on the binary relational approach entails putting together many items that are perceived by users as separately tabulated items residing in tables that have just two columns. This recomposition entails either many key-based **natural joins** of carefully selected binary relations, or else an extended version of **natural join** that collects all the desired properties into a single *n*-ary relation [Codd 1979].

Considering together the reasons in Sections 30.3.2 and 30.3.3, one wonders what the purpose of decomposition was, if it is followed later by as many recompositions as there are reports to be generated and queries for which replies are needed.

30.3.5 Composite Domains, Composite Columns, and Composite Keys Abandoned

The concepts of composite domains, columns, and keys fit quite naturally into the relational model. These concepts appear to have been abandoned in the binary relational approach. Any attempt to fit them into this approach is bound to result in bending the approach and in unnecessary complexity. The example of a person's home address or work address cited earlier illustrates the need for composite domains and columns. The example of the capability relation cited earlier also illustrates the need for composite domains and composite primary keys, and therefore for composite foreign keys.

The absence of these concepts from the binary relational approach means that users must manipulate information in the database in terms of pieces that are smaller than the user's customary perception. Thus, it should be expected that user productivity will decrease.

30.3.6 The Heavy Load of Joins

The binary relational approach places an unnecessarily heavy load of joining on the DBMS. In the regular relational model, database designers occasionally must de-normalize parts of the database to reduce the time spent in executing **joins** and, in this way, obtain good performance. The binary relational approach is likely to cause an order-of-magnitude increase in the execution of **joins** over that required by the relational model.

30.3.7 Joins Restricted to Entity-based Joins

In [Mark 1988], the author says that in the binary relation approach, "Relationships between object types are derived through entity-joins rather than symbol-joins." This is equivalent to taking the regular relational model and permitting key-based **joins** only, since keys denote objects, while non-keys denote properties of objects. All **joins** based on non-keys would be prohibited. This is a very severe restriction that would be hard to justify.

Consider the query: Find the employees who live in a combination of city and state in which the company has a warehouse. Given Mark's ground rules, this query could not be handled by a binary relational DBMS, unless every city and state combination were already treated as an object (having its own immediate properties), and consequently this combination would constitute the primary key in some relation.

When designing a database, it is quite likely that the designer will choose to treat the city and state combination as a combination of properties of other kinds of objects. Normally, this combination of city and state will be treated as an object only if the company's business heavily depends upon data maintained about cities (e.g., population, size of market, crime rate, and distribution of wealth).

30.3.8 Integrity Constraints Harder to Conceive and Express

In the relational model, each case of referential integrity frequently involves two distinct relations (although more than two can be involved). Many user-defined integrity constraints can also be expected to involve two or more distinct relations. In the binary relational approach, each of these integrity constraints is likely to involve even more distinct binary relations, and therefore be harder to conceive, more cumbersome to express, and entail more overhead for the DBMS, thus reducing its performance.

As an example, consider any referential integrity constraint that involves a composite key in the relational model. As a second example, consider a user-defined integrity constraint that requires the company's salespeople to be based in city and state combinations for which the market is at least 10% of the company's total market in the immediately preceding year.

30.3.9 No Comprehensive Data Model

So far, the BR approach lacks a solid foundation. No data model for it has been published that supports all the well-known requirements of database management. Until this occurs, companies intending to acquire a DBMS product should be concerned about the risk of investing in the binary relational approach.

30.4 ■ The Entity-Relationship Approaches

Numerous approaches based on splitting objects into two types, entities and relationships, have been proposed. Many of the authors of these approaches identify P.P. Chen as their source of inspiration [Chen 1976], even though he was by no means the first to propose such a split. In fact, this kind of split was an inherent part of the thinking that went into all single-record-at-a-time, pre-relational approaches to database management. Of the five approaches discussed in this chapter, this one is clearly the winner in terms of its lack of precise definitions, lack of a clear level of abstraction, and lack of a mental discipline. The popularity of ER may lie in its multitude of interpretations, as well as its use of familiar but obsolete modes of thought.

The major problem in the entity-relationship approach is that one person's entity is another person's relationship. There is no general and precisely defined distinction between these two concepts, even when discussion is limited to a particular part of a business that is to be modeled by means of a database. If there are 10 people in a room and each is asked for definitions of the terms "entity" and "relationship," 20 different definitions are likely to be supplied for each term.

A good example is an airline flight. An accountant is likely to think of this as an entity. Someone responsible for airplane scheduling or crew scheduling is likely to think of it as a relationship between a type of aircraft, a flight route, a crew, and a date.

A second problem with this approach is that a relationship between objects is not supposed to have immediate properties that are recorded in the database. It should be very obvious that relationships can have any number of immediate properties. Consider as an example a database containing information about parts and suppliers. Two quite distinct relationships between parts and suppliers are as follows:

1. the CAPABILITY relation, in which each assertion states that a particular supplier *can supply* a particular kind of part;

2. the SHIP relation, in which each assertion states that a particular supplier *has supplied* a particular kind of part to the pertinent company.

Each of these relations is likely to have a distinct collection of numerous immediate properties. For example, CAPABILITY may have estimated speed of delivery, the number of units supplied as a non-divisible package, and the cost of each such package. SHIP may have date of shipment, quantity of parts shipped, and an identifier for the destination warehouse.

Even though a relationship may begin life with no immediate properties, it is extremely unwise to establish the database design and the development of application programs on the assumption that it will stay that way forever.

If it is proposed to handle the manipulation of entities and relationships by means of distinct commands, then the vocabulary for retrievals, insertions, updates, and deletions is doubled over the vocabulary in the relational model. If no manipulative distinctions are made between entities and relationships, why are they conceived as two different kinds of information? Is this just one more example of a distinction that leads to an increase in complexity, but no increase whatsoever in generality?

No data model has yet been published for the entity-relationship approach. To be comprehensive, it must support all of the well-known requirements of database management. Until this occurs, companies intending to acquire a DBMS product should be concerned about the risk of investing in the entity-relationship approach.

30.5 ■ The Semantic Data Approaches

The claim that an approach is semantic is a very strong claim indeed, strong enough to be considered extravagant. One test that I believe should be made to check such a claim is as follows. Imagine that the computer system is equipped with the five human senses: touch, smell, vision, hearing, and taste. If such a system were also equipped with a DBMS based on some approach that is claimed to be semantic, together with a database concerning suppliers, parts, warehouses, projects, and employees, could this system use its five senses and the database to distinguish these objects from one another in its environment, and recognize the type of each object?

While there have been numerous approaches to database management claimed to be semantic, the one discussed here is that of Hammer and McLeod [1981]. This particular case is chosen, because one United States vendor, Unisys, claims that its product INFOEXEC is based on it, and that "it will become the preferred approach to database management in the 1990s" [Balfour 1988]. The major difficulties encountered by any approach that is claimed to be exclusively semantic are two-fold:

1. there is no known, totally objective boundary to the world of semantics;

2. there is no known way to replace predicate logic by semantic machinery.

Of course, either or both of these states of affairs could change in the future, but in neither case is it likely to be an overnight change. Until such a change occurs, however, both of these states represent sound reasons for all of us to avoid claims that a semantic approach can replace the relational model.

In [Hammer and McLeod 1981, page 353], the authors make the mistake of characterizing the relational model as "record-oriented." They proceed to declare that "it is necessary to break with the tradition of record-based modeling, and to base a database model on structural constructs that are highly user-oriented and expressive of the application environment." This completely overlooks all the integrity constraints of the relational model, as well as their definition by linguistic means independently of application programs. The linguistic approach to defining these aspects of the meaning of data is much more powerful than any known structural approach. It represents a strong step forward from the old hierarchic and network-structured approaches.

In [Balfour 1988], the author lists several properties of the relational model that he alleges are "fundamental weaknesses." I find his supporting case for the allegations to be quite shallow and completely unconvincing. He interposes some criticisms of current SQL and current implementations of the relational model. I agree with his criticism of SQL, but I believe his assertion that "current implementations of the relational model have not performed as well as the older database technologies in high-volume on-line transaction-oriented environments" is not only false [Codd 1987a], but also irrelevant to his defense of semantic data approaches.

No data model has yet been published for the semantic approach. To be comprehensive, it must support all of the well-known requirements of database management. Until this occurs, companies intending to acquire a DBMS product should be concerned about the risk of investing in the semantic approach.

30.6 ■ The Object-oriented Approaches

There are several different approaches in the object-oriented category, and no vendor has yet announced a database management product based on one of them. The ideas in this kind of approach stem from the need in programming languages for more thoroughly defined and more abstract data types. In particular, the concept known as *abstract data type* is the key to most of the research in this area. Such ideas are clearly a step forward in the area of programming languages, but it is not at all clear that they represent a step forward in the technology for database management.

As time progresses, a database is bound to change in terms of the types of information stored in it. In fact, there is likely to be a significant expansion in the kinds of information stored in any database. Such expansion should not *require* changes to be made in application programs. Some kinds of information may be dropped. When any drop occurs, there should be a simple way to detect (1) all the application programs that are adversely affected, and (2) all the commands within each such program that are adversely affected.

If each of these requirements is met, the approach can be claimed with some credibility to be *adaptable to change*. When applied to database management, the object-oriented approaches take a very restrictive and non-adaptable approach to the interpretation and treatment of data.

It is important to ask whether any object-oriented language exists that is as high in level as the relational languages. Without a language that conveys the user's intent at a high level of abstraction, how can the system optimize the sequence of minor operations and the choice of access paths when executing a request? The answer to this question is particularly crucial when distributed database mangement is involved.

Can the OO approach to database management support distribution independence? In other words, can application programs remain unchanged and correct when a database is converted from centralized to distributed, and later when the data must be re-distributed? What support does the OO approach provide for built-in and user-defined integrity constraints that are not embedded in the application programs?

No comprehensive data model has yet been published for the object-oriented approach. To be comprehensive, it must support all of the well-known requirements of database management. Until this occurs, companies intending to acquire a DBMS product should be concerned about the risk of investing in the object-oriented approach.

30.7 ■ Concluding Remarks

Both the SD and the OO approaches emphasize the need for DBMS products to support generalization or type hierarchies. I agree that such support is necessary, and showed with RM/T [Codd 1979] how type hierarchies could be supported without making the data structure concepts more complicated. This is a feature of RM/T that is very likely to drop down into RM/V3 within the next decade.

The five approaches to database management examined in this chapter are just five of many that are now competing for a place in the sun.

Development of the relational model has made researchers aware of the impact a data model can have on the field of data processing. Each new model that comes along must be carefully examined from the standpoint of its technical merit, usability, and comprehensiveness. New theoretical contributions to the field should also be examined carefully, not glibly cast aside as just theory, and therefore not practical—a judgment made many times in the last 20 years about the relational model.

Exercises

30.1 **Joins** and **relational division** are occasionally criticized for requiring users to engage in "logical navigation." This presumably means "finding their way through a logical data model." Discuss the claimed alternatives to logical navigation, and your position regarding how complete each alternative is and its technical pros and cons.

30.2 Does the "universal relation" provide a means of protecting users from the multi-relation operators of the relational model? Defend your position on this issue.

30.3 When insertions, deletions, and updates are applied to the "universal relation," what problems are encountered?

30.4 When a new relation is created in a relational database, what is the counterpart activity in a "universal relation?" Create an example such that the addition cannot be attached to the outer boundaries of the "universal relation."

30.5 Consider this query: find the suppliers, and 10 immediate properties of these suppliers, each of whom can supply every part listed by part serial number in a given unary relation. Assume that the database contains information about suppliers including their supplier serial numbers and 50 other immediate properties. Assume also that the database contains capability information about suppliers and parts, together with 20 immediate properties that apply to each combination of supplier and part. Outline a binary relational database, and express the query in terms of **joins, relational division, projects,** and so forth (but only as these operators apply to binary and unary relations). Do not assume that any relation of degree greater than two can be generated as a derived relation, except as the final "report-presentation" step.

30.6 Take an example of a relation of degree five in which there exists a **join** dependency that is not a multi-valued or functional dependency. Cast this relation into a collection of binary relations that is equivalent in information content. Comment on whether the **join** dependency is easier to detect in this form or in the original form.

30.7 A bank has branches in several cities, and each city has its own DBMS storing the customer accounts. Assume that the accounts are all the same in the kinds of identifying properties and other properties stored for each. Thus, they are union-compatible. Suppose that the DBMS in each city is part of the bank's overall control of its distributed database. If each DBMS is based solely on the binary relation approach and each customer account has 20 distinct properties recorded, how would you obtain at bank headquarters the **union** of all customer accounts?

30.8   Supply six reasons why the "universal relation" will not replace the relational model.

30.9   Supply eight reasons why the binary relation approach will not replace the relational model.

30.10   How prevalent is the *property-not-applicable* mark in a "universal relation?" Take a simple example involving 50 suppliers with 20 distinct properties, 1,000 parts with 40 distinct properties, and 2,000 capabilities with 15 distinct properties. Assume the usual condition that none of the properties of an object of any one type is applicable to objects of the other two types, where the three types are suppliers, parts, and capabilities. In this database, how many items of data are marked *property inapplicable?*

RM/V2 Feature Index

A.1 ■ Index to the Features

This index of the 333 features of Version 2 of the relational model described in this book is intended to make it easy to find each feature of RM/V2.

The features are labeled with consecutive numbers within each of 18 classes. The following table indicates the letters denoting each class and the chapter(s) each class falls in:

Chapter	Class	
18	A	Authorization
4	B	Basic operators
15	C	Catalog
21	D	Principles of DBMS design
3,7	E	Commands for the DBA
19	F	Functions
13,14	I	Integrity
11	J	Indicators
22	L	Principles of language design
12	M	Manipulation
6	N	Naming
20	P	Protection
10	Q	Qualifiers
2	S	Structure

Chapter	Class	
3	T	Data types
16,17	V	Views
24,25	X	Distributed database management
5,17	Z	Advanced operators

In the "priority" column, the letter F or B appears (F denotes fundamental, and hence top priority, while B denotes basic). The phrase "multiple rows" includes zero and one row as special cases that are not given special treatment.

Note that DBMS products can be classified by the features they support. In the early 1990s, a DBMS product that fully supports all the features of both Type F and Type B deserves to be called advanced.

Structure-Oriented and Data-Oriented Features (Chapter 2)

Feature Label	Priority	Feature Title	Page
RS-1	F	The information feature	30
RS-2	F	Freedom from positional concepts	32
RS-3	F	Duplicate rows prohibited in every relation	32
RS-4	F	Information portability	33
RS-5	B	Three-level architecture	34
RS-6	F	Declaration of domains as extended data types	34
RS-7	F	Column descriptions	35
RS-8	F	Primary key for each base R-table	35
RS-9	B	Primary key for certain views	36
RS-10	F	Foreign key	36
RS-11	B	Composite domains	37
RS-12	B	Composite columns	37
RS-13	F	Missing information: representation	39
RS-14	B	Avoiding the universal relation	40

Domains as Extended Data Types (Chapter 3)

Feature Label	Priority	Feature Title	Page
RT-1	F	Safety feature when comparing database values	46
RT-2	F	Extended data types built into the system	49
RT-3	F	User-defined extended data types	50

The ten comparators in theta-select and theta-join are as follows:

1	EQUAL TO	$=$
2	NOT EQUAL TO	$\neq$
3	LESS THAN	$<$
4	LESS THAN OR EQUAL TO	$<=$
5	GREATER THAN	$>$
6	GREATER THAN OR EQUAL TO	$>=$
7	GREATEST LESS THAN	$G<$
8	GREATEST LESS THAN OR EQUAL TO	$G<=$
9	LEAST GREATER THAN	$L>$
10	LEAST GREATER THAN OR EQUAL TO	$L>=$

The Basic Operators (Chapter 4)

The Advanced Operators (Chapters 5 and 17)

Naming (Chapter 6)

Commands for the DBA (Chapters 3 and 7)

Missing Information (Chapters 8 and 9)

Qualifiers (Chapter 10)

Indicators (Chapter 11)

Data Manipulation (Chapter 12)

Feature Label	Priority	Feature Title	Page
RM-1	F	Guaranteed access	229
RM-2	F	Parsable relational data sublanguage	230
RM-3	B	Power of the relational language	231
RM-4	F	High-level **insert, update,** and **delete**	231
RM-5	F	Operational closure	232
RM-6	F	Transaction block	233
RM-7	B	Blocks to simplify altering the database description	234
RM-8	F	Dynamic mode	235
RM-9	F	Triple mode	235
RM-10	F	Four-valued logic: truth tables	236
RM-11	F	Missing information: manipulation	236
RM-12	F	Arithmetic operators: effect of missing values	237
RM-13	F	Concatenation: effect of marked values	237
RM-14	F	Domain-constrained operators and DOMAIN CHECK OVERRIDE	238
RM-15	F	Operators constrained by basic data type only, if one operand or both operands are function-generated	238
RM-16	B	Prohibition of essential ordering	239
RM-17	B	Interface to single-record-at-a-time host languages	239
RM-18	F	The comprehensive data sublanguage	240
RM-19	B	Library check-out	240
RM-20	B	Library return	241

Integrity Constraints (Chapter 13)

Feature Label	Priority	Feature Title	Page
RI-1	F	Domain integrity constraints: Type D	246
RI-2	F	Column integrity constraints: Type C	246
RI-3	F	Entity integrity constraints: Type E	246
RI-4	F	Referential integrity constraints: Type R	246
RI-5	F	User-defined integrity constraints: Type U	246
RI-6	F	Timing of testing for Types R and U	247
RI-7	B	Response to attempted violation of Types R and U	248

User-Defined Integrity Constraints (Chapter 14)

The Catalog (Chapter 15)

Feature Label	Priority	Feature Title	Page
RC-1	F	Dynamic on-line catalog	278
RC-2	F	Concurrency	278
RC-3	F	Description of domains	279
RC-4	F	Description of base R-tables	279
RC-5	B	Description of composite columns	280
RC-6	F	Description of views	280
RC-7	B	User-defined integrity constraints	281
RC-8	F	Referential integrity constraints	281
RC-9	B	User-defined functions	282
RC-10	F	Authorization data	282
RC-11	F	Database statistics in the catalog	282

Views (Chapters 16 and 17)

Feature Label	Priority	Feature Title	Page
RV-1	F	View definitions: what they are	285
RV-2	F	View definitions: what they are not	287
RV-3	F	View definitions: retention and interrogation	288
RV-4	F	Retrieval using views	288
RV-5	F	Manipulation using views	289
RV-6	F	View updating	290
RV-7	F	Names of columns of views	291
RV-8	F	Domains applicable to columns of views	291

Authorization (Chapter 18)

Feature Label	Priority	Feature Title	Page
RA-1	F	Affirmative basis	327
RA-2	F	Granting authorization: space-time scope	327
RA-3	B	Hiding selected columns in views	329
RA-4	B	Blocking updates that remove rows from a view	330
RA-5	B	N-person turn-key	330
RA-6	F	Delayed deletions of data and drops by archiving	331

Functions (Chapter 19)

Protection of Investment (Chapter 20)

DBMS Design (Chapter 21)

Feature Label	Priority	Feature Title	Page
RD-1	F	Non-violation of any fundamental law of mathematics	351
RD-2	F	Under-the-covers representation and access	352
RD-3	B	Sharp boundary	352
RD-4	F	Concurrency independence	353
RD-5	B	Protection against unauthorized long-term locking	353
RD-6	F	Orthogonality in DBMS design	354
RD-7	B	Domain-based index	355
RD-8	B	Database statistics	355
RD-9	B	Interrogation of statistics	355
RD-10	B	Changing storage representation and access options	355
RD-11	F	Automatic protection in case of malfunction	356
RD-12	B	Automatic recovery in case of malfunction	356
RD-13	F	Atomic execution of relational commands	356
RD-14	B	Automatic archiving	357
RD-15	F	Avoiding **Cartesian product**	357
RD-16	F	Responsibility for encryption and decryption	358

Language Design (Chapter 22)

Feature Label	Priority	Feature Title	Page
RL-1	F	Data sublanguage: variety of users	362
RL-2	F	Compiling and re-compiling	362
RL-3	F	Intermixability of relational- and host-language statements	362
RL-4	F	Principal relational language is dynamically executable	363
RL-5	F	RL is both a source and a target language	363
RL-6	F	Simple rule for scope within an RL command	363
RL-7	F	Explicit BEGIN and END for multi-command blocks	363
RL-8	B	Orthogonality in language design	364
RL-9	B	Predicate logic versus relational algebra	364
RL-10	B	Set-oriented operators and comparators	365
RL-11	B	Set constants and nesting of queries within queries	365

Feature Label	Priority	Feature Title	Page
RL-12	F	Canonical form for every request	366
RL-13	B	Global optimization	366
RL-14	B	Uniform optimization	367
RL-15	B	Constants, variables, and functions interchangeable	367
RL-16	B	Expressing time-oriented conditions	367
RL-17	F	Flexible role for operators	368

Distributed Database Management (Chapters 24 and 25)

Feature Label	Priority	Feature Title	Page
RX-1	B	Multi-site action from a single relational command	393
RX-2	B	Local autonomy	394
RX-3	B	Global database and global catalog	396
RX-4	B	N copies of global catalog ($N > 1$)	397
RX-5	B	Synonym relation in each local catalog	398
RX-6	B	Unique names for sites	399
RX-7	B	Naming objects in a distributed database	399
RX-8	B	Reversibility and redistribution	401
RX-9	B	Decomposition by columns for distributing data	403
RX-10	B	Decomposition by rows for distributing data	404
RX-11	B	General transformation for distributing data	404
RX-12	B	Replicas and snapshots	405
RX-13	B	Integrity constraints that straddle two or more sites	406
RX-14	B	Views that straddle two or more sites	407
RX-15	B	Authorization that straddles two or more sites	408
RX-16	B	Name resolution with a distributed catalog	409
RX-17	B	Inter-site move of a relation	410
RX-18	B	Inter-site moves of rows of a relation	411
RX-19	B	Dropping a relation from a site	412
RX-20	B	Creating a new relation	412
RX-21	B	Abandoning an old site and perhaps its data	413
RX-22	B	Introducing a new site	414

Feature Label	Priority	Feature Title	Page
RX-23	B	Deactivating and reactivating items in the catalog	415
RX-24	B	Minimum standard for statistics	421
RX-25	B	Minimum standard for the optimizer	422
RX-26	B	Performance independence in distributed database management	422
RX-27	B	Concurrency independence in distributed database management	423
RX-28	B	Recovery at multiple sites	423
RX-29	B	Locking in distributed database management	423

A.2 ■ Summary of RM/V2 Features by Class

Table of features fundamental and basic

Feature Class	Fundamental (F)	Basic (B)	Totals		
RS	9	5	14		
RT	3	6	9		
RB	31	6	37	104	
RZ	2	42	44		
RN	7	7	14		221
RE	8	14	22		
RQ	3	10	13	63	
RJ	0	14	14		
RM	14	6	20		
RI	14	20	34	54	
RC	8	3	11		
RV	8	0	8	35	
RA	6	10	16		
RF	3	7	10		112
RP	1	4	5		
RD	8	8	16	77	
RL	9	8	17		
RX	0	29	29		
Totals	134	199	333	333	333

A.3 ■ Classes of Features and Numbers of Features in Each Class

Class	Number of Features			
Z	44			
B	37	115		
I	34		186	
X	29			
E	22	71		
M	20			333
D	16			
L	17	77		
A	16			
S	14			
N	14		147	
J	14			
Q	13	38		
C	11			
F	10			
T	9			
V	8	32		
P	5			

A.4 ■ Principal Objects and Properties in RM/V1

Structure

Domains
Relations (same as R-tables)
Attributes (same as columns)
Primary keys
Foreign keys
Information portability

Data Types

See Features RT-1–RT-6.

Operators

Each operator can be expressed in at most one command, and without circumlocution or circumconception.

    Theta-select (restrict)

    Project

    Theta-join

(Where **theta** is any of the comparators 1–6 for theta-select, and any of the comparators 1–10 for **theta-join**.)

    Union

    Set difference

    Intersection (inner types)

    Left, right, and **symmetric outer join**

    Relational division

    Relational assignment

Qualifiers

Qualifiers include the temporary replacement of missing elementary database values, as well as the MAYBE qualifiers.

Indicators

    Empty relation

    Empty divisor in relational division

Manipulative Features

See Features RM-1–RM-5.

Integrity Constraints

Each integrity constraint can be expressed in one command per constraint, and without circumlocution or circumconception. Each such constraint is stored in the catalog, not in an application program.

    D   Domain integrity

    C   Column integrity

    E   Entity integrity

R   Referential integrity

U   User-defined integrity

Catalog

See Features RC-1–RC-4.

Views

See Features RV-1–RV-5.

Authorization

See Features RA-1–RA-4.

A.5 ▪ Additional Features for "Adequately Relational" 1990–1994

These additional features beyond RM/V1 are required to be fully supported by a DBMS, if that system is to be called "adequately relational" in the 1990–1994 period.

Functions

See Features RF-1–RF-3.

Investment Protection

See Features RP-1 and RP-2.

DBMS Design

See Features RD-1, RD-2, RD-4, RD-6, RD-11, and RD-13.

Language Design

See Features RL-1–RL-6.

A.6 ▪ The Rules Index

The following table shows the features of RM/V2 that correspond to the twelve rules published in 1985 [Codd 1985]. The text of any selected rule can be found by first using this table to determine which feature(s) of RM/

V2 corresponds to the selected rule, and then by using the index to the features at the beginning of this Appendix to find the text in the book.

1985 Rule	RM/V2 Feature	Name
1	RS-1	Information rule
2	RM-1	Guaranteed access
3	RS-13, RM-10	Missing information
4	RC-1	Active catalog
5	RM-3	Comprehensive data sublanguage (DSL)
6	RV-4, RV-5	View updatability
7	RM-4	High level language
8	RP-1	Physical data independence
9	RP-2	Logical data independence
10	RP-3	Integrity independence
11	RP-4	Distribution independence
12	RI-16	Non-subversion

■ *APPENDIX B* ■

Exercises in Logic and the Theory of Relations

The following exercises are included in this book to help the reader test his or her own knowledge in these two branches of mathematics. Although these topics are not covered in this book, knowledge of them is important for the designers of DBMS products and for database administrators.

B.1 ■ Simple Exercises in Predicate Logic

In the following exercises, P, Q are predicates, x is an individual variable, c is a constant, (∃) denotes the existential quantifier, (∀) denotes the universal quantifier, and → denotes logical implication.

Which of the following pairs of formulas in predicate logic are logically equivalent?

1a.	∀x(Px ∨ Qx)		1b.	(∀xPx ∨ ∀xQx)
2a.	∀x(Px ∧ Qx)		2b.	(∀xPx ∧ ∀xQx)
3a.	¬ (Pc ∨ Qc)		3b.	(¬ Pc) ∧ (¬ Qc)
4a.	Pc → Qc		4b.	(¬ Pc) ∨ Qc
5a.	¬ ∀xPx		5b.	∃x(¬ Px)
6a.	∀x(Px → Qx)		6b.	(∃xPx ∨ ∀xQx)
7a.	∃x(Px → Qx)		7b.	∃x(¬ Px) ∨ ∃xQx
8a.	¬ ∃xPx		8b.	¬ ∀x Px

B.2 ■ Simple Exercises in Relational Theory

In the following exercises, R, S, and T are union-compatible relations. The three operators are **relational union** (denoted ∪), **relational difference** (denoted −), and **relational intersection** (denoted ∩).

Which of the following pairs of expressions are guaranteed to yield identical results?

1a.	R ∪ S	1b.	S ∪ R
2a.	R − S	2b.	S − R
3a.	R ∩ S	3b.	S ∩ R
4a.	(R ∪ S) ∩ T	4b.	(R ∩ T) ∪ (S ∩ T)
5a.	(R ∪ S) − T	5b.	(R − T) ∪ (S − T)
6a.	(R ∩ S) − T	6b.	(R − T) ∩ (S − T)
7a.	(R ∩ S) ∪ T	7b.	(R ∪ T) ∩ (S ∪ T)
8a.	(R − S) ∩ T	8b.	(R ∩ T) − (S ∩ T)

B.3 ■ Exercises Concerning the Inter-relatedness of RM/V2 Features

No claim has been made that all 333 features of RM/V2 are independent of one another; such a claim would be false. This kind of independence would make the relational model, whether Version 1 or Version 2, difficult to understand. It would be similar to trying to learn an IBM 3090 by first learning a universal Turing machine.

Suppose that F and G are two features of RM/V2. The notation F → G means that the DBMS must support F if it is to provide full support for G.

1. Let F be view updatability and G be logical data independence. Show that F → G.

2. Let F be domains as extended data types and G be view updatability. Show that F → G.

3. Let F be primary keys and G be view updatability. Show that F → G.

4. Take each distinct pair of features F and G in RM/V2. Examine whether F → G or G → F, or neither. Explain your answers.

■ *REFERENCES* ■

This list of references is not claimed to be complete. The list, however, does include most of the works by the author of this book that concern database management (Codd 1969–Codd 1988b). (Codd 1968) illustrates levels of abstraction, but applied to a different subject.

The reference list includes the following database management papers by other authors: (Beeri, Fagin, and Howard 1977), (Bernstein and Chiu 1981), (Bernstein, Hadzilacos, and Goodman 1987), (Buff 1986), (Casanova, Fagin, and Papadimitriou 1984), (Chen 1976), (Date 1984 and 1987), (Dayal and Bernstein 1982), (Ganski and Wong 1987), (Goodman 1988), (Hammer and McLeod 1981), (Heath 1971), (Keller 1986), (Kim 1982), (Klug 1982), (Lindsay 1981), (Lipski 1978), (Maier, Ullman, and Vardi 1984), (Mark ⸺ 1088), (Vardi 1988), (Vassiliou 1979), and (Wiorkowski and ⸺ ɔɔ).

Several texts dealing with predicate logic also appear in the reference list. In descending order of difficulty, they are as follows: (Church 1958), (Suppes 1967), (Exner and Rosskopf 1959), (Stoll 1961), and (Pospesel 1976).

The remaining entries in the reference list consist of database management system prototypes and products. (IMS n.d.) was a leading DBMS product in the late 1960s and early 1970s. Note that the Peterlee relational test vehicle (Todd 1976), listed as operational at the end of 1972, preceded all other systems based on the relational model. These entries are far from complete because of the recent development of many relational DBMS products.

Balfour, A. (1988) *INFOEXEC: The First Practical Implementation of a Semantic Database,* Unisys, Europe-Africa Division. December.

Beech, D. (1989) "The Need for Duplicate Rows in Tables." *Datamation,* January.

Beeri, C., R. Fagin, and J. H. Howard (1977) "A Complete Axiomatization for Functional and Multi-Valued Dependencies in Database Rela-

505

tions." In *Proc. ACM SIGMOD 1977 Int. Conf. on Management of Data* (Los Angeles, 1977).

Bernstein, P. A., and D. W. Chiu (1981) "Using Semi-joins to Solve Relational Queries." *JACM* 28:1.

Bernstein, P. A., V. Hadzilacos, and N. Goodman (1987) *Concurrency Control and Recovery in Database Systems.* Addison-Wesley.

Buff, H. W. (1986) "The View Update Problem Is Undecidable." Personal communication, Zurich, August 4. Published as "Why Codd's Rule No. 6 Must Be Reformulated." *ACM SIGMOD Record* 17:4 (1988).

Casanova, N., R. Fagin, and C. Papadimitriou (1984) "Inclusion Dependencies and Their Interaction with Functional Dependencies." *JCSS* 28:1.

Chamberlin, D. D., Astrahan, M. M., Blasgen, M. W., Gray, J. N., King, W. F., Lindsay, B. G., Lorie, R., Mehl, J. W., Price, T. G., Putzolu, F., Selinger, P. G., Schkolnick, M., Slutz, D. R., Traiger, I. L., Wade, B. W., Yost, R. A. (1981) "A History and Evaluation of System R." *Comm. ACM* 24:10.

Chen, P. P. (1976) "The Entity-Relationship Model—Toward a Unified View of Data, *ACM TODS* 1:1.

Church, A. (1958) *Introduction to Mathematical Logic.* Princeton University Press.

Codd, E. F. (1968) *Cellular Automata.* Academic Press.

Codd, E. F. (1969) *Derivability, Redundancy, and Consistency of Relations Stored in Large Data Banks.* San Jose, IBM Research Report RJ599.

Codd, E. F. (1970) "A Relational Model of Data for Large Shared Data Banks." *Comm. ACM* 13:6.

Codd, E. F. (1971a) "ALPHA: A Data Base Sublanguage Founded on the Relational Calculus." In *Proc. 1971 ACM SIGFIDET Workshop* (San Diego, Nov. 11–12, 1971).

Codd, E. F. (1971b) "Further Normalization of the Data Base Relational Model." In *Courant Computer Science Symposia 6, Data Base Systems.* (New York, May 24–25). Prentice-Hall.

Codd, E. F. (1971c) "Normalized Data Base Structure: A Brief Tutorial." *Proc. 1971 ACM SIGFIDET Workshop* (San Diego, Nov. 11–12, 1971).

Codd, E. F. (1971d) Relational Completeness of Data Base Sublanguages." In *Courant Computer Science Symposia 6, Data Base Systems* (New York, May 24–25). Prentice-Hall.

Codd, E. F. (1974a) "Interactive Support for Non-Programmers: The Relational and Network Approaches" and "Data Models: Data-Structure-Set versus Relational." *Proc. 1974 ACM SIGMOD Debate* (Ann Arbor, May 1–3).

Codd, E. F. (1974b) "Recent Investigations in Relational Data Base Systems." *Proc. IFIP* (Stockholm, August). Also published in *Information Processing 1974.* North-Holland.

Codd, E. F. (1974c) "The Relational Approach to Data Base Management: An Overview." Third Annual Texas Conference on Computing Systems (Austin, November 7–8).

Codd, E. F. (1974d) "Seven Steps to Rendezvous with the Casual User." *Proc. IFIP TC2 Working Conf. on Data Base Management Systems* (Cargese, Corsica, April 1–5).

Codd, E. F. (1978) "How about Recently?" *Proc. Int. Conf. on Databases: Improving Usability and Responsiveness.* (Haifa, Israel, August 2–3). Academic Press.

Codd, E. F. (1979) "Extending the Database Relational Model to Capture More Meaning." *ACM Trans. on Database Systems* 4:4.

Codd, E. F. (1980) "Data Models in Database Management." ACM SIGMOD, SIGPLAN, SIGART meeting (Pingree Park, Colorado, November 1980).

Codd, E. F. (1981) "The Capabilities of Relational Database Management Systems." Proc. Convencio Informatica Llatina (Barcelona, June 9–12).

Codd, E. F. (1982) "Relational Database: A Practical Foundation for Productivity." *Comm. ACM* 25:2.

Codd, E. F. (1985) "How Relational Is Your Database Management System?" *Computerworld,* October 14 and 21. Also available from The Relational Institute, San Jose.

Codd, E. F. (1986a) "Missing Information (Applicable and Inapplicable) in Relational Databases." *ACM SIGMOD Record,* Vol. 15, no. 4.

Codd, E. F. (1986b) *The Twelve Rules for Relational DBMS.* San Jose, The Relational Institute, Technical Report EFC-6.

Codd, E. F. (1987a) "The Beginning of a New Era in Data Processing" (review of Tandem's NonStop SQL). *InfoWeek,* May 4.

Codd, E. F. (1987b) *Fundamental Laws in Database Management.* San Jose, The Relational Institute, Technical Report EFC-27.

Codd, E. F. (1987c) "More Commentary on Missing Information in Relational Databases." *ACM SIGMOD Record,* Vol. 16, no. 1.

Codd, E. F. (1987d) *Principles of Design of Database Management Systems.* San Jose, The Relational Institute, Technical Report EFC-18.

Codd, E. F. (1987e) *View Updatability in Relational Databases: Algorithm VU-1.* Unpublished paper.

Codd, E. F. (1988a) "Domains, Primary Keys, Foreign Keys, and Referential Integrity." *Info DB,* May.

Codd, E. F. (1988b) "Fatal Flaws in SQL (Both the IBM and the ANSI Versions)." *Datamation,* August and September. Also available from The Relational Institute, San Jose (Technical Report EFC-28).

Date, C. J. (1984) "Why Is It So Difficult to Provide a Relational Interface to IMS?" *Info IMS* 4:4.

Date, C. J. (1987) "Where SQL Falls Short," (abridged). *Datamation,* May 1. Unabridged version, *What Is Wrong with SQL,* available from The Relational Institute, San Jose.

Dayal, U., and P. A. Bernstein (1982). "On the Correct Translation of Update Operations on Relational Views." *ACM TODS* 7:3.

Exner, R. M., and M. F. Rosskopf (1959) *Logic in Elementary Mathematics.* McGraw-Hill.

Ganski, R. A., and H. K. T. Wong (1987) "Optimization of Nested SQL Queries Revisited." *Proc. ACM SIGMOD Annual Conference* (San Francisco), May 27–29.

Goodman, N. (1988) Letter regarding the outer set operators, July 15.

Hammer, M., and D. McLeod (1981) "Database Description with SDM: A Semantic Database Model." *ACM TODS* 6:3.

Heath, I. J. (1971) Memorandum introducing the outer join. Fall.

Hutt, A. T. F. (1979) *A Relational Data Base Management System.* Wiley.

IBM (n.d.) *IMS Reference Manual.* IBM Corporation, White Plains, N.Y. (any post-1971 edition).

IBM (1988) *SQL Reference Manual.* IBM Corporation.

Keller, A. M. (1986) "Choosing a View Update Translator by Dialog at View Definition Time." 12th Conference on Very Large Databases (Tokyo, August 25–28, 1986).

Kim, Won (1982) "On Optimizing an SQL-like Nested Query." *ACM TODS* 7:3.

Klug, A. (1982) "Equivalence of Relational Algebra and Relational Calculus Query Languages Having Aggregate Functions." *JACM* 29:3.

Lindsay, B. (1981) "Object Naming and Catalog Management for a Distributed Database Manager." *Proc. Second Int. Conf. on Distributed Computing* (Paris, April 1981). Also IBM Research Report RJ2914, 1980.

Lipski, W. (1978) *On Semantic Issues Connected with Incomplete Information Data Bases.* Institute of Computer Science, Polish Academy of Sciences, Warsaw.

Maier, D., J. D. Ullman, and M. Y. Vardi (1984) "On the Foundations of the Universal Relational Model." *ACM TODS,* Vol. 9, no. 2.

Mark, L. (n.d.) *The Binary Relationship Model.* Institute of Advanced Computer Studies, University of Maryland (probably 1988).

Meldman, M. J., D. J. McLeod, R. J. Pellicore, and M. Squire (1978) *RISS: A Relational DBMS for Minicomputers.* Van Nostrand Reinhold.

Ozkarahan, E. A., S. A. Schuster, and K. C. Smith (1975) "RAP: An Associative Processor for Data Base Management." *Proc. AFIPS,* Vol. 44.

Pospesel, H. (1976) *Predicate Logic.* Prentice-Hall.

Relational Technology (1988) *INGRES/QUEL Reference Manual.* Alameda, California, Relational Technology Inc.

Stoll, R. R. (1961) *Sets, Logic, and Axiomatic Theories.* Freeman.

Stonebraker, M., ed. (1986) *The INGRES Papers.* Addison-Wesley.

Suppes, P. (1967) *Introduction to Logic.* Van Nostrand.

Sweet, F. (1984) "What, if Anything, Is a Relational Database?" *Datamation (USA)* Vol. 30, no. 11.

Titman, P. J. (1974) "An Experimental Data Base System Using Binary Relations." *Proc. IFIP TC-2 Working Conf. on Data Base Management Systems,* eds. Klimbie J. W., and Koffeman, K. I., North-Holland.

Todd, S. J. P. (1976) "The Peterlee Relational Test Vehicle: A System Overview." *IBM Systems Journal* 15:4.

Vardi, M. Y. (1988) "The Universal-Relational Data Model for Logical Independence." *IEEE Software,* March.

Vassiliou, Y. (1979) "Null Values in Database Management: A Denotational Semantics Approach," *Proc. ACM SIGMOD 1979 Int. Conf. on Management of Data* (Boston, May 30–June 1).

Williams, R., Daniels, D., Haas, L., Lapis, G., Lindsay, B., Ng, P., Obermarck, R., Sclinger, P., Walker, A., Wilms, P., and Yost, R. (1981) *R*: An Overview of the Architecture.* IBM Research Report RJ3325.

Wiorkowski, G., and D. Kull (1988) *DB2 Design and Development Guide.* Addison-Wesley.

Zloof, M. M. (1975) "Query by Example." *Proc. of AFIPS,* Vol. 44.

■ INDEX ■

511

Q

R

S

Safety feature(s), 238–240
  functions and, 342–344
Safety Feature when Comparing Database Values *(RT-1)*, 46–49, 71–72, 105
SAVE qualifier *(RQ-12)*, 218
Scalar functions, 338–340
  applied to marked arguments, **185**
Security problem, alleged, duplicate rows and corrupted relations and, 378
Select operator, 7:
  algebraic, 69
  missing information and, 183
  of SQL, 69
  user-defined, 137–138
  view updatability and, 302–303
Selecting Columns within Relational Commands *(RN-4)*, 148
Semantic data approaches, relational approach versus, 478–479
Semantic distinctiveness, analysis of, 379
Semantic equality, missing information and, **178**
Semantic features, **150**
Semantic notions of equality
Semantic ordering, 183, 184
Semantics, duplicate rows and corrupted relations and, SQL and, 373–374
Semi-archive and Semi-delete Operators *(RZ-43, RZ-44)*, 321
Semi-insert Operator (RZ-41), 320–321
Semi-join operator, 104–106
Semi-Theta-Join *(RZ-3—RZ-12)*, 105–106
Semi-update Operator *(RZ-42)*, 321